"Greytown is no more!"

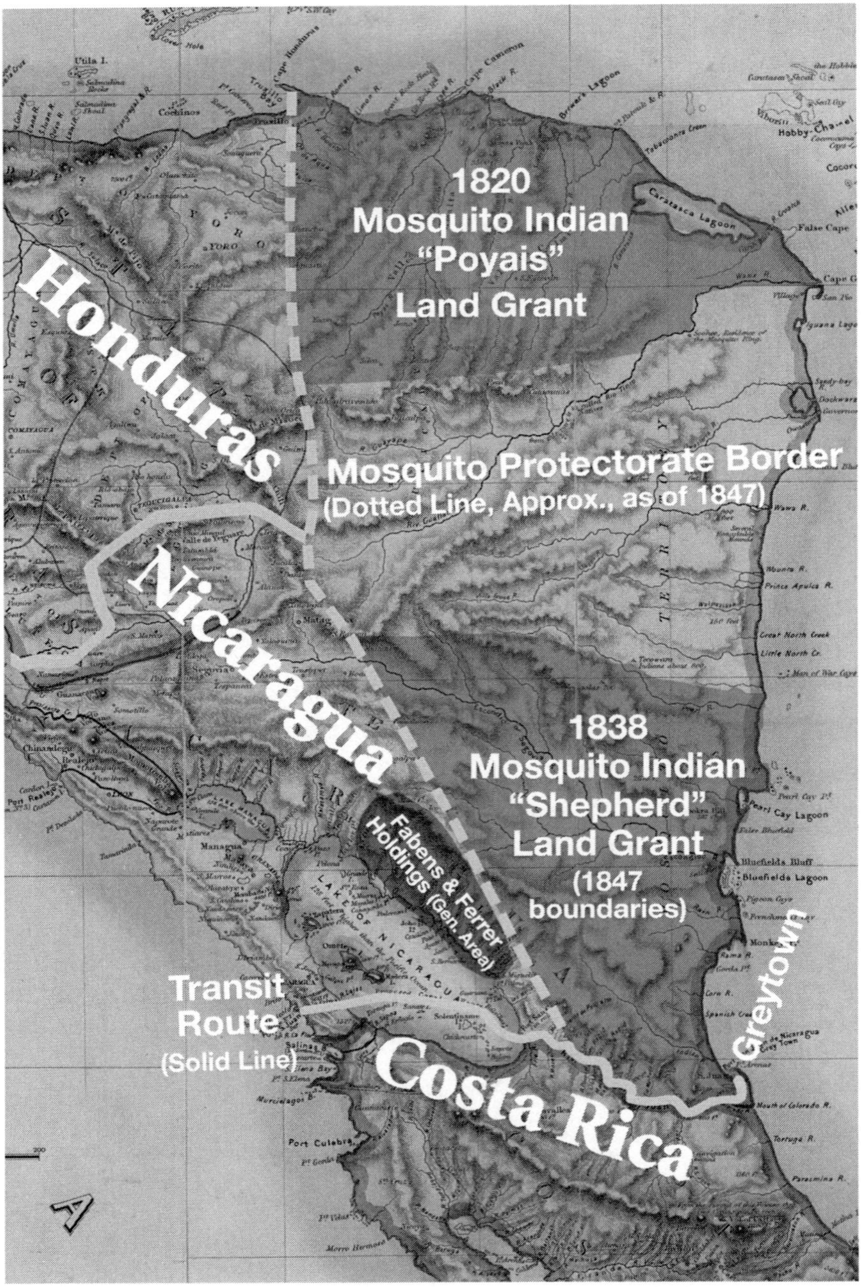

1820
Mosquito Indian
"Poyais"
Land Grant
Honduras
Mosquito Protectorate Border
(Dotted Line, Approx., as of 1847)
Nicaragua
1838
Mosquito Indian
"Shepherd"
Land Grant
(1847
boundaries)
Fabens & Ferrer
Holdings (Gen. Area)
Transit
Route
(Solid Line)
Greytown
Costa Rica

"Greytown is no more!"

*The 1854 Razing
of a Central American Port,
the U.S. Businesses Behind
Its Demise, and the Lasting
Foreign Policy Legacy*

WILL SOPER

McFarland & Company, Inc., Publishers
Jefferson, North Carolina

Frontispiece: Baily's Map of Central America 1850 (partial),
with topic-specific overlays by author.

LIBRARY OF CONGRESS CATALOGUING-IN-PUBLICATION DATA

Names: Soper, Will, 1946– author.
Title: "Greytown is no more!": The 1854 Razing of a Central American Port,
the U.S. Businesses Behind Its Demise, and the Lasting Foreign Policy Legacy
Description: Jefferson, North Carolina : McFarland & Company, Inc., Publishers, 2023 |
Includes bibliographical references and index.
Identifiers: LCCN 2022059834 | ISBN 9781476690575 (paperback : acid free paper) ∞
ISBN 9781476648583 (ebook)
Subjects: LCSH: San Juan del Norte (Nicaragua)—History. | Bombardment—
Nicaragua—San Juan del Norte—History—19th century. | United States—History,
Naval—19th century. | Offenses against property—Nicaragua—San Juan del Norte—
History—19th century. | Port cities—Nicaragua—History—19th century. | United
States—Foreign relations—Great Britain. | Great Britain—Foreign relations—United
States. | BISAC: HISTORY / United States / 19th Century | HISTORY / Military / Naval
Classification: LCC F1536.S2 S67 2023 | DDC 972.85/31—dc23/eng/20221223
LC record available at https://lccn.loc.gov/2022059834

BRITISH LIBRARY CATALOGUING DATA ARE AVAILABLE

ISBN (print) 978-1-4766-9057-5
ISBN (ebook) 978-1-4766-4858-3

© 2023 Jon Soper. All rights reserved

*No part of this book may be reproduced or transmitted in any form
or by any means, electronic or mechanical, including photocopying
or recording, or by any information storage and retrieval system,
without permission in writing from the publisher.*

On the cover: illustration showing the razing of Greytown, from a French newsmagazine
(*L'Illustration, Journal Universal*. From the author's collection).

Printed in the United States of America

McFarland & Company, Inc., Publishers
Box 611, Jefferson, North Carolina 28640
www.mcfarlandpub.com

Table of Contents

Acknowledgments viii
Preface 1
 1. "I Must Shoot the Fellow!" 5
 2. "Impaired by the Folly of an Individual" 24
 3. "Git the English Banks to Help Us" 32
 4. "It Will Be an American Town" 36
 5. "A Mortal Feud Had Arisen" 49
 6. "I Shall … Bombard the Town" 58
 7. "Act of … Cruelty … Upon a Helpless … Village" 65
 8. "The Great Theatre of Speculation" 72
 9. "I Will See the President Again Today" 86
10. "The Greatest Confidence Trick of All Time" 93
11. "Am Grateful … And Entirely Satisfied" 100
12. "They Might Take His Office & Stick It" 110
13. "I Shall Surely Hang Him" 119
14. "No Capacity to Transfer … Title" 122
15. "Make Certain Officials at Washington Wince" 130
16. "The Mormons Had Better Go" 138
17. "As If 'Usurpers' Had Taken Possession" 147
18. "Regarding Constituent Will Soper's Claim" 168
19. "Too Valuable … To Waive or Impair It" 173
20. Whither the Principals? An Epilogue 187

Chapter Notes 197
Bibliography 225
Index 237

The One Duty We Owe to History Is to Rewrite It.
—Oscar Wilde, *Intentions*
(United States: T.B. Mosher, 1904), 117.

To Robert E. May,
professor emeritus of history, Purdue University,
who got where I was going with this before anyone else
and then—for eight years—helped me get there.

Acknowledgments

When one researches a subject for 13 years, debts of gratitude accrue by the truckload.

To Robert E. May, professor emeritus, Purdue University, I owe the existence of this book, which is why it is dedicated to him.

Also thanks to: Stephen Kinzer, former *New York Times* correspondent, and currently (2022) Senior Fellow in International and Public Affairs at Brown University's Watson Institute, who's been answering my emails since 2016; Bruce Baker, the then-editor of the British journal *American Nineteenth Century History* (aka *BrANCH*), who taught me historiography when I could barely pronounce it and then—*and only then*—accepted my 2017 Greytown article; Professor Alan Lessoff of the Illinois State University Department of History, who recommended I submit my article to (*BrANCH*); Rick Shenkman, who accepted my 2018 op-ed about Greytown for publication on the History News Network; and Rep. Adam Schiff's Burbank office staff, who got my journal article to the CRS.

Then there are what I like to call my "Great Eight" email encouragers: Rick Shenkman (see above); the late Walter Nugent, professor of history, emeritus, Notre Dame; George Herring, professor of history emeritus at the University of Kentucky; John M. Belohlavek, professor of history at the University of South Florida; Matthew Karp, associate professor of history, Princeton University; Stephen Kinzer (see above); Greg Grandin, professor of history at Yale University; and Jay Sexton, professor of history, University of Missouri.

Of similar note are the legal minds who have enlightened me in lively email exchanges as to the layman-baffling workings of American jurisprudence: Louis Fisher, scholar in residence at the Constitution Project; Peter Raven-Hansen, professor of law emeritus at George Washington University School of Law; and William C. Banks, Syracuse University College of Law professor emeritus.

I'd also like to thank all the amazing librarians I've encountered on my searches, but most especially: Greg Reynolds, librarian III, at Los Angeles Central Library, whose sleuthing wizardry never ceased to amaze; also, Kate Collins, research services librarian, David M. Rubenstein, Rare Book & Manuscript Library, Duke University, who found crucial documents for me.

And I salute my English researchers, Roger E. Nixon and Liz Evans, who provided important documents from Britain's The National Archives (known by the acronym TNA).

Acknowledgments

As for image provision, Stephanie Arias and Morex Arai at the Huntington Library come prominently to mind for five 160-year-old pictures that I felt were crucial in telling this story. Also, Moira Allen of Victorian Voices who helped me track down the source of the splendid *bungo* illustration.

A special mention needs to be made of Tom R. Halfhill, whose insights informed my endnote about converting mid–19th century dollar amounts to "today's money." See his excellent "Tom's Inflation Calculator" online.

And there's Dr. John Patrick Martin of Kaiser Permanente, who kept me in good working order.

Friends who contributed encouragement and sometimes even real work, in the form of reading passages, etc., include: Anthony Cromwell Hill, Bella Rosenberg, Peter Carlson, Dick Cluster, Ellen Cantarow and her husband, Jack Cole, Janny Scott, Robert "Gunner" Reider, Freddie and Myrna Gershon, and Mike Hughes, whose sympathetic ear got bent on an almost weekly basis. Then there's my brother, Doug, and his wife, Beatriz, whose moral support, emailed jokes, and holiday phone calls are always perk-me-ups. And, most poignantly, if it wasn't for my late friend, author/historian Charles Rappleye, asking me in 2007 what his next book should be about, this book would not exist.

Alphabetical List of Research Contacts, Sourced on a Limited Basis

What follows is a compendium of email pen pals whom I queried regarding my research between 2008 and 2022 and who replied helpfully. They are listed alphabetically by their last names (but with first names first). Their names are followed by the date of one of our emails (in case they want to check their records to recall what our exchange was about). Abbreviations: HR, US House of Representatives congressional staffers; LAPL, Los Angeles Public Library; LOC, Library of Congress; NARA, National Archives and Records Administration; OCLC, Online Computer Library Center; TNA, The National Archives (of the United Kingdom); UCLA, University of California at Los Angeles; USC, University of Southern California; and UNT, University of North Texas. (Those without institutional association are noted by a brief reference to the subject matter discussed or by their profession.)

A Susan Abbott—NARA, 9 Jun 2015; Bruce Abrams, New York County Clerk's Office, 4 Jan 2014; Alex Adrian, OCLC, 12 Feb 2019; Steven Aftergood, Federation of American Scientists, 3 Dec 2019; Samantha Agbeblewu, U. of North Carolina Library, 20 Jun 2013; Alexis Akervik, Minnesota Federal Reserve Bank, 30 Dec 2014; Joel Allen, Queens College, 21 Jun 2017; Dr. Mona Alshamary, USC, 9 Sep 2016; April C. Armstrong, Princeton U. Library, 12 Nov 2018; Alyssa Augustine, Minnesota Federal Reserve Bank, 20 Jul 2020 ; Kyle Ayers, U. of Texas Library, 16 Jan 2014; Irene V. Axelrod, Peabody Essex Museum Library, 3 Jun 2011.

B Shahla Bahavar, USC Library, 11 Apr 2013; Phil Bansner (free-franking), 22 Aug 2018; Donna Barbour, University of Virginia Library, 8 Feb 2016; Gibb Baxter,

Tennessee State Library & Archives, 23 Mar 2010; Sabina Beauchard, Massachusetts Historical Society, 8 May 2015; Adam Berenbak, NARA, 12 Feb 2019; Lori B. Bessler, Wisconsin Historical Society, 22 Jan 2013; Nicholas Beyelia, LAPL, 27 Nov 2019; David Alex Bilodeau, NARA, 14 Mar 2018; Jennifer Boles, *Diplomatic History*, 4 Feb 2015; Judy Bolton, Louisiana State U. Library, 27 Jan 2014; Sara A. Borden, Historical Society of Pennsylvania Library, 7 Dec 2015; Sarah Bost, U. of North Carolina Library, 19 Apr 2013; Brianne Boucher, Government of Canada Library, 13 Jan 2017; Jennifer Brathovde, Library of Congress, 9 Apr 2012; Christopher Brennan, UCLA Library, 7 Jul 2017; Anita Braun, Taylor & Francis Group, 28 Feb 2018; Janice Brown (historian & genealogist), 5 Jun 2014; Laura Brown, New England Historic Genealogical Society, 16 Apr 2014; Lauren R. Brown, U. of Maryland Library, 8 Jan 2013; Denice Bruce, Wichita State U. Medical School, 18 Dec 2015; Marta L. Brunner, UCLA Library, 21 Apr 2014; Nicole Bryan, National Library of Jamaica, 23 Jul 2008; James S. Burns, Union Club of Boston, 20 Jun 2013; Steven "Doc" Butler (Mexican-American War veterans), 17 Jul 2017.

C   Ana M. Campos, LAPL, 16 Nov 2016; James Capobianco, Harvard U. Library, 14 Oct 2011; David Castillo, NARA, 20 Aug 2020; Olivian Cha, LAPL, 11 Apr 2013; Lucas R. Clawson, Hagley Museum and Library, 27 Jan 2014; Neil Cobbett, TNA, 15 Dec 2018; Bonnie B. Coles, LOC, 7 Aug 2008; Patrick Connelly, NARA, 7 Sep 2010; Lynn Conway, Georgetown U. Library, 9 Jan 2014; Geoffrey S. Corn, South Texas College of Law, 5 Dec 2019; Emily Couvillon, U. of Texas, 5 May 2012; Dolores D. Craig, U.S. Consulate, Guayaquil, Ecuador, 24 Apr 2014; Andrea Cronin, Massachusetts Historical Society 19 Apr 2011; Karen Cronmiller, U. of Nevada, Reno, 31 Aug 2015.

D   Kim Damian, Taylor & Francis Group, 24 Apr 2017; Jill M. D'Andrea, NARA, 15 Sep 2008; Damani K. Davis, NARA, 24 Feb 2014; Loretta Deaver, LOC, 16 Apr 2014; Elaine Dickinson, OCLC, 14 Dec 2020; Joseph Ditta, The New-York Historical Society, 24 Oct 2011; Bridget Donahue, New England Historic Genealogical Society, 27 Jun 2013; Eleonora Drury, U. of Kansas Library, 3 Jun 2011; Cheryl Dynan, *Ancestry*, 19 Apr 2013.

E   Esther Eastman, LA Law Library, 20 Apr 2015; Malia Ebel, New Hampshire Historical Society, 19 Jul 2014; Chris Edelson, American U., 26 Jun 2020; Jon Edmondson, UCLA, 10 Jul 2017; Paul Espinosa, Johns Hopkins U. Library, 8 Jan 2013; Vann Evans, State Archives of North Carolina, 17 Apr 2014; Kelley Ewing, Library of Virginia, 30 Jun 2016.

F   Bruce Fein, 21 Feb 2018; Christopher Fiorillo, Yale U. Library, 18 Dec 2015; Connie Fleischer, HathiTrust, 12 Jul 2016; Randall D. Fortson, Navy Department Library, 10 Apr 2017; Kathy Fowler, Arkansas State Library, 3 Dec 2013; Molly French, Charleston County Public Library, 10 May 2013; Rodney French, TNA, 27 Oct 2015; Thomas Frick, *Journal of American History*, 4 Nov 2013.

G   Jean Galbraith, U. of Pennsylvania Law School, 17 Jul 2017; Jenna Galper, HR, 10 Oct 2017; Glenn Gillespie, UC Berkeley Library, 17 Aug 2015; Helen Gilmour, Taylor & Francis Group, 6 Feb 2019; Michel Charles Gobat, U of Pittsburgh, 18 Dec 2017; Simon Goudarzi, TNA, 9 Apr 2011; Miki Goral, UCLA, 31 Jul 2013;

Acknowledgments

Dave Grabarek, Library of Virginia, 1 Jul 2016; Esther Grassian, UCLA Library, 6 May 2011; Elizabeth Gray, NARA, 4 Mar 2011; Patrice R. Green, LOC, 19 Jun 2018; Bobby Griffith, UNT Library, 18 Jul 2016; Richard Grocock, TNA, 23 Sep 2011; James Grossman, American Historical Association, 31 Oct 2017.

H Shannon Hadley, Historical Society of Pennsylvania, 26 Feb 2014; Tina (Rose) Hagee, U. of Kentucky, 14 Jan 2019; Emilie L. Hardman, Harvard U., 27 Oct 2011; Doris Helfer, CSUN Northridge Library, 13 Apr 2013; Sam Haselby, Aeon, 9 Jul 2018; Christine D. Helmlinger Stewart, U. of Virginia Library, 8 Feb 2016; Mallory Herberger, Maryland Historical Society, 19 Jul 2019; Christine Hernández, Tulane U. Library, 3 Apr 2014; Walter V. Hickey, NARA, 26 Mar 2013; Wesley E. Higgins, in re David Francis Keeling, 6 Jun 2015; Michael Hironymous, U. of Texas Library, 21 Oct 2008; Sean P. Hogan, The Catholic U. of America Library, 19 Jul 2011; Aziz Huq, U. Of Chicago, 24 Oct 2018; Cary Hutto, Historical Society of Pennsylvania, 19 Jun 2015.

I & J Suzanne Isaacs, NARA, 2 Mar 2018; James R. Jacobs, Stanford U. Library, 12 Nov 2018; Joseph Jackson, LOC, 20 May 2010; Susan James-Morrow, Minnesota Historical Society, 27 May 2013; Zoe Jarocki, San Diego State U. Library, 4 Jan 2013; Andrew Johns, Brigham Young U., 13 Jul 2020; Greg Johnson, U. of Virginia Library, 21 Feb 2011; Morgan Jones, U. of North Carolina Library, 26 Jun 2013; Kathy Jordan, Library of Virginia, 22 Jun 2016; Morgan Jones, U. of North Carolina Library, 26 Jun 2013.

K Tessa Kale, Columbia U. Press, 13 Jun 2014; Brenda-Lee Kahler, HathiTrust (Jira), 15 Feb 2022; Tom Kanon, Tennessee State Library & Archives, 17 Jun 2015; David Kessler, Bancroft Library, 26 Nov 2012; Chris Killillay, NARA, 17 Aug 2010; Lindsay Alissa King, UCLA, 12 Nov 2018; Bruce Kirby, Library of Congress, 16 Aug 2012; Brian Kiss, Yale U. Library, 11 Aug 2015; Tammy Kiter N-YHS, 6 Jul 2011; James Allen Knechtmann, Navy Department Library, 5 Mar 2014; Tracey Kry, American Antiquarian Society, 8 Jan 2013.

L Kent LaCombe, HathiTrust, 15 Jul 2016; David A. Langbart, NARA, 18 Nov 2013; Dona LaValle, historian, Town of Hornellsville, 22 Jul 2008; Ronald A. Lee, Tennessee State Library & Archives, 23 Mar 2010; Simon Lee, UCLA Library, 7 Sep 2012; Gail Lelyveld (independent researcher), 16 May 2019; Thomas Lester, Massachusetts Historical Society, 18 Apr 2013; Daniel Lewis, The Huntington Library, 3 Jan 2017; Tab Lewis, NARA, 17 Aug 2011; Dan Linke, Princeton U. Library, 12 Nov 2018; Becky Willems Livingston, Panhandle-Plains Historical Museum, 17 Jan 2014.

M Angela Maani, Cal State Library, 29 Mar, 2018; David Martinez, USC Library, 20 Jan 2016; Veronica Martinez, Corpus Christi Public Libraries, 20 Jun 2019; Haley J Maynard NARA, 7 Mar 2018; Kelly McAnnaney, NARA, 8 May 2018; Paul McCardell, Baltimore Sun, 3 Mar 2015; Scott R. McEathron, U. of Kansas, 9 Jan 2012; Bob and Joe Ann McIver, The Descendants of Mexican War Veterans, 21 Jul 2017; Kim Y. McKeithan, NARA, 4 Feb 2013; Cynthia McNaughton, LAPL, 4 Jan 2018; Aaron McWilliams, Pennsylvania State Archives, 1 Apr 2015; Peggy McPhillips, Norfolk City Historian, 28 Jun 2016; Veronica Ronnie Mevorach LAPL, 8 Jun

Acknowledgments

2011; Danielle Mihram, USC Library, 16 Mar 2016; Sam Miller, Historical Society of Pennsylvania, 17 Mar 2016; Romie Minor, Detroit Public Library, 6 Jun 2012; Katherine Mollan, NARA, 7 Sep 2016; Anna Mae Moore, Washington & Jefferson College, 18 Dec 2012; Hayley Moreno, WorldCat, 22 Feb 2019; David N. Myers, UCLA, 4 Feb 2019; Lyndsey D. Myers , U. of Texas Library, 16 Jan 2014.

N   Lisa Nachreiner, HathiTrust (Jira), 8 Mar 2022; Jasper Navarez, Taylor & Francis Group, 1 Aug 2017; Eric Nelson, literary agent, 30 June 2014; John Norvell, author, 15 June 2017; Darlene Nowak, San Diego State U., 8 Jan 2013.

O   Megan O'Connell, Duke U., 6 Aug 2013; Susan O'Donovan (BrANCH co-editor, 2017), 27 Feb 2018; Nicole Oglesby, U. of Texas, 4 Jan 2018; Francis P. O'Neill, Maryland Historical Society, 19 Feb 2016; Susan O'Neill, Pennsylvania State Library, 2 Apr 2015; Natalie O'Neal, U. Press of Kentucky, 10 Jul 2020; F.P. O'Neill , Maryland Historical Society, 12 Feb 2014; Ted O'Reilly, New-York Historical Society, 30 Apr 2010; Jennifer Osorio, UCLA Library, 8 Jul 2014.

P   Barbara Packard, TNA, 27 Oct 2015; Katharin Peter, USC Library, 9 Aug 2012; Kaitlyn Pettengill, Historical Society of Pennsylvania, 26 Feb 2016; Joe Pettican, Taylor & Francis Group, 14 Jul 2017; Elaine Pierce, Ancestry, 5 Sep 2015; Barbara Pilvin, Free Library of Philadelphia, 28 Jun 2013; Rob Platt, OCLC, 29 Nov 2018; Gregory J. Plunges, NARA, 5 Feb 2014; Chris Powell, U. of Michigan Library, 22 Apr 2021.

R   Sally K. Reeves, Louisiana Historical Society, 12 Jan 2014; Kevin Reilly, NARA, 27 Apr 2018; Nancy K. Reis, UNT Library, 13 Jul 2016; Kimberly Reynolds, Boston Public Library, 7 Jan 2013; Andrew Rhodes U. of Southern Miss, 25 Jul 2017; Susan A. Riggs, College of William and Mary Library, 24 June 2013; Gerlinda Riojas, Corpus Christi Public Library, 10 July 2019; Laurie Rizzo, U. of Delaware Library, 25 Oct 2011; Emma Roberts, LAPL, 6 Apr 2015; Mark Roberts, U. of Washington Library, 31 Aug 2015; Rita M. Romero, USC Library, 11 Apr 2013; Valerie Rom-Hawkins, UCLA Library, 24 Apr 2014; Rita Rosenkranz, Literary Agent, 3 Mar 2020; Rodney A. Ross, NARA, 1 Apr 2014.

S   Timothy Salls, New England Historic Genealogical Society, 30 April 2014; Shawn Sambile, Taylor & Francis Group, 14 Jun 2017; Abby L. Saunders, USC Library, 25 Nov 2013; Renee M. Savits, The Library of Virginia, 28 Dec 2018; Carol Savo, NARA, 14 Jan 2014; Gerald D. Saxon (Mexican-American War Veterans), 10 Jul 2017; Lisa Schloss, LAPL, 20 May 2016; Thomas D. Schoonover U. of Louisiana, 4 Oct 2016; Craig Schroer, U. of Texas, 2 April 2010; Eileen Scully, Bennington College, 25 Oct 2018; Andrew Seddighi, HR, 5 Oct 2017; Ruth Selman, TNA, 15 Sep 2020; Nancy M. Shawcross, U. of Pennsylvania, 29 Mar 2011; Elizabeth Shulman, U. of North Carolina, 18 Feb 2015; Mark Silver, National Endowment for the Humanities, 1 Feb 2019; James Similuk, USC Library, 26 Sep 2016; Ganesh Sitaraman, Vanderbilt Law, 6 Jul 2018; Robbie Sittel, UNT, 23 Dec 2018; Rebecca Smith, The Historic New Orleans Collection, 11 Oct 2017; Steven Smith, The Historical Society of Pennsylvania, 16 Jun 2015; Errol S. Somay, Library of Virginia, 25 Jun 2016; Kyla Sommers, History News Network, 19 Sep 2019; Jonathan R. Stayer, Pennsylvania State Archives, 19 Dec 2012; Caitlyn Stephens, U. of

Acknowledgments

Washington School of Law, 28 Nov 2018; Suzanne M. Stewart, New England Historic Genealogical Society, 26 Jun 2013; T.J. Stiles, author, 12 June 2017; Warren Stricker, Panhandle-Plains Historical Museum, 22 Jan 2014; Marten Stromberg, U. of Illinois at Urbana, 4 Feb 2013; Alison Stucke, U. of Wisconsin Library, 16 Dec 2010; Carey Stumm, NARA, 26 Mar 2018; Duane P. Swanson, Minnesota Historical Society, 10 June 2013; Lara Szypszak, LOC, 3 Dec 2019.

T Dace Taube, USC Library, 24 Apr 2014; Scott S. Taylor, Georgetown U. Library, 16 Jan 2014 ; Scott Tiffney (free-franking), 24 Aug 2018; Lee Anne Titangos, UC Berkeley Library, 20 Dec 2013; Charlotte Toney, U. of Virginia, 24 Mar 2011; Jim Toplon, Vanderbilt Library, 20 Jun 2013; Sarah Traugott, U. of Texas, 11 May 2012; Gary Treadway, U. of Virginia, 16 Feb 2011; Kareen Turner, U. of Arkansas, 8 Aug 2013.

V & W Peter Vlahakis, JSTOR, 24 Mar 2011; Elizabeth Vuna, HR, 30 Ag 2018; Peter Wallner, author, 27 June 2017; Bob Walther, U. of Pennsylvania Library, 24 Mar 2011; Matthew Waxman, legal scholar, 29 Oct 2019; Guido Weiss, HR, 22 Feb 2018; Lara Westwood, Maryland Historical Society, 16 Feb 2016; Martin Willis, TNA, 8 Jan 2019; Mary Wirths, Wichita State U. Library, 31 Aug 2015; Ryan J. Woods, New England Historic Genealogical Society, 25 June 2013; Lewis Wyman, LOC, 22 April 2011.

Y & Z Trina Yeckley, NARA, 13 Jul 2011; Jonathon Youssefnia, U. of Texas Library, 16 Jan 2014; Natalie Zacek, U. Of Manchester, 4 Feb 2019.

* *   * *   * *

Preface

I first encountered the story of Greytown's demise more than 50 years ago. It was 1969, and I was writing for an alternative fortnightly newspaper in Cambridge, Massachusetts. The paper would soon reprint a list that had recently appeared in the *Congressional Record* as part of a debate on the Vietnam War. It was called, "Instances of Use of U.S. Armed Forces Abroad, 1798–1945," and was issued by the State Department. (See Chapter 17.) Some of the list's 160 or so entries were mundane. For instance, Iceland was occupied by the United States during World War II "with consent of its Government." One was even funny: "1842, Mexico—Commodore T.A.C. Jones … occupied Monterey, Calif., on October 19, believing war had come. He discovered peace, withdrew, and saluted."

Many entries were of the "to protect American lives and interests" sort. Here is one such that escaped the euphemism filter altogether: "1899–1901, Philippine Islands—To protect American interests following the war with Spain, and to conquer the islands by defeating the Filipinos in their war for independence." And then there was the entry for Greytown, which the list simply said "was destroyed to avenge an insult to the American Minister to Nicaragua." I was astonished. The razing of a whole town for a slight to a diplomat seemed unconscionably heavy-handed.

I wrote a draft article about Greytown in October 1972, but the only searchable source at the time was the *New York Times* on microfilm, which was not as thoroughly indexed in its early years as it was later. I also found some relevant, contemporary Senate executive documents on microform and some germane passages in an 1859 book on Nicaragua. I still have this draft but no record of submitting it anywhere. In 1982 I offered it or some variant to a popular-audience magazine (now defunct) called *American History Illustrated*. It was rejected.

After twenty years as a journalist in the Boston area, I moved to Los Angeles in 1985 to try writing movie and TV scripts. I supported myself as a typesetter, working on some of the earliest pre–PC, pre–Mac desktop electronic typesetting devices. By 1991, having failed at scriptwriting and

Preface

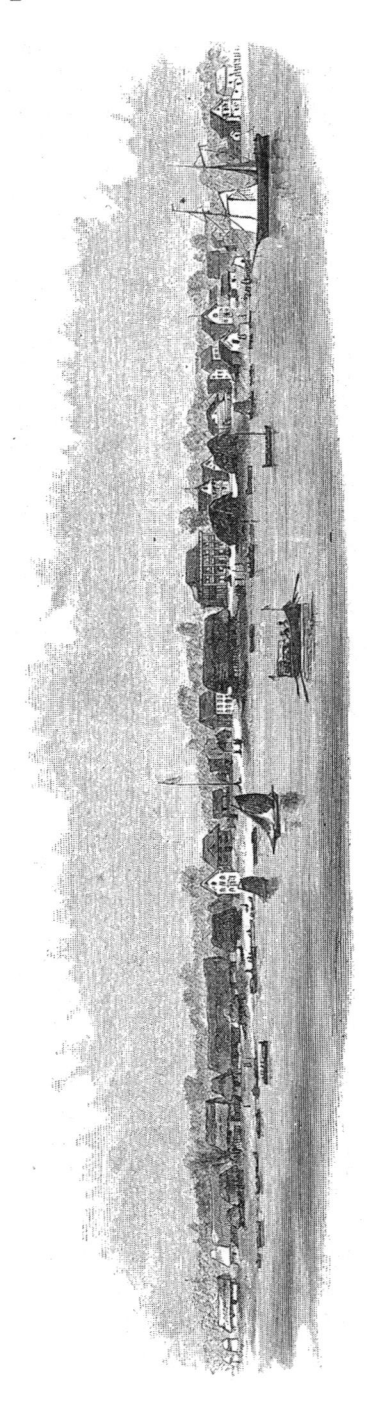

having become enamored of the sophisticated visuals the Mac was capable of, I became a graphic artist, making a freelance living at it for the next 30 years or so.

Along the way, I befriended an historian named Charles Rappleye, with whom I mostly played tennis. (See his page at Amazon or Simon & Schuster.) One day in 2007, he asked me across a tennis net what his next book should be about. I said, setting him up for a fall, "How about Greytown?" And he replied, as I expected, "What's Greytown?" I spent the next three years gathering research materials—from the now increasingly word-searchable internet—and convinced him to take a shot. He wrote a book proposal in July 2010, but when he hadn't had "a lot of success getting commercial interest in it," he said, "you're welcome to have your material back." (Charlie was a great friend and a more than passable tennis player. He died in September 2018, age 62. I miss him dearly.)

When he returned my Greytown research, I hadn't written anything in 20 years, but I decided to take it on. From 2007 until 2014, I researched the incident and wrote multiple drafts of an article I finally submitted in 2014 to one of America's most prestigious scholarly history journals, the Organization of American Historians' *Journal of American History*. Two of the three readers in the journal's

Left: View of Greytown, 1853, from across the harbor (*Harper's New Monthly Magazine*. Reproduction courtesy of the Huntington Library, San Marino, California—AP2_H3_p54).

Preface 3

```
Patricia L. Faust, Editor
American History Illustrated
The National Historical Society        17 February 1982
Editorial Offices
Box 3200
Harrisburg, PA 17105        QUERY: The Greytown Affair

Dear Ms. Faust:
    There was bad blood between T.T. Smith and Albino
Paladino--the American steamer captain had rammed the
```

Salutation and date from author's 1982 pitch letter to *American History Illustrated* in re Greytown draft article (author's collection).

double-blind "peer review" roundly condemned my piece and advised outright rejection—but not the third. Although not without criticisms, the third reviewer wrote: "There is much to recommend this essay, starting with its mastery of published primary sources. The author gives unusually clear accounts of the Greytown incident … among the best I have ever read. It will be good for specialists to have readily available for reference such a cogent and compelling analysis of these important episodes in US diplomatic and business history. This is a tangled story. The author does a wonderful job in relating it."

This reader recommended a rewrite and resubmission, but the editor rejected the piece outright. I emailed him and asked if he would forward an email from me to that reader. He agreed and I offered Anonymous Number Three a co-authorship of any subsequent outing we might collaborate on and half of any proceeds, including from a book or a documentary. I soon received a revelatory reply directly from Mystery Three; he was Robert E. May, professor of history at Purdue University, a titan among chroniclers of 19th-century America and its Latin American policies at the time. He said he was too busy to collaborate but would, gratis, consult on any project I might pursue. He subsequently read and suggested changes, including extensive line edits, to a half-dozen-or-so subsequent drafts of the rewritten article. I submitted this to the British journal *American Nineteenth Century History* (*BrANCH*) in August 2015, which published it in May 2017, under my title, "Revisiting nineteenth-century U.S. interventionism in Central America: capitalism, intrigue, and the obliteration of Greytown."[1]

That article would not have happened without Bob May, nor would this book, which is why I dedicated it to him. As of this writing, he continues to advise me on Greytown, eight years on.

My journal article was a revisionist history of the Greytown razing, exposing the insult-avenging explanation as a pretext or *casus belli* and revealing the real reasons why Greytown was destroyed. According to American historian William O. Scroggs in 1916, it was in the interest of a Nicaraguan-based U.S. corporation "that Greytown be wiped off the map, and it had succeeded in inveigling the [U.S.] government into doing this bit of dirty work." Actually, two groups of American businessmen "inveigled" Washington into destroying the port. The one Scroggs was referring to ran a local steamboat company; the other, in league early on with the first, ran a local land-speculation scheme. The *New York Tribune* of July 28, 1854, captured the essence of these twin intrigues: "That [U.S.-owned steamboat] company [had] long desired to get rid of the town, which … was a hindrance to their supremacy and had defied their power. [Greytown] also stood in the way of a great project for the establishment of a colony … which is entertained by several speculators, and for which they have a [land] grant.… The town being removed, it is supposed that project may be carried out with greater facility."[2]

In October 2018, the website History News Network published my op-ed entitled "Can an Amateur Historian Rewrite History?" This expounded on my failed efforts to get the official cause of Greytown's demise corrected, from the "avenged-insult" distortion to the sub rosa plots by the U.S. steamboat company operatives and the land-grant colonization speculators. The op-ed also described (as did my 2017 *BrANCH* journal article) a court case called *Durand v. Hollins*. In this case, one Calvin Durand unsuccessfully sought damages for property destroyed in the razing. This precedent has been used for decades to justify U.S. military interventions undertaken without securing—as required by a strict interpretation of the Constitution—prior authorization from Congress.[3]

Besides seeking to correct the official record as to the cause of Greytown's destruction, challenging *Durand* is the other pillar of the brace that holds this book upright and righteously thematic. Greytown's *Durand* case law, upon which much of U.S. interventionism is justified and sanctioned, is based on a gross misapprehension of the events attendant and, therefore, on an inappropriate attribution of cause. And this, in turn, should call into question the historical and legal validity of *Durand v. Hollins* as precedential law. In the 2020 edition of their book, *National Security Law*, Stephen Dycus, William Banks, Peter Raven-Hansen, and Stephen Vladeck invoke this very question with a reference to my HNN op-ed: "One observer believes that the real motivation for the attack on Greytown was not protection of American property, but removal of the town itself as an obstacle to the business of U.S. investors. See Will Soper, 'Can an Amateur Historian Rewrite History,' *History News Network*, Oct. 23, 2018. If true," the authors ask, "would that alter the value of *Durand v. Hollins* as a precedent?"[4]

Chapter 1

"I Must Shoot the Fellow!"

(Author's note: The Preface is an essential preamble to this chapter. Please read first.) From 1849 to 1850, Ephraim George Squier had been the U.S. chargé to all the Central American states, posted to Nicaragua. Now, in 1853, he was back, exploring Nicaragua as a private citizen—or at least trying to. At this moment his immediate concern was finding Antonio Paladino, a celebrated black Nicaraguan river and lake skipper, or *patrón*. Squier had befriended him, possibly when U.S. minister, and now had hired him for this prospective trip down the San Juan River to the town of San Juan del Norte in his "pet" *bungo, La Granadina*.

Bungos were big barge-like canoes ubiquitous on the Isthmus of Nicaragua, and the city San Juan del Norte was the port at the mouth of the San Juan River on the Atlantic coast. Even though the town had been seized from Nicaragua by the British in 1848 and renamed Greytown (after their governor of Jamaica, Charles Edward Grey), Americans and Nicaraguans preferred the old name.

Squier was to meet Paladino on a beach on the San Juan River. "The only new or novel object in the picture," Squier later wrote, "was one of the steamers of the Transit Company, with its plume of escaping steam and its starry flag streaming in the wind." Squier probably took considerable pride in this "new or novel" sight. If it weren't for him, that steamboat might not be there at all. In 1849, Squier had, as envoy, deftly liaised an agreement between the Nicaraguan government and the aforementioned—and U.S.-owned—Accessory Transit Company, then known as the American Atlantic and Pacific Ship Canal Company. The agreement gave the company the exclusive right to carry passengers across the isthmus on its almost coast-to-coast natural waterway, the eastern half consisting of the San Juan River and the western half, of Lake Nicaragua. (See map before title page.) This inland water route linked up with oceangoing steamers on both coasts of Nicaragua, cutting the 10,000-mile trip around South America—and so, four or five months—from the voyage between New York and San Francisco. This proved to be a godsend during the early years of the Gold Rush.[1]

6 "Greytown is no more!"

Above: A *bungo* on the Rio San Juan, about 1849. These were often made of dug out 40-foot-long half-logs of the Guanacaste tree, with, in this case, two or three courses of strake planking, building up the sides to increase freeboard (*Century Magazine*).

Left: A recognized archeologist and ethnologist, E.G. Squier wangled an appointment as an envoy just so he could study Central America's ancient peoples and artifacts. He became an able diplomat, a prolific travel writer and America's leading expert on the region (Library of Congress).

1. "I Must Shoot the Fellow!"

Star of the West, which was typical of the ocean-going sidewheeler steamships that linked up with the Nicaraguan isthmus inland steamers, taking their passengers on to New York or San Francisco (*Harper's New Monthly Magazine*).

"I had hardly landed," Squier recalled in a piece for *Harper's New Monthly Magazine*, "before I was nearly caught from my feet in the Herculean embrace of Antonio Paladino, my ancient patrón, who took this elephantine way of evincing his joy at meeting me again."[2]

Squier soon left Nicaragua for a project (never realized) to build a railroad across Honduras. So, this trip to Greytown may have been the last time the two friends ever saw each other.

"A Perfect Desperado"

One of the Accessory Transit Company's American riverboat captains, T.T. Smith, did not share Squier's kind regard for Paladino. A U.S. diplomat later described Smith as "a perfect desperado, and totally unfit for the position he ... occupied. He came very near being thrown overboard ... several times, for his brutality and insolence to passengers." About a year after Squier and Antonio embraced on that beach, Paladino and Smith would have a confrontation on that same river that would trigger events that have influenced American foreign policy to the present day. The two watermen would often quarrel during their regular encounters on the San Juan River, and the clash on May 16, 1854, would differ only in its denouement.[3]

Smith was piloting his steamboat, the *Routh*, on the last leg of the west-to-east trans-isthmian trip to Greytown Harbor. Because the

A river steamer in Greytown Harbor, about 1853 (*Frank Leslie's Illustrated Newspaper*. Reproduction courtesy of the Huntington Library, San Marino, California—RB499751_v1_p21_top).

A lake steamer at Granada in western Nicaragua, about 1856 (*Frank Leslie's Illustrated Newspaper*. Reproduction courtesy of the Huntington Library, San Marino, California—RB499751_v2_p85_bottom).

steamboats could not negotiate the river's three sets of rapids, they had to run, back-and-forth, within the confines of that part of the river demarcated by the rapids up- and downstream from their boat. On the east-to-west traverse, for instance, steamers carried passengers who debarked from an ocean steamer in Greytown Harbor to the Machuca

1. "I Must Shoot the Fellow!"

The port of San Juan del Sur on Nicaragua's west coast (*Frank Leslie's Illustrated Newspaper*).

Rapids. Here the passengers walked around the rapids on a path while *bungos* carried their baggage to a steamer above. At the next rapids, the Castillo—the most difficult—the company had built a small railway to portage passengers and their baggage to the next steamer waiting above. After the last rapids, the El Toro, passengers were met by a much larger Lake Nicaragua steamer, which took them up the rest of the river and then across the lake to Virgin Bay. There, carriages on a macadamized road only 12 miles long took them the rest of the way to the port of San Juan del Sur and the ocean steamer that would carry them on to San Francisco. If all this sounds unacceptably tedious, it should be borne in mind that this only took a day or day and a half and saved the three-to-four months the rounding of Cape Horn would require.[4]

On the fateful day of May 16, 1854, the *Routh* was carrying passengers, west-to-east, returning from California. But not all the *Routh*'s passengers that day began their journey in California. At least one started in western Nicaragua. Solon Borland was a doctor, ex-soldier, and former senator from Arkansas. Most recently, he had served about eight months as the American minister to Nicaragua and was now on his way home. He had

This is the American Hotel, on the 12-mile macadamized road between Lake Nicaragua and the Pacific Coast port of San Juan del Sur (*Frank Leslie's Illustrated Newspaper*).

resigned, effective two weeks earlier, in response to a reprimand from Secretary of State William L. Marcy.

"Solon Is Destitute of a Particle of Discretion"

The New York correspondent of the *Charleston Courier* wrote of Borland: "Solon is destitute of a particle of discretion, is something of a braggart, fulfills his destiny in eternally getting into rows. His [fist] fight with Senator [Henry S.] Foote [D–MS] in Washington, and the pitiful nose-wrenching he gave Mr. [Joseph C.G.] Kennedy, of the Census Department, were not very brilliant trophies of his Legislative career.... He has made botch-work of every official act of his life."[5]

1. "I Must Shoot the Fellow!"

In March 1850, then–Senator Borland had met Senator Foote, apparently by chance, on a Washington street, telling him, according to the *New York Herald*, "General, I understand you said to a friend of mine, to-day, that you considered me a mere tool to Mr. [Senator John C.] Calhoun." Angrily, Senator Foote replied, "Really, I have no recollection of saying so; but if you suppose I was capable of making such a declaration, you are welcome to it." Whereupon "Mr. Borland struck Mr. Foote in the face with his fist, cutting him with his ring, so that he bled." A Colonel Walton of Alabama then separated the men. "Both parties are warm-blooded ... but ... there is no danger of any bad results following the affair, as the parties have become reconciled."[6]

A power first in New York State politics, William L. Marcy moved easily into federal offices. As a young senator he coined the expression, "To the victor belong the spoils" (Library of Congress).

About two years later, in early February 1852, Borland had made some remarks during a debate "upon the census tables." According to the *New York Tribune*, "Mr. J.C.G. Kennedy, Superintendent of the Census ... had come into [the Senate] to make some explanations" to the senators, including Borland. "When I want information from you," Borland responded, "I will ask for it." Kennedy replied, "Those most in want of information are not always the ones to seek for it." At this point "Mr. Borland rose ... and struck Mr. K. a very severe blow on the side of the nose, inflicting a severe wound, and breaking the bridge of the nose.... While Mr. Kennedy was nearly insensible, Mr. Borland sprung at him, but being restrained by bystanders, cried out, 'Let me go, and I'll cut the d—d rascal's throat!' Mr. Kennedy is a very small, slight, delicate man, and an invalid besides, and unable to cope with a man of Mr. Borland's size and vigor even if he had an opportunity.... Mr. Kennedy is laid up, and is severely injured."[7]

Given Borland's backstory, the *New York Times* wrote of his posting to Nicaragua with haunting prescience. "Mr. Borland's public services at the Isthmus must be limited to the collection of information.... If he attempts to interfere at all with the delicate web of diplomacy with those clumsy hands of his ... [we will have] an armful of troubles [in] six months." Of the 62 men in the Senate, the *Times* concluded, "61 men in it [were] better qualified to fulfill the duties of the post."[8]

Little more than a month into his posting, Borland announced to a crowd of Nicaraguans that it was his "greatest ambition to see the State of Nicaragua forming a bright star in the flag of the United States." And as the *Times* had feared, he also tried to make policy rather than just collect information. Washington learned that he was making promises to the Nicaraguans and Hondurans regarding their relations with the British that were threatening delicate Anglo-American negotiations involving the region. In many of his dispatches, Borland urged repudiation of the prevailing treaty with the British, with Secretary Marcy countering that the United States considered it a "subsisting contract and feels bound to observe its stipulations.... Your course in relation to it," Marcy admonished Borland, "will be observed until you receive notice of their modification."

Marcy also objected to Borland complaining about the "devilish machinations" of the British without saying what these were. "There are, running through all your dispatches," Marcy told Borland, "complaints of the conduct of Great Britain, but these complaints are not accompanied with any specification of acts, and I

A Mexican-American War veteran, the irascible Solon Borland was also a physician, pharmacist, newspaper editor and U.S. Senator from Arkansas (Library of Congress).

am left in doubt as to the foundation of them." This long note from Marcy in late December 1853, historian James M. Woods writes, "was not a gentle reprimand, but a general rebuke of his mission. Whether or not Marcy's note was actually intended to induce Borland's resignation, it had that effect."

Borland resigned on February 22, 1854, effective as of May 1; he was so furious at Marcy that he sent his resignation over Marcy's head, to President Franklin Pierce himself. "I most respectfully request you to relieve me," Borland asked Pierce. Marcy, he wrote, "has required of me what, as an honorable man, I cannot consent to do; and has chosen to indulge in a tone of remark to which I cannot continue in a position to be subject, while so much of self-respect remains to me as becomes a man."[9]

"Two Colored Boys Came In and Took Out Three Pistols"

The initial confrontation on May 16, 1854, between the *Routh*'s Captain Smith and river pilot Antonio Paladino began when Smith spotted Paladino's *bungo* tied up with others to the riverbank, the crews all having lunch. Smith turned the *Routh* toward these *bungos*. Aboard the *Routh* that day besides Borland was another diplomat, a German named Henri Wiedemann, who watched anxiously as the little steamer ran up against Paladino's *bungo*. The steamer damaged the *bungo* "by the collision, whether designedly or otherwise, I am unable to say," Wiedemann noted later. "The *patrón*, or master, of the *bungo* thereupon commenced to abuse Captain Smith in Spanish, to which the latter retorted fully in English." A *Routh* crewman then threw a rope to someone on one of the other *bungos*, who tied it to a tree. But when that *bungo*'s crew saw some of the steamboat's crewmen brandishing firearms, they started untying the rope. Captain Smith tried to convince them to wait a "*poco tiempo*" (little time). But that *bungo* crew had seen enough; they threw the line back and "ran into the woods."[10]

The *Routh* drifted away, downstream, towards Greytown Harbor. Neither vessel was badly damaged, no one had been hurt, and the incident seemed over. But then, as the diplomat Wiedemann watched in disbelief, Captain Smith inexplicably turned the *Routh* around and, after "two ineffectual attempts, frustrated by the strong current," took the boat "back up the river for about half an hour." While all this was going on, a New Yorker named William Millar was sitting in his hammock below-decks. "Presently, two colored boys came in and took out three pistols, two of which they concealed in their breast. I asked them what was the excitement?" The boys told Millar that Captain Smith was turning the boat around to go back and shoot Antonio, the patrón of the *bungo* they had just passed.

When Millar asked them why, one of them replied, "Captain Smith and he quarreled every time they met."[11]

Curious about the boys arming themselves and their comments, Millar rose from his hammock and made his way to the upper decks, where he was as surprised as the diplomat Wiedemann by the *Routh*'s slewing about to return upstream. During this interval, according to Wiedemann, "Captain Smith had fetched a rifle from the cabin, and repeatedly vociferated, 'I must shoot the fellow, he has used threatening language that shall cost him his life' and other expressions of that nature, which had better be passed in silence." After a half-hour, the *Routh* was upstream of Antonio's *bungo*; she turned back downstream again, and "was now going under full steam toward the *bungo*." Picking up the story, Millar said that the *Routh* "ran right down, bows into the broadside of Antonio's *bungo*.... [Paladino] did not rise until the steamer struck his *bungo*. When he did rise, he held up his left hand to Capt. Smith, and said, '¡Cuidado, capitán, usted rompe me bungo!'" ("Take care, captain, you break my *bungo*!")[12]

As Smith prepared to fire his rifle at Paladino, the diplomat Wiedemann "did everything in my power to persuade him not to carry out his design. I went even so far as twice to prevent him from firing; the third time he exclaimed, 'I am captain of this boat, and I will not permit even my best friend to interfere.'" Then, according to Millar, a Nicaraguan soldier in charge of the mail onboard "put himself before Smith and tried to prevent his shooting Antonio. While in the act, Smith's mate struck the guard with the butt end of a blunderbuss on the back of the neck and knocked him down. After getting him down, he tried to roll him off the hurricane deck into the river, when Mr. Wiedemann drew him off." Millar added that as Paladino was about the repeat the "you break my *bungo*" expression and "got out the word '*cuidado*' ... a ball entered the nipple of the left breast." The *Routh* then continued its downstream journey. "As far as I saw in looking back," Millar said, Paladino "remained in the same position with his feet up." Captain Smith then turned to Wiedemann and said, somewhat oddly, cryptically, and surprisingly, "I am sorry for this, but I could not help it."[13]

"Poor Antonio!" E.G. Squier later wrote, lamenting the loss of his ancient *patrón*. "He was ... wantonly assassinated by a brutal captain of one of the Transit steamers. There never was an honester and truer heart than that which beat beneath the swarthy breast of Antonio Paladino."[14]

"He Wouldn't Have Done It If 'Borland' Had Not Told Him To"

As for Borland's actions during the murder, Wiedemann reported, "Mr. Borland witnessed, if not from the beginning, yet the greater part of this ... act, from the upper deck, and during the whole time, I have not heard him make any remarks in relation to it. So much on this subject." But there *was* more on the subject, albeit imperfectly supported by second-hand accounts. "Most of the passengers disapproved of the act of Captain Smith," William Millar wrote later, "and the talk was that Mr. Borland told him to shoot [Paladino]." An unidentified Greytown resident repeated this accusation in a letter to the *Boston Atlas* newspaper (parentheses in original): "[The] immortal Solon Borland ... said to the Captain, 'Why didn't you shoot the d—d black _____.' (The language is too gross for publication.)"

The letter writer also corroborated, albeit possibly as hearsay, Wiedemann's story of grappling with Smith, Smith expressing contrition to Wiedemann, and Millar's statement that Smith said, "he wouldn't have done it if 'Borland' had not told him to do it." (On May 30, just two weeks after the murder, the *New York Herald* had written, "Incredible as it may appear, it is said the captain of the steamer was abetted by a person who afterwards figured in the affair in a very conspicuous manner.") Immediately after the murder, Millar confronted Borland: "I asked Mr. Borland if he thought it was right for Captain Smith to shoot the captain of the *bungo*." Borland replied that "it was very wrong to shoot him" and said he had urged Smith "to bring Antonio on board and whip him."[15]

Another American onboard the *Routh* during this fateful and fatal trip was a Kentuckian named George Wiley, whose letter to a newspaper said that "so far as I heard among the passengers, there was a universal feeling of sympathy and regard for the fate of Antonio, and that the deed was cowardly and brutal. However, my motive is not to enlist either prejudice or sympathy, but to state the facts of the case, as far as they came under my own observation. I am sure my countrymen would scorn to get out of a bad scrape by any suppression of truth or perversion of facts. Let God's justice be done."[16]

Justice, whether God's or man's, was eventually thwarted, and when the *Routh* reached Greytown Harbor, George Wiley would witness the opening maneuvers of that foiling firsthand.

"The Mortal Feud"

The *Routh* did not tie up at Greytown proper but at a large, sandy spit of land called Punta (or Point) Arenas across the harbor from the town. Here the transit company had all its Atlantic coast facilities. (Nearby was the *Northern Light*, the ocean steamer preparing to leave for New York the next day.) While it was only a rowboat-ride from Punta

Arenas to Greytown, the distance was a politico-economic abyss, leading as it did to what *Harper's New Monthly Magazine* called a "mortal feud" over, of all things, shopping. A sizable international community of English, German, French, and American entrepreneurs had moved to Greytown hoping to sell goods and services to in-transit passengers. But the steamboat company, *Harper's* noted, would not allow passengers to go into Greytown, keeping them at Punta Arenas and thereby diverting such business "into the hands of the company's favorites and officers."[17]

Punta Arenas was owned by Great Britain's Mosquito Protectorate, a geopolitical contrivance that included Greytown and what otherwise would have been the eastern halves of Honduras and Nicaragua. (See map before title page.) Here lived (and still live) the Miskito, or Mosquito Indians with whom the English had traded for some 200 years. The British claimed that since the Spanish had never conquered the Indians their lands had not become part of Honduras and Nicaragua when those states freed themselves from Spanish rule. Great Britain also claimed that the Indians governed the protectorate under a succession of "kings" (a line the English established and carefully nurtured), but this was only nominally so. "The Mosquito question," noted one U.S. diplomat, "has been a subject for discussion & negotiation for nearly

Punta (or Point) Arenas, 1853, across the harbor from Greytown. Here the U.S.-owned steamboat company had its Atlantic Coast facilities (*Harper's New Monthly Magazine*. Reproduction courtesy of the Huntington Library, San Marino, California—AP2_H3_p55).

two centuries. It is now questionable, to whom this insalubrious sweep of Country on the Atlantic belongs; while in view of our policy in regard to Indian tribes [insisting no Western Hemisphere Indians had sovereign rights to the land they occupied] the Protectorate of Mosquitia must be taken, as a shift & subterfuge."[18]

Early on, in 1851, the U.S.-owned transit company had approached the Mosquito Protectorate to lease part of Punta Arenas as the Atlantic terminus for its inland steamer service, and the authorities (Englishmen acting for the reigning king) agreed. But the British leased just *part* of Punta Arenas to the transit company and *only* for a coaling station. The protectorate charged "a nominal rent of sixpence sterling per month" and reserved the right to cancel the lease if it needed the land for something else. In 1852, after Greytown declared independence from the protectorate, it continued the same lease agreement. Now, in a bid to gain access to their hoped-for customer base, the Greytowners canceled the lease, claiming the land was needed for a quarantine, and then offered the company generous incentives to move into Greytown proper.

When the company refused to move, the city council, on February 8, 1853, ordered the mayor to have the company's buildings removed, one immediately, which was done, and the rest beginning thirty days hence. This gap between "ejectments" gave the company enough time to alert Washington, which sent a U.S. Navy sloop-of-war called the *Cyane* (pronounced SIGH-uh-KNEE or SIGH-ANNIE). The ship arrived just one day before the town was to carry out the second ejectment, which Hollins prevented by landing Marines. (See Chapter 5 for more about the "mortal feud" and this foiled ejectment.)[19]

An uneasy truce prevailed for about a year, until May 5, 1854, which, for context, was 11 days before the Paladino murder. That night, four persons purportedly stole an improbably large amount of basic foodstuffs from the company at Punta Arenas in a 20-foot-long ship's boat, called a yawl. They rowed it over to Greytown, the company alleged, where the residents supposedly hid the food and covered for the "thieves." (The *New York Tribune* intimated that this food theft, "whose whole existence is a matter of uncertainty," probably never took place. There is more about this incident in Chapter 5.)[20]

"I ... Laid Hands on Him"

Word of Paladino's murder reached the port before the *Routh*, and, as George Wiley watched for justice to prevail, Greytown's deputy marshal, Edward Patton, boarded the *Routh*. Captain Smith "shortly appeared with his shirt off," Patton later testified, "as if washing himself; I shook hands with him and laid hands on him, telling him he was my prisoner."[21]

Tensions immediately mounted. An American bystander chided Patton for his role in "such business as this." The deputy was then pushed back, and the prisoner was released. "I was warned to quit the boat immediately; the prisoner ran and got a sword, which he dropped; he then ran and got a blunderbuss, swearing he would shoot me; the pistol in my hand was wrenched out of it, and then I was hustled over the side. We then came away."[22]

Patton reported these events to his superior, Marshal Thomas Codd, "a mulatto man," who went out himself to Punta Arenas with several armed deputies, "mostly Jamaican negroes," to press the matter. George Wiley continued to watch as the marshal and his deputies clambered aboard the *Routh*. Codd later testified that Smith "had in his hand a loaded blunderbuss but appeared willing to come when I arrested him." But by then Borland, who was already on the *Northern Light*, had been alerted as to events and was soon back aboard the *Routh*. Wiley said Borland "was very boisterous and bullying to the officers ... [his language] embellished with many expressions that would be novel in any diplomatic correspondence I ever read." Nor, added Wiley, was Borland very complimentary to the Pierce administration, maintaining, somewhat ambiguously, that if it "had a spirit equal to that of a louse, [it] would have exterminated the damned scoundrels long ago."[23]

As the marshal held Smith, Borland knocked his hand away and threatened his life. "The American Government did not recognize this place," the marshal quoted Borland as saying, "nor any authority in the place; and he, as American Minister, could call to his command every passenger on the steamer [*Northern Light*] to shoot down every one of us."[24]

Just at this moment, the confluence of events brought the situation near to critical mass. Some Americans, standing "coolly around, got their guns ready for action." At the same time, a *bungo*-load of Greytonians approached the *Routh*, with their leader "exhorting the men to pull briskly" on their oars. Then Borland "took a gun from somebody, cocked it, and leveled it, and was about to fire" at the approaching men when the marshal turned it aside with his hand. "[Borland] then said: 'If you respect your lives, do not allow the boat to come any nearer, or I will fire and kill every one. I shall have a man-of-war here in a very short time,' Borland shouted, 'to settle all this matter!' Seeing the numbers around," Marshal Codd later testified, "and the tenor of the remarks made, I was obliged to come away and leave him, the prisoner. I asked him [Borland] to communicate with the American Consul and bring the man over. He said it was not my business, and to leave the ship directly or he would use me as he would any other. I then left and came away."[25]

"Respected by ... [U.S.] Citizens ... Resorting Thither"

As touched upon earlier, Greytown, a tiny village of 500 souls, had belonged to Nicaragua and was known as San Juan del Norte (or San Juan de Nicaragua) until the British seized it in 1848 and then appended it (reattached it, they would insist) to their Mosquito Protectorate. (There is more on this in Chapter 2.)[26]

In 1852, after four years under the nominal rule of the Mosquito Indian kings and the de facto governance of English consuls, the residents of Greytown had, as noted earlier, declared their independence from the protectorate. They set up, in effect, an independent city-state not unlike Bremen in the Hanseatic League of Northern Europe. Instrumental in changing Greytown's political status had been the self-same American and European entrepreneurs who were now involved in the "mortal feud" with the transit company. The British approved of this new city government, usually dominated by American expats, but still exercised some lingering, quasi-official oversight.[27]

Former Minister Borland's offenses at Punta Arenas—obstruction of justice; assault and battery on the town marshal; threatening the lives of several officers—were compounded by his insistence that the American government did not recognize Greytown or its authorities. Marshal Codd knew this was untrue, and so did Borland—or at least he should have. Two years earlier, in 1852, the State Department declared that the "endeavors [of] the existing authority of the place [i.e., the new city-state government] ... to preserve the public peace and punish wrong-doers, would not be inconsistent with the policy and honor of the United States." Accordingly, a U.S. Navy commodore was directed "to repair to Greytown," and, in conjunction with an English admiral, "see that all reasonable municipal and other regulations in force there were respected by the vessels and citizens of the United States resorting thither." After Pierce took office in 1853, his administration renewed this Anglo-American agreement.[28]

"Murder, Without a Shadow of Palliation"

One of the Americans waiting to depart Greytown Harbor on the *Northern Light* the next day was the legendary American army officer and explorer John C. Frémont. He was coming from California and had recently arrived at Punta Arenas but not on the *Routh*'s deadly trip. He told the *New York Times* two weeks later that "this homicide was considered by the Americans [at Greytown], almost without exception, a deliberate, cold-blooded murder, without a shadow of palliation." Nonetheless, Frémont defended Borland's thwarting of Smith's arrest. "To permit the Greytown officers to arrest an American citizen and try him for crime," Frémont told the *Times*, "would be to recognize the authority of the Town Government in the fullest sense." (Apparently, Frémont was unfamiliar with the two Anglo-American agreements sanctioning the town's authority to "punish wrong-doers.")

Frémont also told the *Times* that Borland had made a speech later that same fateful day, May 16, to a crowd of *Northern Light* passengers and other Americans, urging them to aid him in "crushing out" the town, "this scion of the Mosquitos." None heeded his call, and Borland went into Greytown alone. He was rowed across the harbor to the town and made his way to the residence of the only American diplomat assigned to the port, U.S. Commercial Agent Joseph W. Fabens.[29]

"Chosen ... By ... the Transit Company"

Before this assignment Fabens had served nine years as the U.S. consul to French Guiana. Some Greytonians would later write that Fabens at first declined the Greytown commercial agency because it would not pay well enough. The transit company then assured him that if his income fell below $2,000 per annum ($59,000 in 2022), the company would make up the difference. This and a couple of lucrative contracts with the company itself sealed the deal. (U.S. commercial agents were allowed to engage in trade to make extra money.) Later, the *New York Tribune* reported that "there is good reason to believe that it was for the purpose of producing a decided rupture with the town that Mr. Fabens was sent here as Commercial

U.S. Commercial Agent at Greytown, Joseph W. Fabens, aka, J. Warren Fabens (from *"The Last Cigar" and Other Poems*, a book of his poetry published posthumously in 1887).

Agent. It can be shown that he was chosen and recommended by the leading men of the transit company in New-York, who promised him all their influence and support."[30]

When it was rumored that the murderer, Captain Smith, had accompanied Borland to Fabens' home, the mayor ordered that Smith, if found there, be arrested. The rumor proved untrue, so Marshal Codd, accompanied by some very angry townspeople, decided instead to arrest Borland for his prevention earlier that day of Smith's arrest. Borland confronted them, reportedly with pistol in hand. The ex-minister again invoked diplomatic immunity and then undiplomatically called the assembled "the off-scouring of hell." And he repeated—erroneously or deceitfully—that Greytown officials had no authority recognized by the United States to arrest American citizens. When the mayor got wind of the marshal's intent to arrest Borland in lieu of Smith, he rushed to Fabens' house, hoping to defuse the situation by overruling the marshal's decision. He informed Borland that he had not ordered any such proceeding and apologized. Just as the marshal and the crowd seemed ready to withdraw, someone threw a piece of broken bottle at Borland and then ran away; Borland's cheek was slightly scratched. The mayor and another Greytowner offered, on the spot, a reward of fifty dollars each ($1,500 × 2 in 2022) for the discovery of the perpetrator.[31]

After the mayor, the marshal, and the crowd withdrew, Henri Wiedemann, the German diplomat who had been aboard the *Routh*, learned of the assault on Borland. He and several others offered fifty dollars each toward a reward for the assailant's apprehension. Fearing that "evil consequences might result … by this act of rudeness," Wiedemann, who was the consul for Hamburg and Bremen at Greytown, "took the liberty" of calling on Borland at Fabens' house later that night "to see whether this affair could not be adjusted." Wiedemann offered to draft an apologetic "address signed by all the respectable inhabitants, expressing their indignation." Borland replied, "It is not I who has been insulted, but the government of the United States in my person." This, Wiedemann knew, "naturally cut off all further endeavors to redress the matter." (The city attorney addressed a note the next morning to Commercial Agent Fabens saying he had been informed "that a mob under the pretense of law, violated last evening your domicile, and insulted the person of the Hon. S. Borland. The authorities of this city … are determined to punish the offenders with the utmost rigor of the law.")[32]

"Take the D——d Town"

That same night, while Borland remained safely ensconced in his house, Fabens asked an American shipmaster called Wm. H. Rogers (or

Rodgers) to row him and three compatriots over to the *Northern Light*. (While he was on board the steamship *"Northern Light,"* Captain Rogers later told the *New York Tribune*, "several of the passengers told me that Smith would not have shot the man if he had not been encouraged by Borland.") Here Fabens told the captain and passengers that Borland "had been seriously injured by a parcel of rebels and pirates, and niggers in the town, and … called for volunteers to go and burn the town." One passenger said Fabens claimed, "Mr. Borland was very much cut up" and had been put "in the stocks" by the townspeople. Fabens exhorted, unsuccessfully, the *Northern Light*'s crew and passengers to "go, and take Mr. Borland out of the stocks and take the d——d town at the same time."[33]

The passengers doubted Fabens but "appointed a committee of three to go learn the facts." Rogers told the *New York Tribune* that the Fabens party, numbering 11 in all, was "not permitted to land, the people having got wind of the intention to burn the town. They, however, told Fabens that he might land, but not the others." Meanwhile, said Rogers, Borland "remained ashore at the Commercial Agency, and there was no guard around the house and no restraint on Borland. The only guard was along the beach, to prevent parties landing, and burning the town as threatened by Fabens. [Some U.S. officials and newspapers later construed this beach patrol as the town holding Borland prisoner that night.] The next morning Borland went on board the steamship at about 6 o'clock, and there were no marks on his head, as represented by Fabens to the passengers."[34]

"Got a Lick with Something on the Lower Part of His Right Cheek"

Shortly after Borland boarded, *Routh* passenger William Millar approached him "and remarked that I was glad to see that his face was not cut and abused as Mr. Fabens had stated." Borland replied that he "had got a lick with something on the lower part of his right cheek, and that he felt it a little sore." Millar said later that "he did not perceive any marks." Then Millar asked Borland "if he had been in the stocks all night. He said 'No,' that he had been in Mr. Fabens' house all night." The word was, Millar pressed Borland, that Greytowners "had locked him up in the stocks." Borland replied that "he only wished they had tried to do it."[35]

Aboard the *Northern Light*, Fabens and a transit company employee named Joseph Scott told Borland "of the violent and lawless disposition manifested" by the people of Greytown. They recounted the purported food theft just 11 days earlier and the building destruction of about a year earlier. Fabens and Scott said they feared for the safety of those persons and that property associated with the transit company. Borland called a meeting of the ship's passengers to assemble a kind of ersatz constabulary until Washington, notified of events, sent "a proper force for this purpose." He offered 50 Americans returning from California $150 each for the first month ($4,500 each in 2022) and $100 ($3,000 each in 2022) per additional month, if necessary, to remain in Greytown and protect the transit company's personnel and assets. (An additional item of expense, Borland reported, was "the cost of arms to supply a portion of the men.") The *Northern Light* then left with its passengers, including Borland and Captain Smith of the *Routh*, for New York, from where Borland entrained for Washington "to lay this matter before the Government."[36]

The day the *Northern Light* departed, Greytown's city council resigned over Borland's actions. As the *New York Tribune* put it: "If they could not be allowed to exercise the most necessary functions, even the arrest of murderers, ... or if they were to have an armed force raised against them on their own soil by such a fellow as this Borland, why, clearly they were superfluous, and could properly do nothing but abandon all nominal power and responsibility." Now Greytown's 500 residents were left to ponder what retribution might befall them for the assault on Borland and the alleged depredations against the transit company.[37]

For his part, Fabens urged Marcy to seize Greytown *and* the whole of the Mosquito Protectorate to compensate the transit company: "I am of an opinion that no suitable indemnity can be obtained ... except by taking possession of, and holding, the territory of Mosquito ... beneath whose flag the outrages in question were perpetrated." This made almost no sense and risked an Anglo-American war. Future chapters will reveal possible ulterior motives for Fabens' suggestion.[38]

What Borland hoped for the Greytowners was annihilation. On May 30, 1854, he recommended to Marcy that the entire population of Greytown be killed. "I am unable to regard them in any other light than as pirates and outlaws," Borland told Secretary Marcy, "upon whom punishment, to the extent of extermination, may be rightfully inflicted." As with Fabens, Borland may have had ulterior motives for a recommendation that was extreme even for him.[39]

Chapter 2

"Impaired by the Folly of an Individual"

Of the 11 U.S. diplomats sent to Central America before E.G. Squier in 1849, wrote historian J.B. Lockey,

> three died *en route*; another succumbed before he started on his mission; one escaped with his life by being dismissed before he embarked; another survived by contriving to draw his salary for more than a year without going near the Central American capital; and another traveled over the length and breadth of the country, unable to find a government to receive him. Though the remaining four reached their destination and were received, only one of these prolonged his stay beyond a few months, and he committed suicide soon after his return to the United States.[1]

Before his posting, Squier had been an engineer, a newspaper editor, a political organizer, and an ethnologist and archaeologist who began his explorations with the ancient Mound Builders of the Mississippi Valley. In 1848 the Smithsonian Institution was so impressed with his research that they published a book on the subject he coauthored. Then the American Ethnological Society urged him to seek a diplomatic appointment to Central America as a means of studying the region's archaeological remains, as had U.S. diplomat John Lloyd Stephens ten years earlier when he helped rediscover the Mayan civilization in Honduras.

Squier had friends who were well connected politically, and he told these backers, "*Now* is the time to bring the *big guns* to bear" (emphasis in original). They did, and it worked, although, to be sure, U.S. officials were desperate to fill the post. They had no problem with Squier pursuing diplomatic and archaeological objectives in "double harness." While Squier hoped his diplomatic duties would be "nominal," they were anything but. He lived in Nicaragua from June 1849 until June 1850, "during which time," according to one biographer, "he ... aggressively promoted American interests in the region and conducted archaeological and ethnological investigations with great enthusiasm and bravado."[2]

2. "Impaired by the Folly of an Individual"

Squier had received his marching orders a month before he arrived in Nicaragua. "It has been represented to this Department," Secretary of State John Clayton told him, "that certain citizens of the United States are desirous of entering into a contract with the Government of Nicaragua for the purpose of constructing a canal between the Atlantic and Pacific by the way of the River San Juan and Lake Nicaragua." And while the river and lake provided a natural water route across almost the entire Isthmus of Nicaragua, no regular service was yet possible in 1849. For instance, at least two groups of Americans brought disassembled boats to the isthmus, both of which failed to reassemble, forcing them to hire *bungos*. One of these groups took over seven months to reach San Francisco from New York, having been stranded on the isthmus for more than four. To be a reliable shortcut for travelers to and from California, the waterway would need river steamboats (like the *Routh* in Chapter 1) and bigger ones for Lake Nicaragua. Also, there would have to be regularly scheduled ocean steamers (like the *Northern Light* in Chapter 1) to link up with the steam-powered, inland transit.[3]

Clayton wanted Squier to quickly secure the contract because half of Oregon Territory had been acquired from Great Britain in 1846, and Mexico had ceded California to the U.S. in 1848, about six months before the Gold Rush began. "A passage across the isthmus may be indispensable," Clayton told Squier, "to maintain the relations between the United States and their new territories on the Pacific, and a Canal from Ocean to Ocean might and probably would empty the treasures of the Pacific into the lap of this country." (Any such U.S.-controlled route, Clayton added, would be open to "all nations, on the same terms.")[4]

Until this Nicaraguan shortcut was up and running, there were only three other ways most travelers were reaching the California territory from the East Coast: By sailing ship around South America; by rail to St. Louis and then wagon train across the Great Plains and over the Rocky Mountains; or by using a shortcut at the Isthmus of Panama in conjunction with ocean vessels. All three of these were unpredictable and could take six months or more. Also, while Panama, like Nicaragua, saved the 10,000 miles "rounding Cape Horn" required, it was an arduous, dangerous, and pestilential travail by mule and canoe. As a young army officer in 1852, for instance, Ulysses Grant led troops across Panama and suffered weeks of delays due to poor transportation and watched 150 fellow travelers die of cholera. Nicaragua was 300 miles north of Panama and, so, that much further from the Equator, making it far healthier. Even without the proposed canal, this passage—improved with inland steamboats and scheduled ocean steamer link-ups—was rightly predicted to become a strategic boon to the United States.

"Cheaper, Safer, and More Pleasant, Than ... by Panama"

Secretary of State Clayton told Squier that one of the "certain" American citizens seeking this exclusive route contract with the Nicaraguans was Cornelius Vanderbilt, one of America's richest men and a pioneer in steam vessels. Nicknamed the "Commodore" in his youth, for his early success running a New York ferry service, the moniker stuck as he acquired a fleet of ocean-going steam vessels.

By August of 1850, Squier, as touched upon in Chapter 1, had adroitly negotiated the exclusive contract between the Nicaraguan government and Vanderbilt's company. Nicaragua awarded the company the exclusive right to build a canal in return for $10,000 a year ($300,000 in 2022), 20 percent of the annual profits from the completed canal, plus a stake in the business in the form of stock. Moreover, during the 12 years it had to build the canal, the company was given the "exclusive right" of navigating the "waters of the said State by means of Steam vessels, from one sea to the other." For this interim privilege, the company agreed to pay $10,000 a year, plus 10 percent of the net profits. This, Squier exulted, "will enable the company to open a route at once across this isthmus, more rapid, easier, cheaper, safer, and more pleasant, than that by Panama." In other words, while the Nicaraguans wanted a canal large enough to accommodate ocean vessels, they agreed to the inland steamer service in the meantime.[5]

Born to Dutch parents on Staten Island in 1794, Cornelius Vanderbilt ran a ferry service to Manhattan as a teenager, which eventually led to fabulous wealth as a steamship and railroad magnate (Library of Congress).

"He Was, in Short, a Fixer"

Despite this contractual success, Squier nonetheless feared the arrangement might be "impaired by the folly of an individual." He was referring to Vanderbilt's partner, the volatile, bombastic, and injudicious Joseph L. White. In a private letter to Clayton, Squier captured White's character in remarkably prophetic terms: "The US Govt. was a simple machine to register and execute his high decisions. 'I stipulated this,' and 'I did that' are the burthen of every sentence. Mr. White is … a most inveterate, indiscriminating, and indiscreet talker." Squier told Clayton he worried that White would destroy Nicaraguan confidence in the company. He could not have possibly imagined the impact White would eventually have on the transit company and on Greytown.[6]

Joseph Livingston White was born in New York state, the year given variously as 1806, 1813, 1814, or "unknown." He was raised and studied law there. By 1840 he had made his way to Indiana, where he worked in the successful presidential campaign of William Henry Harrison. White was "the most fascinating orator that ever mounted a stump in the state," according to one newspaper. He won election to the House that year as a Whig but only served one term. He possessed "a genius," one writer observed, but "lacked the balance of character to be one of the most powerful men in the nation." After leaving Congress, White moved to New York City, where he practiced law. "He was one of the most social and genial men I have ever met and a most engaging and eloquent conversationalist. His apropos speeches, his witty and good-humored repartees, were inimitable," remarked one New Yorker. White, wrote Vanderbilt biographer, T.J. Stiles, "emerges from these accounts as a highly confident man of sharp wit, a sophisticated and well-connected charmer, a master of both courtroom histrionics and backroom negotiations. He was, in short, a fixer."[7]

"A Few Dozen Huts of Thatch"

Besides the Vanderbilt contract, Squier looked out for American interests in general and explored the region, seeking out and finding "the monumental remains of Central America and [studying] the presumed relations and ethnic affiliations of its little-known Indian peoples." He also kept an eye—both gimleted and jaundiced—on British activities in the area. Of great concern, as noted in Chapter 1, was England's Mosquito Protectorate. The U.S. had been comfortable dismissing the protectorate as a "subterfuge" until the British seized San Juan del Norte in 1848. "San Juan was [then] almost utterly unknown to the world," *Harper's New Monthly*

Magazine, reported later, "a few dozen huts of thatch, built in a narrow opening in the dense forest which burdened the low shore, comprised all that there was of a town."

The seizure was not without historical precedent. The English had long considered San Juan as belonging to the Indians. In 1841, according to historian John Bigelow, an English force from Belize landed at San Juan del Norte, carried off the Nicaraguan port commandant, and "abandoned him on an uninhabited coast." The object "was to assert the majesty of the Indian King as sovereign over the Mosquito Coast, including the mouths of the San Juan." The Nicaraguans later ousted the Mosquito forces, but the English made their 1848 re-seizure stick, renaming the port, as noted, Greytown.[8]

This time the British wanted the port as a bargaining chip to prevent the United States from seizing the entire isthmian watercourse. Greytown Harbor and its appurtenances, San Juan del Norte and Punta Arenas, were the only possible sites for any transit route's Atlantic terminus. "In its tropical seclusion and miserable insignificance," *Harper's* noted ironically, "one might suppose San Juan would have escaped complication with … great events." But the recent American acquisitions of Texas and California made the British foreign secretary, Lord Palmerston, fear that the burgeoning young colossus would now turn south. According to American historian Mary Wilhelmine Williams, "The aggressive movement of the United States towards the southwest, accompanied by the talk of 'manifest destiny,' had given the British good reason to suspect the Americans of designs upon the territory of the isthmus, and to fear that they might attempt to monopolize the Nicaragua route." British historian Kenneth Bourne put his take on the situation more succinctly, "Neither side … aimed at exclusive control but each feared that this was, in fact, the other's real intention."[9]

"The 'His X Mark' of One Savage…"

On one of his trips around the isthmus, E.G. Squier made his way to Greytown. "Most small communities have in their midst one or two resident notabilities, who are regarded something in the light of oracles," Squier wrote, and Greytown was no exception. Captain Samuel Shepherd and his brother, Peter, had lived in San Juan/Greytown since 1811. Often assumed to be English, the brothers were actually Americans from Georgia. "Now old and nearly blind but hale, cheerful, intelligent, and communicative … [Samuel is] capable of giving more information relative to the coast than any man living," Squier noted. "He seldom leaves his hammock

2. "Impaired by the Folly of an Individual" 29

Miskito Indians preparing tortoise shell (*Frank Leslie's Illustrated Newspaper*).

which is swung in the principal room of his house and in which he receives all his visitors."

On the occasion of Squier's visit, however, Samuel made an exception. He rose from his hammock to retrieve "from a very closely locked and substantial case, a variety of parchment grants and conveyances." These were signed with the "His X Mark" of Mosquito King Robert Charles Frédéric, who preceded "the little Sambo boy now wearing the Mosquitian purple." These documents, the captain told Squier, gave the lie to England's continuing presumption of a "protectorate" over the Mosquito Indian lands. The English no longer had authority over the lands, said Shepherd, and neither did the Indians. He, his brother, and a partner named S.T. Haly owned them—or at least two-thirds of them.[10]

Beginning in 1824 the Shepherd brothers and Haly traded with the Miskito Indians, exchanging merchandise brought from Liverpool by way of Jamaica for tortoise shell, mahogany, and sarsaparilla. The market for these Miskito goods collapsed around 1830 and left the Shepherds and Haly badly in debt to their Liverpudlian suppliers and Jamaican go-betweens. In 1839, nine years later and still burdened by this debt, the Shepherds and Haly secured from Mosquito King Robert Charles Frédéric, who was indebted to them, a vast land grant in exchange for discharging his obligations. The three men bought other such "Mosquito grants" until their combined holdings equaled some 22.5 million acres, roughly two-thirds of the king's dominion—or an area about the size of Maine. Henceforth, they lived in the hope of dividing up their holdings, known collectively as the "Shepherd grant" (and later, in U.S. newspapers, as the "Mosquito grant") and selling parcels to settlers. By doing so, they could pay off their creditors and turn a handsome profit for themselves as well.

For the next decade or so, British diplomats vacillated over how to deal with the Shepherd and other grants issued by King Robert Charles Frédéric. Then on October 8, 1846, the English consul to the Mosquito Protectorate, Patrick Walker, moved against all the grants issued by this king, including the Shepherd. He did this as regent to the granting king's underaged son and successor. Walker issued an annulment, over the boy's "His X Mark" of all his father's grants. "The young Sambo," Squier wrote, unfairly ignoring Walker's regency, justified the revocations by "setting forth, in a most unfilial way, that 'his late majesty was not in his right mind when he made them,' that is, was drunk!"[11]

When Patrick Walker accidentally drowned three years later, his successor, one W.D. Christie, sent the British foreign secretary, Lord Palmer-

"The Nigger Emperor of Nicuragua [sic] on his throne." **An 1852 racist caricature of a Mosquito king, perhaps George Frédéric Augustus II (Library Company of Philadelphia).**

2. "Impaired by the Folly of an Individual" 31

ston, a 64-page categorical denunciation of his predecessor's "royal" revocations. Christie's defense of the grants led to a general move to annul the annulments, as the Crown began viewing these grants, especially the Shepherd, as worthy of "an adjustment." The turnabout was perhaps influenced by pressure from the Liverpool creditors of the grant's owners, hoping to be repaid from revenues that might accrue from the re-legitimized grant. Even Foreign Secretary Lord Palmerston thought the Shepherds and Haly had a claim and may have undertaken an adjustment had it not been for the "embroilment with the United States over the political status of Mosquito." In the end, Palmerston let the annulments stand, scribbling at the bottom of one letter on the subject, "I don't see why we should interfere in this matter." Shepherd told Squier that "his titles are in no degree impaired by" Palmerton's decision because "the 'His X Mark' of one savage [the father] is as good as that of another [the son]."[12]

Chapter 3

"Git the English Banks to Help Us"

While Secretary of State Clayton thought that a canal at the Isthmus of Nicaragua was essential to the national interest, he also knew that Congress would never fund its construction. Nor would—or could—Cornelius Vanderbilt. Even though the Commodore was well on his way to becoming the second richest man in America, neither he nor a possible consortium of U.S. capitalists led by him would have had the wherewithal. Or as Vanderbilt himself put it, he'd have to "git the English banks to help us." To facilitate such loans, Vanderbilt and other U.S. capitalists touted the advantages of cooperating with the British. The U.S. minister to England, Abbott Lawrence, told Foreign Secretary Lord Palmerston that "no other nations in the world have so important interests to be affected by it—no others have the requisite capital at command—no others have shown a willingness to guaranty the neutrality essential to its safety—and capital, always timid, would shrink from it without such guaranty."[1]

This, in turn, led to the Anglo-American Clayton-Bulwer Treaty of 1850, which, it was hoped, would facilitate the quick construction of a canal. "Article V," says historian Jay Sexton, "made both nations' commitment to investors crystal clear by guaranteeing that 'the canal may forever be open and free, and the capital invested therein secure,' while Article VII extended special privileges to a pre-existing canal company—presumably that of Cornelius Vanderbilt." With the Clayton-Bulwer Treaty virtually guaranteeing the Vanderbilt company's monopoly contract with the Nicaraguans and rendering any capital investment in it "secure," the Commodore and Joseph White set off for England, to "git" the banks there to help.[2]

"White's Own London Fog"

While this chapter might seem unnecessary for the advancement of the narrative, it serves to illuminate further the rapacious, devious, bull-in-a-china-shop personality of Joseph L. White, who will figure so prominently in Greytown's demise. It also provides a general historical context for some of the narrative-specific events.

Vanderbilt and White arrived in London in October of 1850 and made their way to the offices of the powerful Baring Brothers & Co., offering them half the canal company. But the lack of information in their proposal surprised Baring Brothers. There was no way to gauge profitability or construction costs. Other London banks felt the same. "The matter," one noted, "is not ripe for the present."[3]

"The next day the Baring partners were surprised to see a gross distortion of their position in the financial columns of the *London Times*," wrote Vanderbilt's Pulitzer Prize–winning biographer T.J. Stiles, who said the piece was the handiwork of Joseph White. "His kind of hyperbole and insinuations echoed throughout the piece," Stiles noted. "It is the grandest physical work the world can witness," the *Times* wrote. "A promise was given ... that an equal participation in the enterprise should be offered to this country on reasonable terms." The *Times* went on to say that through the efforts of "Messrs. White and Vanderbilt ... a satisfactory arrangement" had been reached. "It was a planted story," Stiles concluded, "White's own London fog."[4]

"Not One Cent of Capital Subscribed or Paid In"

Vanderbilt and White arrived back in New York on October 31, with a scathing story appearing in the *New York Herald* two weeks later. The canal company was a mere "speculation," the *Herald* wrote. "A delegation of gentlemen from the [canal] company ... lately visited England, for the purpose of securing the co-operation of British capitalists." But, the *Herald* noted, no previous action "relating to the grand canal had been effected. No stock had been taken—no stock books opened—not one cent of capital subscribed or paid in, beyond ... for the secondary purpose which we have specified." This secondary purpose the paper referred to was the river and lake transport by small steamers, "a speculation, which promised, and still promises to be successful, and which, so far as we can learn, has been *the sole direct object* of the company, or to the accomplishment of which any *bona fide* efforts have been directed" (emphasis added).

This suggestion by the *Herald* was reinforced when it was revealed that Vanderbilt had planned "to go cheap on the canal construction by making it only seventeen feet deep," insufficient for ocean vessels of large "burthen." While such a canal would be a significant improvement over the natural route, it would have meant that, as with the current transit route, every arriving sea-going ship would have to transfer its cargo or passengers to isthmian steamers, only to be reloaded onto another ocean ship at the other terminus. This would be useless for ships in international commerce like, say, those in the China trade. To the *sole* direct object noted above, the *Herald* added another. "The whole affair was an experiment," the paper suggested again, "in which a few lawyers in Wall Street were the principal movers, their original purpose being to obtain a [canal] charter, and afterwards dispose of it at any good price."[5]

Vanderbilt's decision to make the canal too shallow for "ship communication between the two oceans" violated both his contract with the Nicaraguans and the Anglo-American Clayton-Bulwer treaty sanctifying that contract. Britain's U.S. minister, John Crampton, wrote to Secretary of State Edward Everett that England no longer felt obligated to honor Clayton-Bulwer and was now "at liberty … to withdraw their protection from that [Vanderbilt's] Company and to transfer it to any other Company which should undertake to construct such a canal."[6]

What soon became apparent was that Joseph White had an idea for dodging this bullet. "I fear," John Bozman Kerr, E.G. Squier's successor in Nicaragua, wrote to Secretary of State Daniel Webster, "from the excited state of the public mind in León [Nicaragua's then-capital] … that an imprudent step has been taken by Mr. J.L. White, in his zeal to bring about a modification of the terms of the Charter and act of incorporation of the Canal Company, more favorable to those interested in the mere transit route."[7]

"The Strange Propensity … for Cutting Each Other's Throats"

Knowing now that the canal was not going to happen, White wanted to separate the "mere transit route" from the canal charter because the deadline for starting on the canal had just passed a few weeks earlier (on July 4, 1851, the month before the transit opened for business). He knew that this lapsed contractual deadline gave the Nicaraguans—now with British support—justification to cancel the charter and take fresh bids on the contract by new investors, thus threatening the Vanderbilt's company's monopoly of the lucrative "mere transit route."

Fortunately for White, Nicaragua was, yet again, in the throes of civil war. In these years, civil strife there was endemic. "Nicaragua," one historian noted, "was torn apart by … civil wars … so frequent as to be almost continuous." Another pointed out, "During a period of six years

Nicaragua had had no fewer than fifteen presidents." And a British diplomat wrote home that "it must be difficult to understand the strange propensity of these people for cutting each other's throats."[8]

In this most recent upheaval, the warring factions, the Liberals and the Conservatives, each claimed they were the legitimate government, so there were, basically, two governments. White bet on the Conservatives, making promises and paying out bribes that resulted, on August 14, 1851, in their agreeing to charter what White named the Accessory Transit Company (ATC), authorizing "the American Atlantic and Pacific Ship Canal Company to divide and separate all the powers, privileges, rights and duties ... relating to the navigation of the waters of Nicaragua, not essential to the construction or use of the said Ship Canal" to the ATC. The contracting parties agreed that neither was relieved from "the performance of all the obligations imposed upon them, respectively, by the [Canal] Charter."

This meant, basically, that the Nicaraguans were still promised $10,000 a year and 10 percent of the net profits "of any route which the Company may establish between the two oceans." According to David Folkman in his book, *The Nicaragua Route,* the company paid the $10,000 for the years 1849 through 1852 but claimed they made no profits those years. Then the Nicaraguans found out the company issued a two percent dividend to their shareholders in June 1852. "As dividends implied profits," Folkman wrote, the Nicaraguans "demanded a statement of accounts." Negotiations ended in a stalemate. The Nicaraguans never saw any profits payments and, apparently, the flat $10,000 annual payments also stopped.[9]

Chapter 4

"It Will Be an American Town"

In June of 1849, possibly soon after he met with Samuel Shepherd (see Chapter 2), E.G. Squier wrote to the State Department with a suggestion for "Mr. White ... and Vanderbilt's Co." Squier knew that Costa Rica might challenge Nicaragua's unilateral granting of the Rio San Juan right-of-way because the river constituted much of their shared border. In this letter Squier recommended the company hedge its bets by buying the Shepherd grant, which, he pointed out, included "both sides of the San Juan." Squier said that the canal company "might obtain all desirable rights of passage, etc., through the disputed territories, from the proprietors of these grants."

Squier knew of the boy king's Patrick Walker–dictated grant annulment but minimized it by suggesting—in an almost perfect parroting of Samuel Shepherd's words to him (see Chapter 2)—that "the 'His X Mark' of one Savage, is, I presume, quite as potential as that of another, and quite as worthy of regard." Squier may have also known of W.D. Christie's 64-page pro-grant screed sent to England's foreign secretary just a month earlier. And while Squier must have known his suggestion flew in the face of the long-established U.S. policy of not recognizing any Indian tribe's sovereignty over the land they occupied, he apparently thought both Britain's upholding of its annulment decision and America's disapprobation of the Mosquito kingdom were surmountable obstacles. As will be seen, he was, to a large extent, correct.[1]

It's not known whether Squier's land grant advice reached Joseph White or Vanderbilt directly. But in late 1853 the *New York Herald* reported that an American named David Keeling bought a one-quarter share of the Shepherd grant that year and another quarter earlier, in 1851. (Whether the remaining half was ever purchased is unclear. The circumstantial evidence is mixed, and the provenance of this crucial document, often ethereal.) "We have lately learned," the *Herald* continued, "that Mr. Keeling has associated with him, for the purpose of improving the lands embraced in these grants, several gentlemen in Virginia, Pennsylvania, and New York, and that measures are now being taken to forward the enterprise."[2]

4. "It Will Be an American Town"

"Placed in the Hands of ... 'a Mr. Keeling'"

About a year later, the British consul at Norfolk, G.P.R. James, fleshed out Keeling's role when he wrote home to Whitehall that Keeling was a long-time resident of Norfolk, Virginia, where he had managed a hotel and owned a restaurant and may have fallen on hard times:

> I should not presume to enclose the accompanying extract from an American Newspaper, but that the whole of the plan for taking possession of a large part, if not the whole of the Mosquito country, originated in this City of Norfolk. The projector is a person of the name of Keeling who kept a public house in this place, became bankrupt, and went to Central America. He returned to Norfolk, having obtained from a person in Central America, a large share, of a so-called grant of some millions of acres from the Mosquito King.... The project of colonizing the tract by a company, has been on foot for between two and three years.[3]

The "company" was called, "Central American Land and Mining." About five months earlier, on July 4, 1853, a British official at Greytown named Dr. James Green quoted a Shepherd brother as saying that he had placed in the hands of an American, "'a Mr. Keeling,' copies of all the documents relative to his claims in Mosquito, and that the gentleman held out strong hopes of recovering everything for him." (Green's report also added, without substantiation, that Shepherd's grant documents had been laid before U.S. Secretary of State Edward Everett.)

Keeling, however, was soon subordinated to a more prominent character. Another British diplomat at Greytown, Henry Grant-Foote, declared that "a Judge Bryce" has become Mr. Shepherd's agent and "no mention is made of the former lawyer" (i.e., Keeling, although he was not a lawyer) and that "Judge Bryce is to receive half of whatever may be recovered (at least such is the report)." Grant-Foote followed this with a letter to the foreign office stating that a "Mr. Bryce ... will shortly visit London for the purpose of communicating with Her Majesty's Government on the subject." (No record of Secretary of State Everett's involvement or of Bryce visiting England was found.)[4]

To establish the personal connections involved here further, it is worthy of note that a "J.G. Bryce" and a "D. Keeling" were listed together as passengers aboard a ship leaving New York for Greytown on May 5, 1853. And two other passenger lists show a "J.G. Bryce" returning to New York from San Juan (Greytown) on June 24, 1853, without Keeling. But the latter had returned earlier, on June 9, with "Loomis L. White," who was the younger brother of Joseph L. White of the Accessory Transit Company.[5]

"Thus Giving an Importance to the Grant"

Although Keeling was eclipsed by this "Judge Bryce," who took over his role as liaison and factotum in all matters grant related, they worked together early on, and Keeling kept his hand in. Sometimes referred to as "Judge Bryce of Louisiana," this was Judge James G. Bryce, a middle-echelon Democratic Party functionary who owned a large plantation and fifty or more slaves in Rapides Parish, Louisiana. In the 1844 election, Bryce gave speeches in Tennessee for James Polk, at least once in the company of Stephen Douglas. In 1850 he spoke at a meeting in New Orleans honoring South Carolina Senator John C. Calhoun at which Governor John Quitman of Mississippi also spoke.

According to the *New York Tribune,* and a later pamphlet by former Greytowners, one of the ways Bryce tried to advance the cause of Central American Land and Mining, the Shepherd-grant-owning company, was to walk around Greytown (which was part of the Shepherd grant), making proposals "to the citizens" to purchase "from the company, lands which they already occupied by virtue of titles derived from other sources." Here, from that referenced pamphlet, is a detailed account of how this worked. Bryce allowed the agreeable owners to set their own price for buying (re-buying?) their lands from the company "for which they were to give notes." If the Company, upon maturity of the notes, was not in "a position to grant a perfect title … the payment of the principal and interest was to be deferred."

The company said that American immigrants, forming a government whose courts would validate the Shepherd grant, would, in turn, ensure the "perfect title" of company land sales, "as the government, court, and people would have an equal interest therein." Because the Greytowners very much desired this colonization, the pamphlet continues, "a few of its citizens gave their notes and received the Company's title to the lands they occupied; thus, giving an importance to the grant in the eyes of strangers who would be influenced by seeing the early occupants thus respecting the Company's title."[6]

"Sensible of the Serious Consequences Which Might Result"

Soon after the U.S. endorsed Greytown's "city-state" independence declaration in 1852 (see Chapter 1), Secretary of State Webster issued a warning to some disaffected U.S. expat residents of the port who were planning to approach the Nicaraguans to ask them to retake Greytown.

When Webster learned of this, he requested that Secretary of the Navy William Graham give the American citizens among these schismatics a timely warning "that they would not be countenanced by this government in any attempt, forcibly or otherwise, to subvert the acting authorities" of Greytown *and that they were not fully sensible of the serious consequences which might result therefrom.* But then Webster added, "They should be informed that a further ... reason for forbearance ... [is] that negotiations are on foot here [Washington] ... by which the objects they have sought ... [regarding] Nicaragua may, perhaps, be compassed [i.e., brought about or achieved]" (emphasis added).[7]

Webster was talking about the Webster-Crampton Treaty or Agreement then being negotiated in Washington by England, the U.S., and Costa Rica. This was primarily aimed at resolving outstanding disputes between Nicaragua and Costa Rica over borders, and between Nicaragua and England over the return of Greytown and the ceding of Nicaragua's "half" of the Mosquito Protectorate. (The other, or northern, half being within the assumed, prospective purview of Honduras. [See map before title page].) Incredibly, Nicaragua was not invited to join these negotiations. Their minister to the U.S., José de Marcoleta, a perennial burr beneath Washington's saddle, had finally been declared persona non grata by the State Department, which asked Nicaragua to recall him, and which Nicaragua, in turn, refused to do. When the U.S. and England signed the agreement, Costa Rica and Nicaragua did not. (Although Costa Rica later did.)

"The Means Which Never Fail of Success Among Spaniards"

With the Nicaraguans refusing to sign the Webster-Crampton Agreement, the ATC's Joseph White interceded—in typical White style. He wrote a confidential letter to U.S. Minister Kerr. "The Company have requested me to go to Nica ... [but] cannot reach Nicaragua before August. Long ere then however, you will I hope have procured the signature of Nica. to the treaty—If she proves obstinate & refuses to sign, *don't send the treaty back before I come, but protract the negotiations until I come with the means* [i.e., bribes] *which never fail of success among Spaniards.*" White added that "These [the bribes] the Govt. will not of course furnish, but *my associates & myself will*" (emphasis in original).[8]

"To his credit," noted historian Karl Bermann, "Kerr sent a letter to the State Department with an indignant repudiation of White's presumptions. But the incident nevertheless suggests the close relations that existed between the US administration and the Transit Company." Bermann points out it did show that U.S. Chargé Kerr's analyses indicated "apprehensions" among the Nicaraguans "were afoot":

> Referring to Nicaragua's rejection of the agreement, Chargé Kerr had written Webster that "strong motives may be found for this decided course in the sneers & insinuations of the other States, conveyed in the oft repeated sentiment, that Nicaragua was already lost to Central America, having been passed over into the hands of Americans." By attributing Nicaragua's recalcitrance to the attitudes of other states, the Yankee diplomat displayed a lack of appreciation for the value Nicaragua placed on its own territory. But his analysis did show that apprehensions were afoot even at that early epoch of US involvement in the region.[9]

And, as Kerr pointed out in the same dispatch, almost channeling his predecessor Squier's characterization of White from three years before, those apprehensions were not without foundation:

> There seems to be some obliquity [deviation from moral rectitude or sound thinking] regulating the conduct of Mr. White.... I have had occasion in a previous communication to deprecate the evils likely to result from the loose & unguarded conversations of Mr. White even during his short stay. It is this same imprudent talking among Americans, that has caused an immense amount of injury to commercial interests. There are two or three Americans only in the interior and a few others settled at Punta Arenas, yet this sentiment of vague apprehension [among the Nicaraguans] has become a settled conviction, altogether traceable to [Americans] blurting words of conquest & possession in due course of time [emphasis added].[10]

"To Act in Concert to Defend the ... Free City"

Soon after the 1852 declaration of Greytown independence, the then–British foreign secretary, the Earl of Malmesbury, wrote, "It is evident that the ultimate result to which it [Greytown] looks is a sort of Hanseatic [League] independence under the joint guardianship of the United States and Great Britain." Referring to these comments by Malmesbury, his successor, Lord Russell, wrote in a dispatch of January 19, 1853, "I have to state that the Committee of Government of Greytown are in fact the real power which exercises authority in that part of Central America."

Then Russell added this hair-splitting proposal, "Great Britain and the United States, without guaranteeing Greytown, should be ready to act in concert to defend the independence of the free city or port of Greytown, from whatever quarter it might be attacked." And "for this purpose" both England and America, if she "should concur in these views," each send a person there "at the same time and for the same purpose" (i.e., defending

Greytown as a free city)." Russell also noted that rather than compensate Mosquito monetarily for its loss of Greytown, the protectorate might be paid "in greater security ... which the free port of Greytown, assisted by Her Majesty's ships of war, might engage to defend the Mosquito nation."[11]

President Fillmore's secretary of state, Edward Everett, interpreted all this to mean that England was "disposed to relieve itself from the protectorate of the Mosquito Indians." But both Everett and Fillmore acknowledged England's insistence that this could only take place, in Fillmore's words, "on terms consistent with her honorable engagements to the Indians of that name."[12]

The British acquiesced in this "dispose of protectorate ... but" interpretation, their U.S. minister telling Lord Russell:

> I have now the honour to inclose the copy of a message from the President to Congress on this subject, in which your Lordship will perceive that Mr. Fillmore has embodied the information which I conveyed to him.
>
> I have reason to believe that the publication of this document has already produced a salutary effect.[13]

But all this only scratched the surface of a conundrum as entangled as the Gordian knot. For a prime example of this, one need only look to a month later.

"Little New Republic"

With the advent of the Pierce administration in March of 1853, Secretary of State Edward Everett resigned and was quickly appointed a U.S. senator by the state legislature of Massachusetts. On March 21, 1853, the brilliant, if long-winded, orator gave a speech on U.S. Central American policy that took up more than five pages in the *Congressional Globe*. (It was about 14,000 words long, or about the same length as his 13,500-word, two-hour speech at Gettysburg ten years later, which preceded Lincoln's two-minute address there.)

In his Senate speech, Everett characterized Greytown remarkably like Britain's Earl of Malmesbury did, that is, as an independent free city. He even echoed the earl's reference to the Hanseatic League by adding that it was "like one of the Hanse towns of Germany." This "little new republic," Everett prophesized, would become if a canal was built, "a great American city, inhabited, for the most part, by citizens of the United States." Everett then referenced the controversial Webster-Crampton Agreement of a year earlier that the Nicaraguans refused to accept. If Nicaragua was to now change its mind and sign the agreement, he cautioned his fellow senators, it might mean allowing Nicaragua "to establish her sovereignty over the city." But then he added—as if speaking from between a duplicitous rock and a hypocritical hard place—"I feel, it is true, that there will be some inconvenience in that course, if this town is to grow. For, mind you, sir, it will be an American town." It almost sounds as if Everett was speaking directly to the Nicaraguan president, urging him to give up any thought of recovering Greytown.

And that is just how the *New York Times* would eventually interpret Nicaraguan leanings when the paper reported in 1855, "This idea of Mr. Everett would seem to have been acted upon by Don Fruto Chamorro, president of Nicaragua, who in a message to the legislative body of that State, in March 1854, recommended that the frontiers, being mostly occupied by foreigners, should be allowed their own local government."[14]

If Secretary of State Marcy was aware of his predecessor's—and fellow Democrat's—speech, he doesn't seem to have taken it to heart. On June 9, 1853, just two and a half months later, he wrote this to U.S. Minister to England Joseph Ingersoll, "The President does not ... regard any instructions heretofore issued from this or the Navy Department ... for the temporary recognition of an authority for the mere purpose of ... punishing wrongdoers by the anomalous settlement at San Juan as sanctioning the pretensions of the people of that place to be considered a de facto Government."[15]

Eight days later Marcy said much the same in instructions to Solon Borland, then still minister to Nicaragua. "The anomalous condition of the town of San Juan de Nicaragua—or, as the British call it—Greytown—requires some explanation. Great Britain regards the settlement at that place as a political organization emanating from the Mosquito power, and hence derives her pretensions to extend her protection over it. This is not the view here taken of that subject," Marcy concluded.[16]

It is important to note that, in telling Ingersoll this, he did not abrogate the two agreements, one entered into by Webster in 1852 and one by himself in 1853, that the authorities at Greytown had Anglo-American backing, temporary or not, in any efforts it undertook to "punish wrongdoers." Nonetheless, as Marcy insisted in his letter to Borland, the United States "has never acknowledged that these authorities were a rightful government to be sustained against the State [Nicaragua] within the limits of which the town was situated."[17]

This is hard to reconcile, as well, with Everett discouraging the Nicaraguans from ever seeking Greytown back. ("It will be an American town.") Nor does it square with Nicaragua seemingly accommodating Everett's fondest wish when President Chamorro suggested that "the frontiers, being mostly occupied by foreigners, should be allowed their own local government." But most amazingly, as shall be seen in Chapter 14, it flies in the face of Marcy's own total, de facto abandonment of this position during Anglo-American treaty negotiations in 1856.

"If the Anglo-Saxon Once Sets His Foot"

The *New York Herald* article of November 10, 1853, mentioned earlier in this chapter, which first publicly disclosed David Keeling's purchases of half the Shepherd grant, also noted that "Mr. Keeling has associated with him ... several gentlemen in Virginia, Pennsylvania, and New York." The *Herald* then went on to wax effusive, as did other U.S. papers, about what Keeling and his associates' ownership of the grant might mean for the future of the United States in Central America. "Measures are now being taken to forward the enterprise. From the character of the gentlemen whose names have been mentioned to us as associated with the Messrs. Shepherd, Haly & Keeling, in this enterprise, we doubt not that it will be carried forward with vigor; and if it should be, it can hardly fail to mark an era not only in the history of the Central American States, but of the United States."

The *Herald* called it the largest private enterprise in 150 years and that the "new impulse" it would give to trade, human thought and action in the Americas will make it rise to "the dignity" of a world event.

> If the Anglo-Saxon once sets his foot on Central American soil, to occupy it permanently, it will, from that moment, give birth to a new and larger ideas; industry, faith, and progress will be stimulated into a new and more vigorous life, and the advantage of situation, climate, and soil will all be laid hold of, and developed by the energy which is inherent in this race, and especially in that type of it which *by virtue of its crosses* exists in the New World [emphasis added].[18]

"To Extirpate the Inferior and Mongrel Races"

This "by virtue of its crosses" reference to American Anglo-Saxonism is an odd-ball, counter-intuitive wrinkle in American 19th-century racism that should not pass without comment. Here is another example of it, phrased another way, from *Harper's New Monthly Magazine* in 1854, "The great composite race, which in our own country has achieved such marvels of progress, will attain to its highest development and greatest power." Put simply, this theory states that if pure Anglo-Saxonism is good then a commingling of different strains of Anglo-Saxon blood is even better, and America boasts the greatest "composite" of that. Here's an explanation of how this purportedly works, from *The New International Encyclopedia*, initially published in 1905. (Note that the word "composite" appears below, as it does in the second sample above.)[19]

> The French population is highly composite. The Anglo-Saxon race is equally or still more so, and *the American people so in a still more marked degree*; the [U.S.] inter-mixture being the result of emigration from the countries of northern and central Europe. It is not only that the old mixes with new stock, but the latter comes from regions differing in soil, climate, etc. Intermarriages between the … strains of the white race are happy in their effects, resulting in increased vigor and fertility; *and so with the stocks of the yellow, brown, or black races.* [Note that the author does *not* limit this benefit to the white race but that crossbreeding *within* the other races also improves them.] "But when marriage is between individuals of widely different races, i.e., *a high and a low* race or variety, its effects *are bad physically and morally*, since the product, *like mules* or hybrids between species, is inferior to the higher though superior to the lower race" [emphasis added].[20]

While sightings of this "crosses/composites" variant seem rare in American 19th-century periodicals, Anglo-Saxon superiority and general white racism were rampant. Witness this cringe-worthy embarrassment from the *New York Times* of January 30, 1857:

> It seems to be settled that *the superior races of the Caucasian family are destined* to control, and eventually *to extirpate the inferior and mongrel races*…. In the organization of the world, as of society, natural and individual right must yield to the exigencies of sound government, and the advantage of the total body politic…. On such principles, intercourse has been opened, to some extent, and will presently be thrown wide open, with China and Japan. On the same principle, the enlightened communities of Europe took possession, and appropriated, the entire Western Hemisphere, ignoring native rights unfounded upon anything better than mere occupation…. The strongest will continue to rule the weak, to the world's end; and the wisest and most cultivated are the strongest [emphasis added].[21]

"For the Purpose of Planting There an American Colony"

The *New York Herald* article of December 10, 1853, which first broke the story of David Keeling's purchase of half the Shepherd grant, was followed quickly by two pieces in the *New York Times*. On January 5, 1854, the *Times* reported: "The Mosquito King … has sold out to a Company of American citizens one half of the entire territory over which he claims to exercise dominion. The Company (of which Senator [James] Cooper, of Pennsylvania, is a member) has purchased 35,000 square miles for $50,000! [$1.3 million in 2022.]"[22]

Cooper was named president of the company. Having a sitting senator—even one as ineffectual and controversial as Cooper—at the head of the board of directors must have given the company a certain cachet. According to a 1905 bio article by A.K. McClure, Cooper "was a weak man, and speedily proved to all that he was unbalanced by the distinction [U.S. senator] he had attained. He was a fluent and adroit speaker, but he was not a man of forceful intellect and was greatly lacking in the important attribute for a political leader of well-balanced judgment.... At the end of his term ... there was little in his record to be memorable." In 1854, Cooper took such vehement issue with newspaper editor Morton McMichael's criticisms that he challenged the man to a duel (which never took place).[23]

The board of directors' first choice for company president had been another sitting senator, James Shields of Illinois. Shields was offered the "appointment of agent of the company in the Mosquito country," according to the *Richmond Dispatch*. But he held the offer "under advisement," hoping to see if he was re-appointed to the Senate in March 1855. The company did not want to wait that long, and, so, offered the position instead to Cooper.[24]

A week after the *Times's* article of January 5, the paper wrote, "We have accounts of a recent grant of [Mosquito] land ... to an American company ... sufficient to enlist the sympathies and the support of Senators in Congress, men prominent in financial and commercial circles, and Government officials." Then a month later, Nicaragua's U.S. envoy, Don José de Marcoleta, received a letter from his minister of foreign relations, stating that "it has been announced in several News papers of the United States of North America, that a company formed of citizens of those states, has purchased a great portion of the Mosquito territory ... for the purpose of planting there an American Colony."[25]

Marcoleta then wrote to Secretary of State William L. Marcy that while he had "not been able, as yet, to produce a document to prove the reality of said project ... there is nevertheless a Moral conviction of the real and positive existence of such a project, as well as of the company, at the head of which there are persons sufficiently well known; the strangest part of the affair being, that several of the principal members of the Board of directors of the Accessory Transit Company of Nicaragua, are those who appear mostly interested in this matter." Marcoleta set forth the name of the "pretended" company as "Central American Land and Mining" and promised to use Nicaragua's "moral force" and laws to prevent the company from carrying out any "illegal project" it "may venture upon."

Again, all this bluster by Marcoleta was predicated on the

Nicaraguan's insistence that they still owned the Mosquito Territory, where the colonists were headed. In any event, he was "getting the word out." Just having such a U.S. colony in a contiguous polity was a threat to Nicaraguan security. Witness Texas. Current U.S. news accounts only confirmed his fears. Marcoleta ended on a conciliatory note, assuring Marcy that Nicaragua will always "be ready to listen to ... propositions which may be made in due form, concerning any project of colonization ... provided that such propositions emanate from respectable persons or companies, who can give competent securities, etc."[26]

"The Party Principally Interested in the Criminal Game"

Then on May 4, 1854 (which, for context, was twelve days before the Paladino killing and Borland's confrontations at Greytown), Marcoleta, who had now connected the dots even further, sent a letter of outright protest to Secretary of State William Marcy. He pinned down the Mosquito scheme's genesis and offered a variant on Bryce's cajoling of Greytown property holders to "re-buy" their holdings from the company:

> In the beginning of 1853 ... some American Citizens, among them, a lawyer of the name of Bryce ... went to San Juan de Nicaragua in search of adventures [and] ... for the purpose of negotiating and speculating on the grants which had been previously annulled.
> It appears that Mr. Bryce induced ... [the Shepherd brothers and Haly] to promise him certain portions of land in the port, notwithstanding that said lands are now occupied by their proper owners, who have been in possession of the same.[27]

Then Marcoleta excoriated the Central American Land and Mining Company, calling it "a fraud, an abuse, and a deception, through which it is proposed to delude and to seduce the American people, it being the most remarkable and strangest thing, that persons in high places, are likewise accomplices in an affair of this kind." And, Marcoleta added, the transit company "is the party principally interested in the criminal game in question." (Although not revealed until later, two transit officials were on the Shepherd grant company's board, including Joseph White, the man E.G. Squier feared would destroy Nicaraguan confidence in the transit company; he was the transit company's chief legal counsel. The other transit man on the grant company board was Charles Morgan, president of the transit company.)[28]

"The ... Expedition ... Appears ... a Peaceful Enterprise"

Marcoleta's challenge to the Mosquito grant/scheme lay dormant for six months until the *New York Herald* armed him with a public corroboration on November 17, 1854. (In the interim, Greytown had been razed, an event which will, of course, be covered in all its particulars and consequences in subsequent chapters.) In late November of 1854, he wrote Marcy from New York City that he now had proof the Central American Land and Mining Company's "members and associates are disposed to violate the laws of this [American] Republic and the territory of Nicaragua. The *New York Herald* ... confirms previous suspicions and presents proofs.... If there can be any exaggeration ... in the article, it is so trifling that it does not destroy ... the reality and existence of the danger."

He praised "the American Union" for its harmonious relations with countries "with whom it is at peace." And he castigated Great Britain for maintaining its Mosquito Protectorate, which, he said, the U.S. had declared as Nicaragua's and that this had been "re-asserted and confirmed by the diplomatic agents of the Union in Nicaragua, in their frequent official interviews and communications with the Government of that Republic."[29]

Given that "the invasion ... will be carried into effect by American citizens," Marcoleta implored Marcy "to withhold them from participation" by using the U.S. neutrality law, which rules "in matters of this kind." Marcy replied that "the association referred to is not understood to be an expedition fitting out for any hostile object against any Government with which the United States are at peace." He said, "it professes to be an association for business purposes." And, so, in his view, "it is not a proceeding in violation of the laws of the United States or of the duties of neutrality. When these citizens, having a peaceful pursuit in view, arrive in another country they will be subject to the laws of that country, and their conduct must be in conformity to those laws. This Government has no authority to prohibit or interpose to prevent them from going out and no control whatever over them after they have gone beyond its jurisdiction."[30]

Here are excerpts from the *Herald* article of two weeks earlier, and touched upon above, to which Marcoleta was referring: "We understand that an expedition of Americans is about ... to establish a republic in the territory purchased in the Mosquito country. We should anticipate a brilliant future, not only for the territory in question, but for all the Central American States. Will the people of Central America understand what is 'manifest destiny,' and what is for the good of their States?"[31]

On December 15, 1854, the *New York Times* wrote, "If this enterprise is carried forward ... its political results will necessarily be very important.

Central America is destined to occupy an influential position in the family of nations if her advantages ... are availed of by a race of 'Northmen,' who shall supplant the tainted, mongrel and decaying race which now curses it so fearfully. That the influence of [the enterprise] ... will speedily spread itself all over Nicaragua and absorb the whole of that State with its inefficient Government, there can be little doubt."[32]

"The Filibustering Spirit"

The Nicaraguans and Costa Ricans obviously feared that a colony of Americans "next door" in Mosquitia might be a pretextual precursor for the U.S. to spread itself throughout Central America. (American news reports like those from the *Herald* and the *Times* above validated their worst fears.) Previously, for example, there had been a series of incursions by small, quasi-military American civilian units called "filibusters," into Baja California in 1853 and the Mexican state of Sonora in 1854.

The term "filibustering" today means "to act in an obstructive manner in a legislature, especially by speaking at inordinate length"; but in the mid–19th century, filibusterism had a completely different meaning, "the attempt," according to the *Encyclopædia Britannica*, "to take over countries at peace with the United States via privately financed military expeditions." This, according to historian Albert K. Weinberg, led to a "decade ... enlivened by the private encroachment called filibustering. Mexico, Nicaragua, and Cuba all felt the tread of impetuous American filibusterers, bands of ambitious and romantic individuals who, despite the neutrality laws of their country, attempted daringly the overturn of backward tropical governments."

On the eve of the 1852 election, which the Democratic candidate Franklin Pierce won in a landslide, this is what the *Democratic Review* said of the filibustering phenomenon, "If there be one thing more than another which 'the gentlemen at Washington' dread, and which they plume [pride] themselves on suppressing, it is what they call 'the Filibustering spirit.' Yet we solemnly forewarn them that in private enterprise will be found the most active agent and instrument most congenial to our age, our people, and the genius of our government, in working out the Destiny of this Republic." Not surprisingly, the *Democratic Review* magazine, a mouthpiece for the Democratic Party, also first published the term "manifest destiny," coined by its columnist and editor, John L. O'Sullivan. This term has come to be defined as the "doctrine or belief that the expansion of the US throughout the American continents was both justified and inevitable." It is to the "filibustering spirit" of Manifest Destiny, to which this narrative shall return, beginning in Chapter 8.[33]

Chapter 5

"A Mortal Feud Had Arisen"

Two U.S. Navy sloops-of-war arrived off Nicaragua in March 1853, the *Portsmouth* on the west coast and the *Cyane* at Greytown on the east. (The *Portsmouth* was sent to dissuade the Nicaraguans from moving against the ATC for violations of its charter.) As noted in Chapter 1, "a mortal feud" had developed between the transit company and Greytown, and the *Cyane* was sent to deal with that. The *Cyane's* mission was so similar to the *Portsmouth's* in spirit that the language in Navy Secretary Dobbin's order was, in places, identical to that of the *Portsmouth's*: "The impression should be very distinctly made, that the United States are both able and determined, etc." Both ships had been sent to "show the flag" and intimidate the powers-that-be into withdrawing challenges "to the property and rights of American citizens."[1]

As noted in Chapter 1, the transit company would not let passengers visit Greytown from their facilities on Punta Arenas, thus denying the entrepreneurs there the customer base needed to sustain their businesses. But, since the company leased Punta Arenas from the town, and since the lease could be canceled at any time, the town canceled it. This, the authorities hoped, would force the company to move to Greytown proper and, thereby, give the port's merchants access to their hoped-for customer base. When the company ignored the cancellation, Greytown's court ordered on February 8 that the company remove all their buildings within 30 days, or the town would remove them. Perhaps to show intent, the town carried out a one-building ejectment on February 21, 1853.[2]

The machinations that followed are murky, but it seems the transit company sought succor from the U.S. commercial agent at Greytown, Joseph Fabens' predecessor, H.L. Stevenson, who referred the question to Washington. Secretary of State Marcy asked Joseph White his opinion. White lied, telling Marcy that Nicaragua, not Greytown, owned Punta Arenas and that the company leased it from Nicaragua. Based on White's word, Marcy sent the *Cyane* to Greytown, which arrived on March 10, the day before the town had scheduled the removal of the rest of the buildings.

King Street, Greytown, looking Southward, 1853 (*Harper's New Monthly Magazine*. Reproduction courtesy of the Huntington Library, San Marino, California—AP2_H3_p56).

"Who Was King Here?"

"All was quiet," wrote a *New York Herald* reporter at Greytown that day. "Many of the workmen, carpenters, &c., had left the company's employ, and, as I said in my last [report], instead of siding with the company, rather sympathized with the people, feeling and knowing, as they did, what just cause the latter had for their indignation, and for the legal steps they had taken against the company." Despite the *Cyane*'s arrival, ominously at "the eleventh hour," the town authorities expected no trouble in removing the transit company's remaining buildings on Punta Arenas. Immediately upon the *Cyane*'s anchoring, the town leaders repaired on board "to tender the usual courtesies, &c., to the commander, Capt. Hollins."[3]

George N. Hollins, a native of Baltimore, entered the navy during the War of 1812 as a midshipman in 1814 at the age of 15 and served on the sloop-of-war *Erie* in her unsuccessful attempt to break the British blockade of Chesapeake Bay. He was assigned to the frigate *President* under Stephen Decatur, which was captured by the British, and he was a prisoner of war in Bermuda until peace was established. He served again under Decatur in the Algerian war in 1815 and received from him a Turkish saber for his bravery in the capture of an Algerian frigate.

The town authorities were anxious to give Hollins their side of the dispute with the transit company "to make any explanation which might be required." Apparently, Hollins didn't ask for any but did make "some inquiries as to the form of government here, extent of territory, &c., and among other questions, 'who was king here?' The President of the Council replied, 'the people,' and then explained the local and independent form of government."[4]

When Commander Hollins asked if the town had any militia, he was informed that there were three volunteer companies. Upon hearing this, Hollins suggested an exchange of gun salutes, a common courtesy of the day. Hollins "intimated that if the town was prepared to return a salute (of which he was assured,) he would fire one." The town authorities were elated. Not only would they have "the gratifying opportunity" of returning the salute of an American vessel and the validation the exchange would bring generally, but it would imply Hollins was not going to interfere in the next day's ejectment of the transit company from Punta Arenas.[5]

Commander George N. Hollins was a native of Baltimore who entered the navy during the War of 1812 at the age of 15 (courtesy of the Naval History & Heritage Command—NH 49028).

"The Mute Language of Those 'Big Guns'"

"In vain," wrote the *Herald* reporter, "did the inhabitants listen the whole [remainder] of that day" for the firing of the *Cyane*'s guns in salute.

King Street, Greytown, looking Northward (*Harper's New Monthly Magazine*).

In the afternoon a Lieutenant Green from the *Cyane* came onshore and delivered a verbal message "on the part of Captain Hollins" to the mayor. Hollins' message did not explain why he failed to salute as promised. Instead, he just had Lieutenant Green state that "no writ of ejectment could be executed against the Accessory Transit Company." The *Herald* reported that the mayor replied that the city government was legally constituted and that the lands occupied by the Accessory Transit Company belonged to the city. Moreover, the lands were now needed for a quarantine, and the ATC had been notified according to law to quit those lands.

Now, the Mayor, while willing to wait until after further discussions with Hollins, would enforce the law "unless prevented by superior force." Hollins' envoy, Lieutenant Green, then inquired that if Captain Hollins hadn't asked for more talks by 11 a.m. the next day, that "the law would be executed? To which the Mayor replied in the affirmative." The *Herald*'s correspondent recounted that "with blank amazement" did the townsfolk witness on the following morning the *Cyane* take a "position immediately opposite the company's depot." In other words, Hollins placed his ship between Punta Arenas and the town. "All understood the mute language of those 'big guns' staring at them, from the vessel's ports."[6]

Despite this cautionary threat, at ten o'clock that morning, March 11, the marshal and a "posse of carpenters" were scheduled to cross to Punta Arenas and remove all the company's remaining buildings. But when that hour arrived, so did Hollins, doubtless responding to the mayor's ultimatum that if no word from the commander were received by 11 a.m., the ejectment would proceed. They met in the town's "commercial chamber" in the presence of the members of the government and a few American citizens. "We the undersigned," their written record of the meeting began, "certify to the following conversation as having taken place in an interview between the Mayor of this city and the Commander of the United States sloop-of-war *Cyane*." The mayor, a man named T.J. Martin, stipulated that Hollins' orders were to protect the buildings and property now occupied by "the Accessory Transit Company of Nicaragua."[7]

Firstly, the mayor pointed out to Hollins that if the town government were illegitimate, neither the U.S. nor England would post diplomats there. (As noted, both countries signed agreements in 1852 and 1853, promising to support the town government, especially in its efforts to "punish wrong-doers." See Chapter 1.) Secondly, that the ATC "never yet plead in Court want of jurisdiction," using the court in cases where the company was both plaintiff and defendant before it. Thirdly, that the ATC had "ample time to remove" itself. And, fourthly, that the ejectment would be carried out "unless prevented by force."[8]

"The mayor ... requested a statement in writing of my intentions to prevent the execution of the 'process,'" Hollins reported later, "which I acceded to, and withdrew to the ship."[9]

"Muttering Anathemas Against the *Cyane*"

Despite the warnings by Hollins that he would prevent the ejectment by force if necessary, the town marshal proceeded toward Punta Arenas by boat with his "posse of carpenters." According to the *Herald* reporter mentioned above, as they rowed past the *Cyane*, Hollins gave the order to "prepare for action, the boats were manned, and in a twinkling of an eye, forty marines, armed *cap-à-pie* [head-to-foot], were ready." They followed the marshal and his carpenters to Punta Arenas. As the marshal commenced reading the writ of ejectment, he was ordered to desist by a Lieutenant Hurst, who said he was there to protect the property and warn off all intruders. The would-be ejectors then left, with the marshal "muttering anathemas against the *Cyane* and her commander."[10]

"Every One of Whom Was an American"

That evening at a public meeting, the Greytown city council, "every one of whom was an American, presented ... their resignations" and "surrendered the city" to Hollins, who they felt had utterly usurped their authority to govern. Local British officials talked the council into retracting their resignations. Hollins not only voiced no objections to this, but, astonishingly, he quoted from the late secretary of state's "resorting thither" order of the year before (see Chapter 1). "I send you the words of the late Daniel Webster, by which I am guided, 'Meanwhile a temporary recognition of the existing authorities of the place, sufficient to countenance any well-intended endeavors on its part to preserve the public peace and punish wrong-doers, would not be inconsistent with the policy and honor of the United States.'" Hollins ended with, "I am pleased to hear you have again formed a government."[11]

"Mr. White Is the Very Incarnation of American Attorneyism"

Whatever Nicaragua's pretensions regarding Greytown, they definitely *did not* lease Punta Arenas to the canal/transit company. The original lease was signed on July 12, 1851, between an agent for the company and the Mosquito authorities at Greytown. Joseph White had to know this.[12]

The British informed Marcy of White's lie with a letter from Foreign Secretary Lord Clarendon to his U.S. minister, John Crampton, dated July 22, 1853. After opening with a reminder of the 1852 Anglo-American agreement supporting "the de facto Government of Greytown ... pending the negotiations for the settlement of the Central American question," Clarendon pointed out that in 1851 the transit company had "by written request" asked the Mosquito Government to lease them land on Punta Arenas. "The Government of Greytown had ceded that portion of land to the Company at a nominal rent, 'until the land in question might be required for the purposes of the Mosquito Government.'" Clarendon wrote that "this agreement therefore clearly shows that the Accessory Transit Company considered the land in question as dependent on Greytown, and that they were bound to evacuate it whenever required by the Government of Greytown." Despite this, his Lordship continued, they refused to move; and "the United States' commander not only supported them in that refusal but landed an armed force to protect them against the authorities of Greytown."[13]

Crampton replied to Clarendon that "I found upon conversing with Mr. Marcy that he had in fact been misinformed upon this subject, as he stated to me, by Mr. Joseph L. White, the legal adviser and agent of the [Transit] Company at New York, who asserted that no such contract had been entered into by the Company; and I therefore felt anxious to correct the erroneous impression under which Mr. Marcy was labouring."[14]

Corrected by the British, Marcy was furious at White and wrote him the following on August 9, 1853:

> I defended the conduct of Capt. Hollins in landing his Marines to protect the property of the transit company on the ground that the people of Greytown had no right to Punta Arenas. I felt safe in taking this position on account of what you said to me on that subject.
> You will see by the extract I sent you that the British Government represent the Transit Co. as lessees of San Juan/Greytown. If this be so, his Lordship shows me to be in error in the assertion I made that Punta Arena was not the property of that town, and that its municipal authorities had no right to interfere with the occupying of it by the Transit Co. This was certainly the view of the subject you presented to me.[15]

Marcy then asked White for "facts and documents" to "controvert" Clarendon. It seems none were forthcoming. "Mr. White is the very incarnation of American Attorneyism," Crampton wrote home, "and his conscience therefore did not oblige him in the least to tell the whole truth when the enquiry was made of him." Of course, Marcy didn't find out White had lied to him until well after the USS *Cyane* had interceded on the company's behalf. All that remains to end the narrative of this sordid affair is to discover what Secretary of State Marcy did when he learned White deceived him. Did he recommend White's disbarment? Did he suggest the ATC fire White? Did Marcy apologize to the Greytonians? Did he suggest to the ATC that they abide by the laws of the duly constituted polity under which they were living? Did he ask the ATC to accommodate the town and move into the city proper—or just let their passengers shop there, which is all the Greytowners wanted anyway? There's no record he did any of this.[16]

"An Employé of the Company … Began to Break His Head"

The transit company remained at Punta Arenas and there was an uneasy truce for about 14 months. Then on May 5, 1854, three men and a woman reportedly stole a 20-foot-long rowboat (called a yawl) from Punta Arenas, filled it with transit company basic foodstuffs, like cornmeal and flour, and rowed it across the harbor to Greytown. There the food was supposedly hidden, and the alleged perpetrators protected by the residents. There is good reason to believe this theft never took place. Key to the theft accusation was an official protest lodged by Joseph Scott, a previously mentioned employee of the transit company (see Chapter 1).

The *New York Tribune* characterized Scott by the "passion, exaggeration, bombast, and whatever other qualities a senseless and blustering bully would be likely to exhibit on such an occasion." A servant and his wife, the *Tribune* continued, who worked for the company were falsely accused of stealing a piece of clothing and fleeing to Greytown, fearing a beating. Or they simply decided to leave the ATC's employ and had permission to use the yawl boat to get to Greytown, taking two others with them to row it back. They were pursued until "an employé of the company named Sloman fell upon him [the servant] and began to break his head." Greytown marshals intervened, saving the man, arresting Sloman, and taking possession of the boat's contents, which were examined in the morning and found to be just the couple's clothing and not the "flour, cornmeal, &c., alleged to have been stolen." (The boat was returned.)[17]

"The Disagreeable Necessity of Taking Any Action"

With the bottle-assault insult to Borland, the one-building destruction during the first ejectment, and now this alleged food theft all considered unresolved by the Pierce administration, Commander Hollins and the *Cyane* were sent back to Greytown ostensibly to exact an apology for the Borland attack and reparations for the company losses. Also, about this time, on June 9, 1854, Secretary of State Marcy asked Fabens whether Greytown's city council was still "dissolved" after resigning over Borland's prevention of Captain Smith's arrest in the Paladino murder. (See Chapter 1.) If this were so, Marcy implied it might be difficult to hold anyone accountable for the assault on Borland or apologize for it or to hand over to Hollins the reparations destined for the transit company. "Should this prove to be true there will be no organized body upon which a demand for redress can be made or from which a proper indemnity for injuries or insults can be received."

Then Marcy addressed specifically the alleged yawl boat food theft. "You were instructed in my former letter to notify the people of San Juan [Greytown] to repair the injury they have caused to the Accessory Transit Company by withholding from it the property which had been stolen and taken to San Juan and by protecting the persons who were guilty of the felony. It is hoped that the town will have adjusted that matter to the entire satisfaction of the company and in that way Commander Hollins will be relieved from the disagreeable necessity of taking any action in regard to that subject."[18] The town authorities had concluded no theft had taken place.

5. "A Mortal Feud Had Arisen" 57

Curiously—perhaps, tellingly—Joseph White wrote Fabens at this same time that "nothing will please" Washington more than if the food thieves were to "runaway [sic]":

> Major Borland's letter to you does not state what course the government will pursue in this case. You will find the information in my letter to Mr. Scott, which I have instructed him to send to you. I made the suggestion to the President in the presence of Mr. B. [Borland] and the Secretary of State, that the information of what the government designed to do had better leak out to the people of San Juan, as in that event the guilty parties would runaway [run away], and thus bloodshed be prevented. To all this he [the president] assented, as did all parties present. Hence my letter to Scott. You can advise him as to the best mode of accidentally communicating the information (or confidentially) to some honest man in San Juan, if he can be found. Unless the guilty rascals runaway or be delivered up to Captain Hollins, bloodshed is certain; and this all of us wish to avoid, if possible. I am well assured that nothing would please the government more than that these men should escape punishment by running away.[19]

If the city council was still "dissolved" (and it still was), "there will be," in Marcy's words just above, "no organized body" to apologize for the Borland insult or to compensate the transit company for its losses. *And*, if Fabens could get the food "thieves" to "run away," then the *Cyane*'s marines could not capture them. Therefore, the *Cyane* captain's only retribution option might be to destroy the town.

"Borland Is an Honest Enthusiast"

About the same time as Marcy's and White's letters above, an unrelated but equally noteworthy piece of correspondence was sent between two friends in the state of Virginia. Henry A. Wise was a prominent Democrat and his friend, George Booker, owned a large plantation. Booker was also one of the owners of the Shepherd grant and was, or later would be, on the board of Central American Land and Mining. He had asked Wise for aid and advice about his investment. Wise's reply seems to implicate Solon Borland in the Shepherd Mosquito land grant speculation, "I can't bear 'Mosquitoes!'" wrote Wise, trying for a pun. "I am the worst speculator in the world, but I will see to your interests cheerfully, and give you my advice—it is needless, I know, to say to you not to go too deep in such matters. Borland is an honest enthusiast" (emphasis in original).[20]

The *New York Tribune* would later note, "It is supposed Borland ... holds a lot of unassessable stock" in Central American Land and Mining and "that this fact contributed to render him rampant at San Juan."[21]

CHAPTER 6

"I Shall ... Bombard the Town"

When the *Cyane* arrived at Greytown on July 11, 1854, Commander Hollins carried with him his orders from Navy Secretary James C. Dobbin: "It is very desirable that these people should be taught that the United States will not tolerate these outrages. It is, however, very much to be hoped that you can effect the purposes of your visit without a resort to violence and destruction of property and loss of life." Other instructions also awaited Hollins at Greytown, addressed not directly to him but to Joseph Fabens. These were from Joseph White, and they are an eerie conjuring of E.G. Squier's characterization of White four years earlier as a man who regarded the U.S. government as "a simple machine to register and execute his high decisions." White told Fabens, "You will see from [Hollins'] instructions that much discretion is given to you. If the scoundrels are soundly punished, we can take possession and build it up as a business place, put in our own officers, transfer the jurisdiction, and you know the rest."[1]

Commander Hollins met with Commercial Agent Fabens to set a course of action. They would demand an apology for the Borland affront and set preposterously inflated demands for reparations for the alleged food theft just two months earlier and for the building destroyed in February 1853. They demanded $8,000 ($239,000 in 2022) for the building incident and $16,000 ($477,000 in 2022) for the recent, purported food theft. (Some questioned whether that much cornmeal and flour could fit in a 20-foot rowboat which also contained four people.) This totaled $24,000 ($716,000 in 2022). In a letter on July 11, 1854, addressed to "those now or lately pretending to [exercise] authority" in Greytown, Fabens laid out the demands. These called for the apology to be "promptly made" and that the $24,000 in reparations be made "forthwith."[2]

At 9:00 a.m. the next day, July 12, Hollins sent marines ashore to confiscate the port's three small brass cannons and to post notices declaring that if the demands were not met, "I shall, at 9 am of to-morrow ... proceed to bombard the town." That gave the Greytowners 24 hours to come up with about $716,000 in today's money. (England's then-minister to the U.S. noted later that Hollins "might as well have thought of finding 20 [million pounds] Sterling as 24,000 dollars" among the 500 inhabitants.) As probably intended, the money demands went unmet. Nor was the apology forthcoming, possibly because there still was no one in authority to give it—which Secretary of State Marcy might have been hoping for, given his earlier query about whether the "civil authority at that place is [still] dissolved." Fabens wrote later, "I received no official reply, the town being without political organization." As conjectured in Chapter 5, if the city council was still "dissolved," there would be "no organized body" to apologize for the Borland insult or to compensate the transit company for its losses. Therefore, it might be speculated, Hollins' only retribution option was to destroy the town itself.[3]

"Is Not Doubly Equal to That of the *Cyane*"

In Greytown's harbor the day Hollins posted his notices was a much smaller British warship called the *Bermuda*. Hollins had himself rowed over to her to deliver notice of his intent to her captain, Lieutenant W.D. Jolley. "The inhabitants of this city," Jolley replied, "are entirely defenseless and quite at your mercy. [A] large amount of property of British subjects, as well as others, which it is my duty to protect, will be destroyed; but the force under my command is so totally inadequate for this protection against the *Cyane*, I can only enter this my protest." Hollins responded with this archly dismissive and derisive braggadocio: "I ... sincerely regret ... exceedingly [that] the force under your command is not doubly equal to that of the *Cyane*."[4]

There was no landside egress from Greytown, a Nashville paper reported, and so, "on the morning of the 13th, the inhabitants of the town took to the surrounding woods, leaving all their property behind them."[5]

"The Alligators ... Were the Greatest Sufferers"

When his deadline expired at 9:00 a.m. on July 13, Hollins commenced firing. The *Cyane*'s cannons poured 177 solid shot and explosive shells into the tiny, defenseless town. Two days later, someone aboard the *Cyane* wrote the following account of the events, which was printed in the *New York Herald* a week or two later.

> We hauled abreast of the town and opened a fire on it from our starboard battery and continued firing several hours ... but the houses being frame, we

The razing of Greytown, from an English newsmagazine (*Illustrated London News*).

could not do much injury, therefore we ceased firing, and sent a party on shore to burn the town, and in a few hours the whole place was in ruins. Greytown has at last received her full deserts. No respectable man can regret her annihilation. Her rulers were entirely anti–American in feeling and principle. Capt. Hollins conducted the affair throughout in a most creditable manner. He is remarkable for his judgment and good sense. The navy and the government may well be proud of such an officer. I learn that the *Cyane* sails for Boston on Monday. She takes Mr. Fabens, commercial agent, home.[6]

Jolley, the *Bermuda's* master, had a different take on why the *Cyane's* cannonade failed to destroy the buildings. His ship's log records that at 9:10 a.m., "*Cyane* commenced firing shot & shell into the town and continued until noon, with two intervals of half an hour each. Obs'd the town but little damaged, few houses being perforated with shot and all the shells having exploded clear of the buildings." Another British account reported that the *Cyane's* "ball practice" was "very inferior and, if we might judge from the appearance of the houses not one being knocked down and from the number and distances of shot and shell afterwards picked up, the alligators in the Lagoons, at the back of the town, were the greatest sufferers from their fire." (The explosive shells had timed, not contact, fuses, so if they hit buildings, they would probably have passed through and through before blowing up behind them.)[7]

Commander Hollins later reported that "the execution done by our shot and shell amounted to the almost total destruction of the buildings." He explained that the subsequent torching was the best way "to make the punishment of such a character as to inculcate a lesson never to be forgotten by those who have for so long a time set at defiance all warnings and satisfy the whole world that the United States have the power and determination to enforce that reparation and respect due to them as a Government in whatever quarter the outrages may be committed."[8]

A British packet ship (mail carrier) called the *Dee* arrived in the middle of the bombardment and afterward towed the *Bermuda* out of the harbor, carrying some British residents to safety. The transit company offered some others passage, but it's unclear how many or on what terms; few took up the offer, the townspeople generally blaming the company for the razing. Most sheltered in place in the woods.

"Our ... Town Lies in a Heap of Smoldering Ruins"

One of the Americans at Greytown that day was 25-year-old Alexander Wood. He wrote the following to his father, Samuel Smith Wood, who was temporarily back at the family home in upper New York State.

> Capt. Hollins said he would blow & bombard the town to atoms ... this threat was actually & faithfully carried into effect & our once pleasant little town lies in a heap of smoldering ruins. There is scarce a house remaining ... and among the rest is our own. Scarce a vestige left; our books and papers are safe and that is all.... Our stock on hand is totally destroyed. I, however, believe that we shall be indemnified by our government to the fullest extent of our loss.... I believe it will be all made right. Tell Ma so too.[9]

Alexander and his father were among the many U.S. and European entrepreneurs who had flocked to Greytown. Fifty-five-year-old Samuel Smith Wood, prominent among the Americans who dominated the political economy of the place, had five years earlier left his wife and six children in New York to join the California Gold Rush. According to a 1906 "family pedigree," Wood went to California "by way of Nicaragua, where he and a small group attempted to cross the isthmus in a disassembled boat they brought with them. It failed to assemble, and the group crossed Nicaragua [probably on *bungos*] and only after many hardships. Despite this inauspicious introduction to Central America, Wood returned there in 1852 and used his California proceeds to establish a trading post at Greytown." Like all the other entrepreneurs, Sam Wood lost everything in the destruction of Greytown. For years, he and others would submit "memorials" to Congress, seeking reparations from the United States for their losses at Greytown. (See Chapter 7 for more on these "memorials" and the "memorialists" who submitted them.)[10]

Hollins kept the *Cyane* in Greytown Harbor for three days after razing the port—time mostly spent painting the ship. On the second day, July

15, a cryptic entry appears in the ship's log: "A party landed on Pt. Arenas and destroyed 69 cases and 2 kegs of powder." This was later reported to be 21,000 pounds or $12,000 ($357,000 in 2022) worth of gunpowder. Hollins ordered the powder destroyed to prevent Greytown residents from taking revenge on the transit company by blowing up its buildings after he sailed. (There will be more about this incident, and the case law it gave rise to, later in Chapter 19.)[11]

"Intimations Have Been Thrown Out"

After the first ship from ravaged Greytown reached New York, the *Times*'s front page for July 25, 1854, declared: "Startling News from Nicaragua. Bombardment and Burning of San Juan or Greytown by US Sloop-of-War *Cyane*. The Town Totally Destroyed. NO LIVES LOST. GREYTOWN IS NO MORE!!!"[12]

Just six days later, on July 31, the *New York Times* reported, "Intimations have been thrown out that Hon. Joseph L. White, of the Transit Company, dictated in part the movement of the *Cyane* upon Greytown. The action of Capt. Hollins followed the intermeddling of Borland and White, and the instructions of the Administration prepared under their dictation." The paper noted that "claimants" who lost property had the "expectation" of proving this. "A private letter from Washington informs us that claimants for property sacrificed by the inglorious transaction at Greytown are now at the Capital, looking after the facts, with the expectation of connecting the Transit Company with the responsibility of the order to Capt. Hollins, and determined to make them joint trespassers, and to look to them for indemnity accordingly."

Three of those claimants who would later emerge prominently were Calvin Durand of New York City and, from France, Charles Augustus Trautmann-Perrin and his wife, Marie Louise. Durand's struggle for reparations lasted six years and the Trautmann-Perrins' for three decades. (There is more about Durand in Chapters 8 and 17 and the Trautmann-Perrins in 19.)[13]

About a month after the bombardment, Henry A. Wise wrote again to his friend George Booker (see Chapter 5 for the first letter): "I had no time to see to the Mosquito affair [while in Washington]. I fear ... [Greytown's destruction] will not aid the speculation. I fear the Cooper project may savor of filibustering & if so, it will fail." In offering Booker his help and advice, Wise may have expected a *quid pro quo*, because two years later he sent Booker a scathing rebuke for failing to back his positions at the Democratic National Convention of 1856. This letter contained absolutely no mention of the Central American speculation. Still, someone went to the uncommon trouble of keeping with the letter its envelope, upon which was scrawled, "Does this refer to Nicoraga [sic]."[14]

"Greytown Is an Embarrassing Affair"

The same day as the *New York Times* reported that "intimations" indicated Joseph White "dictated in part the movement of the *Cyane* upon Greytown," Secretary Marcy wrote to the U.S. minister to England, James Buchanan. "It is not my purpose in this note to comment upon the transaction at San Juan, and I shall therefore only say that the case is misrepresented in the newspapers." (Marcy probably could not have envisioned the almost universal disapprobation by the nation's press that was to come.) A week later, on August 8, he wrote again to Buchanan—twice on that same day. One of these missives was official; the other was not.

"It may be thought that his [Hollins'] proceedings were too severe," Marcy wrote for the record. "Upon this point I do not propose at this time to express a decided opinion." But in the backchannel note, marked "Private & Confidential," Marcy did express a decided opinion, declaring to Buchanan, "The occurrence at Greytown is an embarrassing affair. The place merited chastisement, but the severity of the one inflicted exceeded our expectations. The Government will, however, I think, stand by Capt. Hollins."[15]

Buchanan also had an opinion about the event. He wrote back to Marcy on August 18:

> I told [Britain's foreign secretary, Lord Clarendon] that I had seen the instructions from yourself and Secretary Dobbin in the Public Papers; and it was evident from them that Captain Hollins had exceeded his instructions and had no authority to proceed to such extremities....
>
> From the very first, I undertook to express [to Clarendon] my firm conviction that it was an act done without authority and I await with confidence its disavowal by the Government.[16]

"If Our Liberties Are Ever Lost"

In the end and despite Buchanan's conviction expressed to Clarendon that "it was an act done without authority," Marcy's private and confidential thought that the government would stand by Hollins proved correct. It could be said that since force was not proscribed in Hollins' orders, his actions were within their bounds. Or it could be said that this was what a tight cabal of government and corporate officials conspired to effect. About a month after the *New York Times*'s July 23 hint that Joseph White "dictated in part" the *Cyane*'s voyage to Greytown, the *New York Tribune* ran a piece that deserves to be quoted at length.

> The enormity of the bombardment and destruction of Greytown ... is such as to stamp the Administration and all concerned, with everlasting disgrace.
>
> It seems that the Nicaragua [read: Accessory] Transit Company are at the bottom of the whole movement. This Company and their associates ... owned or professed to own, a large tract of land running ... across the country ... and the obstacles thrown in the way of this land speculation are the basis of the Government's action, which resulted in the destruction of Greytown.
>
> Soon after Solon Borland returned here, there was a select dinner party got up to discuss and settle the question of the Nicaragua Transit Company's interests and titles to these lands, at which Solon Borland, Caleb Cushing, Sidney Webster, Joseph L. White, and Col. [John W.] Forney were present and perhaps Secretary Dobbin. At this dinner party the bombardment and destruction of Greytown was resolved upon. Here we have the whole affair in a nutshell. We see the action of the Government, in the subsequent bombardment and destruction of Greytown, originating from a dinner party of land speculators, composed of members of the Cabinet and persons surrounding the President and connected with the Nicaragua Transit Company.
>
> It is mortifying that we have a President who is surrounded with, and can be used by, such a set of speculators, and that we should be disgraced as a nation ... to enrich a combination of persons connected with the Nicaragua Transit Company and the administration....
>
> When combinations of wealth or a chartered company can control and direct the Executive of a country like ours, and make war and destroy property and towns, to enrich a company or individuals, it is time that a *Protectorate* should be established to guard the country from the designing schemes of those who surround and mislead a weak Executive. If our liberties are ever lost, it will be through the lust of gain, the thirst for gold of those who may control the Government. A poor President may be tempted, a weak one may be misled or intimidated, and a corrupt one should never be trusted. The present one is FEEBLE.[17]

Chapter 7

"Act of ... Cruelty ... Upon a Helpless ... Village"

Two weeks after the *New York Times* headline announcing, "NO LIVES LOST," the *New York Tribune* reported on the death at Greytown of a "Mrs. Clark," the wife of an American boatman who had fought in the Mexican-American War and was wounded at the Battle of Buena Vista. "Mrs. Clark had been ill of the fever of the country," the *Tribune* reported, "and from exposure and privations during the attack and the burning of her dwelling over her head, a stroke of paralysis was induced, which rendered her utterly helpless—and thus for two weeks had she been, in unspeakable agony, without medical attendance, or comforts of any kind. Her cries could be heard for a considerable distance from the temporary hovel hastily set up to shelter her from the sun and rain." This was the only death reported and the *Tribune's*, the only account of it. Nevertheless, there is some supporting circumstantial evidence.

A "Mrs. Clark" was listed as a passenger on a ship to Greytown in 1851. And of several men named Clark found to have fought at Buena Vista, only one, Henry D. Clark, of the 1st Mississippi Volunteers, was described as having been "dangerously" wounded there. There was no land-side egress from Greytown, so most of the inhabitants who fled to the safety of the surrounding woods had to remain there, without shelter for at least some weeks, and it was the rainy season. "It was indeed a piteous case to see the tears course down the cheeks of this bereaved man and hear his reproaches upon the Government which destroyed his property, in requital for his blood shed in the battles of his country. Surely there is a wrong to be redressed."[1]

"There Is a Clause in the Constitution"

Some newspapers said the Greytown razing violated Congress' right to declare war, e.g., "There is a clause in the Constitution," noted the *Loudon* (TN) *Free Press*, "vesting in *Congress* the exclusive power to declare war, but that the present Administration seem to construe the clause to mean that the ... power ... applies only to the *larger States*" (emphasis in original).[2]

Sixteen days after the incident, Pierce's "usurpation" made the *New York Times* wonder if he had the "faintest recollection" that Congress existed. Three days later, prompted by news of New York merchants petitioning Congress for Greytown remunerations, the *Times* unleashed a censorious article on Pierce and his administration, entitled *Greytown Again*: "There's a complication of 'remunerations' growing out of this unfortunate affair, and the most important one in a national point of view is the 'remuneration' due from the President of the United States to the people for a violation of the Constitution. That instrument provides in Section 8, Article 1, that 'The Congress shall have power,' &c., &c., 'to declare war.'" Saying the razing was "an act of war," the authority for which "is nowhere to be found on the Statute book," the *Times* called it an "act of the President, who is justly responsible ... for this apparent violation of the great character of our liberties," namely, usurping the power "vested in Congress and not in the President, to act upon such cause."[3]

Now the *Times* article opened another argumentative point, noting that the Accessory Transit Company "is a foreign Corporation" (like the canal company before, it was incorporated in Nicaragua). The ATC "had no claims in any sense for the protection of the civil or military power of the Country.... If the citizens of the United States choose to invest their money under the faith of foreign Governments, it is their business, and not the affair of the United States."[4]

While the *Times* thought the Greytown sufferers "have a fair claim upon Congress for remuneration," their article continued that they had "no reliable chance" until a change in administrations that involved also a change in the party in power. "And, therefore, remuneration will probably be looked for in other quarters, and the rightful quarter in this respect seems to be the parties who ... appear to have involved the country ... in this untoward and disgraceful affair." (In another article that same day, the *Times* singled out the transit company as "an important agency in this violent ... proceeding. Their grievance was the cause, and the alleged insult to Borland the pretext.") And, finally, *Greytown Again* closed with a parting shot at Solon Borland. "That his maltreatment and duress were entirely proper, we have never doubted. He unfurled his diplomatic banner and pointed his loaded rifle ... for the protection of an alleged murderer, stepping in between the murderer and the majesty of the law of the country, in which he was accidentally placed." Given the circumstances, the *Times* continued, the Administration "degraded itself and dishonored" the United States by demanding an apology from the people of Greytown. "On the contrary, he should have been sent back, with instructions to apologize himself for so gross an outrage. The dignity of the United States should not be spent upon such kind of people."[5]

"The Pretense Is as False and Base as the Action Is Infamous"

Other news outlets were equally damning, including the *Liberator*. This famous abolitionist newspaper minced no words, "The destruction of San Juan de Nicaragua, by the American sloop-of-war *Cyane* ... is one of the most brutal, cowardly and infamous actions that have ever disgraced a civilized nation. What greater cruelty and crime could be perpetrated by a band of pirates! If this wholesale destruction has been authorized by the Federal Government, ages will not wash out the stain from the national escutcheon. The guilty parties, whether high or low, who have authorized this cowardly act, should be degraded from the stations which they disgrace." The *Liberator* followed this with a round-up of sentiments from other papers.[6]

"We care not which party was in the right," wrote the *National Era*, "in the trifling affair which led to the demand of an apology. It is immaterial. There could, under no circumstances, be the slightest justification of the cowardly vengeance which has been taken. It is preposterous to pretend that the honor of the American nation demanded such satisfaction from an insignificant village. The pretense is as false and base as the action is infamous."[7]

"We give below the comments of leading journals," the *Liberator* wrote in continuing its list. "The *Journal of Commerce*, always unwilling to censure a Democratic Administration ... is compelled to express condemnation, although it does it with all possible gentleness." The *Journal of Commerce* opined, "There are many beside ourselves who will doubt the wisdom of proceeding to such extremities as the bombardment and burning of the village; especially as a considerable portion of the loss of property will fall upon our own citizens. Considered as a naval achievement, the act confers no honor, as the place was without fortifications, we believe, and the entire population not above 400 souls."

The *New York Herald* said: "Had the gallant Hollins come into the North river, and bombarded and burned Hoboken, he could not have damaged his own countrymen more effectually. Those who instructed him—the Administration—could not have struck a more deadly blow at American influence or American enterprise in that quarter of the world.

Excepting the natural feelings of irritation, caused by a disregard of the interests of a few of their own countrymen, we imagine the sardonic joy of the Englishmen on board the British war schooner *Bermuda*."

The *New York Post*, whose devotion to Democracy [i.e., the Democratic Party] who can doubt, styles the proceeding "a great naval victory." It says, "It was probably the first place that was ever taken after a bombardment, whether by land or by sea, without the loss of life on either side. In that point of view, the fall of Greytown will doubtless cover with additional glory the military portion of the Administration, under whose auspices it was achieved."

The *Semi-Weekly Courier and New-York Enquirer* alluded to the razing thusly: "It is with pain and mortification we are compelled to comment upon this act of savage cruelty, committed under the deliberate instructions of the United States Government upon a helpless isolated village."

The *New York Mirror* said, "The Federal Administration has won its crowning victory, and as death in the embrace of victory is honorable, a contemporary suggests that the Administration should die. Such a victory ought to kill it."

The *New York Commercial Advertiser* closed the long *Liberator* review of the whole proceedings with the following comments:

> If no facts are brought to light to relieve the enormity of the transaction, we trust that there are yet pride, manliness, and patriotism enough in Congress, to disavow before the world their approval of such a disreputable mode of making reprisals. This due to the honor of the country, which never before tarnished, has tarnished its fair fame, or so set aside those high principles of honor and humanity which ought to govern nations as well as individuals; and if President Pierce desires to come forth out of the universal disgrace into which this act has plunged him, he cannot do better than immediately send out vessels with lumber and carpenters, and rebuild the town those wantonly destroyed.
>
> The whole transaction on the part of Mr. Borland and our Government is infinitely meaner than bold and openly declared piracy. Just think of the *Cyane*, sent against a little community of some 500 men, women, and children, and firing some six or eight hours at the empty houses and shops from which they had fled; and then, not having been able to destroy the empty town, sending men ashore to set it on fire! Who doubts that we are "the smartest nation in all creation"![8]

Two months after Greytown's destruction, the *Nashville Tennessean* reported, "Very wide differences of opinion still continue to prevail." For instance, it noted that local Democrats in Massachusetts resolved it was "proof to the world that the Administration is determined to ... protect our citizens from injury and insult." In contrast, the *Tennessean* also quoted a rural New York newspaper as mocking the bombardment satirically and poetically:

> Father and mother and I
> And ten good soldiers more,
> Beat an old woman stone blind
> That couldn't see much before.[9]

At least 12 other U.S. papers at the time carried this poem, often called "The Lay of San Juan." It was still appearing, albeit on very rare occasions, to comment on Greytownesque events up to 40 years later.[10]

"All Is Hostility to Our Speculators"

The day before this *Liberator* round-up, the *New York Tribune* unleashed a devastating critique of the whole affair, pointing out the utter failure of both the land-grant and transit schemes and lamenting what might have been if they had not been so belligerent. And while the *Tribune* was a Republican paper (its publisher/editor, Horace Greeley, helped found the party), it was, according to the Library of Congress's website on Historic American Newspapers, "one of the more significant newspapers in the United States," and Greeley "was known as the outstanding newspaper editor of his time."[11]

The *Tribune* stated with savage bluntness, "It does not seem that the Transit Company, in whose behalf San Juan was destroyed is likely to gain anything." The managers, especially Joseph White, the paper contended, "probably supposed that if they could get the town out of the way, they would have a freer time of it, and might control the river and the bay in their own fashion."[12]

The machinations of these intriguers were all for naught, in fact, even less than nil, because of the power vacuum that followed the bombardment. The *Tribune* continued:

> The first practical result of this great warlike exploit ... is to restore to its full vitality the British Mosquito protectorate, which had been virtually abandoned, as [Greytown] had risen into importance and power of self-government. That was to all purposes an American town, with an American constitution, and a predominant American influence governing the feeling of its population. Instead of this, we now have a British force in occupation of the bay, while the town is rebuilding under British protection.
>
> Still less is anything gained by that other body of speculators known as the Central American Land and Mining Company. It was operating on ephemera, a grant "annulled and re-annulled" ... which the British Government has repeatedly refused to recognize. It was at any rate an impudent speculation, fit to be ... engulf[ed] in that bottomless limbo where abortive stock-jobbing humbugs and swindles are forgotten forever.[13]

But then the *Tribune* hedged a bit, saying there *was* a possibility for success in such a project. "Any number of honest colonies planted at suitable points on the Coast, would doubtless have been quietly tolerated by the British Government, which would not have inquired too closely into the validity of the exploded grants under which they [were] occupied." (The English actually hinted at this possibility in early 1853 when Foreign Secretary Lord John Russell let President Millard Fillmore know that "Her Majesty's Government will have no objection to enter into arrangements ... with the United States, both for insuring the more rapid settlement and colonization of the territory in question.") But to this end, the *Tribune* insisted, "it was necessary to conciliate all parties in that quarter, and to bully and disgust none. The contrary course was, however, adopted, winding up with the burning of the town." As for neighboring Nicaragua, the *Tribune* said, "she has not gained anything as yet."[14]

Actually, she at least gained some relief because, as noted earlier, the Nicaraguans feared that a colony of Americans in the contiguous protectorate might just invade Nicaragua or provide a pretext for the U.S. to invade Nicaragua after absorbing the colony. It turns out any relief in this regard was only temporary. (The Shepherd land grant owners were not through trying to establish a colony of Americans in Mosquitia, about which more later in Chapters 9, 11, and 12.)

As for now, however, Nicaragua's indefatigable minister to the U.S., Don José de Marcoleta, could only protest "against the whole transaction"—and seek damages for the loss of his citizens' "numerous and immense interests" in the razing of Greytown. True to his previous comments on Greytown and Mosquito, he totally ignored the fact that Nicaragua had had no legal or political standing in either place, "since," in his own telling words "the time of the usurpation."[15]

"And Thus Acknowledge the Title in This Company"

As the occasional references to reclamations, reparations, and indemnifications in the press coverage indicate, there was an assumption by some—including the aggrieved—that the U.S. government would have to reimburse those whose private property was destroyed by Captain Hollins and the *Cyane*. The sufferers seeking recompense submitted "memorials" to Congress. The term "memorial" derives from the Latin, meaning literally "to remember" or to "keep in mind." In this usage, a memorial is a written representation of facts made to a legislative or other body, like Congress, often accompanied with a petition asking for a redress of

7. "Act of ... Cruelty ... Upon a Helpless ... Village"   71

a grievance which, in this case, the Greytown memorialists thought Congress had the power to correct.

To that end, two major memorials were submitted to Congress, primarily variants of each other, and having as the driving force behind them Samuel S. Wood (see Chapter 6) and a lawyer named W.P. Kirkland. "Memorials" and "memorialists" are referenced throughout the rest of this narrative. These people and their pleas for relief are often the only sources for some critical information regarding these events. In Chapter 4, for instance, appears the only detailed description extant of the American lawyer, Judge Bryce, persuading some Greytown landowners to transfer their titles to the Central American Land and Mining Company; this comes from a memorial. Fortunately, in that case, there were at least brief references, noted earlier, to this event in both the *New York Tribune* and a letter from Marcoleta to Marcy.[16]

Chapter 8

"The Great Theatre of Speculation"

Henry Lawrence Kinney was born in Pennsylvania in 1814 and worked in his father's store from the age of 10. On the last day of 1832, when he was 18, Kinney was attacked in his hometown of Towanda, Pennsylvania, "by an irate husband who fancied that the young man was paying too much attention to his wife. A fight ensued, and Kinney was hauled into court the next day, tried for assault and battery, found guilty, and fined the sum of $1." Possibly still dogged by this scandal, he left for New Orleans in 1833 and by 1834 had made his way up the Mississippi, eventually settling in Peru, Illinois. It was here, at the age of 20, he became a wunderkind in local real estate, partnering briefly with a strange, nefarious character named Hiram Pearson. According to one account, Pearson "was a house painter in the early thirties, went in for real estate and was quite successful in his operations. In 1834 he was severely censured by the people of the community for taking advantage of a German immigrant." He left the state under a considerable cloud in 1834 only to reappear in the early 1850s as a Gold Rush millionaire in San Francisco. Kinney and Pearson stayed in touch and would cross paths again.[1]

In Illinois and at least by 1837, H.L. Kinney was being referred to as "Colonel Kinney." Legend had it that he earned the rank fighting the Indian chieftain Black Hawk during the six-month eponymous war in 1832. But a Pennsylvania land deed made out to Kinney in 1833 found in the 1950s by a Texas researcher named Hortense Warner Ward proves he was not in Illinois by 1832. Ward wrote that Kinney was the source of both this Black Hawk War story and the next tale that falsely puts him in Florida at the scene of the Second Seminole War (1835 to 1842). The *Texas Album of the Eighth Legislature* (1860) lists Kinney as serving in this war. But Ward says he was not in Florida during that period; he was in Illinois until 1838 and then left an unbroken paper trail after arriving in Texas that same year.[2]

8. "The Great Theatre of Speculation" 73

"Great Internal Improvement Scheme of 1837"

Not until 1834, when he turns up in Peru, Illinois, "making a new farm on the west bank of Spring Creek," does "Colonel" Kinney emerge into sharp, documented focus. The following spring Kinney and a new partner erected the first building in Peru, a store. Soon after, Kinney built a hotel. From then on, his reputation, projects, and holdings only grew, reaching their apex on July 4, 1836—he had just turned 22—when ground was broken on a state project, the Illinois-Michigan Canal, which was to extend from Chicago, on Lake Michigan, to Peru, about 100 miles to the south-west. The canal was to link up with a proposed railroad that would carry on to Cairo, Illinois. This would open eastern U.S. markets to Illinois agriculture and was referred to as part of the "great internal improvement scheme of 1837."

The canal was the type of "get-rich and promoter atmosphere that Kinney liked," according to historian Coleman McCampbell. Local Peru chronicler, Henry S. Beebe, later wrote of Kinney: "Upon the letting of work on the canal, he became a contractor for all that portion below the Little Vermillion [River], including locks, basin and channel, amounting to nearly a million dollars ($30 million in 2022). He soon embarked in other speculations and business and became the most influential and noted man in this part of the State. In 1837 and the early part of 1838, everybody's movements appeared to be regulated by those of Col. Kinney. He was the central Sun from whom all lesser orbs borrowed their light."[3]

Born in Pennsylvania, H.L. Kinney worked in his father's store until 18; then he made his way to Illinois, where by 22 he was a real estate wunderkind. An eternal hustler, when his land holdings there collapsed, he just moved on to Texas, where he built another fortune. When that one tottered under a mountain of debt, he sought another—in Central America (Library of Congress).

Get-rich schemes intrigued Daniel Webster, too. In the spring of 1836, the legendary Massachusetts orator and statesman sent his son, Fletcher, to the Ohio and Mississippi Valleys to buy land. This is probably when Fletcher first met H.L. Kinney. Daniel, worried about his son's health, urged him in a letter of June 25, 1836, to return home for a visit, "I hope you will leave some faithful 'land-lookers' to explore for you in your absence. You may go back in the fall with as much capital as you think you can use to advantage." Kinney was doubtless one of the "land-lookers," as "Fletcher could not have escaped being impressed by him." One observer later said this about Kinney in a February 4, 1837, letter from Peru, "And but a few short months ago, the land there was entered by an enterprising Pennsylvanian (one who by his business talents, enterprise, and unspotted reputation, has amassed a munificent fortune)."[4]

Son of legendary statesman and orator Daniel Webster, Fletcher Webster held a minor federal position under four presidents. He is seen here in his Civil War Union Army uniform (Library of Congress).

Fletcher and other agents invested the elder Webster heavily in Ohio, Michigan, Wisconsin, and Illinois. These agents acquired "large farming tracts and town sites on partial payments and credits." In 1836 Daniel Webster, "tired of sacrifices" he was making by remaining in Congress, wanted to resign and return to private law's far more lucrative practice. Powerful friends and associates prevailed upon him to stay in the senate, bestowing upon him considerable emoluments, usually in the form of "loans" that were really wink-and-nod bribes to persuade him to remain in a position of power, to advance their various causes.

"He Did the Only Thing He Knew How to Do—Run Away"

The following year, 1837, Daniel Webster set out, ostensibly to look after his land investments in the West but was also hoping the trip would help make him "the preferred presidential candidate [for 1840] of western Whigs." Historian McCampbell noted, "Due to his scale of living and his heavy land investments, Webster was short on cash in 1837" and borrowed $3,000 ($90,000 in 2022) from U.S. Congressman Caleb Cushing before setting out in May on his western tour.[5]

Several accounts are given of the elder Webster's stop at Peru to visit his farm and Fletcher. One newspaper some months later described the farm this way: "We understand that the Honorable Daniel Webster has lately purchased a large and beautiful farm near the flourishing town of Peru, … from Col. Kinney of that place … and that Mr. Webster intends to convert it into a highly improved country seat."[6]

Webster was given a public dinner in Peru, and Kinney headed a delegation that escorted him from Peru to Chicago. Nathaniel J. Brown, a large-scale promoter in Chicago, noted two other aspects of Kinney's connection with Webster's visit. The colonel presented the senator with horses and a carriage and expressed an interest in marrying his 19-year-old daughter, Julia, who had accompanied him. The senator accepted the gifts and reportedly "was not unwilling that his daughter should become the wife of the handsome and wealthy Illinoisan, but the young lady herself said 'no.' Kinney returned to Peru, sold out his interests there and went to Mexico [actually to Texas]."[7]

"So Deeply Involved in a Financial Morass"

The implication in Brown's reminiscence is that after Julia refused to marry him Kinney left Peru because of a broken heart. But according to researcher Hortense Ward "the real facts behind Kinney's removal from Illinois are far more prosaic." Kinney's speculation in the Illinois-Michigan Canal foundered when the country was hit with what became known as the Panic of 1837, a recession so devastating the name is usually capitalized, like the Great Depression. The government ordered work on the canal suspended. So not only was his canal-building income stopped, all his canal-centric land investments tanked in value as well. "Daily it became more apparent to Kinney," wrote Ward, "that he was so deeply involved in a financial morass that he would never within his lifetime be able to extricate himself.... He was bankrupt, and he did the only thing he knew how to do—run away from his difficulties."

Peru historian Henry Beebe noted, "It was wonderful how many people, in the town and vicinity, were ruined by his failure. Many, who had been brought here from Pennsylvania at his expense, and had lived upon his bounty while here, were suddenly ruined by the treachery and perfidy of their friend, and, as a consequence, were entirely unable to meet their own little engagements."[8]

The Panic of 1837 left Daniel Webster in a bad spot, too. In September 1838, he wrote his son Edward, "I owe a great deal of money." According to Coleman McCampbell, "when pushed (very gently, all things considered) by Caleb Cushing for repayment of loans, Webster would refer to his real estate in the West; and, in November 1849, he deeded more than 600 Illinois acres (known as 'the town-plot of 'Rock Island City/so-called') to Cushing, only to find they had been sold for non-payment of taxes and were of little value anyway."[9]

"Even though Kinney sold his Peru holdings under distressed circumstances," historian Coleman McCampbell wrote, trying to sum up the Illinois fiasco, "he remained friendly with the Webster family for many years. This is especially true of his relations with Fletcher Webster during Kinney's Central American filibuster ventures in the 1850s." As if trying to explain the inexplicable, McCampbell excused such seemingly irrational behavior by saying, "both Daniel and Fletcher Webster always hoped for a financial bonanza; and, to this extent, their ambitions and hopes paralleled those of the adventurous Kinney."[10]

Fletcher Webster's faithful and fateful following of Kinney into his "filibuster ventures" rendered this lengthy description of Daniel and Fletcher's interactions with Kinney in Illinois so necessary. There was the drama of this "all-in" gamble of the elder and younger Webster with Kinney in Illinois and later in Fletcher joining Kinney's filibuster. And then there would also be the X-factor of how Cushing—who was attorney-general during the filibuster—would react to Fletcher's refusal, as executor, to re-pay Cushing's loans from his late father's estate. The one $3,000 loan mentioned above was only the tip of the iceberg; over several loans between 1837 and 1843, the indebtedness had reached $10,000 ($300,000 in 2022), not counting interest, by the time Daniel Webster died in 1852.[11]

"It Was Up to Them to Get Along with the Mexicans"

Kinney was approximately 25 years old when he arrived in Texas in 1838. He may have learned from a newspaper editorial of "opportunities" in the Texas coast country known, then as now, as "the coastal bend." This was at the mouth of the Nueces River, about 200 miles southwest of Houston.

On his way there, he crossed paths with William P. Aubrey of Alabama, with whom he formed a partnership called Aubrey & Kinney. This was intended to combine Kinney's interest in trading, or—more accurately, swindling and smuggling—with Aubrey's, in ranching.

The partners bought a property around which the modern city of Corpus Christi would eventually grow, making the two men, in effect, the co-founders of that city. They built their ranch house on a bluff. The property became known as Kinney's Ranch or Kinney's Trading Post, as he became the more prominent of the two partners.

"The facts are," wrote historian Joseph Milton Nance, "that Kinney and Aubrey were carrying on a clandestine trade in violation of the laws of both countries [Texas and Mexico], and since the Texas government could not afford them protection, it was up to them to get along with the Mexicans." The protection provided by armed men Kinney hired led to the settlement of various parts of the surrounding area. This probably enhanced the Kinney/Aubrey historical cachet as the founders of Corpus Christi. (The name was given in 1847 to the town that grew from their property because it was located near the bay that had been called Corpus Christi since the mid–1700s.)[12]

"Arrested and Charged with Treason"

At this time, the late 1830s, the governments of Mexico and the Republic of Texas were in dispute over the huge swath of land of which Kinney's Ranch was a part. The Republic of Texas said the Rio Grande was its southern border; Mexico said it was the Nueces River, 150 miles north of the Rio Grande. The disputed area between the two rivers became known as the Nueces Strip. Texas claimed it by right of conquest; Mexico claimed it was not a part of the domain surrendered after the Texians won their independence from Mexico at the Battle of San Jacinto.

This unresolved territorial dispute led to constant raids on the area by Mexican forces throughout the summer and into the fall of 1841. Early in June, Kinney & Aubrey were reported doing excellent business with Mexican traders, having come to an "accommodation" with the Mexican government and its forces in the area. This led to considerable hostility between Kinney and Aubrey and their chief trading rival in the area, Philip Dimitt. Later, Kinney and Aubrey were implicated in the death of Dimitt at the hands of the Mexicans. In 1959, a reporter for the

Corpus Christi Caller-Times named Travis Moorman wrote that Kinney and Aubrey were "arrested and charged with treason and complicity in the Dimitt affair." On August 22, 1841, a judge ruled "there was no evidence to incriminate the pair, but on the contrary satisfactory proof to place them on very high and unimpeachable ground as men of probity and citizens of fidelity to the republic."[13]

But Kinney's possible culpability in Dimitt's death was still a point of contention in 1959 Corpus Christi. Moorman made a reasoned case for Kinney having set up his chief trading rival for a fall and the Texas governor covering it up for reasons of personal and political expediency. Moorman's contention was seconded by the previously mentioned local historian Hortense Warner Ward. Mrs. Ward believed, according to Moorman, that Kinney's acquittal was accomplished in part, at least, through influence exerted by Mirabeau B. Lamar, president of the republic. "I can't document this," Moorman quotes her as saying, "but here's the circumstantial evidence."

> Kinney and Lamar were good friends at that time.
> Lamar, in Galveston for his health, hastened to Austin while Kinney's trial was still going on.
> His arrival was timely, to say the least, and he definitely intervened in Kinney's behalf.
> Furthermore, Lamar was completely dependent on Kinney and his private army of about 60 men to police and hold the Nueces region for Texas.
> And finally, Kinney was most useful to Texas when he was in residence at Corpus Christi—for his was the only Anglo-American settlement west of the Nueces and therefore, the only shred of substance in Texas's claim to the country between the Nueces and the Rio Grande.

"Someday, perhaps," Ward concluded according to Moorman, "the details of the circumstances surrounding Dimitt's death will become known to us, but until the Mexican Government allows free access to its historical archives, we can only reason from the few facts and many bits of circumstantial evidence at our disposal."[14]

"The Most ... God-Forsaken Hole in the 'Lone Star State'"

In 1845, in the run-up to the Mexican-American War (1846–1848), more than half of the entire U.S. army was stationed at the future Corpus Christi, in the Nueces Strip, the area claimed by Mexico on the one hand and Texas and the U.S., which had annexed Texas, on the other. Briefly, this war resulted from that U.S. annexation in 1845, with the U.S. declaring their new southern border to be the Rio Grande River, as did the Texas Republic. According to the Library of Congress, "The dispute surrounding assigning the border at the Río Grande or at the Nueces River, coupled with the US annexation of Texas in 1845, set the Mexican-American War into motion." Actually, what set it in motion was President James K. Polk sending troops into the Nueces Strip, between the two rivers. He knew full well the Mexicans would have to respond militarily. Polk used this response as a pretext for an all-out war.[15]

The U.S. force, under General Zachary Taylor, was the largest assembly of U.S. regulars since the Revolutionary War. What began as 1,500 men had burgeoned to 4,000. "The men found Corpus Christi to consist of some twenty to thirty houses and just two bars, a paucity in both instances which soon would be alleviated." A U.S. army history described Kinney's Ranch/Corpus Christi during the seven-month encampment as "the most murderous, thieving, gambling, cutthroat, God-forsaken hole in the 'Lone Star State' or out of it." The soldiers, a Texas reporter noted in 2012, "had nothing to do while they waited for war to break out with Mexico! The enterprising scoundrel [Kinney] exploited this rare opportunity for all it was worth and made money hand over fist by offering a smorgasbord of vices."[16]

Whatever his faults—and they were obviously legion—Kinney managed to acquit himself well in support of the U.S. and Texas forces during the war. He acted as quartermaster to General Taylor's Army. He was cited for bravery by General Taylor in the Monterrey campaign, where he served as a guide, translator, and scout. And the governor of Texas made him a major in the Texas Army. He preferred, however, his fabricated rank of colonel to the genuine one of major, the latter requiring a demotion that would have been hard to explain.

It was here, during the war, that Kinney met and was befriended by a man who would profoundly influence, in a few years hence, the rest of his life—the future president of the United States, General Franklin Pierce.

"Hero of Many a Hard-Fought Bottle"

Franklin Pierce, born in 1804, was from New Hampshire, the son of a Revolutionary War hero and a hero himself to the Granite State when he returned from the Mexican-American War. But the battle exploits of the heavy-drinking Pierce have been questioned by some historians, and his contemporary detractors insisted he was the "hero of many a hard-fought bottle." Before the war he had been a U.S. congressman and then a senator, returning, in 1842, to private law practice in New Hampshire until he went to war as a brigadier general.[17]

At the outset of the 1852 Democratic Party convention, Franklin Pierce, 47, was the longest of long shots for the nomination. At first, he had no shot at all, receiving zero votes until the 35th ballot. By then the convention had become hopelessly deadlocked, dividing its ballot votes among four giants of the party: Lewis Cass of Michigan was the nominee four years before and a former secretary of war and U.S. senator; James Buchanan of Pennsylvania had been minister to both Russia and England, secretary of state, U.S. senator and congressman (and would ascend to the presidency in 1856); Stephen A. Douglas of Illinois, a U.S. senator and congressman, was known as the "Little Giant" because he was short but a force in politics; and William L. Marcy, governor of New York, a U.S. senator, and secretary of war during the Mexican-American War.

After Pierce first got on the board on the 35th ballot, his support remained steady until the 46th ballot, when it began to increase at Cass's expense. He was nominated nearly unanimously on the 49th ballot. As a sop to the Buchananites, Pierce's supporters let them fill the running mate position on the ticket, knowing that they would select Alabama Senator William R. King, to whom Pierce had no objections. During the ensuing campaign, King fell ill, limiting his efforts for the ticket. But he helped sway the South's voters with the statement that New Hampshire's Pierce was a "northern man with southern principles."

It was this quality that carried Pierce. He supported state's rights and was opposed to the abolition of slavery because he felt it was constitutional. His northern roots and southern sympathies meant he would probably appeal to voters in both regions. His Whig Party opponent was none other than General Winfield Scott, the popular hero of the Mexican-American War—and Pierce's com-

Son of a Revolutionary War hero, a general in the Mexican-American War, Franklin Pierce was a northerner with southern sympathies. This made him an ideal presidential candidate in 1852, winning in a landslide (Library of Congress).

manding officer at the time. Pierce won by a landslide, 254 electoral votes to Scott's 42. Scott's overwhelming defeat was the last gasp of the Whig Party, which never recovered from this loss.[18]

"As Whiffling as a Weather-Cock"

Among historians, Pierce is often in contention for "worst president ever." But it's hard to parse out—except through the facile lens of 20/20 hindsight—which wretched failures were visited upon him by fate, and which were purely of his own making. Of the latter, a *New York Post* reporter described him "as whiffling as a weather-cock.... I believe it is [U.S. Minister to Spain Pierre] Soulé, who says that it's the last man that has influence with the President. Everyone goes away with the notion that he will have his wish gratified." This assessment came in the middle of his term. It was accompanied by the accusation he was prone to "soft sawder," a phonetic spelling of soft solder; that is, solder that melts at a lower temperature, a 19th-century saying, that meant, in this case, that Pierce was susceptible "to flattery that has the aim of persuading or cajoling."[19]

As noted, he had a pre-presidency reputation as a hard drinker and post-presidency, as well. But for his White House years, the evidence is mixed. Here is one recorded account of his drinking then, from England's minister to the U.S., John Crampton. In a private and confidential letter to Whitehall, Crampton described Pierce's drinking problem this way (the Latin phrase is from Virgil's *Aeneid*): "Mr. Pierce, you may have already perceived, is given to continual vacillations ... [and] although he has taken 'the pledge' [against drinking] there are moments at which the *veteris vestigia flamma* [ashes of the old fire flare up] and this would partly account for silly speeches which he has made on various subjects."[20]

While an alcohol-addled mind might be considered a self-inflicted decision-making deficit, a man who saw his third and only surviving child's head crushed in a train accident might be forgiven for drowning his sorrows. On January 6, 1853, about halfway between his election and inauguration, Pierce, his wife, and their 11-year-old son, Bennie, were traveling by train when their car went off the tracks and tumbled down an embankment. Pierce and his wife were unharmed but watched in horror as their son was nearly decapitated in the wreck, the accident's only fatality. "My Countrymen," he began his inaugural speech two months later, "it is a relief to feel that no heart but my own can know the personal regret and bitter sorrow over which I have been borne to [this] position."

Historian Roy Nichols wrote in his biography, "Pierce's great justification for assuming the burdens of the Presidency had been the thought of building a heritage which might aid Bennie's advance in life. Now this great station was no longer a half-compensated responsibility, but an impending horror. Much of the difficulty which he experienced in administration during the next four years may be attributed to this terrible tragedy and its long-continued after-effects."[21]

"If Shepherd Would Give Him an Eighth of ... the Territory"

Pierce became the first president to publicly declare territorial aggrandizement an aim of his administration. "The policy of my Administration will not be controlled by any timid forebodings of evil from expansion," he said at his inaugural. Whether Pierce intended to start his foreign conquests amid the ruins of Greytown, the Washington paper, *National Era*, had its suspicions, "We predict that the affair will be found to be merely a pretext for the annexation of the town and the adjacent coast."[22]

This *National Era* piece appeared less than a month after Greytown was razed (see Chapter 6). It was followed within a month by the *New York Tribune* and another paper each leveling stunning accusations at Solon Borland. "I am informed from the best authority," a *Tribune* correspondent wrote, that Borland "went ... to visit old Capt. Shepherd, the person holding the repudiated grant of the entire Mosquito coast, which Great Britain has two or three times refused to recognize." During that visit, Borland "proposed to Shepherd to put through his claim on shares." That is to say, "if Shepherd would give him an eighth of the right to the territory, he (Borland) would undertake to have the grant confirmed, and Shepherd put in possession. This the old man declined doing, on the ground that he had already sold out to Mr. J.L. White and others."

And then there was this from the *Semi-Weekly Courier and New-York Enquirer*. About the time that Borland resigned as minister to Nicaragua, "he made offers of service to the grant-holders, in consideration of a heavy interest in their property. This was held under advisement for some time and would probably have been accepted but for the proceedings of the ex–Minister at Greytown and the subsequent bombardment of the place. It was contemplated to dispatch Mr. B. to Greytown and place him in general charge of the Company's interest. That design has been abandoned."[23]

"I Regret ... To Learn, You Have Been Arrested"

When the *Cyane* returned from Greytown, it docked in Boston, where Hollins received the following from Navy Secretary Dobbin, "You are

8. "The Great Theatre of Speculation"   83

hereby detached from ... command ... and you will proceed to New-York without delay ... [where], I regret ... to learn, you have been arrested." Dobbin assured Hollins that "you retain unimpaired the confidence of the Department in your patriotism, gallantry and fitness for command of a national ship."[24]

Hollins was arrested because Calvin Durand, one of the three "claimants" mentioned in Chapter 6, was suing Hollins—personally—for $14,000 ($418,000 in 2022). The charge was trespass. Today, the most common form of trespass is the self-explanatory, entering upon private land uninvited and unwelcomed. But the word has two other legal meanings: trespass against a person (assault, etc.); and trespass against chattels (seizure of, or "intermeddling" with, another's goods, including destroying them). Hollins was being sued for the "chattels" version. Hollins was bailed out by three men associated with the Federal government. The decision in this case did not come until 1860 and became a precedent that has had a profound effect on American foreign policy and U.S. jurisprudence down to the present day. (See the Preface and Chapters 17 and 18.)[25]

"Not Explaining That They Were Prickly Pear Cactus"

By 1852, H.L. Kinney had amassed a fortune in the 14 years he'd been in Texas. Not in his wildest imaginings could he have seen himself three years hence, meeting with "several of the great men of the nation ... [who] ... all agree.... I shall go down at the head of the New Government of Central America." But in 1852, according to author Charles G. Norton, a financial disaster struck Kinney that put him, inevitably, on just that improbable, and, ultimately, unrealized path. He "organized ... a fair held in Corpus Christi, generally believed the first fair ever held in Texas," wrote author Norton, and it was Kinney who was also the main backer, and when it proved a financial fiasco, he found himself deeply in debt.[26]

Author Norton was the grandson of Judge Milford P. Norton, who was Kinney's lawyer and agent. Writing in an unpublished typescript, around 1938, Judge Norton's grandson noted that Kinney had met his grandfather in the early 1840s when Milford was a lawyer in Refugio, Texas, where Kinney "engaged in frequent litigation." Kinney noticed he was often on the losing end when Norton was representing the other side, so he persuaded Norton, at an annual salary of $1,750 ($52,000 in 2022), to manage his affairs when Kinney was away (which he continued to do, even after being named a judge in 1845). Besides this unpublished typescript about his grandfather, Charles Norton had six articles about Kinney published in the *Austin Times and the Texas Democrat* in 1937 and 12 very similar articles in the *Corpus Christi Caller-Times* during the spring of 1938. All three Charles Norton sources are referenced immediately below, along with some comments by the previously mentioned historian Hortense Warner Ward.[27]

Charles Norton wrote that Kinney's 1852 fair, "was a land-selling scheme by which Kinney thought to attract settlers to the Corpus Christi territory and to sell them land for farming and ranching. He advertised it far and wide, in the eastern and northern states and even in England." (He even included, wrote historian Dan L. Thrapp, "such lures as the statement that 'pears grow wild' in the area, not explaining that they were prickly pear cactus.") "The fair was held in the month of May and included an exhibition of local products, horse racing, cock fighting and considerable speech making. Kinney gave prizes, mostly money, aggregating $3,000 ($90,000 in 2022) and then sought ways to meet the debts he had contracted."[28]

The failure of the fair, as noted, left Kinney deeply in debt, especially to a friend named John Schatzell. "Kinney … persuaded him to move to Corpus Christi to spend the twilight of his life"—and borrowed heavily from him. Beginning in 1850, these sums ranged from $500 to $10,000 ($15,000 to $300,000 in 2022), Kinney "giving his note for a few months or for a year or so, but always failing to pay the notes when due." Given that Kinney paid the interest on time, Schatzell let the principal slide, knowing Kinney had considerable property as potential collateral. Eventually, his fair debt reached $45,000 ($1.4 million in 2022). "Kinney turned over to Schatzell, in partial payment, notes and mortgages amounting to about $21,000 ($626,000 in 2022) and then [later] borrowed another $1,000 ($30,000 in 2022)." (There will be more on Kinney's finances in Chapters 11 and 16.)[29]

"The Most Kind Feelings and Attachment"

In early 1854 (for context, this was about three months before Greytown was destroyed), Kinney, demoralized over the fair failure and burdened by his concomitant indebtedness, was at loose ends as to what to do next in his life. On April 12 he received a letter from a friend in Washington named James Myer, "I saw Genl Rusk [Thomas Jefferson Rusk, an early Texas military and political figure] and [Peter Hansborough] Bell [a former Texas governor] and had a long conversation with them in regard to you…. [They feel] confident … that if you were here [in Washington] that you could succeed, having talked with Genl Pearce [*sic*] about you, whose recollections of you [from the Mexican-American War] are of the most kind feelings and attachment." Two weeks later Kinney received a letter from his lawyer, Judge Norton, which opens with a reference to Myer's earlier missive:

> You can delegate Myer ... to remain at Washington until you reach there. I am so sure that you can accomplish what you please there with Congress or the President.... Do not, Dear Col., let this opportunity to secure and establish your proper position in the world pass by. One day's ride upon the [railroad] cars will do more to drive out of your mind your little ... troubles ... than all the Brandy you & I can drink in a year. [Washington] is now the great theatre of speculation and you will find parties there from the President down as glad to get your assistance as you will be to get theirs.... Why not do it instead of dribbling your life away at Corpus ... and wearing out your life & energies ... with no benefit to your happiness or position in life.[30]

Author Charles Norton noted that in the early 1850s, "Colonel Kinney was considered very wealthy. He owned large tracts of land along the Nueces River, in the coast country below Corpus Christi, in the lower Rio Grande country near Brownsville and in Mexico near Matamoras. He owned cattle and horses, had several ships and operated cross country freight wagons. He was a large borrower and never out of debt, but always was able to make trades that brought him in money with which to pay pressing obligations." (Texas historian J.W. Wilbarger wrote that Kinney seemed to think that his "'strong box' ... would replenish itself automatically whenever it was emptied.")[31]

Chapter 9

"I Will See the President Again Today"

Despite the exhortations by his lawyer/agent Milford Norton in April to visit President Pierce in Washington, Kinney hesitated. He had promised Hiram Pearson, his old friend from the Illinois land speculation, to visit him in San Francisco. (See Chapter 8.) Pearson had moved there at the beginning of the Gold Rush, where he got into a scam that made him a millionaire. (This may have been the reason Kinney was torn between seeing Pierce or going, as planned, to visit his now very wealthy friend.) Pearson had enriched himself via the arcane practice of squatting on "water-lots" around the edge of San Francisco's harbor. Pearson and his like—often by force of arms—would "stake off" areas of water contiguous with the land by using pile-drivers. As one history records, "the pile driver, both the man and the machine, was an institution of San Francisco's babyhood."[1]

"Several ... Great Men ... Attended and Made Speeches"

However appealing this scam may have sounded to a hustler like Kinney, he chose not to join Pearson—although their affinity for each other would lead later to another business association. Kinney did not leave Corpus Christi for Washington until September 1854 and, inexplicably, did not arrive in D.C. until October or November. Once there, the "Shepherd" Mosquito land-grant company, Central American Land and Mining, chose him to lead their expedition to Greytown. (It is tantalizingly unknown if he met with President Pierce before or after this appointment.) "The Central America Company met at my rooms last evening," Kinney wrote his lawyer, Judge Norton, on November 8, still thinking of pile-driving Pearson in San Francisco. "Several of the great men of the nation attended and made speeches. All agree so far that I shall go down at the head of the New Government of Central America. I shall know about it tomorrow.… If I take the management of the new govt, I shall not remain long in San Francisco." Nine days later, on November 17, 1854, the *New York Herald* confirmed this decision to "establish a republic," including Greytown and under Kinney, in the Shepherd-grant lands.[2]

Beneath the headline, "A New Anglo-American Republic in Central America—What's in the Wind?" the *Herald* noted, "We understand that an expedition of Americans is about to start from this city, Texas and other parts, to establish a republic in the territory purchased in the Mosquito country. It is said the purchase covers some twenty-five millions of acres. The purpose is to bring in, also, the town of San Juan, or Greytown, by the consent and co-operation of the authorities. From the character of the gentlemen engaged in this enterprise," the *Herald* enthused, "we should anticipate a brilliant future, not only for the territory in question, but for all the Central American States. This may be the leaven that will leaven the whole lump and give a vigorous government to the feeble and disorganized population of that part of the world. We are informed that the celebrated Col. Kinney … is to lead the expedition, and to be the President of the new republic. Such a man," the *Herald* continued, "who has made his mark wherever he has been, and in whatever he has undertaken—is not likely to fail."[3]

By this time Kinney had definitely met with President Pierce—and canceled his plans to visit Pearson. (They stayed in touch, however. Later, in 1855, when the Central American Land and Mining Company put out a prospectus promoting their colonization scheme, Hiram Pearson was listed as vice president and gave his residence as Providence, Rhode Island.)[4]

"The Arrogant Contumacy of the Offenders"

On December 4, 1854, in his State of the Union message 17 days after the *Herald* article above, President Pierce gave his first public justification for Greytown's demise five months earlier. He characterized the port city as, "This pretended community, a heterogeneous assemblage gathered from various countries, and composed for the most part of blacks and persons of mixed blood, had previously given other indications of mischievous and dangerous propensities." Pierce then recounted the official version of the physics-defying story of how four people in a 20-foot rowboat stole basic foodstuffs worth $477,000 in 2022 money. "Property was clandestinely abstracted from the depot of the Transit Company and taken to Greytown. The plunderers obtained shelter there and their pursuers were driven back by its people, who not only protected the wrongdoers and shared the plunder but treated with rudeness and violence those who sought to recover their property." (See Chapter 5.)[5]

"Not standing before the world in the attitude of an organized political society," Pierce continued, "being neither competent to exercise the rights nor to discharge the obligations of a government, it was, in fact, a marauding establishment too dangerous to be disregarded and too guilty to pass unpunished, and yet incapable of being treated in any other way than as a piratical resort of outlaws or a camp of savages depredating on emigrant trains or caravans and the frontier settlements of civilized states." In that remarkable 83-word sentence, Pierce was trying to insulate himself from the accusation that he made war on a foreign state without consulting Congress, which the Constitution says only that body can declare. Briefly, he was trying to hark back to when this provision was suspended in cases where the enemy was a stateless group, like pirates. Or, if landed peoples, they were regarded as otherwise "uncivilized" by the United States because they lacked an organized government or other qualities of a sovereign state. (There is more about stateless groups and "uncivilized" states in Chapter 17.) By now, this narrative has established Greytown's bona fides as a sovereign polity.[6]

"Seasonable [reasonable] notice was given to the people of Greytown," Pierce continued, "that this Government required them to repair the injuries they had done to our citizens and to make suitable apology for their insult of our minister, and that a ship of war would be dispatched thither to enforce compliance with these demands. Finding that neither the populace nor those assuming to have authority over them manifested any disposition to make the required reparation, or even to offer excuse for their conduct, he [Commander Hollins] warned them by a public proclamation that if they did not give satisfaction within a time specified he would bombard the town. By this procedure he afforded them opportunity to provide for their personal safety." (Pierce didn't mention that Hollins gave the 500 residents only 24 hours to come up with $716,000 in 2022 money.)[7]

"It certainly would have been most satisfactory to me," Pierce continued, "if the objects of the *Cyane's* mission could have been consummated without any act of public force, but the arrogant contumacy of the offenders rendered it impossible to avoid the alternative either to break up their establishment or to leave them impressed with the idea that they might persevere with impunity in a career of insolence and plunder."[8]

"His Guns Are Not Well Shotted with Truth"

The *New York Tribune* noted the next day that "the President opens on the Greytown ... people with a very loud battery, but his guns are not well shotted with truth. The bombardment of Greytown was a foolish act of barbarism, and the President labors hard to palliate it, by exaggeration and distortion, with little success. The fact that he obviously seeks to clear himself of the imputation of having directed or contemplated that bombardment proves that he does not trust to his own argument. What had the fact—supposing it *to be a fact*—that the Greytowners are mostly 'blacks and persons of mixed blood' to do with the merits of this controversy?" (emphasis in the original).⁹

Secretary of the Navy Dobbin also defended Hollins' actions, "I could not reprove this commander for his conduct," wrote Dobbin. "I think that an acquaintance with all the facts and calm reflection will relieve our own people ... from any fear that a wrong has been perpetrated."¹⁰

The day after Pierce's State of the Union, the *Washington Daily Globe* reported:

> The Washington correspondent of the *Semi-Weekly Courier and New-York Enquirer* says, the meditated expedition to Central America, under Colonel Kinney, of Texas, may lead to important results. He is to be the local agent of the Central American Land and Mining Company, which claims to be the sole and rightful possessor of San Juan and all the surrounding territory for three or four hundred miles up and down the coast. The views of Colonel Kinney are understood to be of a filibustering character. He and his rangers will assert the title of their principals to the Mosquito country by a strong hand if necessary; and will receive a million or so of acres as their fee for so valuable a service. But it may be doubted whether, in these degenerate days, working-men are not more essential to the foundation of Empire than fighting-men. The establishment of a few hundred sharp-eyed American riflemen in that region, however, will have a tendency to adjust some of the troublesome questions which have for a number of years disturbed our relations with Central America.¹¹

"Where Then Was the Power Found to Demolish Greytown?"

A week after the State of the Union, the *Baltimore Sun* reported that a New York congressman named John Wheeler offered an amendment to a pending resolution "prefaced by declaring in effect that in the destruction of Greytown, the President has exercised a power violating the Constitution, and providing for the appointment of a Select Committee of Thirteen to report the facts relative thereto, *with power to send for* persons and papers" (emphasis added). This implied the compelling power of the subpoena and would have been a considerable step up from what both houses did immediately after the razing, in "*requesting* the President, *if compatible with the public interest*, to communicate ... copies of any ... etc." (emphasis added). Wheeler's proposal was voted down.¹²

About the same time, another representative, an ex–Whig, now of the American Party, Leander Martin Cox of Kentucky, gave this stirring speech on Congressional war powers regarding Greytown:

> The framers of the Constitution had seen the wretchedness to which a people could be reduced by being involved in the desolation and expense of war by the act of their rulers. They, therefore, declared that Congress should have power to declare war, thereby prohibiting all other powers in the Government from declaring or making war. For it would have been useless to say the President shall not declare war, and, at the same time, give him power to make war by acts. War can be begun without any declaration, and when the sword is drawn, and bathed in the blood of an adversary, the nation is at war and must be responsible for the consequences. Where then was the power found to demolish Greytown? It is said they were a "nest of pirates." If so, why did we send a commercial agent to reside with them; and furthermore, why not capture them and execute them according to law. I am not attempting to justify the people of Greytown. They may have and probably did deserve their fate. But I want to know under what clause of the Constitution the power is found to enable the President to judge the case, pass sentence, and execute it himself.[13]

According to historian David P. Currie, a U.S. Representative from New York named Rufus Peckham (like Pierce, a Democrat) "objected to a proposed appropriation to build an additional warship on the ground that he feared the Administration might use it illegally, as it had used the *Cyane* at Greytown. For in authorizing the bombardment of that settlement, Peckham argued, President Pierce had unconstitutionally 'assum[ed] the right to make war'":

> Did the Constitution, in declaring that Congress shall have power "to declare war, grant letters of marque and reprisal," ever intend to vest any such power in the Executive as was thus conferred upon this naval officer? Was it not intended in thus vesting in Congress the right to "grant letters of marque and reprisal"—a species of distress-warrant among nations to enforce the payment of a debt or the performance of some duty—carefully to avoid conferring on the Executive, under any circumstances, without the consent of Congress, power to involve the country in war?
> If the Executive had authority to direct the destruction of this town, why has he not authority to make war on Cuba? Where is the limit to his power? What but his own will shall prevent his involving the country in war at any time?[14]

"No one answered Peckham's penetrating questions," Currie wrote. "The only response to his argument was that it was out of order, and he withdrew his motion." In summing up, Currie said, "Despite widespread objections on the home front, there was precious little discussion of the incident in Congress."[15]

"The Enterprise Is Not a Filibustering One in Any Sense"

The day after Congressman John Wheeler questioned Pierce's constitutional power to act against Greytown, Kinney wrote to his lawyer that "my arrangements about going to Central America [are] now concluded. I will see the president again today on the subject." The *New York Times* reported three days later: "Col. H.L. Kinney ... is still in town. The Central American enterprise in which he is engaged ... some years ago purchased extensive grants of land in the Mosquito country. This Company propose to establish a new Central American Republic upon the territory thus acquired." Here the paper introduces a former U.S. congressman from Maryland named Wm. Cost Johnson as the president of the company and says Kinney was "to go out and found the projected colony." The paper reassured its readers that in "interviews with the President and other members of the Government" Kinney "has satisfied them entirely that the enterprise is not a filibustering one in any sense, and contemplates neither a violation or evasion of our neutrality laws. Under these circumstances, of course, the Government will throw no obstacles in their way."[16]

As the commenting *New York Times* understood it, the company would give liberal grants of land to the right sort of men. About a hundred colonists were expected to leave New York by January 13, 1855, with others to join them from Pennsylvania, Texas, and New Orleans. Greytown, now being rebuilt under British dominance, had always been part of the Shepherd grant, which had little consequence when the grant had been annulled and moribund. Now, the *Times* pointed out that "the property holders at Greytown, it is stated, desire the success of the enterprise, and are anxious to bring their municipality within its influence, as soon as the new Government shall be established."

Now the *Times* article—just three paragraphs after saying Kinney convinced the Pierce administration that the "enterprise is not a filibustering one in any sense"—revealed, as noted earlier, the true nature of the enterprise:

> That the influence of [Kinney's] new Republic will speedily spread itself all over Nicaragua, and absorb the whole of that State with its inefficient Government, there can be little doubt; humanity will be the gainer by the event and the commercial world will reap great benefit from the settlement of an enterprising, energetic people, and the establishment of a strong Government at a point where promptness and security in interoceanic communication is of primary importance.[17]

This is the same *New York Times* that roundly condemned the razing of Greytown. Now the paper was rhapsodic about this federally encouraged private enterprise and, while parroting Kinney's assurances that it is not a filibustering expedition, saluting its seemingly inevitable conquest of Nicaragua as a boon to humanity and commerce.

Other papers that condemned Greytown's demise also applauded the Kinney expedition—at least early on. An exception was the *New York Herald*:

> It is generally believed that the administration is virtually pledged to see Colonel Kinney safely installed in his new republic. Unquestionably the Kitchen Cabinet hold a large amount of sympathy and perhaps, also, of stock, in this grand adventure. The plan is to send down one or two thousand men, armed and equipped, to plant the colony. Having first obtained a foothold in the Mosquito purchase, they are forthwith to begin "the extension of the area of freedom," and to keep it up till all the Central American States are absorbed in this Cooper, Cost Johnson and Kinney republic.

The next paragraph in this *Herald* story ends by making a direct connection between the razing of Greytown and the Kinney filibuster, both part of a conquest in, or even, *of* the region:

> The sinews [funding needed] of war are to be derived from the stock of the thirty-five million acre tract [size usually given as 22.5 million acres] which the company suppose they own down there. It is also understood … that Secretary Dobbin is to make a diversion in favor of the new colony, in the concentration of all the available ships of the home squadron, as a check upon the English and French, whose naval force in that quarter, as you are well aware, is in process of being largely increased. So, you see that in this Kinney scheme we have the promising nest egg for a naval collision with France and England. [There were rumblings in the press regarding such planned naval face-offs, but they seem to have been illusory.] Thus, too, you will perceive that the bombardment of Greytown had a meaning in it, and an object in view of the largest dimensions, and of the most belligerent character.[18]

This last is reminiscent of an accusation in the *New York Tribune,* as noted before, of some four months earlier. Then that paper said the Greytown razing was preordained, that it "was resolved upon" at a dinner party of federal officials and speculators shortly after Borland returned to the U.S. (See Chapter 6.)

About this time another man was brought into the Kinney project—Joseph W. Fabens, the U.S. Commercial Agent at Greytown who was responsible, along with Joseph White of the transit and land-grant companies, and Captain Hollins, of the *Cyane*, for the destruction of Greytown.

Chapter 10

"The Greatest Confidence Trick of All Time"

Kinney and the Shepherd-grant company were hoping for one or more of three possible results from their efforts. First, an outright validation of the grant, giving the company a piece of Central America the size of Maine, including Greytown. Or, second, to use the grant as a pretext to "colonize" the area with, in reality, filibusters. If successful, they would seize the grant land and perhaps convince the United States to annex it—like Texas—and then spread their influence to Nicaragua and the rest of Central America. Or, third, to make the grant seem valid enough to convince Americans to purchase stock in the company. This last was called "stock jobbing," a pejorative referring, generally, to selling speculative or worthless securities.

In this regard, the Kinney scheme reminded the British of a scam of their own 30 years earlier. While that episode involved bonds, not stocks, the basic concept is the same. In a private and confidential letter to Whitehall in October of 1854, Britain's Minister to the U.S. John Crampton echoed the sentiments expressed in the American press about the Shepherd grant. Crampton concluded that the "whole thing is a stock jobbing humbug … [similar to our] great Poyais swindle." The Poyais dupery was the brainchild of General Gregor MacGregor, a wily Scotsman who served in the Latin American independence movement against Spain. MacGregor parlayed this back-story into a con so deceptive that the London Stock Exchange was actually persuaded to trade in bonds issued by a Central American "country" that literally did not exist.[1]

Poyais is generally considered to be the greatest fraud in history. In 2012, England's prestigious *The Economist* magazine called it just that. Like the Shepherd-grant company, MacGregor had also purchased a large Mosquito land grant, encompassing "a nation" he called "Poyais" (probably after the Poyas, a local river and a small tribe in the area). He described the country, wrote author Maria Konnikova, as "so fertile it could yield three maize harvests a year. The water, so pure and refreshing it could quench any thirst—and as if that weren't enough, chunks of gold lined the riverbeds. The trees overflowed with fruit, and the forest teemed with game."[2]

The Poyais deceit and the Kinney-led scheme were so alike—and ultimately so interconnected—that a detailed description of the earlier event, its antecedents and its chief protagonist are essential to this narrative.

"I Am Sick and Tired of This Bluffer"

Gregor MacGregor was born in Scotland in 1786. At age 25, he became intrigued by the revolts against Spanish rule in Latin America, especially that in Venezuela, when one of its revolutionary generals, Francisco de Miranda, was feted in London society during a visit in 1811. MacGregor romanticized about seeing himself so honored, returning triumphantly to Great Britain after such heroic exploits. MacGregor went to Venezuela and offered his services directly to General Miranda. As a former British army officer, MacGregor was given command of a cavalry battalion, with which he soon routed a Spanish force.

Subsequent engagements were less successful, but, according to a fellow soldier, Michael Rafter, in his 1820 book, *Memoirs of Gregor M'Gregor*, MacGregor "was generally considered, not only by the South Americans but also by the French and German adventurers in Miranda's army, as a man of a daring and excessive courage." But some officers saw him, even

General Gregor MacGregor is credited with the greatest swindle in history and one eerily similar to the later Kinney scheme (General Research Division, The New York Public Library).

at this early stage, as a poseur. One wrote to a friend, "I am sick and tired of this bluffer, or Quixote, or the devil knows what. This man can hardly serve us ... without heaping ten thousand embarrassments upon us."[3]

To be fair to MacGregor, his record was mixed, at least early on, with some failings interleaved with genuine triumphs. The problem was that, later, his failures began to outnumber and eventually eclipse his successes. Inexorably, MacGregor's military skills and courage gave way to serial cowardice and an unbridled pursuit of wealth and fame through a series of con games culminating in the Poyais affair.

"I Shall Sleep Either in Hell or Amelia Tonight"

After several campaigns in the army of Simón Bolivar, the legendary "Liberator" of South America, MacGregor resigned. He was headed for the United States, "where he would attempt to recruit soldiers for an invasion of Spanish Florida." MacGregor set his sights on Amelia Island, just off the northeast coast of East Florida, because he thought its population of stateless pirates would not resist him or aid the small Spanish garrison there in its defense.[4]

In a foreshadowing of Poyais, he raised $160,000 ($4.7 million in 2022) by selling scripts, promising buyers 2,000 fertile acres in Florida for $1,000 ($30,000 in 2022) or their money back with interest if he failed to deliver. In late June 1817, MacGregor left Charleston, South Carolina, in a ship with fewer than 80 men, primarily U.S. citizens. Upon arrival, he exclaimed, "'I shall sleep either in hell or Amelia tonight,' and led the attack." The Spanish commander of the garrison, with 51 men and several cannons, greatly overestimated the size of MacGregor's force and surrendered without either side firing a shot.[5]

"Liberty for the Floridas Under ... MacGregor"

MacGregor announced in his increasingly grandiose manner—from this 18-square-mile island—a "Republic of the Floridas" under his rule. But as Spanish forces assembled on the mainland opposite Amelia, MacGregor, "without giving the slightest notice of his intention ... sent all his baggage on board ... [an awaiting schooner], and, embarking himself with his wife, sailed a few days after, even at the moment when the Spaniards were attacking his deserted and deceived followers." Despite his money-back guarantee on the land scripts he issued to raise funds for the Amelia expedition, he made no attempt to repay the $160,000 he had collected.[6]

Amazingly, after his ignominious escape from Amelia Island, MacGregor signed on with other Latin American revolutionaries in London to lead a "British Legion" in the ongoing struggle against Spanish rule. In two spectacular failures, at Porto Bello, Venezuela, and Rio de la Hacha, then part of New Granada (present-day Colombia and Panama), he deserted his troops again in both instances. After the second debacle, MacGregor issued a lofty proclamation of victory which he signed as "His Majesty the Inca of New Granada." Author Michael Rafter called this an "aberration of human intellect."[7]

"That He Would Convert into the Mythical State of Poyais"

MacGregor disappeared in the face of universal condemnation; his whereabouts for months following October 1819 are unknown. When next he emerged into public consciousness, it was on the Cape Gracias á Dios, on Central America's Caribbean coast, in Britain's Mosquito Protectorate, at the court of the King of the Mosquito Indians, George Frédéric Augustus I. He was there, wrote historian David Sinclair, "negotiating the land grant that he would convert into the mythical state of Poyais." This was just one of many such grants issued by Mosquito kings down through the years. This Poyasian grant was in the far north of the protectorate; the Shepherd grant was in the south of it. (See map before title page and Chapter 2.) The Poyais was only about one-third the size of the Shepherd.

The English government had mixed, often conflicting reactions to the issuance of these grants. ("The subject of the grants," wrote historian David Hunter Miller in 1936, "has as yet been meagerly treated.") In 1846, as noted, Whitehall's Mosquito representative, Patrick Walker, annulled all those issued by King Robert Charles Frédéric, including the Shepherd, because, Walker alleged, that the king was drunk when he issued them. (Because it was issued, as noted, by an earlier king, the Poyais was unaffected.)[8]

On April 29, 1820, the king signed the grant document that MacGregor called the Poyais; this substantial swath of Mosquito territory, comprising 8,000,000 acres, was larger than New Jersey and Connecticut combined. An early traveler described the land as "poor, and unfit for cultivation, but [it] really appears to have been laid out by some skillful landscape gardener."[9]

"The Most Audacious Fraud in History"

With grant in hand, MacGregor appeared in London in mid–1821, referring to himself as the *Cazique* of Poyais. (This is a Spanish-American word for a native chief, which MacGregor corrupted into "Prince.") He claimed to have been declared such by the Mosquito king, but historian Sinclair wrote that the title and the name Poyais were of his own invention. Despite Michael Rafter's critical book, London society remained largely unaware of MacGregor's failures over the past few years. But they remembered his successes, such as his early triumphs in Latin America and, even earlier, his association with the heroic "Die-Hards" regiment of the British infantry.[10]

So began what David Sinclair called in the subtitle of his book, "the most audacious fraud in history." MacGregor had Poyaisian offices set up in London, Edinburgh, and Glasgow to sell impressive-looking land certificates to the general public and to coordinate prospective emigration to his grant lands. He launched a Poyais loan of £200,000 (£30 million or $40 million in 2022) on October 23, 1822. He mounted an aggressive sales campaign for both these bonds and the plots of Poyaisian land he was selling.[11]

"Globules of Pure Gold"

"Nothing would have been more calculated to encourage belief in Poyais," wrote historian Sinclair, then a "300-page, leather-spined volume" which appeared in Edinburgh and London in mid–1822. The printing cost alone seemed an incontrovertible bellwether of authenticity. "And, yet," wrote Sinclair, "it was a complete fake" (going so far as to claim the rivers of Poyais contained "globules of pure gold"). Represented as a guidebook "chiefly intended for the use of settlers," *Sketch of the Mosquito Shore, Including the Territory of Poyais* was attributed by MacGregor to a "Captain Thomas Strangeways," aide-de-camp to the *Cazique*. But it was, according to Sinclair, actually written either by MacGregor himself or by accomplices. (It included, according to a magazine account from 1912, "a compilation of the most glowing description of the agricultural possibilities of the West Indies transferred to the swamps of the Honduras coast.")[12]

When MacGregor "needed tangible evidence to support the concept of his fraud," Sinclair concluded, "he merely produced the documents himself, knowing that, no matter how implausible, they were likely to be accepted at face value."[13]

The descriptions ranged from misleading to outright lies. But MacGregor's calculation that official-looking documents and the printed word would convince many people proved correct. He was able to increase the price of his Poyaisian land certificates from two shillings and three pence per acre to four shillings per acre without diminishing sales. MacGregor became, to quote one 21st-century financial analyst, the "Founding Father of Securities Fraud."[14]

"Which Cession Led to the Speculation So Notorious"

The first two shiploads of colonists to Poyais found nothing established when they arrived. They languished for months until some residents of nearby Belize (British Honduras) accidentally happened upon them. In the end, of the 240 colonists, only 60 survived the ordeal. (The king of the Mosquitos visited the colonists' encampment and, among other things, "expressed considerable concern to hear of his country being publicly advertised for sale in Europe.")[15]

Fortunately for the next group of colonists, word reached England in time for warships to overtake their five-ship flotilla and return it to England. By then MacGregor had fled to France only to return to England when the furor died down somewhat. He tried to resurrect the scam several times in both countries, getting indicted and arrested on occasion but never convicted. In 1839, Gregor MacGregor moved to Venezuela, where he requested and received a pension as a general who had fought for independence. He died there in 1845.

But the effects of his scheme lingered. And it is here where the MacGregor Mosquito-grant fraud and the Kinney Mosquito-grant scheme enter upon converging paths that would eventually bring them together in an 1856 Anglo-American draft treaty called the Dallas-Clarendon Convention (see Chapter 14). Meanwhile, though, in 1852, when the previously mentioned "Webster-Crampton Agreement" was being drafted, England's foreign secretary, the Earl of Malmesbury, shared a special concern with his U.S. minister. This spoke to the "grants of land made by the Mosquito Government. [Specifically,] the localities of the well-known Poyais or Black River Grant, made by the Mosquito King, George Frederick, in 1820, to General MacGregor, which cession led to the speculation *so notorious* under the title of 'Poyais bonds.' Great numbers of British subjects have long been, *and still are, deeply interested in this grant,*" the Earl continued, "and Her Majesty's Government could not properly lend themselves to such a summary abandonment of British rights, *however questionable the said grants may in some particulars be,* as would be involved in an unconditional transfer to Nicaragua or any other State of the district in which the Black River lands are situated" (emphasis added; the "Black River" reference is explained below).[16]

Ironically, this blatantly cynical and self-serving admission by Malmesbury, in "press[ing] for a modification" to protect the "speculation so notorious," need never have appeared in his letter and, hence, the official record. Apparently, Malmesbury did not know that the Poyais grant was in lands claimed only by Honduras and that Honduras was "no party to the treaty" under consideration. "From [the grant's] position within the limits of Honduras," England's U.S. minister later explained to him, "as those limits are acknowledged by Nicaragua herself, Nicaragua could not advance any claim."

Another historical benefit of Malmesbury's mistake is his reference to the "Black River" grant. He seems to be implying that Black River was another name for the Poyais, but it was really a later attempt to resurrect the "notorious" Poyais under a new name. Around 1838 British speculators convinced the then-reigning Mosquito king to "re-grant" them the Poyais, which they renamed after a river in the area. The owners tried mightily to distance themselves from the Poyais debacle and convince investors that they were serious about colonizing their "Black River" version of these same grant lands, but nothing really came of it.[17]

"In the Bulging Wallets of the 'Alley-Men'"

In 1852, the same year of Malmesbury's letter above—and about *29 years* after MacGregor's fraud was revealed—a highly regarded British gazetteer, commonly called *Johnston's,* was still listing the utterly chimerical "Poyais" as part of Central America, viz.: "Central America ... compris[es] besides the Central Amer. confed., Yucatan, parts of Mexico and New Granada, Poyais, the Mosquito coast, and British Honduras." (By *Johnston's* 1868 edition—then *45 years* on from the fraud—Poyais had been dropped from the gazetteer's Central America description but was still in an alphabetical list of individual places, viz.: "Poyais, a river and district of Central America, Mosquito territory, with a settlement on the river. Lat. 15° 10' N., lon. 85° 10' W.")[18]

In his excellent 2000 book on stock market speculation, *Devil Take the Hindmost*, Edward Chancellor reported that "a half a century later [i.e., the 1870s] Poyaisian land grants and debt certificates were still to be found in the bulging wallets of the 'Alley-men' of the [London] Stock Exchange."[19]

Chapter 11

"Am Grateful ... And Entirely Satisfied"

Now, two years after Malmesbury's letter, Kinney, his compatriots, and assorted prominent American citizens and politicians with financial interests in the Shepherd grant colonization scheme, were poised to cash in.

On December 31, 1854, in what now seems like the expedition's last unmitigated hurrah, Kinney sold 5,000 shares in Central American Land and Mining to Thomas Jefferson Rusk, a sitting U.S. senator from Texas. (As noted earlier, it's unclear whether the company was certified by the New York Stock Exchange to sell shares.) But then, less than 72 hours later, the first crack in the scheme appeared. On January 2, 1855, Thomas Lord, current president of the transit company, told the *New York Herald* that the Nicaraguan minister to the U.S., José de Marcoleta, had been informed that the company had "no interest in, or connection with, the 'Central American Land and Mining Company' whatever.... In fact, they have not made any communication to this company, of any sort, *at any time*" (emphasis added).

Then Lord admitted immediately after that in the same article that "Mr. [Charles] Morgan, our President, was at one time a director of said land company [and] J.L. White, Esq., our counsel, was also a director [but] withdrew. The Transit Company," Lord continued, "beg to assure Mr. Marcoleta that they disapprove any movement on the part of said company ... calculated to disturb the harmony and good understanding so happily existing between them and the government of Nicaragua."[1]

American newspapers speculated as to why the transit company severed its ties with the Shepherd grant company. Marcoleta's shaming campaign in the U.S. press may have had something to do with it. But the most likely reason for the schism, according to historian William Scroggs, was that the transit company had begun to fear what a loose cannon like Kinney might do if he got established in Mosquitia. In his classic 1916 book, *Filibusters and Financiers*, Scroggs wrote:

11. "Am Grateful ... And Entirely Satisfied"

It soon became evident that the Kinney enterprise had met a deadly foe in the Transit Company. It was to the interest of that corporation that Greytown be wiped off the map, and it had succeeded in inveigling the government into doing this bit of dirty work. But it had barely made itself absolutely master of the port before Kinney appeared with a proposition to revive the settlement, introduce a more energetic population, and assert the rights of Greytown to autonomy in a more vigorous fashion than ever before. The Central American Company, if once it got a foothold in Greytown, might grant special privileges to a rival steamship concern and destroy the Transit Company's monopoly. It was rumoured, too, that the Transit Company was maturing a scheme to rebuild Greytown for its own profit. White and his associates, therefore, determined to thwart the Kinney enterprise at all hazards.[2]

"Well Known to Everybody Except the Government"

Whether coincidental to, or a cause of the transit company's abandonment of the Kinney scheme, Secretary of State Marcy finally started questioning the ostensibly peaceful nature of the expedition. To this turnabout, the *New York Herald* responded, cynically, "The character and purposes of the expedition are notorious, and have been, for a long time, well known to everybody except the government." According to historian Robert E. May, "Marcy sent Kinney a copy of a document in the government's possession, endorsed by Kinney, indicating the expedition was to be organized militarily with Kinney as commander-in-chief."

Marcy then asked Kinney for a clarification of his intent, to which Kinney replied on January 28 and which Marcy quoted back to him in his response to Kinney on February 4. "You seem ... to repel the inference that you intend to submit to the existing sovereign authority of any country. Your design in this respect is indicated by the following passage in your letter, 'It is my purpose to occupy some suitable place, and to establish municipal regulations for the immediate government of the Colonists, so that it may be in my power to enforce order and keep up the forms of civilized society from the beginning.'" Marcy chided the disingenuous Kinney, "It is not to be assumed that the country to which you are going is not within the territorial limits of some government." Kinney promised Marcy that he would alter the nature of his expedition, but it was too late.[3]

Another possible reason for the administration's volte-face was Washington's adamant opposition to England's recruitment of American volunteers for their Crimean War. Top U.S. officials regarded this as a violation of American neutrality and perhaps thought that allowing U.S. filibusters to venture forth unchecked at this time would seem hypocritical.

For a short time, some of the powerful men behind the Central American Land and Mining Company, including Senator Cooper and former Congressman Wm. Cost Johnson, stood by Kinney. On March 1, 1855, for instance, the *New York Tribune* reported a published letter from Cost Johnson defending the Kinney expedition "on the ground that it is a pacific undertaking to colonize the Mosquito shore." But then, just 22 days later, the company threw Kinney overboard in a *New York Times* classified advertisement. "To All Whom It May Concern—Having understood that certain persons are under the impression that Col. H.L. Kinney is still Agent of the Central American Company, this is to give notice ... that all power and authority [of said] Kinney have been revoked, and that his connection with the company ceased on the 23rd day of February." (Notwithstanding this, when the company published a prospectus in October, Kinney was listed on the board of directors.)[4]

"A Home in Nicaragua! The Kinney Expedition"

This might seem like the end for Kinney. But within a month of the *Times* classified ad ostracizing him, Kinney had completely re-spun the public image of his efforts and was again making plans to steam for Greytown. In a brochure published in April of 1855 and entitled *A Home in Nicaragua! The Kinney Expedition*, the colonel's thinking is described this way in a news article reprint. "The plans of the 'Central American Company' first engaged his attention. This was an organization professing to hold lands by a grant from the Mosquito King. The title was defective, and Colonel Kinney has now no connection with that company. His whole exertions will be in behalf of the 'Nicaragua Land and Mining Company,' whose lands are held by an unexceptionable title."[5]

In a turnabout that would have been fast even by today's standards, Kinney had thusly denounced the Central American Land and Mining Company in favor of an entirely new corporate entity he created. The Nicaragua Land and Mining Company was based on lands and mines his partner, Joseph Fabens, purportedly co-owned with a prominent Nicaraguan named Fermín Ferrar. These holdings were not in the Mosquito Protectorate but in Nicaragua, just inland of the protectorate (see map before the title page). Fabens and Kinney said they had indisputable titles to these lands and the presumed approval of the Nicaraguan government, which had let other foreign colonizers buy and settle similar holdings. A departure date was set for this new Kinney expedition based on these new land titles. Five hundred "colonizers" were scheduled to sail from New York Harbor with Kinney and Fabens on May 7, 1855, aboard a large, fast steamer called, ironically enough, the *United States*.[6]

"Something Like a Trial Out of Court"

Both before and after being cut loose from Central American Land and Mining and embarking on this new venture, Kinney was borrowing heavily. According to the previously mentioned 1938 unpublished typescript (see Chapter 8) by Charles G. Norton, grandson of Milford Norton, Kinney's agent and lawyer, Kinney "drew drafts" on the elder Norton, "forcing sales of cattle and land." The colonel also borrowed a $1,000 ($30,000 in 2022) from an old friend, J. Pinckney Henderson, then in the United States Senate. In fact, wrote the younger Norton, "he borrowed from one friend after another"—and from total strangers. Two of the latter were Lucien Birdseye, a New York lawyer and, later, on the bench, and from Edward R. Boyle of Pennsylvania and New York. He not only borrowed a total of $25,000 ($745,000 in 2022) in cash from these two but secured a promise by them to pay off about $5,000 ($148,000 in 2022) in debt he had incurred in New York. He gave them "not only a mortgage covering all his real and personal property in Texas but also a power of attorney authorizing them to take over and administer his property until the debt to them had been paid."[7]

It was only several months after Kinney left for Greytown that it dawned on Birdseye that he should "ascertain the value of the Texas property" on which he and his friend Boyle had loaned Kinney $30,000 ($895,000 in 2022). "A correspondence between him [Birdseye] and Judge Norton," wrote Norton's grandson, was "something like a trial out of court, ... a notable contest between two able lawyers. They began fencing cautiously," wrote the younger Norton, "but gradually learning that each was seeking only what was right." About a year later, "both put their cards on the table and a settlement was effected. Kinney had contracted debts that had to be paid and they were paid, but because of Judge Norton's legal ability and straightforward dealings, the larger portion of Kinney's property was saved to him. Judge Birdseye and Judge Norton eventually became good friends and the former made a trip to Texas and was the latter's guest in Corpus Christi for several weeks."[8]

"The Man First on the Ground Would Have the Country"

Four days before Kinney's scheduled departure date of June 6, 1855, the amazing Minister Marcoleta sent Marcy a purloined letter from the president of the Central American Land and Mining company, Senator James Cooper, that was addressed to the company's secretary, a "Mr.

Hopkins" [read: Hipkins]. (Where and how he got the letter Marcoleta did not say, only that "the original ... is now in the hands of Mr. McKeon, US District Attorney of Southern District of N.Y.") Marcoleta told Marcy that "from its contents you will see all the intrigues going on against Nicaragua and the ideas and projects of Kenney [sic]."

In his letter, Cooper implied that he feared that Kinney's new company, "Nicaragua Land and Mining," and newly announced destination, Nicaragua, were possible smoke screens for falling back to his previous plan of exploiting the Shepherd grant in Mosquitia. Cooper wrote that he was informed that Kinney remarked that the "man first on the ground would have the country," and that Kinney was determined to go "unless we should get the start of him." (Cooper must have rightly assumed this implied Mosquitia and not Nicaragua because Cooper and Central American Land and Mining had no holdings in Nicaragua.)[9]

Cooper implied in this somewhat chaotic missive that Kinney waffled between belligerent confrontation with Cooper and benevolent cooperation. On the one hand, he quoted Kinney as saying of Cooper that he "had an oily tongue, & would talk the people into opposition to him [Kinney], & put mischief into the heads of the damned Nicaraguans. But that if he [Kinney] was there in advance [of Cooper], all Hell couldn't root him out &c." But, on the other hand, Kinney was suggesting he'd give Cooper $10,000 ($300,000 in 2022) for a schooner to take Cooper and his men (numbering by Cooper's own admission, only ten) down to Greytown ahead of Kinney "provided we would receive him [Kinney] & his men and allow them to share in the enterprise. He was willing, he said, to recognize me as Governor, if I would make him the Commander in Chief of any Military force that we might see fit to raise." (This letter's contentions could not be confirmed from other sources, but Kinney was notorious for this sort of flimflammery. And, yet, then again, Cooper was no saint, either.)[10]

"By the programme we marked out," Cooper continued in his letter, "we cannot expect under any circumstances to be in the country before the latter end of September. In the meantime, this Scapegrace [a 'rascal,' i.e., Kinney], may, by going South elude the vigilance of the [U.S.] Govt., as he would have done already, had it not been for the superior sagacity & energy of [Joseph] White." Cooper seemed to be conceding bitterly that, while "the only quality Kinney possesses is a Bulldog pertinacity" he had learned that the colonel had managed "to wheedle out of certain parties" the financial means to "go South & get off." Cooper may have been aware of the money Kinney borrowed from Birdseye and Boyle. In any event, he seems to have given up his rivalry with Kinney at this point.[11]

Ironically, Marcoleta sent another letter to Marcy the very same day, denouncing the sailing for Nicaragua from San Francisco of "the so-called

11. "Am Grateful ... And Entirely Satisfied"

Colonel Walker, in company with several armed persons [actually, 58], who are on their way to the territory of the Republic of Nicaragua, in evident violation of the laws of both countries." If Marcoleta thought Kinney was a handful, he could not have imagined what William Walker had in store for Nicaragua.[12]

"Equal to One Twelfth of the Whole of Said Lands"

With Secretary of State Marcy now opposed to Kinney, the latter and Fabens hoped to win over a few key Pierce Administration officials by resorting to an age-old ploy—bribing them. Early documentation of this suborning is sketchy, but three letters housed at the New-York Historical Society shed considerable light. On March 13, 1855, Fabens wrote from Salem, Massachusetts, to Kinney in New York, "You may arrange everything with Nicholson as we talked of." The Nicholson that Fabens referred to was Judge A.O.P. Nicholson, a close confidant of President Pierce and editor of the *Washington Union*, a quasi-official administration newspaper.

Attached to this letter is a draft of a letter Kinney then wrote to Judge Nicholson on March 16, "Dear Judge, I have written to Mr. Fabens our arrangements. When I hear from him, I will write, or dispatch you by telegraph. I think I will meet him in N.Y. & bring him with me to Baltimore to meet you, where we will conclude all our matters." In a March 17 letter to Kinney, Fabens declares he will

A.O.P. Nicholson was a lawyer, newspaper editor, banker, and politician from Tennessee. A Democrat, he was twice a U.S. Senator from that state (Library of Congress).

leave for New York on the 19th and discusses outfitting a ship with lumber and framing materials, presumably to make the expedition's "colonists," look like "the first settlers of California [who] went with their tents, mining tools, &c."[13]

Fabens' reference to arranging everything with Nicholson and Kinney's mention to Nicholson of concluding "all our matters" certainly refer to the arrangement which took place less than a month later. In return "for valuable advice and services," Kinney, Fabens, and Fermín Ferrar, "sold," to Nicholson and two others, for one dollar, a one-fourth share of their "certain lands and privileges now held, or to be hereafter acquired," this "being an interest to each ... equal to one twelfth of the whole of said lands and privileges." Besides Judge Nicholson, the recipients of this largesse were the oft-referenced-here Fletcher Webster and his distant cousin, President Pierce's 26-year-old private secretary, Sidney Webster. The instrument of conveyance was a deed-of-transfer, a copy of which (probably Nicholson's) resides in the New-York Historical Society.[14]

At this time Fletcher Webster held only a minor federal post, as surveyor of the port of Boston. But 11 years earlier, in 1844, he was the secretary of the legation on an important U.S. diplomatic mission to China, which established diplomatic relations and secured most-favored-nation status. This delegation was led by Caleb Cushing, now, of course, President Pierce's attorney general. The connection, wrote historian William Scroggs, "served to strengthen still further the impression that the [Kinney] movement had the sanction of men high in the nation's counsels."[15]

Sidney Webster was a New Hampshire neighbor of Pierce when the newly elected president tapped the then 24-year-old as his private secre-

Sidney Webster used his youthful stint as a president's personal secretary to forge social, political, and financial connections which made him a very wealthy man (source unknown).

tary. (He served in this capacity through Pierce's entire term.) Four days after he received his copy of the deed-of-transfer, Sidney Webster acknowledged receipt in a letter. "My Dear Fabens, I have received the document, and with my associate here [some conjecture that he is referring to Pierce] am grateful to you and your partner, and entirely satisfied." It was not until a court proceeding in early 1857 that the deed-of-transfer and Sidney Webster's thank you note to Fabens were revealed to the public (about which, more later in Chapter 15).[16]

Bribing these three did not work. Just four days after Sidney Webster's thank you note, the U.S. District Attorney in New York City, John McKeon, arrested Kinney for violating U.S. neutrality by recruiting for a filibuster expedition. Four days later Fabens was also arrested and finally fired from his Greytown commercial agency by Marcy—although it took him three tries, two letters from Marcy to Fabens and then another to a New York City federal judge. Marcy sent copies of his two letters addressed to Fabens to this judge and added, "If it has been represented to you that Mr. Fabens was under orders to return to [Greytown] to discharge his duties as an officer of this government, the statement is incorrect." The third time was the charm, and the tenacious Fabens finally accepted his dismissal.[17]

"And Hermaphroditic in Politics"

Fabens and Kinney were arrested reportedly at the instigation of Attorney General Cushing, who was rumored to be a supporter of, or at least unopposed to, the expedition early on but had lately turned against it. As the following suggests, the longstanding debt feud between Cushing and Daniel and Fletcher Webster (see Chapter 8) may have been behind the former's recent opposition to the enterprise.

Born to wealth in 1800, Cushing graduated from Harvard at the age of 17. He served as a Massachusetts congressman from 1835 to 1843. There he gained a reputation as a man devoid of either principle or ideology, blowing whichever way the winds of pragmatic self-promotion and self-aggrandizement carried him. Speaking in 1856 Senator Thomas Hart Benton called Cushing the "master spirit" of the Pierce cabinet, "a man of talent, of learning, of industry" and an "unscrupulous, double-sexed, double-gendered, and hermaphroditic in politics." When Benton heard of Cushing's appointment, "I set down Mr. Pierce for a doomed man, and foresaw the swift and full destruction which was to fall upon him."[18]

As another political commentator, Hermann von Holst, put it, "[Cushing's] opinions on the slavery question had run through all the points of the compass-card." This ability to "invert his thoughts," von Holst noted, might have served him well as the attorney of a client with a dubious case. "But, in an attorney general of the United States, who had to tell the president simply what the law was" it was "incontestably more desirable, that things should not change form before his intellectual eyes with every change of position." In Cushing, as one of the president's political advisers, Holst thought this character flaw might "become a matter of dangerous significance, since he far surpassed Pierce intellectually, and was a master ... of ... persuasion."[19]

Yet another observer, Carl Schurz, the first German-American senator, wrote:

> There was something like a cynical sneer in his [Cushing's] manner of bringing out his sentences, which made him look like Mephistopheles alive, and I do not remember ever to have heard a public speaker who stirred in me so decided a disinclination to believe what he said. In later years I met him repeatedly at dinner tables which he enlivened with his large information, his wit, and his fund of anecdote. But I could never quite overcome the impression ... [that] I could always listen to him with interest, but never with spontaneous confidence.[20]

"Cushing Is Fiercely Opposed to the Enterprise"

As noted in Chapter 8, Daniel Webster was by 1837 deeply in debt due to failed investments, especially from those recommended by Kinney. Also, as noted, much of this indebtedness was forgiven by his creditors. But this was a view not shared by Caleb Cushing, whose loans to Webster totaled about $10,000 ($300,000 in 2022) and which Cushing was seriously, if politely, bent on collecting. Daniel Webster, and later his son Fletcher, as the executor of his will, may have seen these Cushing loans as having been rendered null when Daniel Webster, as secretary of state, appointed Cushing as head of the commercial treaty delegation to China in 1844. While Cushing may have felt he received the plum job based on merit (he was amply qualified), the elder Webster may have regarded the appointment as a quid pro quo debt nullification. Cushing, for his part, may have felt he had repaid the appointment by filling the crucial role of delegation secretary with Fletcher.

Cushing continued pressing first Daniel and then Fletcher for repayment. This became part of the newspapers' guessing game as to why the Pierce administration was so divided over the Kinney expedition. What follows are summaries of three news articles which, though often speculative, are valuable in highlighting just how complex and conflicting were the personal interactions and motivations in these events.

The first, from the *New York Times* of May 12, 1855, addressed the Pierce administration's intramural squabbling over Kinney as it played out in the *Washington Union* and the *Washington Star*. "The case is easy of explanation," the *Times* contended:

> Attorney General Cushing is fiercely opposed to the enterprise or has been so during the last few weeks—and the *Star* is his organ, not the President's. The *Union*, on the contrary, reflects the views of the majority of the Cabinet, who are not ready to interfere with the private business of citizens, until there is good reason to believe those citizens have violated the law.... Mr. Cushing's opposition to the scheme is very bitter, for what reasons we know not, unless to satisfy the country that he was slandered by those who ... charged him with an interest in the scheme.[21]

If the *Times* couldn't offer a reason for the attorney general's opposition, save for disproving rumors of "an interest in the scheme," this next article suggested one, albeit some months later. A *Washington Star* article from October 15, 1855 (reprinted in the *Sacramento Daily Union*, December 5), mentioned the unpaid $10,000 in loans Caleb Cushing had made to the elder Webster and added: "Mr. Fletcher Webster is known to have had some sort of an interest in the Kinney Expedition," the piece went on, making "the opposition of the law officers of the Government to the Colonel's enterprise ... not, therefore, so difficult to understand as it might have been, perhaps, if that ten thousand dollar note had been paid." (As the *Times* article above noted, the *Star* was associated with Cushing. The *Sacramento Union* called it "one of Mr. Cushing's chosen vessels of wrath.")[22]

In addition to the presumptive inferences in the two news pieces above, there is this third article, from the *New York Post* (reprinted in the *Times*) that is worth considering. "The story has not been disputed that gentlemen in official stations, very high in [the administration's] confidence, had last Winter a direct pecuniary [financial] interest in the more objectionable Mosquito expedition [i.e., the one based on the Shepherd grant]; and if it [the administration] be now engaged in strangling the present enterprise [based on Fabens' Nicaraguan holdings], the reason may be that the bantling [baby] comes of different parentage."[23]

Chapter 12

"They Might Take His Office & Stick It"

When Fabens and Kinney were brought to court on May 7, 1855, accused of violating U.S. neutrality, it was the same day their expedition was scheduled to depart, so it was postponed. But when the judge dismissed the case because D.A. John McKeon couldn't locate a couple of his witnesses, Kinney and Fabens renewed plans to depart. Then Kinney was indicted on the same charge in Philadelphia. His attorney, a former vice president (under Polk) and a former minister to Russia (under Van Buren) named George Mifflin Dallas, asked for a delay until the court's next session and the judge agreed.[1]

If Kinney assumed his charter ship would be free to leave, with the New York dismissal and now the Philadelphia postponement, he was in for a rude shock. When he returned to New York, Kinney found his chartered vessel surrounded by three federal ships. (It turns out, the neutrality law allowed a president to act unilaterally, without a court finding.) As a practical matter, however, actually guarding against the *United States'* departure resulted in a comedy of errors that strained credulity, especially considering the U.S. rivaled England, at this time and especially at sea, as the most powerful nation on earth.

The opening move was by Pierce on May 25, 1855, when he sent this order to Commodore Charles Boarman, in charge of the U.S. Navy in the New York area. "Sir, Official information has been laid before me ... that one Henry L. Kinney, and one John [read: Joseph] W. Fabens, have ... set on foot and have prepared a military expedition against the Republic of Nicaragua, with which the United States are at peace." Then Pierce informed Boarman that Kinney, Fabens, and Fletcher Webster had chartered a steamer called the *United States* "for the purpose of being employed in such military expedition or enterprise, in violation of the [neutrality] law to convey the said Kinney and Fabens, [and] their followers" to Nicaragua. "You are therefore hereby directed and empowered, in virtue of ...

[the Neutrality Act] ... to prevent ... the departure of said steamer *United States* from beyond the limits of the said District of New York."[2]

Poor Boarman! Here he was, responsible for the defense of the most important city in the country and, according to historian Robert E. May, all he could muster was "the paddle-wheel steamer *Vixen* available to carry out orders to intercept the expedition. As a result, Boarman hastened repairs on a surveying vessel and got a revenue cutter [used to enforce tariff laws] added temporarily to his command, and asked the army's commanding general, Winfield Scott, to make up the deficiency." Scott oversaw the Army in the New York area. On May 30, Boarman messaged Scott that Pierce had ordered him, Boarman, to prevent the departure of the steamer *United States* from New York. He then asked Scott to order the army commanders at Fort Schuyler and Fort Hamilton at the harbor's two natural choke points, "to be instructed to prevent the departure of the steamers '*United States*' and '*Ocean Bird*' [another Kinney charter, scheduled to leave later], if they should succeed in evading the naval forces now placed in their immediate vicinity."[3]

But there were two problems. One, as historian May points out, was that Fort Schuyler, which stood at Throggs Neck, where the East River meets Long Island Sound, was unfinished, "lacking artillery and garrison at the time of Boarman's request." Fort Hamilton, on the other hand, which overlooked the Narrows, an outlet to Lower New York Bay and the ocean, was operational, but the other problem was that President Pierce withheld approval as to the use of Fort Hamilton's guns, for fear, writes May, "that the soldiers might accidentally fire on the wrong vessel."

When General Scott heard this, he wired the War Department:

> I am not a little mortified at the answer received ... from the President, of yesterday. According to the wires the President says:—"If it is proposed to have the guns, at Fort Hamilton, in readiness to fire into <u>any</u> vessel passing the Narrows, the President would not approve." Nothing so insane had entered my imagination. My communication to which that reply is made was, if the wires did me justice, in these words:
>
> "Commodore Boarman wishes Fort Hamilton to assist him, if necessary, to stop Kinney's expedition. I am inclined to give orders to that effect. Will the President approve?"
>
> I was aware, thro' the Commodore, that it was known, at Washington, that "Kinney's expedition" consisted of the two steamers the "United States" & "Ocean Bird," thence did not give the names of the vessels in my despatch.[4]

Did Pierce withhold permission to fire to increase Kinney's chances of escaping? As noted in the previous chapter, the newspapers of the day were baffled about much of the motivation behind the administration's mixed signals regarding the Kinney expedition.

"Mr. Webster Appeared Excited & Under the Influence of Liquor"

On the evening of June 6, 1855, with his charter ship still blockaded, Kinney stole out of New York Harbor bound for Greytown aboard a sailing schooner called the *Emma*. He had about 18 followers with him, including Fletcher's 15-year-old son, Daniel, but not Fletcher himself or Fabens. Fabens may have been left behind to try to "clear," that is, un-blockade the charter ship or otherwise advance the cause. But Fletcher, although presumably allowing his son to go, was not happy with Kinney.

Two weeks after the *Emma* departed, an assistant U.S. D.A. in New York sent a confidential letter to Attorney General Cushing, writing that he had made inquiry concerning Fletcher's pronouncements at a meeting of the scheme's supporters and "heard that in the presence of … [a] Marshals officer, he used the most vituperating expressions about the President and his officers in the cabinet." And he denounced Kinney for not getting "Cushing [financially] interested as he had the others" (i.e., Nicholson and Sidney Webster) and that if the group wanted it, "they might take his office [in the grant company] & stick it XXXX. Mr. Webster," the assistant D.A. concluded, "appeared excited & under the influence of liquor." Interestingly, it might be that Kinney *did* try to get Cushing "interested."

In Cushing's archived papers, there is a cryptic, undated note to Cushing from a man named March, asking Cushing, "Can't you dine with me to-day at the club [at] five o'clock—Col. Kinney, the founder of a new empire, will be there with one or two others. [signed] C.W. March" According to historian John Belohlavek, this was Charles W. March, a Washington-based reporter for the *New York Tribune*.[5]

"'Jumping and Thumping' Over the Reef"

"It was three weeks ago yesterday evening," wrote William Sidney Thayer, "when Col. Kinney, with eighteen other passengers, set sail in the *Emma*." It was now June 27, 1855, and Thayer was fulfilling his obligations as both a close confidant of Col. Kinney *and* correspondent for the *New York Post*—a conflict of interest that both he and the paper chose to ignore.

The *Emma's* journey to Greytown was uneventful until the captain lost "his reckoning off the Caycos (now, Caicos) Islands" and we were startled by a shout of, "Breakers ahead!" The vessel "made a narrow escape" but came to grief forty miles later, with the schooner "jumping and thumping" over the same hard reef.

12. "They Might Take His Office & Stick It"

"During the wrecking it was rather singular," Thayer noted, "to observe the different ways in which the men behaved themselves. The only one who seemed to have no care at all on his mind was little Daniel Webster [Fletcher's 15-year-old son] who whistled and sang as if he was in his element. An attempt by four men to row the lifeboat over the reef's breakers, to seek help failed but the colonel then stepped in," wrote Thayer. "With the energy of an old Roman written on his weather-beaten visage, he [Kinney] threw off his coat, and ... waded out to the boat, and fairly pushed it over the breakers, whence it carried a store of provisions and little Dan Webster to a shore about three miles off." Eventually, everyone made it to this same shore safely, thanks, Thayer made clear, largely to Kinney's Herculean efforts. "He has never quailed before any obstacles ... to forward his great design," wrote the *New York Post* reporter, and "his conduct ... has only served to increase the confidence of his men in his abilities as the leader in the work of colonizing Central America."[6]

Born in 1830 William Sydney Thayer graduated from Harvard in 1850 and joined the *New York Post* as a staff reporter around 1852. The two parties probably most interested in "Bill" Thayer's espousal of Kinney's cause were Thayer's father, Abijah, and his brother, James. Abijah wrote to his son that the *New York Tribune* had reported that he "had taken stock in the Kinney Expedition [which was true]. Everyone, in any way connected with it is regarded as more or less a filibuster—an outlaw." Historian James Wall noted, "apparently, Thayer's father had never been satisfied with the legality and morality of Kinney's activities in Texas. And Thayer's brother wrote to

William Sidney Thayer. Correspondent for the *New York Post* covering the Kinney scheme while closely tied to same (Library of Congress).

him about having trouble explaining to their friends ... just what 'Bill' was doing on a filibuster expedition."[7]

Kinney and company slept on the beach of North Caicos Island for two nights before being transported to Grand Turk Island by two small vessels. No lives were lost in the *Emma* wreck or subsequent ordeals, and the survivors were given comfortable accommodations on Grand Turk by John L. Nelson, U.S. consul to the British colony of the Turks and Caicos Islands. (To this day, they are a British Overseas Territory and now a popular resort destination.) Consul Nelson resigned his job in this diplomatic backwater to throw in his lot with Kinney. He, his family and two Turks islanders left Grand Turk with Kinney and the others aboard the British passenger ship *Huntress* on June 28, 1855, touching at Port Royal, Jamaica, before arriving at Greytown on July 16—one year and three days after the port's razing by the *Cyane*.

"Fifty Men ... Fully Armed, to Oppose Col. Kinney"

"Our object ... was to get ashore without any one's knowledge," Thayer wrote to the *Post,* aware that Kinney's expedition was suspect due to, Thayer insisted, false stories planted by the transit company or Nicaragua's envoy to the U.S., José de Marcoleta. Before the *Huntress* even dropped anchor, a boatload of men "informed us that some fifty men" had arrived the night before, "fully armed, to oppose Col. Kinney ... standing ready to fire at the *Emma*" (which they did not yet know had wrecked in the Caicos). This 50-man armed force had been recruited off the streets of New York by transit company agents, working in concert with Marcoleta. The force was to travel up the San Juan and lie in wait for Kinney and his small contingent, to prevent them from entering Nicaragua, where the expedition had been declared "piratical." (This scenario seems off-timing. If Kinney hadn't been delayed by the *Emma* wreck, this blocking force would have arrived much too late.) Marcoleta later insisted he had the assurance of U.S. D.A. McKeon that "these proceedings were not illegal." But then, in Marcoleta's retelling, McKeon, "after having maturely reflected upon the question, ... had arrived at an opinion diametrically opposite to that which he had formerly expressed." Red-faced, Marcoleta apologized, and the force was quickly disbanded.[8]

"Walker and His Men in the Interior"

"After the colonel had been safely carried ashore," Thayer wrote that the *Huntress* was boarded by the master of a British war steamer, looking for Kinney. Satisfied with the evasive answers he received, he was about to leave when he "embraced the occasion to tell us of the late defeat of Walker and his men in the interior, with whom, he entertained the belief, the Kinney Expedition was in some way connected."[9]

The "Walker" in question was William Walker, the Tennessean, as touched upon in Chapter 11, who would become the high priest of the dark art of filibustering. He had arrived on the Pacific coast of Nicaragua on June 16, 1855— exactly one month before Kinney arrived in Greytown. Walker, who gained notoriety as a filibuster after ill-fated forays into Baja California in 1853 and the Mexican state of Sonora in 1854, was invited to Nicaragua by one side in a civil war that had begun in 1854. After he and his "American Phalanx" of 58 "Immortals" suffered the one early defeat above, Walker put together a string of victories. These swelled his ranks with new American recruits. He was the de facto ruler of Nicaragua after only four months and its dubiously elected president nine months after that.

The filibuster William Walker, who took over Nicaragua, de facto, in just four months (*Illustrated London News*).

Some observers, including U.S. newspapers—perhaps reading causality into their near-simultaneous arrival on the isthmus—reported that Walker and Kinney were co-conspirators, the jaws of a bi-coastal vice in which to squeeze the isthmus into submission. "It is evident," the *New York Times* declared, "that the Walker forces from San Francisco, and the Kinney immigrants from New-York, will meet about the centre of Nicaragua, and the results of their junction can hardly be doubted, as far as a permanent location of an American colony is concerned." Kinney and Walker had no connection and, as will be seen in the next chapter, soon became bitter antagonists.[10]

"Pierce Poor Devil Is Frightened Half Out of His Boots"

Given the recent arrival of Walker and the opposition of the Nicaraguan government to the "piratical" Kinney expedition (he and Fabens had been banned from the country by name), the colonel decided to remain in Greytown. Awaiting Kinney upon his arrival was a letter from Fabens that seemed sent to reach Greytown just when the *Emma* should have carried him there. His delay due to the wreck probably gave the British authorities at Greytown time to intercept and copy the letter, as their archives seem to have the only extant copy (question marks indicate words guessed at):

> "Sell your cargo … and load the *Emma* at once for New York," [obviously oblivious to the *Emma's* demise]. After you stole off without me, Cahill & I went to sea in an open boat in search of the *Emma*, & at one o'clock at night reached Coney Island, wet thro, took a big drink, got up at 4, started again, couldn't find the *Emma*, came back to Fort Hamilton & got up to N.Y. in Season [on time] for Court—presented myself & couldn't get a trial—of course—yesterday being the last day of the term. I was discharged in full—so ends that farce….
>
> Ted Nicholson [A.O.P. Nicholson, editor of the *Washington Union*, and one of those Kinney and Fabens had bribed] gave the Expedition a good notice while we were there, & we succeeded in getting the US [the *United States*, Kinney's blockaded charter ship] clear [free to leave New York Harbor]. Graham [the ship's owner and captain] has not decided to try[?] the ship again—says it is doubtful if he could get passengers & she might be seized—[?].
>
> Hazard & Eagle will put up a vessel[?] as soon as the news of your safe arrival reaches here. Keep quiet—everything depends upon the character of our movement now. The community here are sympathetic with us. Graham has got 8000 signers to a memorial to Congress in his behalf for damages [his losses from his ship being under federal blockade]. He must prove that we are good citizens & no filibusters. I believe all the property holders of Granada, Leon, are with us. There are many things I would like to write but you will hear of them from other sources. Zacharie [a Kinney Texas colleague] has not sent the $5,000 [$150,000 in 2022] & your drafts on him are all returned protested. This embarrasses us much. He Z says it will be all right after Cahill gets there. [Fletcher] Webster will write to you all about this. Read this letter to Mason & Gaffreau[?], if there, but to nobody else.[11]

In the middle of this letter, Fabens off-handedly dropped a tantalizing bombshell. "[Fletcher] Webster and I have been in Washington for a week. Pierce poor devil is frightened half out of his boots for himself & his companions in arms." This and other such tidbits have long fueled conjectures by even mainstream historians like Roy Nichols of Pierce's direct involvement in the Kinney scheme. In his classic 1931 Pierce biography, for instance, Nichols wrote that the president may have given Kinney, his old Mexican-American War comrade, "the nod" to go ahead with his expedition.[12]

"Now a Ruined Man"

Writing in the *Post*, Thayer declared that "the reception of the colonel and his party by the inhabitants was most enthusiastic." But, according to historian Scroggs, this was simply untrue. "The news of Kinney's coming created no excitement among the enervated population of Greytown." Although partially rebuilt under British tutelage after the leveling by the *Cyane*, Greytown's merchants still had no access to travelers-as-customers because the transit company still kept them out of the town.

Kinney, Scroggs wrote, "was now a ruined man. He had exhausted his pecuniary resources, and there was not the slightest prospect of further aid from the United States, where the government remained obdurate, and the Transit Company continued hostile. Still, he did not abandon hope. The disconsolate inhabitants were inclined to accept his leadership, thinking that no change could be for the worse, and at a public meeting on September 6 and 7, 1855, a provisional government was created, and Kinney was chosen civil and military governor." The British Mosquito Protectorate authorities, who also oversaw Greytown's quasi-autonomy, took a dim view of Kinney's elevation to governor of the port.[13]

In the same edition of the *Times*, August 7, that the Thayer *Post* note above appeared as a reprint, there was an unrelated piece reporting the sailing from New York on July 27 of the steamer *Ocean Bird*, carrying more Kinney "colonists," along with a commercial printing press. On September 15, Kinney issued the first number of a newspaper he called the *Central American*. "The chief object of the journal," noted historian Scroggs, "was to advertise the resources of the country and attract immigrants. There is, however, a kind of melancholy humour in the extensive advertisements of Greytown lawyers, merchants, schools, traders, physicians, hotels, and places of amusement, all of which owed their existence to paper, printer's ink, and a vivid imagination."[14]

On or about September 23, H.L. Kinney's reign as the Civil and Military Governor of Greytown ended in resignation, just 16 days after it began. He realized he lacked popular support because he had been elected at a meeting of only his followers. According to the *New York Tribune*, "another [election] meeting has been called, the English consul having assured him that the English government would recognize him if re-elected." But apparently, he declined to run again and nothing came of this. Within days, another steamer, the *George Law,* arrived, carrying Kinney's right-hand man, Joseph Fabens. "Toward the end of the year," Scroggs noted, "they decided to approach Walker with a proposal of cooperation. This was their last hope," and, as the following chapter will show, "it was destined to bitter disappointment."[15]

Chapter 13

"I Shall Surely Hang Him"

"The new expedition under Walker," wrote Scroggs, "was meeting with notable success." As touched upon in the last chapter, in only four months Walker had taken effective control of Nicaragua. He was soon being called the "Gray-Eyed Man of Destiny" because of a belief attributed to the Miskito Indians during Spanish rule that a "gray-eyed man" would appear and drive the dark-skinned oppressors out. Walker, who did, apparently, have gray eyes, milked this myth for all it was worth in the pages of *El Nicaraguense*, his movement's newspaper. "If we were disposed to believe that the race of prophets did not die with Isaiah and Jeremiah (and why should they?) we could say that this traditional prophecy has been fulfilled to the letter. 'The Grey-Eyed Man' has come."[1]

Scroggs wrote that when Fabens arrived at Greytown, Kinney "resolved to form, if possible, some sort of offensive and defensive alliance with Walker." So, he sent Fabens and 20 others to see Walker, who treated these "ambassadors" courteously until they said they sought "a union of the two adventurers for their reciprocal advantage. There was no hedging in the reply of Walker," Scroggs noted. "'Tell Governor Kinney, or Colonel Kinney, or Mr. Kinney, or whatever he chooses to call himself, that if I ever lay hands on him on Nicaraguan soil I shall surely hang him.'" Or as one reporter archly put it, Kinney's dreams of Central American conquest would end with "his involuntary exit from earth through the instrumentality of a hempen auxiliary." Fabens and the 20 others, Scroggs continued, "decided that it would not be healthy to return to Greytown, and the entire delegation deserted Kinney then and there and enrolled under the rising star of Walker."[2]

"Probably Thinking That He Was Ready to Surrender"

Despite the defection of Fabens and the others, Kinney remained at Greytown but was now drinking heavily. He was visited by a pair of

Walker lieutenants who urged him to see Walker in person, one of them pledging his life for Kinney's security. Kinney "thought this practically an official invitation" and decided to use it to play what he alleged was his recently acquired trump card. He claimed that in August 1855, "Messrs. Shepherd and Haly have disposed of their entire right, title and interest in the celebrated 'Mosquito Grant' to me for $500,000 [$15 million in 2022]." This, of course, was the same grant his erstwhile Central American Land and Mining colleagues claimed they still owned.

Also, newspapers argued over whether he still had the wherewithal to make such a purchase. Under the title "PUFFIFICATION," the *Washington Star*, accused the pro–Kinney *New York Post* of "humbug ... truly sublime" in touting the purchase as valid, and that the *Post* would make an excellent mouthpiece for "companies organized to work copper mines [on] the moon." But the *New York Times*' Greytown correspondent, in a weak analysis, accepted the story at face value, "The Colonel's purchase ... has tended much to increase the confidence of the people in the sincerity of his professions of founding a peaceable colony. No one can suppose he would risk so large a sum as half a million of dollars if his object in coming here were a filibustering invasion of the country. He has now too deep a stake in its material prosperity to compromise himself by any foolish hostilities against the established government of Nicaragua."[3]

Despite Walker aides having invited Kinney, Walker did not know he was coming. Nonetheless, historian William Scroggs noted, Walker received Kinney courteously, "probably thinking that he was ready to surrender and follow the example of Fabens." For his part, Kinney did not know that, just three days earlier, on February 8, 1856, the Walker regime declared the Mosquito protectorate part of Nicaragua. This, Walker's government decreed, rendered "the Rights which the said Kinney pretends to claim in and upon the said Territory ... null, void, and of no effect.... [And Kinney and] all other persons claiming this unlawful acquisition, are declared guilty of an attempt against the integrity of Central America."[4]

"Kinney Retorted That the Land Was His by Purchase"

"The former governor of Greytown proposed recognizing the military authority of Walker over the Mosquito kingdom if the latter would recognize [reinstate?] Kinney's civil government." Walker apprised Kinney of his recent decree making the protectorate Nicaragua's and, thus, rendering the Shepherd grant null. "Kinney retorted that the land was his by purchase; that a hundred thousand dollars [$3 million in 2022] had already been spent in connection with the grant, and that he would not surrender it until legal means had been employed to determine the title." The *New York Times* quoted Kinney as saying here not "legal means" but that "it would have been better for Gen. Walker to have left it to a tribunal competent to judge such matters." As will be seen, either phrase—"tribunal competent to judge" or "legal means"—might be a prescient foreshadowing by Kinney of grant-relevant events to come, which are covered in Chapter 14.[5]

Walker told Kinney that the government "determined such questions for itself and inquired whether Kinney was in a position to render any service to the Rivas [Walker's puppet, Patricio Rivas] administration. Kinney stated that he could bring a large number of immigrants, negotiate a loan, and use his political influence to secure recognition of the new government by the United States."[6]

When the two parted for the evening, it was with the understanding that they were to consult further the next day. Overnight, however, Kinney, according to Scroggs, "committed an egregious blunder." He met with Walker's puppet, Rivas, and some of his cabinet and explained his theory that one colonist was worth five soldiers and that an overgrown army, such as Walker was accumulating, would devour the substance of the country. This belittling of Walker got back to him. When Kinney called the next day, the commander-in-chief said that he had ordered Kinney's arrest for treason and threatened to hang him. He would have carried through with this if not informed of the "safe-passage" promise made to Kinney by the Walker aides who invited him to visit. "Kinney was therefore released and sent away under a special escort," wrote Scroggs. "The passport which Walker furnished him was couched in very insulting language."[7]

CHAPTER 14

"No Capacity to Transfer ... Title"

In early 1856 President Pierce named a minister to England to negotiate a new bilateral Central American treaty with Foreign Secretary Lord Clarendon. Pierce appointed George Mifflin Dallas, who was, as noted previously, a former vice president and former minister to Russia and Kinney's lawyer at Philadelphia eight months before (see Chapter 12). When Dallas and Clarendon began working on the *projet* treaty, the British regarded U.S. hegemony over Central America as inevitable and hoped the treaty would provide them with a graceful means to exit the region (while retaining Belize). But they also wanted a process for adjudicating the validity of Mosquito land grants.

As noted, officials and citizens in both countries had political and economic interests in seeing their respective Mosquito grants—especially the Shepherd and the Poyais (the latter now sometimes referred to as the Black River grant)—validated, however specious those grants might be. And what better way to do that than by following Lord Malmesbury's advice in his 1852 letter about the Poyais grant—by a set of articles in a treaty. (See Chapter 10.) On June 30, 1856, Dallas and Lord Clarendon began working on treaty articles for determining the validity of Mosquito land grants.

That such articles made it into the *projet* at all is astonishing given the total proscription by whites of sovereign rights of Indians to the lands they lived on.

As Secretary of State Marcy told U.S. minister to England, Joseph R. Ingersoll, on June 9, 1853:

> The United States cannot recognise as valid any title set up by the people at San Juan [Greytown] derived from the Mosquito Indians. It concedes to this tribe of Indians only a possessory right—a right to occupy and use for themselves the country in their possession, but not the right of sovereignty or eminent domain, over it.
>
> It is not now made known, for the first time, to Her Majesty's Government, that the United States denies that these Indians have any sovereignty over

the country they occupy. Our Government does not make—nor does it perceive any good reason for making—any distinction between this tribe of Savages and those which occupied parts of our territories or of the territories of the British Provinces in North America. I am aware that Her Majesty's Government regard the Mosquito Indians as an exceptional case [i.e., that since the Spanish never conquered them, their lands remained independent] to the rule generally acted on by itself, as well as other nations; but in this claim the United States has never acquiesced.[1]

Besides this declaration to Ingersoll, and a previous denunciation of England's embrace of "Mosquito power" (see Chapter 4), Marcy also told Kinney, "that the Mosquito Indians ... have ... no capacity to transfer to individuals ... title to the lands in their possession."[2]

Moreover, in January 1854, James Buchanan, Dallas' predecessor at the Court of St. James's, reported to Marcy the following from a conversation he had with Lord Clarendon. "He [Clarendon] then asked what we should do with the grants of land which had been made to individuals by the king of the Mosquitos; and I answered that under the law of all European nations since the discovery of America, as well as by the uniform practice both of Great Britain and the United States, such grants made by Indians were absolutely void. I also stated to him, somewhat in detail, the decision on this point made by the Supreme Court of the United States in the case of *Johnson vs. Mcintosh,* to which he appeared to listen with marked attention."[3]

Four years earlier, in 1850, Secretary of State John Clayton had told E.G. Squier that if Indians had sovereignty, we would not have a country. "We have never acknowledged, and never can acknowledge the existence of any claim of sovereignty in the Mosquito King or any other Indian in America. To do so would be to deny the title of the United States to our own territory." Then Clayton added, "Having always regarded an Indian title as a mere right of occupancy, we can never agree that such a title should be treated otherwise than as a thing to be extinguished at the will of the discoverer of the country." (But, as noted, the English said this rule didn't apply to the Mosquitos because Spain never conquered them. "For centuries," England's *Guardian* newspaper wrote in 2006, "Miskito people have defended their Central American rainforest kingdom. They rebuffed invading of the Spanish settlers in the 18th and 19th centuries.")[4]

But none of these categorical denials of Indian sovereignty from Marcy, Buchanan, or Clayton kept Mosquito Indian land grant articles out of the treaty. Marcy not only did not disallow them but even contributed to Dallas and Clarendon's debates over them. The English, as will be seen, pushed hard for them. As the U.S. *National Era* newspaper noted later, "It should be remembered that the titles of most of the British subjects in the

Mosquito territory rest upon no better foundation, and that the settlement of their titles is the only substantial advantage which England could hope to gain by the Treaty." Why Marcy acquiesced in the inclusion of Mosquito grant validation articles in the treaty is a complete mystery. It was a profound turnabout for him—and for U.S. policy.[5]

"The Commissioners ... Cannot but Decide Favorably"

In their early land-grant discussions, Lord Clarendon suggested to Dallas that, rather than "perplex ourselves with their consideration," the land grants "might be referred to a Commission." Dallas counter-proposed that all bona fide Mosquito grants should simply be "confirmed." Their first draft, dated August 25, 1856, contained both their suggestions. Article IV, §3 confirmed all bona fide grants, while Article VI called for a commission to pass judgment on which grants were bona fide.[6]

When Marcy responded to Dallas in a letter dated September 26, 1856, he suggested:

> (A) Omit No. 3 [i.e., §3 of Article IV] entirely, leaving the whole question to the Republic of Nicaragua.
> (B) Or insert instead of it, this: '3. [§3]: All *bona fide* grants ... lying within.... Greytown ... shall be confirmed, provided that no grant [exceed] one hundred yards square [91 square meters].'
> (C) Or insert instead of it this: '3. [§3]: All *bona fide* grants ... made ... since the 1st of January 1848 [the date England seized Greytown], shall be confirmed, provided the same shall not exceed ... one hundred yards square [91 square meters], if within the limits of Greytown, ... or one league [5.56 kilometers] square if without the same.'[7]

Any of these three options would have precluded validation of either the Poyais or Shepherd grant. In the case of Option A, Walker's puppet regime, as noted, had declared the grants "null, void, and of no effect" seven months earlier; as for B & C, both grants were huge and issued well before 1848.

In the next and final draft, dated October 17, 1856, Dallas and Clarendon opened their revision of Article IV, §3 with a virtual copy of Marcy Option "C" above but then added a sentence near the end of the section which introduced a seeming loophole, "This stipulation is in no manner to affect the grants of land made previously to the 1st of January, 1848." Could this be construed as giving blanket approval to all pre–1848 grants, including both the Shepherd and the Poyais? Events three years later would prove that this was, indeed, the intention here.[8]

Marcy responded on November 10. His words were as suspect as the Dallas/Clarendon phrasing that inspired them:

> It is barely possible that the sentence, "This stipulation is in no manner to affect the grants of land made previously to the 1st of January, 1848," may be interpreted as implying a confirmation of such grants or remove the limitation as to the quantity mentioned in the former part of the same clause of the convention. Such is not, I believe, the understanding of either party to the instrument, nor indeed would such a construction be borne out by the language used by them.[9]

So, Marcy concluded, it would not, therefore, be "deemed necessary to make any change to guard against a misinterpretation."[10]

Just the kind of "misinterpretation" that Marcy saw no need to guard against was not long in coming. On February 9, 1857, the *New York Times* noted "the presence in that treaty of a reservation in favor of *all* grants made by the Mosquito Chief, and the appointment of a Commission to allow them, if verified" (emphasis added). On February 23, the *Times* reported that

> the Colonel [Kinney] is confident that when the Dallas and Clarendon treaty shall have been ratified, he will be in a fair way to proceed with his darling scheme—the colonization of his grant through Sheppard [sic] and Haley.
>
> The grant being for a consideration that can be proven to have been valuable [i.e., evidence of its bona fides], he feels that the Commissioners, when they shall have taken it into consideration, cannot but decide favorably.[11]

"The Only Expunging on Which ... They May Hesitate"

Eight days after James Buchanan was inaugurated on March 4, 1857, as President Pierce's successor, the Senate ratified the treaty but only after making changes that included removing all mention of the Mosquito land grants. In response, Dallas told Lewis Cass, Buchanan's secretary of state, that this was "the only expunging on which it is possible they [the British] may hesitate." But then Dallas quoted to Marcy Lord Clarendon's capitulation on the grant-articles deletions. "The exclusion of the [grant] provisions ... altho' it would necessarily cause much disappointment with both American and British holders of those grants, and occasion a great extent and complication of trouble ... might be acquiesced in." (In the end, other conflicts unrelated to the grants arose between the British and the Senate, and the treaty never went into effect.)[12]

Notwithstanding Marcy's dismissal of the possibility of a "misinterpretation" of the "stipulation," it seems by his begrudging acceptance ("cause much disappointment ... occasion a great ... complication of trouble"), that even Clarendon—one of the *projet's* co-authors—thought, like the *Times* and Kinney, that the commissioners would have been passing judgment on big, pre–1848 grants, like the Poyais and the Shepherd.

"The Dallas Letterbooks. Where Are They?"

In 1951, historian Roy F. Nichols wrote an article entitled "The Missing Diaries of George Mifflin Dallas." According to Nichols, Dallas's daughter, Susan, published—in 1892 and "presumably in full"—her late father's diaries from his ministerial postings to Russia and England. Of the latter, Nichols wrote that "Dallas kept careful notes of the progress [of his treaty talks with Clarendon], but for some reason the diaries published by his daughter do not include this material." In his article, Nichols largely corrected this omission after "most" of the diary entries were found in 1950, but he cautioned that "some interesting questions still remain." Paramount among these for Nichols was the fate of Dallas's letterbooks. Before there were typewriters and carbon copies, a diplomat's letterbooks held the duplicates of his essential correspondence—handwritten reference copies of his handwritten letters. "Perhaps [of] even more interest to historians [than the previously missing diary entries]," Nichols noted, "is the location of the Dallas letterbooks. Where are they?" As of this writing, 73 years on from when Nichols posed that question, Dallas's letterbooks are still, as yet, unsighted.[13]

"Giving British Subjects a Controlling Power"

Further proof, if needed, of England's disappointment over losing the grant articles came to light three years later. This was when England negotiated bilateral treaties with Honduras (1859) and Nicaragua (1860). These treaties ceded to each country that part of the Mosquito Protectorate which would fall into their presumptive jurisdictions (see map before title page)—while at the same time carefully preserving British subjects' Mosquito Indian grants in both treaties. (The Nicaraguan treaty also provided a reservation for the Indians.)

For instance, the convention between Great Britain and Honduras stipulated that "whereas British subjects have by grant, lease, or otherwise, heretofore obtained from the Mosquito Indians, interests in various lands ... the Republic of Honduras engages to respect and maintain such interests." And in the Anglo-Nicaraguan convention, there are grant passages strikingly similar to those in the Dallas-Clarendon *projet* of 1856, including precisely the same size limitations applicable to grants made "since 1 January 1848." And, as in the 1856 *projet*, there is also the same exemption from such restrictions for all grants before 1848—only the language was inverted. In 1856, that passage said, "This stipulation is in no manner to affect the grants of land made previously to the 1st of January 1848." The 1860 British/Nicaraguan treaty said, "This stipulation only embraces those grants of land made since the 1st of January 1848."[14]

"While the Filibusters Were Hovering About"

It might be conjectured as to why the Nicaraguans and Hondurans were so accommodating to the British on the land-grant issue. A possible answer might be: William Walker. The erstwhile president of Nicaragua from Tennessee, who had been driven out twice by now, was rumored to contemplating a return in 1860. These two states may have been currying favor with England in return for protection against Walker. For instance, in the same Anglo-Honduran treaty of 1859 that protected English Mosquito grants, the British agreed to return the Bay Islands—which the British had long claimed as a colony—to Honduras.

By this time, Ruatán (now Roatán), the largest of these islands, held a sizable British settlement. "Bitterly opposed to this transfer," writes historian Regis A. Courtemanche, "they petitioned the Queen to withhold her approval of the treaty—but in vain." This inspired "one of the Bay Islanders" to visit "New Orleans in the spring of 1860" to invite "Walker's 'help.' … Soon, small parties of United States 'emigrants' began appearing on Ruatán. When the British government heard of this, they agreed with the Honduran president, [José Santos] Guardiola, to postpone the transfer of the islands while the filibusters were hovering about."[15]

Walker did, indeed, launch another filibuster, landing in Honduras in August of 1860. The English, under Royal Navy Commander Nowell Salmon, found Walker and his 91 men in the town of Truxillo and offered the protection of "the English Flag" if they surrendered to them. Walker seemed to agree but then fled with 70 of his men under cover of night, forfeiting Salmon's protection. "Some Honduran soldiery now arrived" under General Mariano Alvarez, Courtemanche continues. He and Salmon agreed that the Hondurans would track down the Walker group but then hold back and let Salmon negotiate with Walker. This was done. Salmon demanded that Walker surrender unconditionally and once assured by Salmon that he and his men were surrendering "to a representative of Her Majesty's Government," he agreed.

The implication was that the British would just repatriate Walker and his men to the U.S. But the Hondurans objected, and the best Salmon thought he could do was strike a compromise with them: If he surrendered Walker and his second in command, A.J. (or A.F.) Rudler, to the Hondurans, they would repatriate the remaining 69 Americans. Salmon signed this agreement on September 5, 1860. A week later, the Hondurans executed Walker by firing squad. (Rudler was later pardoned.)[16]

"It Confirmed the Grants of Land ... Made in Mosquito Territory"

The purposes of the British, wrote U.S. Secretary of State Hamilton Fish about thirteen years after these 1859 and 1860 bi-lateral treaties, "were in the main accomplished." (Although he doesn't mention the Anglo-Honduran treaty, this would basically apply to it as well.) The treaty between Great Britain and Nicaragua, he wrote, restored to Nicaragua "the nominal sovereignty" over that territory even though "it assigned boundaries to the Mosquito Reservation probably beyond the limits which any member of that tribe had ever seen, even when in chase of wild animals. Worst of all, however, it confirmed the grants of land previously made in Mosquito territory. The similar stipulation on this subject in the Dallas-Clarendon treaty was perhaps the most objectionable of any [in it], as it violated the cardinal rule of all European colonists in America, including Great Britain herself, that the aborigines had no title to the soil which they could confer upon individuals." This rule, Fish concluded, "has repeatedly been confirmed by judicial decisions, and especially by the Supreme Court of the United States."[17]

In his fourth state-of-the-union, President Buchanan said he found these 1859 and 1860 treaties "entirely satisfactory." *The Digest of International Law of the United States,* also, like Fish, writing about the Nicaraguan treaty but whose words could apply as well to that with the Hondurans, said: "President Buchanan's expressions of satisfaction ... were based on the assumption that Great Britain had ceased to exercise any influence whatever over the Mosquito country. *That this is not the case, however, follows from the ratification, by the treaty, of British titles from Indians ... giving British subjects a controlling power in the territory*" (emphasis added).[18]

But in Buchanan's defense, historian Ira Dudley Travis wrote in 1900 that "it has been asserted, by high authority, that at the time Buchanan penned his message he did not know that the treaty with Nicaragua ... confirmed the grants of land previously made in the Mosquito territory."

Travis suggests that the grant wording in the treaties was somehow "withheld" from Buchanan. "However that may be, his statement that the adjustment was acceptable to the United States Government ... is of more than passing interest, because it has since been seized upon by the British in their efforts to justify their position respecting the Clayton-Bulwer treaty and Central America."[19]

Chapter 15

"Make Certain Officials at Washington Wince"

In early 1857, in the twilight of the one-term Pierce administration, the same U.S. district attorney in New York City who had accused Kinney and Fabens in 1855 of violating U.S. neutrality (see Chapter 12) now arrested Fabens again for the same offense. This time District Attorney John McKeon said it was for Fabens' role as First Director of Colonization for William Walker's filibuster regime in Nicaragua. (As noted in Chapter 13, Fabens had deserted Kinney to join Walker in late 1855.)

Fabens was furious and was going to exact revenge on the waning Pierce Administration. He refused bail, the *New York Herald* reported, to "avoid the vexatious delay to which he was subjected when arrested [with Kinney] in May 1855. It is not probable that [Fabens] will let the matter drop. If unable to obtain a trial, [he will] bring a suit … which will make certain officials at Washington wince. Rich developments may be expected in the course of events," the *Herald* wryly concluded, "and if filibusterism be a crime, we may find some criminals in high places."[1]

Besides providing a welter of detail and documentation about Greytown's demise, Fabens' defense team formulated a parallelism between what they characterized as the Pierce-backed Kinney "colonization" plan and Walker's "colonization" plan (this, notwithstanding that they were both barely disguised filibuster schemes). Fabens' counsel argued that both projects were innocent attempts to aid American emigrants—would-be Central American farmers. (This was a real stretch in the case of Walker; he had insisted that the military contract he was first offered would violate U.S. neutrality laws, but "if … a contract of colonization" was offered instead, "something might be done.") And because President Pierce had backed Kinney's expedition, his administration could hardly find fault with Walker's and, therefore, Fabens' role in it. Also, the defense pointed out that the Pierce administration not only encouraged Kinney early on but also the Walker regime later on by briefly recognizing it, from May to September 1856.[2]

"Threatens to Damage Everybody But the Accused"

This is the 1857 court proceeding where the deed-of-transfer and the Sidney Webster letter were brought to light. (See Chapter 11.) Fabens and colleague Alexander Lawrence's lead attorney was Thomas Francis Meagher (pronounced "Mar"). Meagher was a convicted Irish revolutionary whose death sentence was commuted to life and who then escaped an English penal colony on Tasmania, the island off the south-east coast of Australia. He had made his way to New York City, started a newspaper, and became a lawyer—and a hero to the city's large Irish community. (He would later organize the Union Army's famous Irish Brigade during the Civil War.)

Meagher said he had evidence that, as the *New York Times* hypothesized, "threatens to damage everybody but the accused." And besides the deed-of-transfer and Sidney's letter, he had one more ace up his sleeve—the envelope in which Sidney sent his thank you note. For this had no postage stamp affixed to the front but rather bore there the signature of Franklin Pierce and the word "Free," an example of the then-legal presidential franking privilege. And while it was legal for Pierce to use such an envelope, it was decidedly illegal for anyone else, even if they had his permission. Sidney Webster's use of this Pierce "free-franked" envelope would loom large in the proceedings.[3]

Fabens and Lawrence were arrested on January 28, 1857. "It seems," the *New York Herald* opined sarcastically, "that Mr. Secretary Marcy still continues to honor the friends of General Walker in this city with his pressing attentions." The event that triggered these "attentions" was the imminent departure from New York of a passenger steamer called the *Tennessee*. Fabens and Lawrence characterized the passengers, who signed on at the Nicaraguan Colonization office, "simply as immigrants" who were to receive "a homestead of eighty acres of land." The U.S. government said they were actually recruits for Walker's army, and this made the ship's prospective sailing a violation of U.S. neutrality. But Fabens insisted that the neutrality charge was smoke and mirrors, and "the course pursued by the lower government officials was instigated and brought about by [Cornelius] Vanderbilt and other parties opposed to the present transit line across the Isthmus."

As noted in Chapter 1, Vanderbilt initiated the line in 1849. He was forced out of the company by his partners in 1853, then recovered it, only to lose it again, this time to Walker himself. (Vanderbilt was absent from the company when Greytown was destroyed and, so, blameless in its demise.) Now Vanderbilt was using the rival route across the Panamanian isthmus, which, since 1855, had benefited greatly from an infrastructure upgrade, including a solid railroad. The Commodore also harbored a vengeful hatred for Walker, after suffering slights most observers found inexplicably self-immolating on Walker's part.[4]

Arrested at the same time as Fabens and Lawrence were a Joe Brown and a Robert Fuller, not as co-conspirators but as witnesses against Fabens and Lawrence. (Fuller and Brown apparently knew each other from working on the Panama Railroad.) A defense attorney described them as "two as drunken and worthless vagabonds as could be raked from the lowest purlieus [border areas] of the City."[5]

"To Be Enlisted ... In a Foreign Country ... As a Soldier"

The men had entered Fabens' colonization/recruiting office as ostensible recruits, signed up, and then went to U.S. D.A. McKeon's office. There they signed affidavits that Fabens and Lawrence "did hire and retain [both] to go beyond the limits and jurisdiction of the United States, to wit, to Greytown, with intent to be enlisted or entered in the service of William Walker, in a foreign country, to wit, Nicaragua, as a soldier." In jailhouse interviews, Fabens and Lawrence denied ever seeing Brown and Fuller before. Given that Fabens suspected Vanderbilt was behind their arrest, it is not surprising that the *Herald* reported, "These two witnesses are said to have expressed their surprise why Vanderbilt did not come and bail them out and were confident that he would do so." (That evening, D.A. McKeon released the two witnesses on bail.)[6]

The case was being heard in a U.S. Commissioner's Court. Commissioners assisted federal judges and provided the federal government with local officers to support the enforcement of specific laws. Most commissioners were lawyers who carried out their judicial responsibilities while pursuing their own practice. They were authorized to set bail, take affidavits, and perform other duties. In this Fabens case, the commissioner presiding would decide whether to forward the case to a grand jury which, in turn, would recommend whether the accused should be indicted for violation of Section 2, the neutrality passage of the Act of 1818.[7]

The case began in earnest on February 4. "Defendants Threaten to Expose the Complicity of President Pierce. Rich Developments Ahead" was one of the *Herald*'s headlines on the day following.[8]

"I Hold in My Hand Written Proof"

A significant witness that day was Charles Morgan, president of the Accessory Transit Company and owner of the *Tennessee*. As noted, this

15. "Make Certain Officials at Washington Wince" 133

was the ship about to leave New York with the latest farmers/filibusters recruited by Fabens destined for Walker's Nicaragua. If Fabens wanted to make certain Washington officials "wince," his lead defense attorney, Thomas Meagher, questioning Morgan, cut right to the chase:

Q. Have you understood from Colonel Fabens that parties of rank and high executive standing in this country are [financially] interested in the Mosquito grant?

A. I have.

Q. Have you ever heard that President Pierce had any [financial] interest in the Mosquito grant?[9]

At this point, the District Attorney objected, and Meagher retorted dramatically, "I hold in my hand written proof, and if it is not admitted in evidence, it shall appear in print; but I am willing to say that if the District Attorney admits that the question is calculated to criminate President Pierce, I will not offer it." This was met with laughter, as was the D.A.'s response, "I will admit no such thing." The *Herald* reported that the envelope the president's secretary used to thank Fabens for the bribe document "was superscribed, 'Free, Frank Pierce.'" The paper even went to the trouble of printing a crude facsimile of the envelope, a rare visual aid at a time when newspaper editorial pages were usually a solid sea of type.[10]

Another defense attorney, one Judge Dean, stated that they had a right to have the letter the envelope contained read into evidence.

> Mr. Fabens was arrested on the authority of the President of the United States and here we offer a letter from Sidney Webster, the private secretary of the President, under the frank of the President, which letter is in reference to the colonization of Central America and the interest of Col. Fabens, in which it also refers to the President as "interested" in the subject. This letter is under

> District Attorney — I will admit no such thing.
> The envelope was superscribed:—
>
> Free, Frank Pierce.
>
> J. S. FABENS, ESQ.,
> Washington   Mansion House,
> post mark   New York City,
>   N. Y.
>
> Mr Dean contended that they had a right to have the letter read in evidence. Mr. Fabens was arrested on the

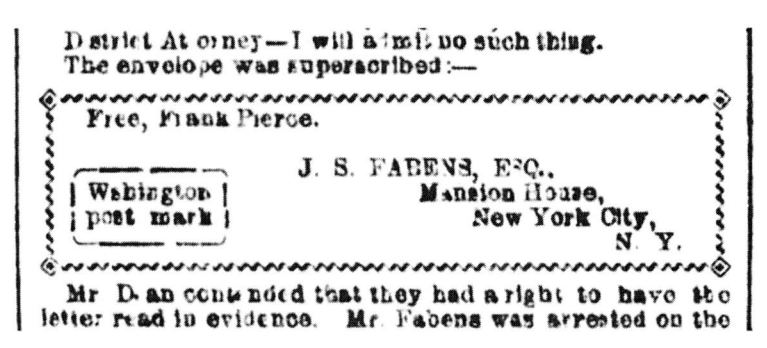

The *New York Herald*'s facsimile of the envelope franked by President Pierce that Sidney Webster used to send his thank you note to Joseph Fabens for the deed-of-transfer bribe.

the frank of the President, and we will prove the signatures of both himself and his secretary. We presume that no one will pretend that the President intended to violate the law, and will it be presumed that Col. Fabens has?[11]

There is much to unpack here. Firstly, the letter doesn't say, outright, that the president was financially interested in the Mosquito grant. But Webster did write "and with my associate here am ... entirely satisfied," which certainly could be construed as referring to Pierce. Secondly, Judge Dean's last sentence reinforces the overall theme of Fabens' defense strategy, implying that Pierce was involved in the Kinney expedition, and no one was accusing *him* of violating the law, so why accuse Fabens of an illegality when he was involved with Walker in the same kind of expedition as Kinney's?

The Commissioner adjourned for the day, saying the letter's introduction as evidence should be deferred until the next day. "Rich developments are expected if the letter is admitted," the *Herald* declared, "at all events it will be published in connection with the proceedings of Thursday. The counsel for the defense did not feel justified in showing it to reporters until it is read in evidence or its admissibility overruled by the Commissioner." The paper concluded that the defendants "will call to the witness stand Mr. Secretary Marcy, A.O.P. Nicholson, editor of the *Union*, and Sidney Webster, Private Secretary of President Pierce." (None of these persons were ever called.)[12]

When court adjourned that day, February 4, 1857 (exactly one month before Pierce left office), McKeon telegraphed the U.S. attorney general, Caleb Cushing, for advice. "Fabens offered a letter under the frank of the President & said to be from Sidney Webster purporting a peculiar [pecuniary, 'relating to money'] interest in Nicaraguan lands & colonization. I objected.... Do you wish to give any directions?"[13]

Cushing telegraphed McKeon a reply that same day. "It is not necessary for me to give you any instructions as to admissibility of evidence. But I am instructed by the President to say that if Mr. Fabens has an envelope with the President's frank upon it, such envelope did not contain a letter from him, nor any letter written with his knowledge. And that he can have no possible wish as to the production or non-production of any letter or other paper in the pending trial except such as may arise from a desire that the facts in the case may fully and truly appear."[14]

"Pierce ... Owns One-Twelfth ... of the Mosquito Grant"

To drive home his argument that Pierce was financially interested in the Mosquito grant, Meagher called William L. Cazneau to the stand.

15. "Make Certain Officials at Washington Wince" 135

Cazneau was a former soldier and politician who joined Henry Kinney in an 1847 Texas land speculation. In 1853 he was appointed by President Pierce as a special agent to Santo Domingo (now the Dominican Republic).

In his opening set of questions, Meagher elicited this response from Cazneau:

Q. *What is the Mosquito grant?*

A. It amounts to from twenty to thirty millions of acres.

Q. *Do you know of President Pierce being [financially] interested in that grant?*

A. I believe he is.

Here D.A. McKeon interjected, "I do not think it respectful to the first magistrate of the country to endeavor to get in hearsay evidence." But, Meagher replied, Pierce is also "an officer" who is as "amenable [susceptible] to the laws as the humblest man in the country." Then Cazneau dropped a bombshell, "I presume that President Pierce would have no objection that it should be known that he owns one-twelfth of the thirty millions of acres of the Mosquito grant."[15]

District Attorney McKeon objected. To which the defense retorted that it was necessary to show "that this colonization was encouraged by our government, and … there are rival interests here [Kinney and Walker], both endeavoring for the peaceful colonization of that country."[16]

Cushing sent McKeon a letter on February 7, basically an expanded reiteration of his telegram three days before. D.A. McKeon asked the commissioner to allow Cushing's letter to be admitted as evidence "as a reply to the base intimations that had been made against the President of the United States, of being [financially] interested in land in Central America."

"I Defy the Other Side to Publish the Letter"

McKeon added that he would not "put in the adjective pecuniary interest as originally used by Mr. Meagher against President Pierce." Meagher retorted, "I adhere still to the adjective 'pecuniary' interest." (See McKeon's telegram above where he attributes the word to Fabens, possibly substituting his name for Meagher's, with whom Cushing was probably unfamiliar.)

McKeon: "Let it go so. Then the present [Cushing] letter must be put in to show the groundlessness of the charge against President Pierce." But Commissioner George W. Morrell ruled it inadmissible. So, a defense counsel suggested that McKeon should "put the letter in the [news]papers."

Mr. McKeon: "I intend to do so, and I defy the other side to publish the letter from Sidney Webster, about which they have made so much splurge."

McKeon then said he would give the Cushing letter to reporters, and, according to the *Times,* "he thereupon threw upon the table, with marvelous projectile force, the following letter." (Excerpted here:)

> If Mr. Fabens possessed [such an] envelope ... it ... did not contain any letter of his [the president's], nor any letter written with his knowledge. The President [has only one] desire ... that the facts of the case might fully and truly appear.
>
> The allegation insinuated ... that the President has connection of any sort in the matter is utterly destitute of shadow of foundation. He has not, and never had, an interest in any lands, grants or property whatever in Central America. He has never, by any act or knowledge whatever, participated, directly, or indirectly, in the proposed colonization project of Mr. Fabens or any other person; and all suggestions reflecting on him in this relation, from whatever quarter they may come, are but false insinuations.
>
> You are therefore instructed to invite and challenge all possible inquiry on this point, and in this respect as in all others to continue to proceed as you have done in such case without fear or favor in the impartial performance of your whole duty as well to the people as to the Government of the United States.[17]

Cushing's categorical denials here are simply unsupportable given the numerous newspaper accounts to the contrary and the reinforcing private letters between Kinney and his lawyer Milford Norton.

"Subsequent to the disposition of the above letter [to reporters]," the *New York Times* noted, "Mr. McKeon renewed his desire to hear the other side produce their Sidney Webster letter." For his part, "Mr. Meagher said he would give the District-Attorney a scent of its contents."

> **Mr. McKeon:** "I thought you would not dare to publish the letter."
> **Mr. Meagher:** "There is time enough yet."[18]

The commissioner did not admit the Sidney Webster letter into evidence, so Meagher released it to the papers. Fabens escaped indictment by the grand jury, even though the commissioner recommended it. He was soon out on a New York street making a bombastic speech at a pro–Walker rally.[19]

Sidney Webster suffered no consequences, legal, political, economic, or social, for his taking the bribe from Kinney and his cohorts, or for—if Cushing and Pierce were to be believed—his unauthorized use of Pierce's free-franked envelope. (At the time, the unauthorized use of a free-franked envelope carried a $500 fine [$14,794 in 2022], although the statute of limitations may have expired by the time this violation came to light two years after the fact.)[20]

15. "Make Certain Officials at Washington Wince" 137

Nor did Sidney's relationship with Franklin Pierce suffer. Surprisingly—or, perhaps, tellingly—Pierce did not distance himself from Sidney when his financial interest in the scheme, via the bribe, and his use of a Pierce-franked envelope hit the newspapers during this court proceeding. Webster's acts of deceit and perfidy behind Pierce's back—if that's what they were—threatened to implicate the president in a potentially devastating scandal. And, yet the two remained fast friends. After Pierce left office, he and Sidney Webster corresponded often. Webster advised Pierce on political matters; Pierce attended Webster's wedding; and Webster, Pierce's funeral. Pierce left Webster valuable keepsakes in his will. (For more on Sidney Webster's charmed, post-administration life, see his entry in Chapter 20: Whither the Principals?)

Chapter 16

"The Mormons Had Better Go"

After the Dallas-Clarendon treaty failure, Colonel Kinney, the 16-day governor of Greytown and purported owner of a land expanse the size of Maine, left the tiny port and turned up on the Island of Ruatán (now Roatán), one of the Honduran "Bay Islands," just off the north coast of that country. Reportedly he was "entirely out of money" and spent his time "enlightening the natives with marvelous stories of the immense number of cattle he possesses in Texas." One account of his time on Ruatán had him joining forces with a fellow American filibuster there named Thomas Adrian. Reportedly, they talked of "swamping the island with sugar planters, asserting 'white government,' and 'driving all the niggers off the island.'" (However serious this Kinney/Adrian threat was, Hondurans and other Central Americans had real reason to fear further filibustering from William Walker. As noted in Chapter 14, he made a third attempt on Central America three years later, in 1860, landing in Honduras, where a British force captured him and turned him over to the Hondurans, who executed him.)[1]

After about a year on Ruatán, Kinney moved to Aspinwall (now Colón) in what is now Panama. It was apparently here, in early 1858, that he hit upon the idea of selling the Shepherd grant—which he probably did not own—to Mormon leader Brigham Young. In mid-1857, President James Buchanan, alarmed by the Mormons' polygamy and their quasi-theocratic governance of the Utah Territory, sent the U.S. Army there. Kinney thought this would make Young desperate to get his followers out of the United States and that the Mosquito Coast might appeal to him. In late April, this small blurb appeared in many U.S. newspapers:

> [Another] letter dated from Panama, April 16th, [states] that Col. Kinney had been for some time treating with the Mormons, with the view of settling them on the Mosquito Coast. By the last California steamer he received intelligence that his proposition had been favorably received by the Mormons, and this information enabled him to raise $30,000 cash [$900,000 in 2022] and $80,000 [$2.3 million in 2022] more in merchandise and supplies, with which, accompanied by twenty followers, he has sailed for Greytown.

16. "The Mormons Had Better Go"

He expects to obtain through Gen. [Mirabeau Buonaparte] Lamar [U.S. minister to Nicaragua, former president of Texas, and, as noted in Chapter Eight, a close Kinney friend] permission to colonize the country under the Nicaraguan flag, obligating the colonists to help to defend Nicaragua against "the encroachments of filibusters." Failing to obtain this privilege, he will hoist the Nicaraguan flag, and as this is under British protection, he expects no serious opposition from any quarter.[2]

Kinney sailed for Greytown in mid–April, not with twenty followers, but only six, to carry out what historian Robert E. May calls "one of filibustering's strangest incidents." After some routine commerce, the bark that brought Kinney and his six followers left Greytown at noon on the 25th of April but without them. These seven men were seen just an hour later at the flagstaff in the town plaza, striking the Mosquito flag and hoisting the Nicaraguan colors in its place. The municipal authority ignored this seemingly provocative act, a correspondent for the *New York Herald* on scene reported, because the flag "is entirely under the English Consul's authority." (Most of what follows is from this *Herald* reporter's lengthy account.) The city authority, which was made up of Americans, English, Germans, French, &c. "has no flag." What followed was a brilliant two-day exercise by Kinney in bluff and braggadocio that would not have lasted two hours in the modern era of instant communication.[3]

"Seeing the Strangers with Guns in Their Hands"

If the flag incident didn't get the town's attention, what followed did. Kinney and his six cohorts went to the town's station house, where one of them read an address aloud, and then the six Kinney men, sans Kinney, formed themselves into an armed "posse" and proceeded toward the residence of the mayor. They were bent on arresting him on a "warrant" issued by Kinney. "Seeing the strangers with guns in their hands, closing in on his home, the mayor," the *Herald* reporter related, "closed his door against them." While one of the Kinneyites guarded the front door, the others, "by oaths and threats, endeavored to gain admittance, swearing that they would break open his doors if the Mayor did not open them." They vowed "to arrest him or die in the attempt."

One of the doors was finally breached and "the Mayor was dragged through the streets … to the station house, where Kinney endeavored to compel him to resign his office. Kinney stated to the assembled crowd that Capt. [C.H.] Kennedy, of the United States [war]ship *Jamestown*, [then in the harbor] had ordered the Mosquito flag pulled down and the

Nicaraguan colors hoisted, and that the Nicaraguan flag had been made on board the *Jamestown* for that express purpose."

Kinney then warned the crowd of townspeople that if the town's governing authorities "dared to resist him or his men, the *Jamestown's* guns would immediately open on the town." The mayor responded by asking the crowd, "who had elected him, ... if they wished him to resign." The *Herald* reporter said they replied, "in one chorus, 'No! and we await your orders to turn out these strangers.'" In an inexplicable anticlimax, the mayor simply left the station house and went home.[4]

"Towards evening," the *Herald* reporter's account continues, "Captain Kennedy came on shore ... and called on Kinney, and afterwards informed the English consul that Kinney had promised to send the mayor and other authorities a written apology the next morning for what he had done." But Kinney didn't send an apology. He sent, instead, an unabashed defense of his actions, claiming he had been encouraged by the townsfolk. Then he declared the former government was "abrogated" and reassured the inhabitants and the Kinney-displaced authorities they had nothing to fear from him and his men. "Sir, I beg to inform you, agreeably to the wishes of the citizens of this place, the flag of Moschito [sic] has been hauled down and that of Nicaragua substituted; and although the former government has been abrogated, you need fear no act of violence to any of its agents or inhabitants of San Juan [Greytown]."

The authorities, "being perfectly paralyzed" at Kinney's earlier announcement that "he was supported ... by the United States naval force stationed at this port," reacted by drawing up a protest against him, "with a view of sending it to Capt. Kennedy." Meanwhile, the *Herald* reporter claimed that "Kinney and his associates were constantly threatening the Mayor and others with hanging, banishment, and the like."

"The Game Which Had Been Played Off on Him by Kinney"

When Captain Kennedy arrived with four armed boats and was received by Kinney, as Kinney's envoys had predicted, the townsfolk assumed the commander and the colonel were, indeed, in league. But then Kennedy met with the authorities and, the *Herald* reported, he "began to get an insight to the game which had been played off on him by Kinney, and the awkward position he had appeared to assume."

Kennedy retreated to the *Jamestown* and drafted an air-clearing letter to the mayor. "A report ... industriously circulated and believed ... that [Kinney's] acts ... were countenanced by me ... [has] no foundation in truth." Then Kennedy referenced "a certificate" written by Kinney, which Kennedy left earlier that day (April 26) with the authorities. In it, Kinney absolved the commander of the very collusion the colonel had attributed to him. Kinney, Kennedy concluded, "acts entirely on his own individual responsibility, or at any rate not under my protection or authority, and the only part that I desire to take in the matter is to prevent the shedding of blood."

Upon receipt of this note the following morning, the authorities "having no further fear of the guns of the *Jamestown*," arrested Kinney and four of his associates. (What happened to the other two is unknown.) Kennedy came ashore and congratulated the mayor "that the arrests had been made without violence." Then, to help the town "get rid of Col. Kinney and his associates," Kennedy refereed negotiations which led to the colonel and his now four-man army agreeing "to accept the asylum" of the *Jamestown* until they could leave "for the interior of the country … and not return to the town except with peaceable and friendly intentions." For reasons unknown, the Kinney party did not travel to the interior; Commander Kennedy, instead, put them aboard an English passenger ship, which returned them to Aspinwall.[5]

"Kinney Appears … Shocked, at the Turn Affairs Had Taken"

Kinney continued on to Corpus Christi, where his Central American odyssey had begun four years before. Despite his failure, he was something of a celebrity when he returned.

According to M.P. Norton's grandson's account (see Chapter 8), his grandfather had continued "the management of Colonel Kinney's property until the latter's return from Nicaragua in the summer of 1858, when he turned it back to him with an accounting that proved Kinney yet fairly wealthy, notwithstanding the debts he had contracted in New York before starting for Central America and other debts contracted in Nicaragua."[6]

The younger Norton may have been oversanguine in his estimates of Kinney's remaining wealth. Besides the New York and Nicaraguan debts, he still had the Schatzell borrowing to contend with. According to historian Hortense Ward:

> When the colonel left Corpus Christi to filibuster in Central America, he was heavily indebted to John P. Schatzell, the former U.S. consul at Matamoros. This indebtedness had been incurred mainly through his celebrated Lone Star Fair in 1852—a financial fiasco.
>
> Schatzell died suddenly very shortly after Kinney left Corpus Christi. James

W. Zacharie of New Orleans, who was Shatzell's agent and banker, was adamant in his demand that Kinney should pay up his debts.

Kinney appears to have been shocked, or at least he pretended to be, at the turn affairs had taken. He owed Schatzell something like $70,000 [$2 million in 2022], and he protested that Schatzell, who had no heirs, had told him that he never intended that Kinney should pay back the money he had borrowed, and had so stated in his will.

Unfortunately, the will was not to be found, and Kinney was forced to mortgage almost the entire block of his holdings in order to satisfy the claims of the Schatzell estate.[7]

There is no way to assess accurately the state of Kinney's financial affairs when he returned to Corpus Christi in 1858. Purportedly, the Shepherd grant holding company had no monetary assets; its only asset was the grant itself, the provenance for which was vaporous. The 18 or so owner/directors, some of whom were wealthy, refused to invest any money in it. It probably fell to Kinney—especially after Central American Land and Mining ostracized him in March of 1855—to cover his own, i.e., the second, or *United States/Ocean Bird/Emma*, expedition's costs. For instance, who paid to house the 500 "colonists" in New York hotels, or keep the ships on standby, first through the expected waiting period and then through the delay imposed by the federal government's blockade? Many references are made to Kinney's agent/attorney, Judge Norton, using Kinney's allegedly vast land and cattle holdings to pay off these debts, but this is not verifiable.

"The Dominancy of the Yankees in That Quarter"

While Kinney was pretty much a broken man, having suffered disappointments that would have crushed most people, he had one more bamboozle up his sleeve. He would rekindle his plan to sell the Shepherd grant to Brigham Young. (Given this turn of events, it might be conjectured, that this is why Kinney undertook his tiny, windmill-tilting assault upon Greytown. If he could re-establish himself there, it might bolster his bona fides as the owner of the grant and make him appear to the Mormons capable of ushering them safely through the port and into the Mosquitian Shepherd grant lands.) As with much that involved Kinney and the Mosquito grant, accounts vary wildly regarding its proffered sale to Young, ranging from a dime-novelesque tall tale to a sophisticated international intrigue.

In the latter category, there is this tantalizing tidbit from the *San Francisco Daily Union*:

16. "The Mormons Had Better Go"   143

> EXTRAORDINARY DIPLOMATIC MISSION.—We are advised that an Englishman recently came from San Francisco by the Tulare route, on his way to the headquarters of the Mormons. He is the representative of the English Government and Col. Kinney, of Central American notoriety, and is commissioned to jointly represent those powers near the Court of the Prophet and extend to him the offer of the Kingdom of Mosquitodom, as a refuge from the insufferable persecution of the American Government. If he cannot translate the Zion of the Latter-day Saints to that paradise, they are willing to accept the establishment of a Vice-royalty in that country by the Revelator, to be supported and sustained by a colony of saints, which, fresh from Utah, will carry hostile anti–American feeling enough into that country to quiet the apprehensions of John Bull respecting the dominancy of the Yankees in that quarter.[8]

The colonel had lived on Ruatán about a year before this purported Anglo-Kinney overture to the Mormons. And the British *did* fear "the dominancy of the Yankees in that quarter," what with William Walker, the twice-failed filibusterer of Nicaragua, planning yet another expedition to Central America (which, as noted, ended in his execution in 1860). But it is unclear where Kinney came down on all this.

"I Set to Work to Do Them a Good Turn"

At the other, the tall-tale, extreme of the Mormon grant-offer accounts, there is this picaresque scenario in an autobiographical newspaper article by one James Madison "Matt" Harbin. He and his family established in northern California what became, in the 1860s, a resort called Harbin Hot Springs. (It is still there.) In 1897, now an old man, he told the *San Francisco Examiner* that in 1858:

> The Mormons were being persecuted, and I reckoned I could help them. I wasn't a Mormon, and you couldn't make me one in a thousand years; but I was a man, and they were of my kind, and I felt sorry for them. I couldn't figure out that they meant any harm, and I could figure out that they were having mighty hard traveling. So, I set to work to do them a good turn and ended by accomplishing nothing for them…. I bought the Mosquito Kingdom in Central America and planned to fix it up for the Mormons. I paid $100,000.00 [$3 million in 2022] down and was to pay the remainder of the purchase price within ten years.[9]

While the author of a Harbin Hot Spring history calls this story "a bit far-fetched," there is no doubt Harbin made his way to Provo, Utah, in the spring of 1858 and was welcomed there by Brigham Young as a selling agent, if not the owner, of the Kinney Mosquito grant. According to Mormon records, no fewer than six such men made this offer to Young. One of them, D.W. Thorpe, set out alone in late 1857 but failed to reach Utah. Then Harbin and a man named John B. Cooper (probably unrelated to Senator

James Cooper) arrived in the spring of 1858 and met with Young on May 24 and 25. In a letter dated May 24, Cooper offered Young thirty million acres at ten cents apiece. Young replied that circumstances "require me to decline entering into any negotiations for purchasing all or any portion of the country claimed by Mr. Kinney in Central America."[10]

Cooper and Harbin were followed shortly by a Colonel Clarkson, a Major Brookie (or Brooky), and a Judge Cliff, all of whom met with Brigham Young on May 30, 1858. The meeting was chronicled in the Mormon's *Journal History of the Church (1830–2008)*:

> Messrs. Clarkson, Booky [sic], of San Francisco, in company with Jefferson Hunt [probably a Mormon] and Robt. Cliff, called upon the president. Clarkson said the proposition to sell Mosquito Coast was known to Pres. Buchanan, and all operations of the army were suspended, until the result of Mr. Cooper's mission was ascertained, as it was expected that we would accede to the proposition; he believed that government would give us from 12 to 12 [sic] million dollars [$360 million in 2022] and pay our transportation, as they had spent eight million dollars [$240 million in 2022] now to no purpose in the war against us.[11]

"If It Was Covered Fifteen Inches Deep with Gold"

There is a fancy, proclamation-like document in the Mormon archives, complete with calligraphy and a be-ribboned seal. Kinney signed it as the "Governor of San Juan del Norte or Greytown, Central America." In it, Kinney invites Brigham Young to establish a "Mormon Government in Central America" and anoints D.W. Thorpe as his authorized agent. Apparently, Thorpe mailed this document to Young. The document, which does not mention the grant, is dated September 20, 1855—over two years before Kinney reportedly got the idea to sell the grant to Young. But its date falls conveniently on one of the only sixteen days Kinney was governor of Greytown. It is not known whether Kinney did think of approaching the Mormons then or purposely backdated the document to the brief period he was Greytown's governor to bolster its bona fides. All the agents and their overtures met with Young's refusal to consider the offer. One Mormon source quoting him as saying, "I would not go to that country, if it was covered 15 inches deep with gold, and we owned it all. We are here, and here we will stay in this territory."[12]

"All Sects Are Persecuted at First"

Oddly, this does not seem to have ended the matter. On June 11, 1858—about two weeks after Young declined the grant offer—he invited

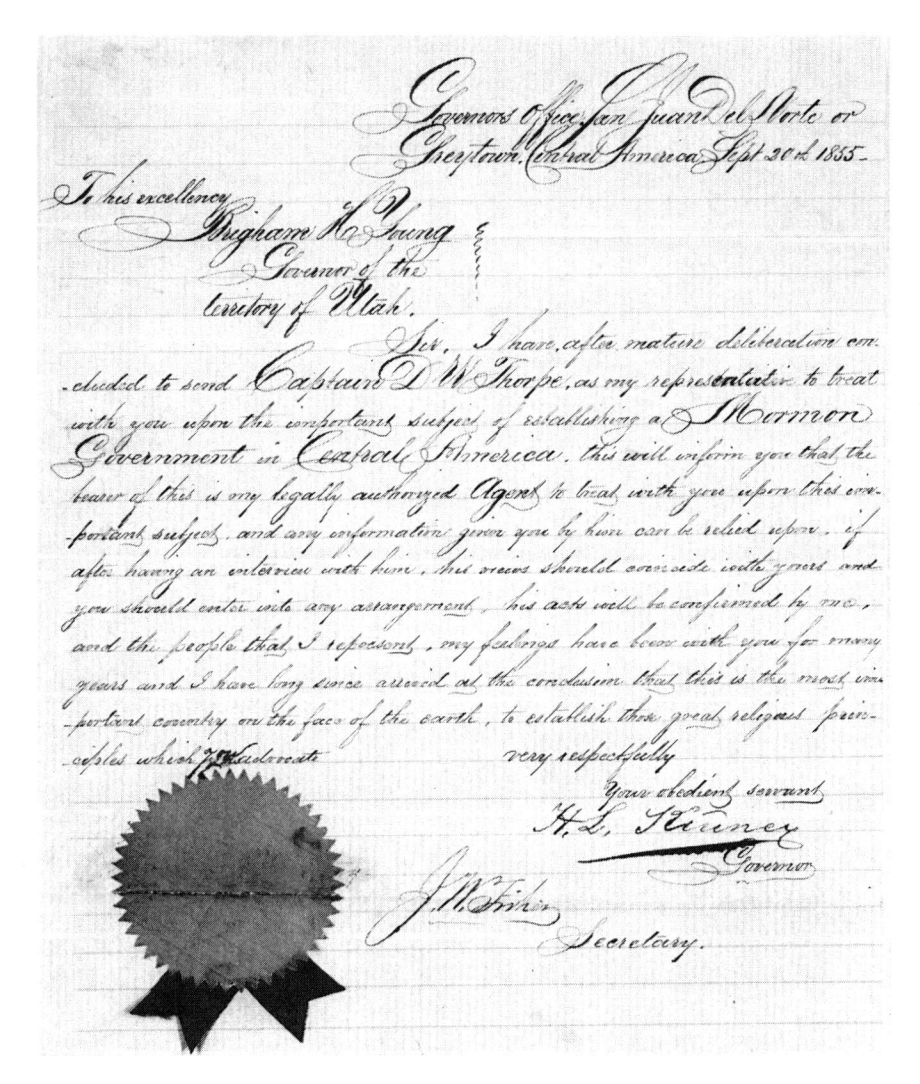

Solicitation by H.L. Kinney to Brigham Young to set up a Mormon government in Central America (courtesy of the Church History Library, The Church of Jesus Christ of Latter-day Saints).

Clarkson to a meeting that included himself, some church elders, and two Buchanan emissaries, Kentucky senator-elect L.W. Powell and U.S. Army Major Ben McCullough. The next day, Young not only asked Clarkson back for another meeting but even "called upon" him to speak, an opportunity which church records indicate Clarkson "reasonably and gentlemanly" declined. Four days later, at supper after another meeting, Major

McCullough, within earshot of Clarkson, said to two church elders, "The Mormons had better go and establish a republic, for the damned Christians will keep on persecuting you." One of the elders, George A. Smith, replied—prophetically—that "it would not be many years before the Mormons could go where they pleased, as any other religious bodies do; all sects are persecuted at first."

Just about this time, the church leaders and Buchanan's internuncios, Powell and McCullough, reached a settlement, and the crisis ended. This now put the grant purveyors in a decidedly buyer's market. "The pending difficulties having been satisfactorily settled between the government and your people," John Cooper wrote to Young, grasping at a straw. "I have taken the liberty of addressing you again on the subject of my mission here, and should you feel disposed to renew the negotiations, I think we might come on terms that would be agreeable to both parties." Apparently, Clarkson and Brookie were still sniffing around, too, because six weeks later they rented "a mansion" in Salt Lake City. Whether Young encouraged lingering hope among these agents or they, too, were just grasping at straws is unknown. But, in any event, nothing came of it.[13]

The next and penultimate reference to the grant in Mormon archives is this anonymous note to Young signed, "A Friend of the Saints," and dated February 17, 1859. "An attempt will be made by Mr. Cooper or his agents, to sell you the Mosquito Country. I am well assured that Col. Kinney will not ratify any sale made under Cooper's authority, and I write this as a *confidential* caution. Kinney will visit you himself soon or send a confidential agent." Two months later, this mystery missive was, indeed, followed by an offer from "Mr. Cooper." The *Mormon History Journal* relates that "George A. Smith received a letter from John B. Cooper, enclosing one to Pres. Young, proposing to sell him half of Kinney's claims in Mosquito for $100,000 [$3.0 million in 2022] in 10 annual installments. Last summer, Cooper wanted three million dollars [$90 million in 2022] for the whole of the claim. John [read: James] M. Harbin, the reputed millionaire, who was said to have bought the whole claim for $2,500,000 [$74 million in 2022], has become bankrupt."[14]

CHAPTER 17

"As If 'Usurpers' Had Taken Possession"

It took six years, but Calvin Durand's suit against Commander Hollins of the *Cyane* for losses he suffered at Greytown was finally decided on September 13, 1860. Presiding was a U.S. Supreme Court justice named Samuel Nelson, who, like every justice at the time, was "riding the circuit," that is, hearing circuit court cases for part of each year. (This practice was abandoned in 1891.)[1]

National Archives and Records Administration personnel tried unsuccessfully to locate for this research the *Durand v. Hollins* case file, which should have been in NARA's depository at Lee's Summit, Missouri. Nevertheless, some hints as to the Hollins defense strategy can be gleaned from two 1855 letters written by his chief counsel, the federal D.A. in New York, John McKeon, and from three 1857 newspaper articles about the suit.[2]

McKeon's first letter, dated March 16, 1855, was to Solicitor of the U.S. Treasury Farris B. Streeter and had as a prominent theme McKeon's concern for keeping the case from judicial scrutiny. "If ... the alleged misconduct of the people [of Greytown] ... be pleaded ... we then tender an issue ... as to whether the alleged provocation, if it existed, was sufficient to justify the Bombardment. This ... course, in my estimation, ought, if possible, to be avoided as indirectly submitting the action of the Executive to an inquiry before the Judiciary." To avoid this, McKeon insisted that Greytown was still part of Nicaragua, that is, on territory friendly to the United States (a contention, as noted, U.S. officials had been vacillating over for years). To bolster his argument, McKeon quoted from Ex-Minister Borland's accusation in his report to Marcy, that "in their anomalous condition, without a government which any civilized nation recognizes—[Greytown residents], indeed, [are] occupying, by usurpation, territory which our government recognizes as belonging to Nicaragua."[3]

McKeon ran with this concept. "I have therefore prepared a Plea which I enclose and which covers the positions assumed by Mr. Borland in his dispatch [to Marcy]. It is, perhaps, the safest ground to take. I put the case as if 'Usurpers' had taken possession [of Greytown] and the Government had ordered Captain Hollins to bombard their stronghold." This plea made it into Justice Nelson's decision, "There was … a plea setting forth … that the community at Greytown had forcibly usurped the possession of the place, and erected an independent government, not recognized by the United States."[4]

This plea is insupportable by the evidence; there was no instruction in Navy Secretary Dobbin's order to Hollins to bombard Greytown. In fact, here is the relevant passage to the contrary in Dobbin's order to Hollins, "It is, however, very much to be hoped that you can effect the purposes of your visit without a resort to violence." Moreover, Greytown's government had not "forcibly usurped the possession of the place," and it *was* recognized by the United States, through two Anglo-American agreements and having posted a minor diplomat there.[5]

McKeon followed this first letter with another five days later, this time writing to Attorney General Caleb Cushing. This one is difficult to follow, possibly because the pleas themselves are missing. Nonetheless, there is a clear indication McKeon was worried Hollins might lose the case, especially if heard by a jury. For the sake of completeness, the whole substance of the letter is offered here:

> These pleas must go off tomorrow—they were brought in by the Solicitor after you went out to-day.
> The second plea is probably demurrable [disputable as a legal pleading on the grounds the facts put forward do not support it], while the 3rd presents a question of fact for the consideration of the jury (the usurpation &c & the acts of war) which I should be unwilling to submit to a New York jury at this time. The plff [plaintiff] will offer evidence to disprove these points, notwithstanding what may appear in Hollins instructions, as the determination of the Executive upon them. I should prefer pleading his adjudication, & let the question come up on demurrer to the plea, to raising it upon the admissibility of evidence at the trial….
> *If the evidence should be admitted, a verdict would follow for plff, & although it might be set aside, still the effect would be bad* [emphasis added].[6]

"Congress, Which Body Holds the War-Making Power"

Two and a half years later, in the fall of 1857, at least three newspapers carried stories indicating court proceedings were held at the time regarding these pleas. ("This case came on to-day.") One article was from the

New York Journal of Commerce (as reprinted in the *Nashville Union* of September 29, 1857):

> The case ... involves a number of interesting questions, and especially the broad one of the constitutional power of the President to order the bombardment and destruction of a town in a foreign country without the authority of Congress, which body holds the war-making power.... It has been suggested by some ... that the orders to Capt. Hollins did not justify the extreme measures of hostility which he resorted to, and that he is, therefore, liable for the consequences of those measures. But a reference to the orders will sustain the construction which Capt. Hollins put upon them; and besides, his act was afterwards assumed, avowed and justified by the Executive Government.[7]

Another, similar article was written by the *Baltimore Sun's* New York correspondent in the September 21, 1857, edition. "Captain Hollins, of the *Cyane*, ... sets up that he simply obeyed the orders of his government, but to this the plaintiff demurs, on the ground that the President of the United States had no right to direct the bombardment without the concurrence of Congress. The question involved is an important one, politically as well as pecuniarily."[8]

Two days before this *Sun* piece, there appeared in the *New York Tribune* an article far more detailed than the two above. What follows is a summary of this *Tribune* article.

> This case came on to-day. The plaintiff, a large property-holder there, sued the Captain for damages. The defendant pleaded execution of orders, to which the plaintiff demurred on the ground that the President had no right to give any such orders.
> It was on this demurrer that the case came up, Mr. [John A.] Manning appearing for the plaintiff and District-Attorney McKeon for Capt. Hollins.

Firstly, the plaintiff's attorney, Mr. Manning, argued that neither the President nor the Secretary of Navy "had power to give such orders, and the defendant cannot justify them." Secondly, the people of Greytown are not alleged to have given any provocation for the bombardment. Thirdly, the "bombardment was a gross violation of the sovereignty of Nicaragua, a friendly country and an ally." [As noted, U.S. authorities dithered over who owned Greytown.] Fourthly, no state of war existed, so its people could not be treated as enemies. Fifthly, "it does not appear that the people of Greytown were pirates." And, sixthly, "this proceeding was not authorized under the law of reprisals."

The District Attorney, on behalf of Capt. Hollins, traversed the above points with the following:

> The act of the defendant was the act of the supreme executive power of the State. The President of the United States, under the Constitution, possesses

the lawful power of the Government. He is the Commander-in-Chief of the Army and the Navy of the United States. That he is, under the United States, entrusted with a discretionary power as to the employment of the naval forces, and had a right to use the public force of the country to protect the persons and property of American citizens from injuries, *or compel punishment on marauders who are not recognized by the United States or by Nicaragua as a foreign power* [emphasis added].[9]

As noted previously and below, there was incontrovertible evidence that the Greytonians were not marauders and were recognized, if not by Nicaragua as a foreign power, then by the U.S. and Great Britain, at least temporarily.

"This ... Generally Wretched Episode"

According to historian Kenneth E. Shewmaker, "Arthur M. Schlesinger, Jr., has suggested that the erosion of congressional control over the war power began in the nineteenth century, when the executive was permitted to undertake military actions against such nongovernmental entities as bandits and pirates." Schlesinger implied in his 1973 book *The Imperial Presidency* that President Franklin Pierce and Justice Nelson were categorizing the Greytowners as a "piratical" and "irresponsible" group to counter the accusation that Congress's power to declare war had been expropriated by the executive branch in this case. McKeon was probably doing the same when he called the Greytonians "marauders" in response to Calvin Durand's lawyer raising the same charge, namely, that "neither the President nor the Secretary of War [read: Navy] had power to give such orders." (And while the executive branch, through Navy Secretary Dobbin, didn't actually "direct" the bombardment, it did not rule out the use of force, which, in retrospect, was seen, in effect, as authorizing Hollins to attack at his discretion.)[10]

After Schlesinger noted that "both Pierce and even Nelson himself said with the utmost clarity that the action was undertaken, not against a sovereign state, but against a 'piratical' and 'irresponsible' group," he added, "nevertheless this ... generally wretched episode was cited in later years by lawyers in desperate search of constitutional justification for presidential war against sovereign states." The Greytonians were neither "piratical" nor "irresponsible."

As noted in Chapters 1 and 5, two Anglo-American agreements, one in 1852 and one in 1853, recognized the government of Greytown and its power to "punish wrong-doers," at least temporarily, until a treaty could settle the fate and status of the port permanently. Besides, both England

and the U.S. had posted minor diplomatic officials there, something neither country would do in a lawless and stateless society. Moreover, in 1853 Senator Edward Everett (who had previously been secretary of state briefly between Webster and Marcy) seemed to have established Greytown's permanent status already. As touched on earlier (in Chapter 4), he called the port, "a little new republic" and "an independent free city ... like one of the Hanse towns of Germany."[11]

"The Interposition of the Executive Abroad"

Justice Nelson found for Hollins, saying, in part:

> As the executive head of the nation, the president is made the only legitimate organ of the general government, to open and carry on, correspondence or negotiations with foreign nations, in matters concerning the interests of the country or of its citizens. It is to him, also, the citizens abroad must look for protection of person and of property, and for the faithful execution of the laws existing and intended for their protection. For this purpose, the whole executive power of the country is placed in his hands, under the constitution.
>
> Now, as it respects the interposition of the executive abroad, for the protection of the lives or property of the citizen, the duty must, of necessity, rest in the discretion of the president. Under our system of government, the citizen abroad is as much entitled to protection as the citizen at home. The great object and duty of Government is the protection of the lives, liberty, and property of the people composing it, whether abroad or at home; and any government failing in the accomplishment of the object, or the performance of the duty, is not worth preserving.
>
> And it is quite clear that, in all cases where a public act or order rests in executive discretion neither he nor his authorized agents is personally civilly responsible for the consequences.[12]

"A nation's use of armed force," Schlesinger wrote, "to rescue, for example, citizens endangered by the breakdown of order in a foreign land had ample sanction in international practice. Presidents therefore decided that such police actions, *not directed at sovereign states* ... did not rise to the dignity for formal congressional concern" (emphasis added).[13]

So, early on, such policing actions by U.S. forces against "uncivilized" states and stateless actors, like pirates, were, de facto, exempt from the proviso that only Congress can declare war. But civilized foreign countries were another matter. In 1841, for instance, Secretary of State Webster wanted the U.S. Navy to undertake military reprisals against Montevideo for Uruguay's brutal treatment of an American citizen. President John Tyler responded, "The idea is that a movement on Montevideo if redress was refused either in the form of blockade or otherwise would be equivalent to a declaration of war against a civilized nation which is exclusively intrusted to Congress."[14]

"Paying with the Foretopsail"

A telling example of this distinction between sovereign, or civilized, states, and those polities perceived to be uncivilized came in 1851. The United States was confronted with almost simultaneous, though unrelated, offenses against two citizens abroad, one in Greece and the other on the Indian Ocean island of Johanna (now called Anjouan or Nzwani). Secretary of State Daniel Webster ordered that the Greek affair be settled solely by negotiation, ruling out the use of force because he considered Greece a civilized, sovereign nation. According to historian Shewmaker, Dr. Jonas King, a fiery American missionary, had had valuable property he owned near the Acropolis "sequestered" without compensation and was ordered banned from the country after reviling the Greek Orthodox Church.

On April 29, 1852, Secretary of State Webster directed George Perkins Marsh, the U.S. minister to the Ottoman Empire, to undertake a special mission to Greece. "Although a naval vessel was detached from the Mediterranean Squadron and placed at Marsh's disposal," wrote Shewmaker, "he was not authorized to threaten Greece with military reprisal. However unfairly King may have been treated, Marsh could not go beyond investigating and writing a report. Marsh performed his task brilliantly; King was allowed to remain in Greece and received an indemnity of $25,000 [$750,000 in 2022] for his property."[15]

"The United States did not have formal diplomatic relations with either Greece or the island nation of Johanna in 1851–52," Shewmaker continued, "but it dealt with Johanna quite differently when a problem arose." Johanna was a favorite resupplying stop for American whaling vessels. Some 25 to 40 touched there yearly for fresh supplies, as the island had abundant fresh water, vegetables, and beef cattle, goats, and chickens. The American whaling ship captains and the island's leader, a sultan named Selim, often clashed. The incident in question resulted from a common practice among Yankee whalers at Johanna and elsewhere— the 19th-century maritime equivalent of "dine and dash." The culprits would take the supplies aboard and then just leave without paying. It was called "paying with the foretopsail," purportedly because that was the last thing the suppliers would see as the absconding ship disappeared over the horizon.[16]

In April 1850 an American whaling ship called the *Phoenix,* captained by Thomas Bloomfield, stopped at Johanna for supplies. After obtaining them, he carped about their quality and then set sail in the middle of the night without paying. The next American whaler to visit the island was the bark *Maria*, commanded by Charles C. Mooers. According to historian Kenneth R. Stevens, when Mooers went ashore … the sultan indignantly complained about Americans who had taken supplies and left without paying. He ordered Mooers to reimburse him for every U.S. captain who had done this. The sum totaled around $700 ($20,000 in 2022). When Mooers refused, Selim told him, "You shall not go until you pay me all the Americans owe me … & if you make any resistance, I will tie your hands & feet." Mooers still refused but avoided being tied up when an Englishman interceded on his behalf and convinced the sultan to let Mooers stay with him. Mooers ordered his crew to take the *Maria* out to sea for four or five days. Selim reduced his demand on the captain from $700 to $154 (to $4,500 in 2022), the amount of one bolting captain's bill, and threatened to "take all the American captains that come into this place & keep them until paid." By the time the *Maria* returned to Johanna, Selim had released her captain without getting any extra money from him. Mooers and the *Maria* sailed soon after, continuing their whale hunt.[17]

"Open the Battery of This Ship Upon Your Town"

While still on the island, Mooers had written a letter demanding Washington exact damages for him from Selim. This letter made it to Secretary of State Daniel Webster, who did not know Mooers had been released unharmed after about nine days. Webster asked Navy Secretary William Alexander Graham to look into the matter. It was possible, he warned Graham, that there might be "some degree of misrepresentation" in Captain Mooers' account, but if it were accurate, "such an outrage cannot be permitted to go unpunished by this Government. It has been its habit to let it be known, all over the world, that it protects its citizens, in their lawful commerce, by its power."

According to historian Stevens, Webster urged Graham to send an American warship to restore Mooers to liberty and secure him just compensation for his imprisonment. "On one point Webster seemed contradictory," Stevens continued in his excellent 1985 article on this incident. "He suggested that the 'actual application of force is to be avoided' except in case of 'absolute and indispensable necessity' yet clearly he intended that the naval officer who dealt with the sultan should be intimidating and was authorized by this wording to use force if he saw fit. He advised Graham that 'a firm demand made by the Commander and a conviction which the presence of the vessel will inspire of his ability, to enforce that demand, will, it is to be presumed, produce all necessary effect.'" (Neither force nor intimidation was authorized in the Greek affair noted above, but both options were on the table when it came to "uncivilized" Johanna.)[18]

The U.S. sloop-of-war *Dale* was dispatched, under the command of William Pearson, Stevens wrote, "to investigate the situation there." Pearson was to exercise his "own sound judgement" in the case. Pearson didn't arrive at Johanna until some fifteen months after Mooers' release. He demanded redress for the "unlawful imprisonment and detention" of Captain Mooers in the form of a $20,000 reparation ($600,000 in 2022) and Selim's promise that neither he nor his subjects would again molest an American citizen. Selim replied that he regretted the incident, but he could not pay that amount because there was not that much money on the island. Pearson held firm. He replied that the sultan had to accede to his demand for $20,000 or he would "resort to violent measures to enforce it," threatening to "open the battery of this Ship upon your Town" and to keep firing "until it is demolished." After two fusillades, first of six and then 29 projectiles, the bombardment ceased, and Pearson offered to reduce his demand to $5,000 ($150,000 in 2022). The next day, Selim counter-offered with a $1,000 ($30,000 in 2022) and 30 head of cattle. Pearson accepted the money but declined the "bullocks" for logistical reasons and then sailed away. (An eyewitness account in the *New York Times* indicated that Pearson warned the sultan prior to the bombardments to remove women and children from the town. And, then, when he did fire, it was only at a fort in one corner of the town. Stevens, however, reported that Johanna was "demolished.")[19]

"So Consistent in All Its Parts … That I Believe It True"

Several weeks later Captain Pearson of the *Dale* met Captain John H. Aulick, commander of the U.S. East India and China Seas Squadron and informed him of his actions. Subsequently, Aulick visited Johanna, and, unlike Pearson, he took the time to listen to Selim's side of the story, which, historian Stevens recounted, "differed in many particulars from Captain Mooers's version."

> Selim informed Aulick that Mooers and the captain of the *Phoenix*, who had departed without paying, had come together to purchase provisions which, Selim believed, they had divided between them. Aulick had no means of knowing whether Selim's account was more accurate than Mooers's. But he advised the Navy Department that the sultan expressed himself "with so much

simplicity, earnestness, and sincerity, and it was, at the same time, so consistent in all its parts, and likely in its incidents, that I believe it true." Captain Aulick had no doubt that the sultan frequently was cheated by American whalers, and he recommended, out of a "sense of justice," that the United States return the $1,000 that Pearson had collected.

Selim's money was not returned.[20]

Secretary of State Edward Everett told Captain Mooers that the money was obtained "under threat of bombarding the town."[21]

"Executive War Against … Small [Uncivilized] States"

In terms of historical significance, Johanna—counterpoised with the Greek affair involving Jonas King—was crucial in setting an important precedent. The island had a legitimate government recognized by Western nations (the English even posted a consul there). By the earlier rules of intervention-sans-Congressional-approval, orders should have precluded the use of force at Johanna, as they did in the Greek case. "By 1851," wrote historian Shewmaker, "it seems, the precedent of executive war against nongovernmental groups … and small states such as Johanna that were considered to be uncivilized was … well established. Where these two categories were concerned, the war powers of Congress had been 'exercised beforehand' by the executive branch of the government with the tacit acquiescence of the legislative branch." Historian Kenneth Stevens ended his Johanna piece with this, "The phrase 'gunboat diplomacy' is generally associated with a later era, but its fundamental source—condescension toward those regarded as less civilized than ourselves—was already well established in the middle of the nineteenth century."[22]

"With the Exception … As to President Buchanan"

Perhaps the earliest codification of this policy drift from only attacking "pirates" without consulting Congress to such war-like assaults on legitimate, if lesser-light polities like Johanna can be traced back to 1912. In that year, the State Department's solicitor, J. Reuben Clark, wrote a memorandum entitled, *The Right to Protect Citizens in Foreign Countries by Landing Forces*. According to the Congressional Research Service (CRS), he lists "47 instances in which force had been used, in most of them without any congressional authorization." The list included the Greytown and Johanna affairs and the descriptions of both hewed closely to the official U.S. line. Clark, for example, parrots the lie that Captain Pearson exacted an indemnity from Sultan Selim of Johanna "under threat of bombarding the town," when, in fact, as noted above, Pearson bombarded the town twice.[23]

The only fly in Clark's argumentative ointment for unilateral presidential war power was, in fact, one of the presidents. James Buchanan refused to exercise such power because he thought it belonged, constitutionally, in the hands of Congress. "It will not be denied," Buchanan said in his third annual message, "that the general 'power to declare war' is without limitation, and embraces within itself not only ... a public or perfect war, but also an imperfect war, and, in short, *every species of hostility however confined or limited*. Without the authority of Congress," Buchanan insisted, "*the President cannot fire a hostile gun in any case except to repel the attacks of an enemy*" (emphasis added).[24]

Clark must have known there were other strict constructionists who would agree with Buchanan and take issue with his position. He concluded his memorandum with the following odd exercise—half hedged bet, half trial balloon. "The above observations ... are made *merely by way of suggestion* and with no thought or pretense of more than a *cursory consideration. It is entirely possible that a more detailed and careful study would lead to other or modified conclusions*" (emphasis added).[25]

A more detailed and careful study might, indeed, have led to other conclusions. But what followed instead was another monograph, this time by a Johns Hopkins graduate student named Milton Offutt, who created it from his Ph.D. thesis. It is called *The Protection of Citizens Abroad by the Armed Forces of the United States*. Its three-page description of the Greytown affray follows the official line, including writing that "Mr. Solon Borland ... was surrounded by a mob, the leaders of which tried to arrest him" but without saying what Borland did to prompt the arrest attempt, a revelation which would have crippled his argument.[26]

Offutt's, like Clark's, was what authors Francis Wormuth, Edwin Firmage and Francis Butler call an argument that "derives not from legal sources, but from a literary tradition." In their book, *To Chain the Dog of War,* the authors state that "Offutt discarded Clark's misgivings and adopted his argument." These two booklets—and not political debate or case law—formed some of the earliest underpinnings of the concept that presidents could make war without seeking the consent of Congress. Other lists of interventions followed. The authors have a whole chapter entitled "Lists of Wars" in their book, enumerating Clark's, Offutt's, and the lists that followed.[27]

"The United States Wished to Constrain and Manipulate"

By 1914, the Greytown affair was 60 years old and largely forgotten. In April of that year, President Woodrow Wilson was casting about desperately for a pretext upon which to intervene militarily in Mexico to remove the president. Mexico was in the throes of revolutionary chaos, which, according to historian Hans Schmidt, "the United States wished to constrain and manipulate," given that it had $1 billion ($30 million in 2022) worth of investments there, much of it in oil. The U.S. Army massed on the Mexican border, and warships carrying marines stood off Vera Cruz (now Veracruz), Mexico's main port. These bellicose acts of intimidation were what President Wilson called "watchful waiting."[28]

Wilson found neither the present dictator, Victoriano Huerta, nor any of his rivals acceptable; nor did the U.S. Army Chief of Staff Leonard Wood, who thought "some form of intervention" was "absolutely necessary." Wilson agreed with Wood but was uncertain as to what extent and under what excuse the intervention should be carried out.[29]

A fortuitous precursor to Wilson's wished-for *casus belli* presented itself at the Mexican port of Tampico on April 9, 1914. Huerta's troops arrested nine American seamen whose longboat came ashore in a restricted area. The sailors were not harmed and were soon released. However, the U.S. Navy commander offshore, Rear Admiral Henry T. Mayo, demanded a formal apology from Huerta's government for this insult to U.S. honor. Huerta quickly proffered a written one, but Mayo demanded more, "I must require that you send me ... a formal disavowal of and an apology for the act. Also, that you hoist the American flag in a prominent position on shore and salute it with 21 guns, which salute will be duly returned."[30]

Huerta counter-proposed that the salutes be simultaneous, which Wilson refused. This impasse was pretext enough for Wilson. But as pretexts go, it was going to be a bit thin. So, Wilson asked his counselor to the State Department, Robert Lansing, to find an historical precedent—an affront to America's dignity by an impenitent and unapologetic polity that the U.S. punished with military action. As writer Robert Quirk noted, "It had been necessary to go back more than sixty years, but Lansing found a precedent ... Greytown."[31]

On April 15, 1914, Wilson used Greytown to help justify an intervention to congressional leaders; this put Greytown's destruction back in the press, however briefly. Among the newspapers carrying Wilson's Greytown reference was the *New York Times,* under the headline, "Precedent from Greytown. Wilson Cites Episode of 1854 in Connection with Present Crisis." The *Times* noted that "in that case demands for an apology and an indemnity were duly made upon the local authorities of Greytown, but they were not answered by them. Failing to obtain an apology, Capt. Hollins of the USS *Cyane*, after public proclamation of his intention, bombarded and destroyed Greytown. His course was upheld by the American Government."[32]

On the same day of this publication, the *Times* received the following letter from one W. Cecil Durand:

> I have read with interest your account of the bombardment by Commodore [sic] Hollins of the town of Greytown.... Among the Americans who owned property in that town at the time was my father, the late Calvin Durand.
> He, like all others, had to suffer the entire loss, the Committee on Claims in 1876, Washington, D. C., deciding adversely in the Trautmann Perrin bill for damages, this being a test case. It was said at the time that Lord Palmerston in Parliament denounced the bombardment and called it a "hen roost robbery." The Greytown claims were just and should have been paid in full by the United States Government.[33]

The intervention at Vera Cruz began on April 21, 1914, ironically—or perhaps tellingly—the day b*efore* Congress expressed its approval of it; the intervention lasted six months.

"Just Why the President Should ... Ask What He Did"

During World War I, on February 26, 1917, five weeks before the United States declared war on Germany, President Wilson appeared before Congress and requested authorization to arm U.S. merchant ships to defend themselves against German submarines. "Accord me," he said, "by ... definite bestowal ... [this] authority." The next day, Representative Edward John King (R–IL) told the House that he "wanted to call ... attention ... to a certain decision of one of the courts of this land.... It may help some of us in arriving at a conclusion as to just what the President of the United States asked yesterday." King then ordered the entire *Durand v. Hollins* decision reprinted in the *Congressional Record*.

The *Jamestown* [ND] *Alert* newspaper said the *Durand* case allowed "the interposition of the President to protect the lives and property of citizens of the United States" overseas and that it was "a matter resting in his discretion." King, the paper added, "professed to be somewhat puzzled as to just why the President should come to Congress and ask what he did." King told the House, "In light of this [*Durand*] decision, it appears to me that the request of the President for authority to act in the premises is superfluous and is, in effect, a request of Congress to declare war in disguise."

King's comment got no play in the prominent newspapers, and no other members of Congress chimed in. But, as will be seen, by at least 1940, this use of *Durand* had become common coinage in the scholarly and popular press. What follows is series of writings and events in which *Durand v. Hollins* has been raised to justify U.S. foreign military interventions undertaken without congressional approval.[34]

"Refusal to Pay ... Recalls Shelling of Greytown"

In the first, 1940, edition of his book, *The President: Office and Powers* (considered a classic on the subject), Edward S. Corwin, the first chairman of the Department of Politics at Princeton, wrote: "Far more important is the question whether the President may, without authorization by Congress, take measures which are technically acts of war in protection of American rights and interests abroad. The answer returned both by practice and by judicial doctrine is yes. The leading precedent was an outgrowth of the bombardment in 1854, by Lieutenant [*sic*] Hollins of the USS *Cyane*, of Greytown."

This book appeared in five editions: 1940, 1941, 1948, 1957, and 1984. The 1941 edition also contains the same passage quoted here. But it disappeared from all the subsequent editions, replaced—in the same surrounding context—with this more oblique Greytown reference: "The first question to be considered in this connection is whether the President may, without authorization by Congress, ever use force abroad.... Such action has received the highest judicial sanction. One of the precedents relied on by Justice Miller in the *Neagle* case was the outgrowth of the bombardment in 1854 by Lieutenant Hollins of the U.S.S. *Cyane*, of Greytown, Nicaragua."[35]

In the same year as Corwin's first edition, 1940, a flurry of newspaper accounts appeared about American property being destroyed by Japanese forces then occupying large areas of China. The articles centered on Japan's reaction to American citizens' demands for reparations, as encapsulated in this *Boston Globe* headline and story, "Japan Follows US Precedent on Damages, Refusal to Pay Many Claims Recalls Shelling of Greytown, Nicaragua."

> Japan has brushed aside scores of claims of Americans for injuries to themselves or their properties in China. She argues that since the damages occurred during military operations, international law and American precedents clear

her of liability. She is saying to the Americans, in effect, Seek damages from the Chinese Government. China was responsible for you and your property. The more legally minded American officials concede that Japan is acting in accordance with international law and that she had several potent American precedents to back her up. Japan has not hesitated to call to the attention of American officials the celebrated Greytown case. The question of whether the Sino Japanese conflict is a declared or undeclared war is also ruled out by the same decision. An identical precedent also developed from the American bombardment of Vera Cruz, Mex.[36]

"Turn the Congo into a Communist Satellite"

In 1960, a CIA-inspired coup overthrew the charismatic, leftist leader of the former Belgian Congo, Patrice Lumumba, who was murdered soon after. Four years later, resurgent "Lumumbists," now calling themselves "Simbas" (or "Lions"), took nearly 2,000 U.S. and European civilians hostage in the town of Stanleyville, hoping to use them as bargaining chips in their efforts to regain power. Belgian commandos, carried in on U.S. planes, rescued about 1,600 of the 2,000 hostages. According to Richard Holm, a then-29-year-old CIA paramilitary operative, the CIA thought the Chinese and Soviets were supplying the Simbas "in order to ... turn the Congo into a communist satellite."[37]

In the run-up to the rescue mission, Arthur Krock, a columnist for the *New York Times,* had reported that "anxious consultations" between Belgium and the U.S. were held "to cushion against the effect on neutrals and quasi-neutrals of Communist charges of 'colonialism' and 'imperialism' the mission was sure to evoke." In one exceptional 57-word sentence, Krock managed to both craft a moral imperative for the rescue and set up the legal justification for America's involvement: "Nor did the hesitation of Washington and Brussels to perform what *the United States Supreme Court has described as 'the great object and duty of Government'* dissuade [UN Secretary-General U] Thant from dwelling on 'undesirable consequences' of the landings, without mention of the highly 'desirable consequences' of rescuing from torture, murder and cannibalism hundreds of innocent non-combatants engaged in humanitarian endeavor" (emphasis added).[38]

"Justice Nelson Spoke for the Supreme Court"

The "great object and duty" quote Krock attributes to the U.S. Supreme Court is from *Durand v. Hollins*. As noted, this was a U.S. Circuit Court decision, heard by one Supreme Court justice, Samuel Nelson, "riding circuit." President Johnson's supplying air transport for the Belgian military rescue mission, wrote Krock, "was in performance of one of the highest duties and responsibilities imposed on civilized government. The duty and responsibility of the President to render whatever protection he deems required to American nationals abroad ... is firmly established in constitutional history and in the record of such occasions. But this obligation was never more emphatically stated than in its affirmation by the Supreme Court in 1860 in the case of *Durand v. Hollins*."[39]

Continuing his erroneous attribution, Krock added that "Justice Nelson spoke for the Supreme Court as follows. 'Under our system of government, the citizen abroad is as much entitled to protection as the citizen at home ... and [the means of this protection] rests in the discretion of the President. The great object of and duty of Government is [this] protection ... and any government failing in the accomplishment of the object, or the performance of the duty, is not worth preserving.'"[40]

"His Old Mentor, Arthur Krock"

An interesting sidelight to Krock's propounding on the Stanleyville hostage crisis was his references to Moise Tshombe, the Congo's prime minister, who was, earlier, the pro–Western leader of the breakaway province of Katanga, where Lumumba was murdered. Tshombe, according to the *Britannica* website, "was an adroit politician, who used his foreign supporters to help him achieve his personal ambitions in the Congo." One of these foreign supporters, according to American journalist Richard Reeves, "was his old mentor, Arthur Krock." And one of Krock's efforts on Tshombe's behalf was to lobby President Kennedy to provide Tshombe with a U.S. entry visa. This led to a confrontation so legendary in American politics that it made it into *Bartlett's Book of Anecdotes*. Both Kennedy and Krock had been members of Washington's exclusive Metropolitan Club, but Kennedy, upset over the club's refusal to admit blacks, had quit. Krock had not. When Krock continued to pester Kennedy for a Tshombe visa, the president responded, "Arthur, I'll give Tshombe a visa if you'll take him to lunch at the Metropolitan Club."[41]

"The Greytown Case Is Still Good Constitutional Law"

After North Vietnam began what was called (in the West) their "Easter Offensive" in 1972, President Nixon went on television April 26 to announce his response, "If we continue to provide air and sea support [to the South Vietnamese forces], the enemy will fail." (Nixon resumed bombing North Vietnam on May 10, 1972, and the Navy again began launching strikes against the North.) Nine days after Nixon's speech and anticipating backlash from the President's opponents, Ernest Cuneo, the pro–Nixon writer and editor of the North American Newspaper Alliance (NANA), wrote a piece describing Greytown and *Durand* and using them to defend Nixon's actions.

Cuneo said that "as far as constitutional law is concerned, President Nixon is completely within his powers in ordering air and sea support for terrain on which the American army is under attack. The Senate and House could pass resolutions from here to eternity, but they do not have the constitutional power to limit the constitutional powers of the President, particularly as commander-in-chief of the armed forces. The Greytown case is still good constitutional law."[42]

After the Vietnam War, Congress passed the War Powers Resolution (WPR) in 1973, trying to set restraints on a president's ability to wage war. The WPR requires the president to notify Congress within 48 hours of unilaterally committing armed forces to military action. It then forbids armed forces from remaining for more than 60 days without Congress issuing an Authorization for Use of Military Force (AUMF) declaration or a declaration of war. The WPR's effectiveness has been repeatedly questioned throughout its history, and several presidents have been accused of failing to comply with its regulations. Often, West Wing lawyers since then, to strengthen a president's hand, have invoked *Durand* in their arguments supporting executive branch war-making. Here are a few documents in which *Durand* has been so used: *Report of the Congressional Committees Investigating the Iran/Contra Affair* (1987); *Authority to Use United States Military Forces in Somalia* (1992); *Deployment of United States Armed Forces to Haiti* (2004); *Legal Authorities Supporting the Activities of the National Security Agency Described by the President* (2006); *Authority to Order Targeted Airstrikes Against the Islamic State of Iraq and the Levant* (2014).[43]

Matthew Waxman is, at this writing (January 2023), a Columbia Law School professor and has previously held senior policy positions at the State Department, Defense Department, and National Security Council. On the 165th anniversary of Greytown's razing, July 13, 2019, he wrote an op-ed entitled, "Remembering the Bombardment of Greytown," which concentrated heavily on the *Durand v. Hollins* case law it spawned. "If the United States launches limited strikes against Iran," Waxman wrote, "I will not be surprised if the Justice Department cites this case in its justification."[44]

17. "As If 'Usurpers' Had Taken Possession" 163

Besides using *Durand* to justify military interventions, it has been used at least once to try to thwart the prevention of such a future intervention. On February 6, 2019, Rep. David N. Cicilline (D–RI), introduced a House bill entitled *H.R.1004—Prohibiting Unauthorized Military Action in Venezuela,* which had 78 cosponsors. As the name implies, it was an effort to prevent the executive branch from intervening militarily in Venezuela without congressional approval. "Frankly," said Eliot L. Engel (D–NY), Chairman of the Foreign Affairs Committee, "I would prefer to focus our committee's attention solely on supporting the people of Venezuela in the struggle for a better future. But, unfortunately, we are forced to respond and reinforce the role of Congress under the Constitution and the War Powers Resolution. I do believe that it is Congress' right and ability to declare war and I think for too long we have been abrogating our responsibility to the executive branch no matter who the President was."

Two days after Engels spoke, an assistant attorney general named Stephen E. Boyd wrote to the chairman of the Armed Services Committee that H.R. 1004 "raises constitutional concerns." The bill, Boyd continued, "would not appear to allow deployment of the Armed Forces even when necessary for the President to fulfill his constitutional duty to protect the lives and property of American civilians in Venezuela." He then cited three precedents supporting his argument, one being *Durand*. The other two were the *Slaughter-House* cases and *In re Neagle*. This trio of boilerplate case laws is often cited by executive war-powers defenders— and attacked by opponents of presidential war making.

Although clearly not to be numbered among such opponents, this is, nonetheless, how Richard Nixon's secretary of state, William P. Rogers, characterized *Durand* and the *Slaughter-House Cases* in 1971. "The origin of the notion set forth in *Durand,* that citizens have a right to protection abroad, is unclear. It [this protection] is [also] listed as an unquestionable privilege of federal citizenship in the *Slaughter-House Cases,* with no authority given. It is also mentioned with approval in *In re Neagle*."[45]

Rogers didn't characterize *Neagle,* but others have. In California, on August 14, 1889, a U.S. marshal shot and killed a man who had attacked the Supreme Court justice he was guarding; state authorities arrested the marshal because there was no law authorizing U.S. marshals to protect judges. "Although no federal statute expressly granted the executive authority to assign personnel to protect federal officers by the use of deadly force," wrote law professor Peter Margulies in 2014, "the Court in *Neagle* held that the President had the power under the Take Care [That the Laws Be Faithfully Executed] Clause of the Constitution to ensure the safety of federal officers. The *Neagle* Court asserted that the combination of the President's inherent and delegated power should also cover protection of US nationals abroad. Some scholars," Margulies concluded, "have expressed wariness about the scope of the President's power to rescue US citizens or domiciliaries abroad."[46]

"200 Instances of Use of Force … in the Last 200 Years"

In 1987, Fred F. Manget, a member of the Senior Intelligence Service and a former Deputy General Counsel of the Central Intelligence Agency, wrote that "the President … has the power to order military intervention in foreign countries to protect American citizens and property without prior congressional approval. The theory has been cited to justify about 200 instances of use of force abroad in the last 200 years. The theory was given legal sanction in a case [*Durand*] arising from the bombardment of a Nicaraguan port by order of the President in 1854."

While Manget's math seems absurd on the face of it, an official U.S. list of "Instances of Use of United States Forces Abroad" published just two years later, in 1989, put the total number of such events at 215. Five of these were declared wars (World War I & II, etc.), and six were significant undeclared wars (Korea, Vietnam, etc.) But "the majority of the instances listed," author Ellen C. Collier noted, "were brief Marine or Navy actions prior to World War II to protect US citizens or promote US interests. A number were actions against pirates or bandits." So, it is possible that "about 200" of these instances were undertaken without congressional approval by 1987. But Manget must have been applying *Durand* retroactively to "sanction" the "theory" behind all of them because about 60 pre-date the 1860 *Durand* decision.[47]

This 1989 "Instances" list with the 215 events was put out by the previously mentioned Congressional Research Service. Often called "Congress's think tank," the CRS was founded in 1914 and is the research arm of the United States Congress. It provides background reports on various subjects to members of Congress or their staffers and sometimes—as will be seen anon—answers questions submitted by a constituent through his or her Congress member. This 1989 list was preceded by one by the CRS in 1975. The progenitor of *that* one seems to have been issued by the State Department in 1945. Since about 2001, the "Instances" list has been updated almost every year by the CRS.

What immediately follows are summaries of two CRS reports on the use of *Durand v. Hollins* to justify U.S. foreign military interventions ordered by executive fiat, without consulting Congress.

17. "As If 'Usurpers' Had Taken Possession" 165

"There Is a Dearth of Subsequent Case Law"

In 2007 and 2013, the CRS sent reports to Congress which contain this exact same line: "Only one federal court, in an 1860 opinion [i.e., *Durand*], has clearly held that in the absence of congressional authorization, the President has authority to deploy military forces abroad to protect US persons (and property)."[48]

And in 2017 the CRS had this to say about Greytown and *Durand*:

> This incident and this case were but two items in the 19th century advance of the concept that the President had the duty and the responsibility to protect American lives and property abroad through the use of armed forces if deemed necessary. Although there were efforts made at times to limit this presidential power narrowly ... rather than to the promotion of broader national interests, no such distinction was observed in practice and so grew the concepts which became the source of serious national controversy in the 1960s and 1970s, the power of the President to use troops abroad to observe national commitments and protect the national interest without seeking prior approval from Congress.[49]

As noted, the War Powers Resolution of 1973 called for an Authorization for Use of Military Force or AUMF to follow with 60 days of any presidential military intervention. Two such AUMFs were passed by Congress in 2001 and 2002. The first, passed in haste in the immediate wake of 9/11, gave President George W. Bush virtually a blank check to go after Al-Qaeda, with no time limits. The 2001 law is still applicable as of this writing (2023) against other forces in circumstances totally removed from the law's original intent. This was virtually prophesied by Rep. Barbara Lee (D–CA), the only member of Congress who did not vote for the 2001 AUMF law. "We must be careful," she said at the time, "not to embark on an open-ended war with neither an exit strategy nor a focused target." On May 15, 2018, she and 49 other like-minded members of Congress called for the repeal of the current AUMFs, which, they said, have "resulted in a critical deterioration of Congressional oversight and in perpetual armed conflict for over 16 years, including against groups and in countries and regions where Congress did not intend to authorize force."[50]

The two AUMFs (the second one, in 2002, authorized the U.S. invasion of Iraq in 2003) are, in effect, the legislative successors to their judicial equivalent, *Durand v. Hollins*. They were used by Presidents George W. Bush, Obama, and Trump to justify multiple military interventions beyond the laws' original scope. This same basic "position creep" transformed *Durand* from a mechanism for simply rescuing individual Americans and their property in overseas predicaments into a powerful instrument for effecting political change in foreign polities with unbridled executive war making.

Besides the AUMFs, the CRS report(s) above also mentioned the 1973 War Powers Resolution, the "immediate stimulus" for which "was the widespread dissatisfaction with President Nixon's failure to consult with Congress before ordering US Forces to invade Cambodia in May of 1970." In 1977 "a review of the operation and effectiveness of the War Powers Resolution" led to its opponents invoking *Durand v. Hollins* in their attacks upon it: "The president's authority to act unilaterally with force to protect American lives and property abroad from direct attack has also been upheld" in *Durand v. Hollins*. In the same footnote citing *Durand* in that quoted passage are three arguments this use of *Durand* often bestirs. First, there is this from the 1977 War Powers Resolution hearing, paraphrasing the position of the late Raoul Berger, American attorney and professor at the University of California at Berkeley and Harvard University School of Law. "There is a dearth of subsequent case law to supplement the commonly cited decision in *Durand v. Hollins*"; and [Berger also argued that] "the founding Fathers intended to limit independent presidential war making powers to repelling sudden attacks against the United States." This is followed by a paraphrasing of a countervailing argument by J. Terry Emerson, counsel to U.S. Senator Barry Goldwater, who "espoused a very broad interpretation of independent presidential war making power.

Emerson points to history and argues that repeated past usage of broad presidential authority without objection from Congress gives constitutional validity to continued similar usage." But, then, in counterpoise to Emerson, there is this from a 1969 Supreme Court decision in which Chief Justice Earl Warren stated, "that an unconstitutional action has been taken before surely does not render that same action any less unconstitutional at a later date."[51]

"To Avenge an Insult to the American Minister"

Since at least the 1945 iteration of the "Instances" intervention list, the entry for the Greytown affair has remained, in essence, the same single sentence. In 1945 it said, "San Juan del Norte (Greytown) was destroyed to avenge an insult to the American Minister to Nicaragua." More recently, it has read, "Naval forces bombarded and burned San Juan del Norte (Greytown) to avenge an insult to the American Minister to Nicaragua."[52]

That 1945 version of "Instances" was, as noted, put out by the State Department. At least since 1975, when the Congressional Research Service inherited responsibility for the list, all the legacy descriptions have remained virtually unchanged. The CRS only adds any new U.S.

interventions since the previous iteration. (By at least 2010 they had stopped listing the exact count, replacing it with the word "hundreds.") The next chapter will outline the effort this author made trying to get the CRS to correct the explanation in the "Instances" list as to why Greytown was destroyed, and with that correction, call into question, as a necessary consequence, the validity of *Durand v. Hollins* as a precedential case law.

Chapter 18

"Regarding Constituent Will Soper's Claim"

In 2015, as noted in the Preface, I submitted a 14,000-word article on Greytown to the British Journal of *American Nineteenth Century History* (*BrANCH*), which published it in May 2017 under my title, "Revisiting Nineteenth-Century US Interventionism in Central America: Capitalism, Intrigue, and the Obliteration of Greytown."[1]

"The Book That Literally Rewrote History!"

For roughly a year after my *BrANCH* article was published, I tried to convince one or more staffers of progressive members of Congress to liaise between me and the Congressional Research Service, the "keepers" of the "Instances of Use of US Armed Forces Abroad" list. The CRS does not interact directly with the public, only with members of Congress and their staff. So, I was hoping one of said staffers might persuade the service to read my journal article and use it to correct the list's description of why Greytown was destroyed. I explained to them that correcting the "insult-avenging" explanation for Greytown's demise would benefit their employers, who would get to call into question the purported grounds upon which *Durand* is based. This might be crucial if such Congress members succeeded in their quests to rein in or sunset the previously mentioned AUMFs. (See Chapter 17.)

If *Durand* had *not* been rendered suspect by its origin story by then, executive branch lawyers could just fall back on it. (The CRS literally suggested *Durand* could be such a fallback in a 2007 paper, during the Iraq intervention. They said that "in light of relevant jurisprudence [i.e., *Durand*] and the War Powers Resolution, the repeal of the AUMF ... would likely have little, if any, legal effect on the continuation of combat operations [in Iraq].") Also, I could use the instances list's Greytown correction to bolster my quest for a contract for a book with the prospective cover blurb, "The book that literally rewrote history!"[2]

Such direct email pleas to progressive congressmembers' staffers failed. Then I discovered what is known on Capitol Hill as a "Casework Request." This refers to the response or services that members of congress provide to constituents who request assistance. These are formal pleas for help in dealing with—or understanding the actions of—a federal agency. They can range from "Why did I stop receiving my social security checks?" to one in which a constituent wanted to know why the U.S. Postal Service was "stockpiling ammunition?" (The USPS puts out bids for ammunition because their postal inspectors are law enforcement officers and, therefore, carry guns.)[3]

There is actually a Casework Authorization Form. So, I decided to fill one out and submit it—as a constituent—to the local office of my representative, Adam Schiff (D–CA). In mid–August of 2018, the staff there forwarded the form to the author at the CRS of the most recent "Instances" list, Barbara Salazar Torreon. The package included a copy of my 2017 article and my cover letter describing the error in the "Instances" list and why Greytown was really destroyed. Ms. Torreon replied to Schiff's office with an undated report in mid–September 2018. "Regarding constituent Will Soper's claim that the following entry: '1854 Nicaragua. July 9 to 15. Naval forces bombarded and burned San Juan del Norte (Greytown) to avenge an insult to the American Minister to Nicaragua,' in CRS Report, Instances of Use of United States Armed Forces Abroad, 1798–2017, is factually incorrect, please refer to the following sources referenced below that substantiates [sic] this entry."

What followed were three quotes, two from reputable historians who, like most, just parroted the official line. The third was from President Franklin Pierce, who, as one might expect, defended the action. (See Chapter 9.)[4]

"Amazing Story. And It's Extremely Well Written"

A month later, in response to the CRS spurning of my overture, I submitted an op-ed piece to the online site History News Network entitled "Can an Amateur Historian Change History?" The founder (and then-editor) of HNN, Rick Shenkman, emailed me that it was an "amazing story. And it's extremely well written." The piece summarized my 2017 journal article, chronicled my successful effort to get my article to the CRS, quoted Ms. Torreon's response, and then gave my reaction to it. I offer here the 1,144-word op-ed in full.[5]

CAN AN AMATEUR HISTORIAN REWRITE HISTORY?
By Will Soper

When my article about the US Navy's 1854 razing of the Central American port of Greytown was published in a peer-reviewed journal last year, the editor added the title "Independent Scholar" under my name. I guessed this was the go-to fall back for a non-academic with nothing more than a BA in philosophy.

Once the piece was up I embarked on a quest to both parlay it into a book contract and get the federal government to use it to correct its official explanation of why Greytown was destroyed. These twin pursuits were joined at the hip: If I could get the official description corrected, I would have literally rewritten history, which, in turn, would make it easier for a publishing company to envision a star-burst blurb to that effect on the cover of its next best seller.

Since 1945 the official list of US military interventions has attributed Greytown's utter destruction to the nation's need "to avenge an insult to the American Minister to Nicaragua." (No residents were killed in the bombardment and burning, as they had time to flee.) The insult occurred when an angry town resident threw a piece of broken bottle at the diplomat, which slightly scratched his face. The resident was motivated by the envoy's earlier interference with Greytown's sheriffs when they tried to arrest an American steamboat captain for the cold-blooded murder of a black river pilot. The diplomat—who had witnessed the murder—prevented the arrest by leveling a rifle at the sheriffs and saying they had no authority recognized by the United States to arrest an American citizen, which was untrue.

My article proves the insult was a pretext and that, actually, two groups of American businessmen bent on taking over Greytown, an independent city-state, inveigled Washington into destroying it. One group ran the isthmian steamboat company and wanted to own the port, their Atlantic terminus. The second group (for a time, associated with the first) wanted Greytown as the prospective capital of a new colony based on a huge, dubious Mosquito Coast land grant they owned. This is how the *New York Tribune* of 28 July 1854 captured the essence of these twin intrigues: "That [steamboat] company [had] long desired to get rid of the town, which ... was a hindrance to their supremacy and had defied their power. [The town] also stood in the way of a great project for the establishment of a colony ... which is entertained by several speculators.... The town being removed, it is supposed that project may be carried out with greater facility."

Until now, these plots against the tiny, defenseless port have remained largely hidden for over 100 years.

Besides the "lost history" appeal of a book on this subject, there is also the perennially important legal case it gave rise to, *Durand v. Hollins*. This case law has been used ever since to sanction American military interventions undertaken without seeking the prior congressional approval required by the Constitution's provision that only Congress can declare war. (Googling the exact case name will yield about 2,000 hits. Some of these will also mention the Authorization for Use of Military Force, or "AUMF," laws, which approved the invasions of Afghanistan and Iraq.)

"It's a marvelous piece of detective work," Princeton history professor Matt Karp told me after reading my article, "and perhaps the definitive account of the incident. I really had no idea how important Greytown was as a precedent for executive action … [and] that much of the legal precedent and justification for current US foreign policy is based on a giant error of fact, surrounding a 160-year-old bit of gunboat diplomacy."

Since about 2000, a federal agency called the Congressional Research Service (CRS) has annually updated the interventions list (officially called "Instances of Use of United States Armed Forces Abroad.") So I knew it was to the CRS I must turn to get the record corrected. Trouble is, I couldn't approach them, at least not directly. The CRS doesn't respond to requests from the public, only from members of Congress or their staffers. So, I wrote my congressman, Adam Schiff (D-CA), and his local office staffers forwarded my article to the CRS and asked for a report back.

"Good idea contacting … House staffers," renowned constitutional scholar Louis Fisher told me. "Getting CRS to correct its error is a big and important step." Fisher, who worked for the CRS for 36 years as their "separation-of-powers" expert, viewed *Durand* with an eye both gimleted and jaundiced, given the case law's long-time use by executive branch lawyers to bypass Congress when presidents are bent on unilateral military interventions.

In 2014, Fisher used an amicus brief to urge the Supreme Court in a "separation" case to correct a precedent being applied there. I think he was itching to file another amicus brief. "Please send me a link to the CRS report [when issued]," he emailed me, "so I can see how [they handle it]." If the CRS agreed with my paper and corrected the erroneous description of why Greytown was destroyed, I would have literally rewritten history and Fisher could have used that correction to challenge the factual basis of *Durand* and ask the Supreme Court to abrogate it. Not only is *Durand* still taught in law schools and still cited in intervention apologia, but if it remains unchallenged and the AUMF laws are ever repealed or sunsetted, West Wing attorneys could just fall back on it.

Well, I'll have to wait a while longer to rewrite history and Lou Fisher, to rewrite foreign policy jurisprudence. In mid–September Schiff's office got the report from CRS on my challenge to the insult-avenging explanation of Greytown's demise: "Regarding constituent Will Soper's claim that the [Greytown] entry … in [the CRS 'Instances' Report] is factually incorrect, please refer to the following sources referenced below that substantiates [sic] this entry." What followed were three random quotes, two from credible historians but basically parroting the official line. The third was from a less-than-neutral observer, President Franklin Pierce himself (who, early on at least, was involved in one of the plots against the port). In his defense of its razing—not quoted in the report—he called Greytown a "pretended community ... composed for the most part of blacks and persons of mixed blood ... too dangerous to be disregarded and too guilty to pass unpunished ... a piratical resort of outlaws or a camp of savages."

The report's author is the CRS's Information Research Specialist (Foreign Affairs, Defense, and Trade Division) Barbara Salazar Torreon. She not only didn't address the evidence in my paper, she didn't even mention the paper itself.

My tax dollars at work—and yours.[6]

Soon after this op-ed appeared, I began work on the draft of this book.

CHAPTER 19

"Too Valuable ... To Waive or Impair It"

In addition to *Durand v. Hollins*, the Greytown affair spawned two other legal precedents, *Wiggins v. United States* and *Perrin v. United States*, both of which were to impact American legal history. *Wiggins* was largely consequential in understanding other cases, including *Perrin*. But *Perrin* has been cited in decisions making fundamental changes to how U.S. military damage to private property was compensated—or, ultimately, not. This included a case almost 150 years after Greytown's demise, when it played a key role in the aftermath of a major international incident that also involved a headline-grabbing presidential sex scandal.

On August 7, 1998, near-simultaneous terrorist attacks on the U.S. embassies in Kenya and Tanzania killed over 300 people. On August 20, President Bill Clinton—then embroiled in the Monica Lewinsky scandal—launched retaliatory cruise missile strikes against Al-Qaeda bases in Afghanistan and a pharmaceutical factory in Sudan called El-Shifa, which he claimed was making chemicals for terrorist weapons.

"A Party ... Destroyed 69 Cases and 2 Kegs of Powder"

Like Calvin Durand (see Chapter 17), none who suffered losses at the hands of Commander Hollins ever received reparations from the United States—except for a Boston company called Dexter, Harrington, & Co. It was first represented before the U.S. Senate by its consignee at Greytown, William H. De Forrest, and later in court by James S. Wiggins, presumably an owner of the company.[1]

Wiggins and the other company owners eventually received $6,000 in 1867 ($180,000 in 2022) in restitution from the federal government. This is in sharp contrast to the outcome of the other Greytown precedent case covered in this chapter, *Perrin v. United States*. In *Perrin*, a French couple who had lost around $13,500 ($400,000 in 2022) in destroyed merchandise during the razing received not a dime in indemnification from Washington.[2]

Two days after Commander Hollins destroyed Greytown, he noted in the *Cyane*'s log that he sent "a party [which] landed on Pt. Arenas and destroyed 69 cases and 2 kegs of powder." This was gunpowder that Dexter, Harrington & Co. owned, and Hollins had ordered it dumped into the harbor (see Chapter 6). "He believed," Senator James Mason later said, "that, if it were not destroyed, the people of Greytown would, by going there and exploding the powder [21,000 pounds of it], destroy the whole property of the Transit Company." These details were revealed during a Senate debate on March 2, 1855, concerning whether to authorize the Treasury to pay $12,000 ($360,000 in 2022) in restitution for the destroyed powder. The exchanges on the Senate floor were both heated and revealing, with some senators chary of paying for the destroyed powder, lest it set "a very dangerous precedent."[3]

By December 31, 1855, the Senate still had not acted on the matter. So, Senator William H. Seward raised the question again, presenting "the memorial of William H. De Forrest and others [including, presumably, Wiggins], praying compensation for property destroyed." Whereupon it was, "Ordered, that it be referred to the Court of Claims." When the Senate decided to foist this knotty problem on the U.S. Court of Claims, the focus there became whether the destruction of the gunpowder was covered under the Fifth Amendment clause stating, "Nor shall private property be taken for public use, without just compensation." (This is known as the "Takings Clause" and can include damage to or destruction of property.) In its decision, the *Wiggins* court cited another case, which grew out of the Civil War:

> We do not see how this case can be distinguished in principle from that of [William S.] *Grant v. United States*. There the property of a citizen, in one of the Territories of the United States, was destroyed to prevent it from falling into the hands of the insurrectionary forces. Judge [David] Wilmot [in the *Grant* case] reviews at length the grounds of the claim, and the authorities bearing upon the subject, and shows most clearly and conclusively that ... the party is entitled to compensation. ... We are entirely satisfied with the grounds there assumed, so far as they are applicable to the facts of this case [*Wiggins*], and can add nothing to the cogency or conclusiveness of the reasoning. Nor is it necessary to support it by further citations of authorities.[4]

For all of U.S. history under the Constitution and through the Civil War, such military applications of the Takings Clause of the Fifth Amendment were guided by the thinking of an 18th-century Swiss philosopher, diplomat, and legal scholar named Emer de Vattel (1714–1767). According to legal expert Charles Covell, Vattel wrote "one of the single most influential treatises in the history of modern international law," *The Law of Nations* (1758). Much of early American law was influenced by Vattel. For instance, said noted U.S. legal scholar Charles G. Fenwick, a case was decided in the Supreme Court in 1814 "in which the authority of Vattel was claimed by both the majority and the dissenting minority."[5]

Vattel's most important pronouncement regarding the impact of military events on private property will be considered here. When "damages [are] done by the state itself [to its own citizens' property] *deliberately and by way of precaution*, as, when a [citizen's] house … is taken for the purpose of erecting a … fortification, or when … his store-house [is] destroyed, to prevent [its] being of use to the enemy, [then] such damages are to be made good to the individual [i.e., the citizen is to be compensated for the loss]." On the other hand, when the damage inflicted by the state on its own citizens' property is "caused by *inevitable necessity*," as when the state's artillery destroys that property "in retaking a town from the enemy," Vattel regarded such events as "merely accidents—they are misfortunes which chance deals out … on whom they happen to fall." Consequently, for Vattel, state compensation is not required "*for misfortunes of this nature*—for losses which she has occasioned, *not willfully, but through necessity*" (emphasis added).[6]

As will be seen later, the reason why Wiggins got compensated and the Perrins did not is classic Vattel.

"To Seek a More Quiet Location in the Interior"

In May 1854, just two months before Greytown was destroyed, Frenchman Charles Augustus Trautmann-Perrin, arrived, followed by his wife, Marie Louise, about a month later. They intended to establish a "Commercial House" there, selling "Silks and other Dress Goods, Fancy Articles, Plated Jewelry, Embroideries, Mantillas, Laces, Shawls, Cassimeres, Cravats, Linen and Silk Handkerchiefs, and Sewing Silk, packed in eighteen large trunks." However, finding conditions at Greytown unsatisfactory, the couple decided "at once to seek a more quiet location in the interior [i.e., in Nicaragua] for the transaction of our business, and the establishment of our [commercial] house."

Trautmann-Perrin left Greytown in mid–June 1854 for western Nicaragua, only about a month after arriving, taking with him some sample goods "of the cost value of $1,500 in gold [$446,000 in 2022]." His wife "remained alone with the balance of the truly valuable stock which we had opened and offered for sale for the purpose of defraying our expenses."

Trautmann-Perrin successfully sold all his samples within 25 days "at a large profit and selected a most advantageous place of permanent residence in Nicaragua." While returning to his wife, he was "first informed on the river of the bombardment and burning of Greytown." He arrived to discover Marie Louise unharmed, but all their goods destroyed.[7]

The couple and other French victims immediately asked their government to seek redress from the U.S. government for their losses. An official French appeal was made, but not until January 1857, and then only to America's "sense of equity." The federal government rejected this. The Trautmann-Perrins had left Greytown soon after the razing, moving to Nicaragua as planned, where they opened a dry goods store with new stock, perhaps paid for with loans from friends and relatives. However, the store was destroyed in the following two years in the wars waged between the American filibuster William Walker (see Chapter 13) and the forces opposed to him. "In the general ruin," Trautmann-Perrin later wrote, "our last resources from France were in that convulsion irretrievably lost."

Where the couple went immediately after this *déjà vu* calamity is unknown, but by 1862 they were in Venezuela. In 1863, they moved to the United States, probably settling first in Boston (or certainly by 1865), where Trautmann-Perrin worked as a "teacher and translator of foreign languages." After five years in the country, it was in Boston on June 19, 1868, that the couple received their naturalization papers as U.S. citizens. It was at this time that they renewed their quest for indemnification, about which, more later. They moved to Philadelphia around 1871, where the husband advertised in the city directory for that year as an "accountant, translator, interpreter & teacher of modern languages." The couple had returned to Boston by 1876 and remained there until 1880.[8]

Sometime before or during 1868, and for reasons unclear, the Trautmann-Perrins became known as "Marie Louise Perrin" and her husband "Trautmann [or Trautman] Perrin." In the American city directories in which the husband advertised, he referred to himself simply by his hyphenated surname, "Trautmann-Perrin." Had he done the same in conversation, it is likely that Americans might have assumed, with the hyphen lost in the ether, that "Trautmann" was his given name. Eventually, the couple began referring to themselves by their new names in some—but not all—legal documents. (Henceforth in this narrative, they will for the most part be named as Trautmann and Marie Louise Perrin.) It was also by at least this year, 1868, that Marie Louise Perrin had become "a confirmed invalid," having developed "rheumatic affections" (most likely today's rheumatoid arthritis). Trautmann was desperate to get his wife out of Boston and to a warm climate to ease her suffering but did not have the wherewithal.[9]

19. "Too Valuable ... To Waive or Impair It"

In 1868, the Perrins petitioned Secretary of State William H. Seward, through Massachusetts Senator Charles Sumner, for reparations for their Greytown losses. Denying their appeal in his letter of reply to Sumner, Seward enunciated the core premise governing all such cases: "The principle affirmed is, that one who takes up a residence in a foreign place and there suffers an injury to his property by reason of belligerent acts committed against that place by another foreign nation, must abide the chances of the country in which he chose to reside; and his only claim, if any, is a personal one against the government" of the country where he took up residence.[10]

Curiously, in his rejection of the Perrins' plea, Seward added: "The only discrimination suggested in Mr. Perrin's case is on account of the very temporary nature of his sojourn at Greytown." As noted above, the couple were in Greytown for just two months, half of which Trautmann had spent looking for a place to move. So, had the Perrins "chose[n] to reside" in Greytown? Or were they just transients, passing through? Secretary of State Seward must have been aware that prominent legal thinkers, like the British scholar Travers Twiss, had addressed this very question. "If [a person] resides in a given territory permanently," wrote Twiss, "he is regarded as adhering to the Nation to which the territory belongs, and to be a member of the political body settled therein. If he is only resident in a given territory for temporary purposes, he is regarded as a stranger thereto."[11]

Seward continued that the transience of the Perrins' stay at Greytown "cannot affect the principle, which is too valuable *in the present circumstances of this country*, to allow us to waive or impair it" (emphasis added). This is an odd—and perhaps telling—turn of phrase. Why did Seward dismiss his own exemptive conditional ("very temporary nature") in favor of some timely expedient ("the present circumstances of this country")? What may have concerned him was that this case, as a precedent, might justify wholesale dismissals of certain kinds of Civil War damage suits, thus saving the federal treasury considerable amounts of money. While Seward seems not to have pursued this himself, others took up the cudgel, using the eventual *Perrin* case and other legal machinations to do just that.[12]

"The United States ... Were in Violation of the Laws of War"

After this setback with Seward in February 1868, "Marie Louise Perrin and Trautmann Perrin, her husband," filed a case later that year in the U.S. Court of Claims against the United States. (Uncommonly for the day, much of the litigation was named for the wife. She had been alone at Greytown when their losses occurred and, therefore, "the reclamation was subscribed in her own name.") One of their attorneys was W.W. Boyce, a former U.S. Congressman and Confederate Congressman from South Carolina who moved to Washington, D.C., after the Civil War, where he practiced law until the late 1880s. Amazingly, alongside Boyce, their primary lawyer was Caleb Cushing, the former attorney general on whose watch Greytown was razed.[13]

Citing *Wiggins*, Cushing and Boyce based their case first and foremost on the Takings Clause of the Fifth Amendment. This line of argument is incomprehensible. As noted, *Wiggins* was won because the property in question was destroyed deliberately and with premeditation "to prevent it from falling into the hands" of a public enemy. But the Perrins' property at Greytown was destroyed in an actual, direct hostile attack. In addition to this argument, and again incomprehensibly, Cushing and Boyce raised the argument that the leveling of Greytown was illegal. "We submit that the United States are liable ... [because] the bombardment and burning of Greytown were in violation of international law ... [and] in violation of the laws of war." Cushing must have known this would be dismissed out of hand as "a political question," which U.S. courts were loath to consider. Moreover, Cushing's declaration that the razing was a violation of law was supremely ironic, given that, as attorney general, he was the nation's chief law enforcement officer when the port was destroyed.[14]

"Which No Court of This Country ... Is ... Empowered to Decide"

Upon rendering its opinion, the Court did dismiss Cushing's argument that Greytown's destruction violated "the law of nations." It said this did, indeed, raise an international political question, "which no court of this country in a case of this kind is ... empowered to decide." As to the Takings Clause, the Court declared that the *Wiggins* case was different from *Perrin*. "[This] case, we think, bears no resemblance to that of ... *Wiggins* ... [where] the claim was for property of citizens taken by the United States and destroyed to prevent it falling into the hands of the public enemy. It was not destroyed in hostile operations against the public enemy, but for the purpose of preventing the aid and succor it would have afforded him if it had been permitted to fall into his hands."[15]

The Perrins appealed to the Supreme Court, which, in December 1870, simply affirmed the lower court's decision. In 1875, the Perrins submitted a request for relief to the Senate's Committee on Claims, but it was dismissed in 1876. In 1884, they tried a final appeal to the same committee. This, too, was rejected, ending their 30-year quest for indemnification.[16]

The *Perrin* court codified a long-established legal concept when it said: "No government, except as a special favor bestowed, has ever paid for the property of even its own citizens in its own country destroyed in attacking or defending against a common public enemy." (The court based this on Seward's "The principle affirmed..." statement in his Perrin denial letter.) This long-established legal concept, dating back even to Vattel, seems to have become part of U.S. precedential law by way of *Perrin*, allowing jurists to cite it in the future when dealing with similar cases.

In 1968, for instance, in *National Board of Young Men's Christian Ass'n v. United States*, the Court of Claims considered "whether the destruction of a YMCA building" in which American soldiers took cover from snipers during a 1964 Panamanian riot "constitute[d] a compensable taking." The Court dismissed the case, saying that "it is axiomatic that the fifth amendment is not suspended in wartime, but it is equally well recognized that a destruction of private property in battle or by enemy forces is not compensable." As the Supreme Court "declared long ago," the Court in *National Board* concluded, quoting *Perrin*, "no government ... has ever paid for the property ... destroyed in attacking or defending against a common public enemy."[17]

Used in 1868 and 1968, this same argument was applied again in *El-Shifa Pharmaceutical Industries Co. v. United States* (2003) when the owner of the Sudanese factory destroyed by President Clinton in 1998 sued for his losses. As noted, Clinton claimed the factory was making chemicals for terrorist weapons. He told the U.S. public on the night of his attacks that the targets were "terrorist-related facilities in Afghanistan and Sudan" associated with Osama bin Laden. The next day Clinton told Congress that El-Shifa was "a facility in Sudan being used to produce materials for chemical weapons." This was disputed almost immediately.

"Within days," the *New York Times* later reported, "Western engineers who had worked at the Sudan factory were asserting that it was, as the Sudanese claimed, a working pharmaceutical plant. Reporters visiting the ruined building saw bottles of medicine but no signs of security precautions and no obvious signs of a chemical weapons manufacturing operation." The same article also noted that Secretary of State Madeleine Albright and a senior deputy "encouraged State Department intelligence analysts to kill a report being drafted that said the bombing was not justified."[18]

El-Shifa's owner, Salah El Din Ahmed Mohammed Idris, filed suit on July 27, 2000, asking $50 million ($85 million in 2022) in damages in the

U.S. Court of Federal Claims; his original suit, decided in 2003, and its 2004 appeal are considered below.[19]

"A Nauseating 'Bounce' in the Opinion Polls"

Clinton's evidence against the El-Shifa factory is questioned to this day, with speculation continuing over a possible ulterior motive for the attack. With what a cynic might consider impeccable timing, the strikes came on the very day White House intern Monica Lewinsky completed her testimony before a grand jury investigating whether President Clinton had urged her to lie under oath about their affair. Just three days earlier, Clinton himself had appeared before the same grand jury, and had publicly admitted later that day to having had an inappropriate relationship with Lewinsky. According to CNN at the time, some members of Congress "suggested the attack could appear to be designed to divert attention from Clinton's personal problems."

In an article in *The Nation* on October 4, 2001, Christopher Hitchens wrote: "The bombing took place as Miss Lewinsky was returning to the grand jury and secured him [Clinton] a nauseating 'bounce' in the opinion polls." In 2005, the *New York Times* published the following: "American officials have acknowledged over the years that the evidence that prompted President Clinton to order the missile strike on the Shifa plant was not as solid as first portrayed. Indeed, officials later said that there was no proof that the plant had been manufacturing or storing nerve gas, as initially suspected by the Americans, or had been linked to Osama bin Laden."[20]

"An Allegation That the Attacks Were a 'Wag the Dog' Exercise"

About eight months before the El-Shifa factory was destroyed, a major U.S. motion picture entitled *Wag the Dog* was released, starring Dustin Hoffman and Robert De Niro. In it, a fictional president in the run-up to his bid for a second term is accused by a teenaged "Firefly Girl" of groping her during her scouting group's tour of the White House. In response, the president's political consultant enlists a Hollywood producer to fake a small war in a film studio to distract the public from the scandal for several days, until after the election. In a case of life imitating art, when the *El-Shifa* suit came to court, Idris's lawyers actually made reference to the film in their filing. The Court accused them of "none-too-subtle an allegation that the attacks were a 'Wag the Dog' exercise," with Idris' counsel countering that "the strikes ... were ordered to distract America from a breaking scandal involving the President's affair with a White House intern."[21]

According to attorney Ilana Tabacinic in her 2008 article "The Enemy-Property Doctrine: A Double Whammy?," the Court in the original *El-Shifa* case (decided in 2003) cited the *Perrin* case "at length." (The name "Perrin" appears in the decision 16 times.) The Court concluded: "Thus, the *Perrin* case, never overruled, qualified, or distinguished, would seem to end the matter. And we think it does." In her article, Tabacinic added that "following *Perrin*, the principle that the government is not responsible 'for injuries to or destruction of private property in necessary military operations during the Civil War, ... [was] thus considered established.' Later cases merely polished the contours of the doctrine." (One such later case, *United States v. Pacific Railroad* (1887), is the source of the above quote about "operations during the Civil War.")

Tabacinic continued that "compensation provided in prior cases was generally stated by the President to be 'a matter of bounty rather than of strict legal right.'" This principle will be addressed at some length here. This idea of "bounty" rather than "strict legal right," came from President Ulysses S. Grant and misrepresents the legal history of these matters and empowered Grant and subsequent parties to act as if the real history had never transpired.[22]

"Governments Do Not Admit a Legal Obligation"

As mentioned earlier, much of America's early judicial history was profoundly influenced by the Swiss thinker Emer de Vattel. Relevant here is his classic distinction, again, as noted earlier, between those "damages ... done by the state ... [to its own citizens' property] *deliberately and by way of precaution*, ... [which] are to be made good to the individual," and those "*caused by inevitable necessity*," which do not require compensation. The *Perrin* decision apparently obliterated this *deliberately cautionary* versus *inevitable necessity* distinction. In the words of Ilana Tabacinic: "The reluctance of courts to award compensation in cases following *Perrin* demonstrates that the earlier understanding of the doctrine as one providing for compensation became the exception rather than the default."

Or, as the U.S. Court of Appeals (Federal Circuit) put it in the 2004 appeal of the *El-Shifa* suit referenced above: "*Perrin* is a seminal case ... the first case in which the outlines of an enemy property doctrine applicable to takings jurisprudence can be recognized.... The Supreme Court applied enemy property doctrine to a number of military takings cases that followed *Perrin*." If, however, the Supreme Court did so, it apparently didn't refer to it as such. According to Tabacinic, "The Federal Circuit [in the 2004 *El-Shifa* appeal] created a new doctrine. The opinion is the first time a court refers to the existence of an enemy-property doctrine." And in his 2021 book *War*, Andrew Clapham writes: "The [2004 *El-Shifa*] litigation has drawn critical commentary due to the repeated reference [nine times] to an 'enemy property doctrine,' as if this were an established precedent."[23]

"It Is a Matter of Bounty Rather Than of Strict Legal Right"

Debate over the Vattel-inspired *deliberately cautionary* versus *inevitable necessity* distinction continued in Congress for 17 years following *Perrin*, from 1870 to 1887. The compensable, *deliberately cautionary* argument was defended by those Congress members who were convinced the nation's sense of equity and fair play required that it remain in place. In 1872, for instance, a bill was introduced to compensate Dr. J. Milton Best, a loyal citizen in the loyal state of Kentucky, for his Civil War loss. His house had been seized by Confederates for use as a snipers' nest, then recaptured by Union troops, and then destroyed by the latter *deliberately and by way of precaution* to deny the rebels the *possibility* of recapture. Dr. Best's property loss was a classic Vattelesque situation, crying out for compensation, and Congress voted for it—including one of Grant's fellow Republicans, Congressman and future President James A. Garfield, who stated the following:

> I know the history of this claim, and I do not much care how many others like it come before us. Sir, as an American citizen I should be proud the more we could find like this.... Dr. Best ... ought to have the best hearing the House of Representatives can give him, and I hope we shall pay this claim. I only fear that there are but few others in the country that can plead this as a precedent. I wish there were more, even if they cost the Treasury much.[24]

Dr. Best's supporters in Congress also included Senator Timothy O. Howe of Wisconsin, chairman of the Senate Committee on Claims and, like Grant, a Republican. As to this question of cost, he said: "He who regards law or loves justice will be reluctant to see a loyal citizen reduced by the deliberate act of his government to absolute destitution, and then turned away from the full tills of the treasury, which carry from year-to-year unused millions, a single year's interest on which would compensate for every injury coming within the principle of Mr. Best's claim."[25]

Yet, President Grant vetoed Congress' award to Dr. Best, writing the following.

> It is a general principle that all property is held subject not only to be taken by the Government for public uses, in which case, under the Constitution of the United States, the owner is entitled to just compensation, but also subject to be temporarily occupied, or even actually destroyed, in times of great public danger, and when the public safety demands it; *and in this latter case governments do not admit a legal obligation on their part to compensate the owner.* The temporary occupation of, injuries to, and destruction of property caused by actual and necessary military operations are generally considered to fall within the last-mentioned principle. *If a government makes compensation under such circumstances, it is a matter of bounty rather than of strict legal right* [emphasis added].[26]

In his Committee on Claims report, Senator Howe found that Dr. Best's was "*not* a case of the destruction of property by what is termed by law-writers [and Grant elsewhere in his veto] as 'the ravages of war.' This property was actually appropriated by the Government to public use two and a half years before it was really destroyed. All the necessary steps required by the laws of war for the appropriation of private property to public use were taken long prior to the destruction of the property. It was therefore a taking of private property for public use by the commanding officer of an army in the field—*a deliberate taking, and not the result of a conflict of armies*" (emphasis in the original).

Then Howe challenged Grant's assertion that as "a general principle ... all property is ... subject to be temporarily occupied, or even actually destroyed ... when the public safety demands it; and, in ... [that] case, governments do not admit a legal obligation." The committee, Howe asserted, "has not found any such general principle affirmed either in international or municipal law, but has found the very reverse of that to be affirmed by all law, international and municipal."[27]

To prove this point Howe then detailed six cases dating back to 1818 supporting this unanimous conclusion of the committee, which, by the way, consisted of six of Grant's fellow Republicans (including Howe) and just two Democrats. Of one of the cases, Howe wrote:

> In 1870 Congress passed an act to pay Otis N. Cutler $50,000 for cotton taken ... [by General Grant's order] to pack the machinery of the steamer *Tigress*, to enable her the more securely to run the rebel batteries at Vicksburg. The boat and the cotton were sunk on the trip.... That act [to pay Cutler] was approved by President Grant. The papers in the case show that he examined its merits while acting as Secretary of War, and that although he refused to pay the claim for want of authority, he pronounced it 'meritorious,' and referred the claim to Congress....

> To the foregoing precedents a great many might be added. Not a single case has been found in which Congress has denied the liability assumed in the precedents cited. Not a single authority has been found controverting the principle asserted ... by Vattel ... by the Court of Claims, and by the Supreme Court of the United States.[28]

Deconstructing Grant's veto even further, Howe countered the president's contention this payment would open the floodgates for similar "claims that may be made against the Government for necessary and unavoidable destruction of property by the Army." To this, Howe replied

> that the act passed for the relief of Dr. Best does not provide for the payment of property unavoidably destroyed. On the contrary, it clearly discriminates against and disclaims liability for such payment. The injury done to Best's house by firing upon it while in possession of the enemy was deemed to be unavoidable. For such injury the Committee on Claims held the Government was not obliged to make compensation. What the committee deemed to be the amount of such damages it deducted from the claim, and only reported for payment that which was supposed to be equal to the value of the property which was deliberately destroyed by the military authorities to promote the security of the [nearby] garrison.[29]

With its line-blurring, tortured prose, Grant's veto naysayed Vattel's precept of "damages ... done *deliberately and by way of precaution*," which, over the previous 21 years, had been used to find in favor of wronged citizens in one Supreme Court case, *Mitchell v. Harmony* (1851), and two Court of Claims cases *(William S.) Grant v. United States* (1863) and Greytown's *Wiggins v. United States* (1867). In 128 words, President Grant had nullified two decades of precedent, made a mockery of decisions by Congress and the highest echelons of the U.S. court system, and, finally, denied loyal citizens like Dr. Best the compensation they were due for Civil War damage—and he did all this without acknowledging he was doing any of it. It was an Orwellian manipulation of facts and events, 75 years before George Orwell would write, in his classic *1984*, "Every record has been ... falsified.... History has stopped."[30]

Howe's committee recommended that Congress compensate Dr. Best, "the objections of the President to the contrary notwithstanding." But the two-thirds majority needed to override Grant's veto could not be marshalled.[31]

Following the veto message, long-time Grant confidant and U.S. minister to France Elihu B. Washburne wrote to the president: "There is no act of your administration which has afforded me more satisfaction. I early saw a tendency among the loose Congressmen to sanction that extraordinary principle [of compensating loyal citizens for precautionary Civil War damages].... You will receive the gratitude of all loyal and patriotic men in the north for thus taking the bull by the horns and squelching the most dangerous assault ever made on the public treasury."[32]

Writing just two years earlier, Judge Charles C. Nott, Sr., future chief justice of the U.S. Court of Claims, noted that "in the great arrogance of great ignorance, our popular orators and writers have impressed upon the public mind the belief that in this republic of ours private rights receive unequalled protection from the Government." But the fact is, he continued, that "the legal redress given to a citizen of the United States against the United States is less than he can have against almost any government in Christendom. The mortifying fact is judicially established that the Government of the United States holds itself, of nearly all governments, the least amenable to the law."[33]

"The Nation as It Pieced Itself Back Together after the Civil War"

In a 2015 *Michigan Law Review* article entitled "Emergency Takings," Professor Brian Angelo Lee offered what might make an illuminating coda to all this. In referencing the *Pacific Railroad* case, he noted: "The Court itself quoted, with apparent approbation, Vattel's general assertion that compensation in fact is owed for property destruction 'done by the state deliberately and by way of precaution.' Thus, *Pacific Railroad* is properly understood not as stating a universal principle of non-compensation, but rather only a judgment tailored to the particular circumstances of the nation as it pieced itself back together after the Civil War." Lee's reference might make a fitting bookend to Secretary of State Seward's dismissing as unimportant the "temporary nature" of the Perrins' "sojourn" at Greytown. Perhaps Seward saw here a "principle" in the Perrins' situation that was "too valuable *in the present circumstances of this country*"—piecing itself back together after the Civil War—"to allow us to waive or impair it."[34]

Legal scholar Stephen I. Vladeck writes (emphasis in original): "Even though the *Pacific Railroad*'s suit did not even *raise* the question of whether the destruction of property in conjunction with active combat operations would give rise to a takings claim, Justice [Stephen Johnson] Field clearly stated, albeit in dicta, that it would not." (Dicta are observations of a judge that are not a part of the legal reasoning needed to decide a case. Although dicta may be cited in a legal argument, they are not binding as legal precedent.) Some 65 years later, Vladeck continues, the Supreme Court "expressly approved Justice Field's dicta in another case." This was *United States v. Caltex (Philippines), Inc.* (1952), in which the Court wrote,

"Whether or not the principle laid down by Mr. Justice Field [in *Pacific Railroad*] was dictum when he enunciated it, we hold that it is law today."[35]

The Supreme Court's decision in *Caltex* overturned a Claims Court's previous award of compensation to the plaintiff; the lower court calling *Pacific Railroad* "the chief reliance" of the government's defense, had written the following.

> Like *Mitchell v. Harmony*, and, indeed, all the authorities upon the point except the *Grant* and *Wiggins* cases, the language applicable to the instant case is dictum. And the dictum is contrary to the dictum in *Mitchell v. Harmony* and to the holdings [the legal principles to be drawn from the opinions] of the *Grant* and *Wiggins* cases....
>
> We are of the opinion ... that the reasoning of the *Grant* case, where the court necessarily met the very issue involved here and considered it fully, together with Chief Justice [Roger] Taney's dictum in *Mitchell v. Harmony*, present sounder precedents upon which to found our decision today than does the dictum of the *Pacific Railroad* case.[36]

Given its importance, it is worth examining the relevant dictum passage from Justice Field's decision in *Pacific Railroad*: "The Government cannot be charged for injuries to, or destruction of, private property caused by military operations of armies in the field, or measures taken for their safety or efficiency." As the Claims Court quote above suggests, Field's dictum disregards three precedent cases, including *Mitchell v. Harmony*. Take, for instance, Field's use of the word "efficiency." In finding for the property owner in *Mitchell*, Chief Justice Roger Taney wrote: "The property was seized [by the officer], not to defend his position, nor to place his troops in a *safer* one ... but to insure the *success* [or 'efficiency'] of a distant and hazardous expedition, upon which he was about to march" (emphasis added).[37]

By the time of the Supreme Court's decision in *Caltex*, it seems the metaphorical polishing of *Perrin*, to which Ilana Tabacinic refers in "The Enemy-Property Doctrine: A Double Whammy?," had finally relegated Vattel's *deliberately cautionary/inevitable necessity* distinction to the metaphorical dustbin of U.S. judicial history.

Chapter 20

Whither the Principals? An Epilogue

Henry Lawrence Kinney

Kinney was elected to the Texas state legislature after the sale of the Shepherd grant to the Mormons failed, but he opposed secession, and so resigned in March 1861. He then moved to Matamoros, Mexico, possibly to work on a newspaper owned by his brother, Somers. In 1861, 1862, or 1865, Col. Kinney was shot and killed in Matamoros, either as an innocent bystander hit by a stray bullet, or as a victim of a vengeful murder carried out under cover of factional chaos in that city, or as a targeted victim of one of the gangs involved in that factional chaos, or as a man on the amorous make, paying a "social call" at three a.m. who was "met by a gun instead of a girl." The most likely scenario is the last and took place in 1862 when he was about 48. (A variant of this last story is that he was looking for his common-law wife in an attempt to see the daughter they had had years before. Instead, he ran into her husband, words were exchanged, and gunfire erupted.)[1]

Joseph Livingston White

In 1861 White was shot and killed by a rival for a monopoly on Nicaraguan India (natural) rubber. His age at death is unknown, his birth year being uncertain. Here is the opening of the *New York Times* account of White's murder, published February 4, 1861. "Joseph White has been assassinated! A sad and mournful sentence that will blanch the cheek of many who only knew him as a friend and fall with crashing weight upon the hearts of loved ones who will never see him more!"[2]

Whether by chance or otherwise, White had wound up staying at the same hotel as a Canadian named Jonathan Gavitt. The latter was also in Nicaragua trying to secure the India rubber monopoly and thought White was trying to cut in. They passed the evening in quiet but unpleasant conversation, "swinging in their hammocks, under the piazza of the hotel." Then Gavitt ordered "a servant to bring him his revolver from an upper room." As White took his leave to retire for the night, Gavitt fired at him, hitting him in the leg, just below the knee, "shattering the limb dreadfully." A surgeon amputated White's leg, and he lived "in great pain" for seven days. He died around January 12, 1861. He was buried at El Realejo, Nicaragua. He left a wife and three children. At trial, Gavitt claimed he fired accidentally. And even though witnesses testified he had made death threats against White the day before, he was acquitted. (The *Detroit Free Press* said Gavitt was sentenced to a chain gang, implying he was found guilty.)[3]

Joseph Warren Fabens

In May 1857, barely two months after escaping indictment for violating the neutrality act, Fabens became involved in yet another adventure, this time not over land but what birds deposit upon it. He became an early applicant under the U.S. "Guano Islands Act of 18 October 1856." Guano, or seabird droppings, is an excellent fertilizer. American farmers were desperate for cheap reliable sources and Congress passed the Guano Islands Act to make it legal for U.S. entrepreneurs to "mine" guano-covered islands that no sovereign nation claimed. Washington facilitated this by the legal nicety of appurtenance, defined by Webster's in 1913 as "something annexed to another thing more worthy." (Ironically, this entry adds that "In a strict legal sense, land can never pass as an appurtenance to land.")[4]

Suffice it to say, disputes ensued, with nearby nations claiming that the islands "appertained" by the United States were theirs. This included Honduras in the case of the Swan Islands, which the U.S. awarded Fabens' company the right to exploit. Fabens and his partners "mined" guano on these islands under U.S. protection from 1858 until 1862, when they sold out to another U.S. company, the first of several which would continue the operation for more than forty years. The United States finally ceded the islands to Honduras in 1972, after having used them to prepare for the CIA's Bay of Pigs invasion of Cuba in 1961. In 1987, after the cession to Honduras, the CIA and other American governmental agencies reportedly had a covert training facility on the Swan Islands for Nicaraguan Contras.[5]

In another scheme, Fabens signed a sweetheart deal with President Buenaventura Baez of Santo Domingo (now the Dominican Republic), who commissioned Fabens to survey all the country's public lands—in return for one-fifth of all the lands he surveyed. Fabens formed companies based on this windfall and lobbied the U.S. hard to annex the country. In September 1869, Baez agreed to cede the whole country to the United States for $1.5 million ($44 million in 2022). A formal annexation treaty was signed on November 29, 1869, but it was defeated in the U.S. Senate. Early in 1873, Baez leased what could have been a U.S. naval base to yet another Fabens company, but Baez was overthrown soon after, and his successor canceled the concession. Fabens died two years later; he was about 54. In 1887 his widow published a book of his poetry. It was called *The Last Cigar and Other Poems*.[6]

Solon Borland

Borland returned to Little Rock, Arkansas, in October 1854, resumed his medical practice, opened a pharmacy with a partner and went back to being a newspaper editor. He declined a nomination from President Pierce to be governor of the New Mexico Territory. He remained active in local politics, switching his allegiance from the Democratic Party to the new, anti-immigrant, anti–Catholic, pro-slavery, and semi-secret American Party (nicknamed the "Know-Nothings" because when members were asked about the party, they were supposed to reply, "I know nothing").

At the start of the Civil War, Borland was appointed as a commander of the Arkansas state militia. While in his command position for the Northern Arkansas Militia, he ordered an embargo of goods to end price speculation, but the governor rescinded his decision. Borland protested that a governor could not countermand an order from a Confederate official. Still, in January 1862, his order was overturned by the Confederate States Secretary of War Judah P. Benjamin. In declining health and resenting that slight, Borland resigned from further service to the Confederacy in June 1862, moving to Dallas County, Arkansas. He died in 1864; he was 53.[7]

Ephraim George Squier

In 1853, as noted in Chapter 1, Squier returned to Central America as a private citizen to explore Nicaragua some more and examine a route for a projected interoceanic railroad through Honduras. In 1858, at age 37, he married Miriam Florence Folline, a 22-year-old former actress. About 1860, he became editor-in-chief for Frank Leslie's publishing house, including *Frank Leslie's Illustrated Newspaper,* one of the most popular publications of its time. In 1863 Squier was appointed as U.S. commissioner to Peru, where he studied Inca ruins.

In 1873, his wife, who had become the editor of Leslie's magazine for women, divorced him and married Leslie. According to the wife's biographer, "less than a month after the Leslie wedding—an inquisition taken at the New York City Courthouse found that [Squier] ... 'was a lunatic, not having lucid intervals, so that he was incapable of the government of himself or of the management of his goods and chattels.' On application by his brother Frank, E.G. had been ordered to an asylum for the insane." He recovered somewhat but was never able again to do original work. He died in 1888, aged 66.[8]

George Nichols Hollins

Despite Secretary Dobbin's assurance, noted earlier, that Hollins still retained the navy's "unimpaired" confidence, he did not receive another sea command for six years, despite lobbying hard for one. In March 1855, for instance, about eight months after Greytown, Hollins wrote to his friend, the influential U.S. Navy captain, Samuel Francis Du Pont, "In one of your ... talks, with [Navy Secretary] Dobbin, find out if he will let me have a ship, I have no home. I want to show Englishmen I can get a ship ... any ship, to show the world the Dept. has confidence in me. Now I do think the Navy Dept. owes it to itself to stand by me in an open, above board way, 'face the music,' give me a ship, I feel a little sore and nothing but being sent to sea will heal it."

Du Pont may not have been the best man for Hollins to enlist in this quest. Just four weeks after the Greytown affair, Du Pont had written to a friend, "What the end will be I know not—a greater nest of pirates and freebooters never existed, but whether it was worthwhile to be so fierce with them may be questioned."[9]

Hollins did, however, receive two shore appointments in these interim years. One of them was in a backwater known as Sacket's Harbor, in upstate New York, which, he found "suits me exactly. No officers, and no men, and as a matter of course no Government work, a first-rate house and garden, sufficient for all purposes." He lived there with his children by his first wife, by then deceased, and with his second wife, the sister of his first wife. His only complaint about his life at Sacket's Harbor was the abolitionist preacher he found there. "A fellow got preaching in our church ... abusing the South. I walked out of the church but came back that night and stood up and gave him a quar[ter]deck sermon, not only him but the elders of the church for permitting such a man to preach, and I stuck to it until they turned him out or got rid of him. We have now a very clever man [who] leaves the 'niggers' outside of his sermons."[10]

Hollins finally got another sea command on July 24, 1860, six years and 13 days after he razed Greytown. This was the frigate USS *Susquehanna*, which he took on a patrol of the Mediterranean. Upon arriving back at Boston in early June 1861, he promptly resigned from the U.S. Navy. According to the *New York Times*, the Navy Department did not accept his resignation (perhaps anticipating his defection to the Confederacy) but struck his name "from the Navy list." Soon after, Hollins made his way south and joined the Confederate Navy.

Barely in the rebel navy more than a few weeks, Hollins achieved the South's first naval victory of the Civil War, on June 29, 1861, when he seized a U.S. commercial vessel on Chesapeake Bay. Hollins and another rebel naval officer disguised themselves as a married couple—history dithers over who was in drag—and boarded this passenger steamer, called the *St. Nicholas*. They and some compatriots, also disguised as passengers, seized control of the sidewheeler. The idea was to use this ship to get close to and then seize a Union warship called the USS *Pawnee* before the crew got wise to the ruse. But the plan fell through.[11]

Less than a month later, Hollins was put in charge of the naval defenses of New Orleans and the Mississippi River. In October he drove off Union blockaders at the mouth of the Mississippi with the iron-clad ram *Manassas* and a rag-tag flotilla of six armed riverboats nicknamed the "mosquito fleet." The victory was spectacular and humiliating for the Union. But it was unsustainable against the North's superior forces, which returned and overwhelmed the Confederate naval forces, by-passed their forts, and took New Orleans in April 1862. The newspapers, North and South, were full of stories about "Hollins's Ram," and he was regaled as a hero in the Confederacy. But later he supposedly had disagreements with the Confederate Secretary of the Navy and was recalled to Richmond.[12]

After the war he became a crier in the city court of Baltimore, that is, a court officer who makes proclamations like the opening and adjourning of court, the swearing of witnesses, etc. He died in Baltimore in 1878. He was 78.[13]

Daniel Fletcher Webster

After the Shepherd grant debacle, Fletcher returned to his federal job as surveyor for the port of Boston (which he held from 1850 to 1861) and edited a volume of his father's letters in 1857.

Early in the Civil War, Fletcher raised a regiment, the 12th Massachusetts Volunteer Infantry, which he led, including into the Second Battle of Bull Run on August 30, 1862. On that morning, Webster wrote his wife, "If a fight comes off, it will be to-day or to-morrow & will be a most dreadful & decisive one. This may be my last letter, dear love, for I shall not spare myself." He was mortally wounded and captured. His body was returned to Union lines. Fletcher Webster lay in state at Boston's famed Faneuil Hall, and he was buried at the family estate in Marshfield, Massachusetts.

"The value which his friends had for him," wrote Boston lawyer and author George Stillman Hillard, "was higher than the mark which he made upon his times. The course of his life had not in all respects been favorable to his growth and influence, and he had not the iron resolution and robust purpose which make will triumph over circumstance. But when the golden opportunity came, he grasped it with heroic hand. He rose to the height of the demand made upon him, and dormant powers and reserved energies started into vigorous life as the occasion required them." Hillard ended his memorial with, "Colonel Webster left a widow and three children, two sons and a daughter. His eldest son has since died."[14]

Webster's eldest son, Daniel, who, at 15, it will be remembered, accompanied Kinney to Greytown (see Chapter 12), served in the Union army, survived the war, and died, age 25, in 1865, in Massachusetts. The state records attribute his death to "Consumption," that is, tuberculosis. While many newspapers noted his passing without comment, a few indulged in this unabashed violation of the old adage, never speak ill of the dead: "The young man had led a dissolute life and was hopelessly wrecked in health and character."[15]

Sidney Webster

After Pierce left office, Sidney went into a law partnership with Caleb Cushing, Pierce's attorney general and the man rumored to be most responsible for the move against the Kinney expedition. Sidney, as noted, had had a financial interest in the Kinney scheme, by way of the deed-of-transfer bribe (see Chapter 11). In 1858, Sidney was made a federal court commissioner (like the commissioner who presided over the Fabens 1857 proceedings). In a letter, Caleb Cushing boasted of having secured the post for Webster.[16]

In 1860, Sidney married Sarah Morris Fish, a daughter of Senator Hamilton Fish. According to the *New York Times*, when Fish became President Grant's secretary of state "he often sought his son-in-law's advice on delicate political matters." (In 1873, when Fish savaged the land grant articles in the Dallas-Clarendon *projet* treaty [see Chapter 14], he must have known his son-in-law had owned about two million acres of the Shepherd land grant 19 years before.) Reportedly, Sidney received $40,000 a year ($1.1 million in 2022) "as the attorney for Spain [practicing] before his august father-in-law." (In 1907, a sniping columnist for the *Brooklyn Daily Eagle* opined that "having married into the Fish family, he didn't have to exert himself in his profession.") After the Civil War, Webster practiced law in New York for 20 years, and "his advice was particularly sought on matters of constitutional law, on which he was regarded as an authority." According to *Harvard Graduates' Magazine*, Sidney Webster's "law firm, Webster & Craig, had the reputation of receiving the first $1,000,000 fee [$30 million in 2022] in the history of the legal practice."[17]

In 1883 he became involved with railroads and was said to have mentored Edward H. Harriman, who became a giant in the industry and a major contributor to the Republican Party. "It was to Mr. Webster," the *New York Times* noted, "that Mr. Harriman wrote his celebrated 'Where do I stand?' letter in January 1906, which was leaked to the press and revealed that Mr. Harriman had accelerated the collection of a $200,000 ($6 million in 2022) campaign fund to assist the Republican Party in the Presidential campaign of 1904." Harriman charged in his letter, according to the *Times*, that "certain alleged promises on behalf of the Administration which were the quid pro quo for the contributions had not been kept. Mr. Webster's reply was never published."[18]

In 1892, Sidney Webster authored a short book about the Pierce administration. In it, he referred to the razing of Greytown as a "naval episode which … effectually disposed" of the port. He described filibusterism as "one of those fits of epidemic insanity, which from time to time seize on the desperate and reckless." And he added that "President Pierce did not fail to repress and to cause to be prosecuted all such persons and their enterprises." And yet, in this book, Webster doesn't raise, even to dismiss, the accusations made against Pierce and himself in the 1857 court case or mention that he once had a pecuniary interest in the Shepherd grant filibuster.[19] Sidney Webster died in 1910; he was 82.

Charles Augustus and Marie Louise Trautmann-Perrin

In 1880 Trautmann applied, at Boston, for a passport for him and his wife. He probably hoped to relocate to a tropical climate where the year-round warmth might ease his wife's debilitating "rheumatic affections." (See Chapter 19.) Instead of leaving the country, however, they moved to

Charleston, South Carolina—just in time to make the 1880 federal census there. "Chas. A. Trautmann-Perrin" is listed as an accountant. Under the "sickness or disability" category, "Marie L." has "Rheum., Chr." written next to her name. And under the category, "Maimed, Crippled, Bedridden or otherwise disabled," there is a mark. A considerable effort was made to discover their ultimate fate, but no trace of them after 1884 was found.[20]

Samuel Smith Wood

Much of what follows is from two sources, an excellent 1960 paper by Robert Seager, II, in the *Yale University Library Gazette* and a collection of Samuel Smith Wood's papers, which Yale holds.

Wood's fortunes never recovered from the razing. His losses in real estate and merchandise at Greytown totaled $55,000 ($1.6 million in 2022), a financial blow that seriously undermined his credit rating in New York. By early July 1855, Wood had to admit to his sons Alexander and Samuel that "I have had to go as poor people do [to] beg for goods credit." Only by mortgaging the family furniture was Wood able to buy $420 worth of merchandise ($12,500 in 2022) for shipment to Greytown. Compounding this problem was the continued animosity toward the transit company, which Wood and his son blamed for Greytown's ruination. Alexander told his father on October 13, 1854, that he was "not disposed to submit to any abuse from any member of the Co[mpany].... [R]ather than toady and succumb to them I will go home." On top of this were the disruptions caused by the ongoing Nicaraguan civil war, which began that same year. Then, in 1855, when the American filibuster, William Walker, took control of Nicaragua the Woods were forced to supply him goods, whether he had the wherewithal to pay or not—and, increasingly, as his fortunes waned, he did not. "It was," according to historian Robert Seager, "a question of doing business with Walker or doing little business in Walker's Nicaragua." Kinney was no better and, eventually, according to Seager, Walker would stiff the Woods for $2,200 ($66,000 in 2022) and Kinney, $9,000 ($269,000 in 2022). Here is an excerpt from a letter the elder Wood sent to his son, Alexander, dated September 5, 1855: "Inclosed you will find Kinneys draft protested. Mr. Wright showed me other drafts protested on New Orleans to the amount of $5,000 now you see in what credit Col. Kinney stands here don't take any more drafts from him sell for cash alone these drafts. ... he augt to pay the expense when I first presented the draft on the 6 augt he said know [sic] doubt it would be paid as soon as he saw a friend or two."[21]

"By November 1855," wrote Seager, "the family financial position was

20. Whither the Principals? An Epilogue

so desperate that Mrs. Wood took in borders and opened a small bakery in her home." On April 8, 1856, Sam Wood, who was in Washington, pleaded with his son, Alexander, in Greytown, to send enough funds for personal expenses to enable him to continue pressing the Wood bombardment claims in Washington. "You must send me some funds to enable be [me?] to work for us and pay my expenses.... I know from experience your longing for home. You must arrange our affairs there now yourself who is most competent to do so and It would be idle for me there ... and tis of vast importance for me to be here during sessions of Congress, so says the members to me. I am doing everything I can for our good."[22]

Walker was defeated and driven from Nicaragua in May 1857, giving Sam Wood hope a return of normality on the isthmus would again bring some modicum of prosperity for him and other merchants. But on an 1857 trip from Greytown to New York, via Aspinwall at the Isthmus of Panama, Alexander learned that "the Panama transit had forged far ahead of Greytown and the Nicaraguan route during the chaotic Walker period." The Walker-inflamed civil war wasn't the only reason for this. (Interestingly, the Nicaraguan transit remained largely unmolested during the war until near the end.) More important was the successful completion, in 1855, of an efficient railroad across the Panama isthmus, shortening the land transit there from several days to four-and-a-half hours. This provided a now superior alternative to the Nicaraguan isthmus route.[23]

On reaching New York in September, Alexander found more bad news to report to his father. The Panic of 1857 was in full progress. (Like the Panic of 1837, this one was bad enough to have its name capitalized, too.) "Business almost at a stand[still?]," he wrote his father on October 7. "Banks and companies and individuals are failing daily and upon every side—confidence is gone—and no one knows where it will all end."[24]

"Lacking funds, merchandise, and shipping facilities, and dunned by creditors," wrote Robert Seager, "Wood finally gave up in disgust and returned to New York."[25]

The only hope remaining was congressional compensation for the "memorialists" who suffered losses in the razing. And, as noted, that did not happen.

Meanwhile Greytown Harbor filled with silt. On July 26, 1859, a fellow memorialist (see Chapter 7), W.P. Kirkland, informed Wood that "the entire river, from Greytown to the Colorado, is filling up—at the same rate, of the present filling, in less than two years, *bingos* [read: *bungos*] cannot reach this port.... We are now without hope of either Canal or Transit with a certainty of poverty—all of which are the evil fruits of the Old Transit Company's policy and Mr. Pierce's credulity." Finally, on November 17, Kirkland reported that property in the town was selling for

15 percent of its cost and that the population was swiftly melting away. "Greytown," noted Seager, "had become a ghost town." And the fight for reparations got bogged down in "a snowstorm of legal depositions, collected by the Greytown Board of Commissioners." Their "arguing that the Accessory Transit Company had maliciously produced the bombardment by misrepresenting the peaceful and cooperative nature of the Greytowners failed to stir the Congress." And a letter-writing campaign by Wood to New York newspapers, "re-counting anew the story of the bombardment, failed also to agitate public sentiment for payment of the claims."[26]

"Thus," Seager concluded his piece on Wood, "the Greytown claims died a quiet death in the maelstrom of the approaching Civil War." (The Greytown memorialists also suspended their efforts during the war, feeling it inappropriate to be competing with the widows and fatherless children of the war dead for congressional funds.)

When the war began, Seager noted:

> Wood opened a small shop at 450 Pennsylvania Avenue. There he sold flags, patriotic notions, and general merchandise while waiting for the restitution from the United States that never came. He unsuccessfully sought appointment as a secret service agent from Abraham Lincoln, pointing out to the President in an undated letter that Washington was full of traitors and spies. "I have brought some new silk American flags for sale here to enable me to make enough to pay my Expenses," he informed Lincoln. "I could detect Traitors by their bitterness against the Stripes and Stars." On that bizarre note, Samuel S. Wood fades from history.[27]

* *   * *   * *

Chapter Notes

Preface

1. Will Soper, "Revisiting Nineteenth-century U.S. Interventionism in Central America: Capitalism, Intrigue, and the Obliteration of Greytown." *American Nineteenth Century History* 18, no. 1 (2017), 19–44, https://doi.org/10.1080/14664658.2017.1319633.

2. William O. Scroggs, *Filibusters and Financiers: The Story of William Walker and His Associates* (New York: Macmillan, 1916), 102, https://hdl.handle.net/2027/mdp.39015005233559?urlappend=%3Bseq=122%3Bownerid=13510798890071585-126; *New York Tribune*, July 28, 1854.

3. Will Soper, "Can an Amateur Historian Rewrite History?" History News Network, https://historynewsnetwork.org/article/170070. (See also a reprint in Chapter 18.)

4. Stephen Dycus, William C. Banks, Peter Raven-Hansen and Stephen I. Vladeck, *National Security Law,* 7th Edition (New York: Wolters Kluwer, 2020), 372.

Chapter 1

1. E.G. Squier, "Nicaragua, an Exploration from Ocean to Ocean," *Harper's New Monthly Magazine* 11, no. 65 (October 1855, Part 1), 582, https://hdl.handle.net/2027/hvd.hnybh2?urlappend=%3Bseq=596%3Bownerid=27021597768254339-602.

2. *Ibid.*

3. William F. Boone, *W. F. Boone to William L. Marcy, June 7, 1854.* Letter (see page four). *Despatches from United States Consuls in San Juan Del Norte, Nicaragua, 1851–1906* (United States: Department of State, National Archives and Records Service, 21 microfilm reels), OCLC Number: 145079238, Reel 1. Boone was posted only briefly to Greytown in 1852. He wrote this to Marcy in 1854, volunteering his opinion about the "recent difficulties" there.

4. David I. Folkman, *The Nicaragua Route* (Salt Lake City: University of Utah Press, 1972), 50–51.

5. Quoted in the *New York Times*, August 15, 1854.

6. *New York Herald*, March 16, 1850.

7. *Burlington* (VT) *Free Press*, February 12, 1852, reprinted *New York Tribune* article datelined February 7.

8. *New York Times*, July 26, 1853.

9. Charles Wyke to Lord Clarendon, November 27, 1853, in James Woods, "Expansionism as Diplomacy: The Career of Solon Borland in Central America 1853–1854," *The Americas: Quarterly Review of Inter-American Cultural History* 40, no. 3 (January 1984), 408; *ibid.*, 409–410; William R. Manning, ed., *Diplomatic Correspondence of the United States: Inter-American Affairs, Vol. 4, Central America, 1851–1860* (Washington: Carnegie Endowment for International Peace, 1934), 387, https://hdl.handle.net/2027/txu.059172149398109?urlappend=%3Bseq=441%3Bownerid=13510798887257568-461.

10. *Message of the President of the United States Communicating, in Compliance with a Resolution of the Senate, the Correspondence Between the Department of State and the Minister of Bremen, on the Subject of Claims for Losses Alleged to Have Been Sustained by Subjects of the Hanse Towns at the Bombardment of Greytown*, 35th Cong., 1st sess., S., Ex. Doc. No. 10. Senate Docu-

ments, Volume 112. (U.S. Government Printing Office, 1858), 8, https://hdl.handle.net/2027/ucl.b3984741?urlappend=%3Bseq=676%3Bownerid=9007199276160643-834. Wiedemann gave the victim's first name here as "Albino," as did some others. But "Antonio" is much more frequently used and so was substituted here and will be used hereafter; *New York Tribune*, August 16, 1854.

11. *Correspondence Between ... Department of State and the Minister of Bremen*, 8, https://hdl.handle.net/2027/ucl.b3984741?urlappend=%3Bseq=676%3Bownerid=9007199276160643-834; *New York Times*, August 5, 1854, reprinted Millar's letter, which first appeared in the *New York Post*, August 4.

12. *Correspondence Between ... Department of State and the Minister of Bremen*, 8, https://hdl.handle.net/2027/ucl.b3984741?urlappend=%3Bseq=676%3Bownerid=9007199276160643-834; *New York Times*, August 5, 1854.

13. *Correspondence Between ... Department of State and the Minister of Bremen*, 12, https://hdl.handle.net/2027/ucl.b3984741?urlappend=%3Bseq=680%3Bownerid=9007199276160643-838; *New York Tribune*, August 5, 1854; *Correspondence Between ... Department of State and the Minister of Bremen*, 12.

14. Squier, "Nicaragua, an Exploration from Ocean to Ocean," *Harper's*, 582, https://hdl.handle.net/2027/hvd.hnybh2?urlappend=%3Bseq=596%3Bownerid=27021597768254339-602. Squier gives Antonio's surname here as "Paladan"; all other sources say it was "Paladino," so the latter is used here and everywhere else.

15. *Correspondence Between ... Department of State and the Minister of Bremen*, 8–9, https://hdl.handle.net/2027/ucl.b3984741?urlappend=%3Bseq=676%3Bownerid=9007199276160643-834; *New York Times*, August 5, 1854, reprinted Millar's *New York Post* letter of August 4; *New York Tribune*, August 3, 1854, reprinted correspondence in the *Boston Atlas*, July 28, 1854; *New York Herald*, May 30, 1854; *New York Tribune*, August 5, 1854.

16. *New York Tribune*, August 15, 1854, reprinted Wiley's letter, dated August 10, which first appeared in the *New York Post*, n.d.

17. "San Juan De Nicaragua," *Harper's New Monthly Magazine*, 10, no. 55 (December 1854), 56, https://hdl.handle.net/2027/hvd.hnybh1?urlappend=%3Bseq=68%3Bownerid=27021597768256921-72.

18. Manning, *Diplomatic Correspondence*, 4:328, https://hdl.handle.net/2027/txu.059172149398109?urlappend=%3Bseq=382%3Bownerid=1351079888725 7568-402.

19. Samuel S. Wood and William P. Kirkland, *A Memorial to the Congress of the United States, on Behalf of the Sufferers from the Bombardment and Destruction of Greytown, or San Juan Del Norte, by the U.S. Sloop-of-war Cyane, on the 13th July, A.D. 1854; and Narrative of Events Which Transpired at That Place Between the Years 1852 and 1854* (New York: J.A. Gray, 1859), 16, https://hdl.handle.net/2027/loc.ark:/13960/t4dn4zd2m?urlappend=%3Bseq=18. (This a slightly different version of the pamphlet cited elsewhere entitled, *The Greytown and Nicaragua Transit Company Controversy*. It is also dated 1859.)

20. *New York Tribune*, August 3, 1854.

21. Wood and Kirkland, *A Memorial ... of the Sufferers ... of Greytown* (1859), 37, https://hdl.handle.net/2027/loc.ark:/13960/t4dn4zd2m?urlappend=%3Bseq=39.

22. Ibid.

23. *New York Times*, May 26, 1854; Wood and Kirkland, *A Memorial ... of the Sufferers ... of Greytown* (1859), 36, https://hdl.handle.net/2027/loc.ark:/13960/t4dn4zd2m?urlappend=%3Bseq=38; *New York Tribune*, August 15, 1854.

24. Wood and Kirkland, *A Memorial ... of the Sufferers ... of Greytown* (1859), 36.

25. Ibid., 36–37.

26. John Bigelow, *Breaches of Anglo-American Treaties: A Study in History and Diplomacy* (New York: Sturgis & Walton Company, 1917), 51, https://hdl.handle.net/2027/hvd.hx4h21?urlappend=%3Bseq=63%3Bownerid=27021597768403678-71.

27. The once-powerful Hanseatic League of city-states in northern Germany was reduced to just three members by the mid–1850s. As noted earlier, one of the murder witnesses aboard the *Routh*, Henri Wiedemann, was the league's consul at Greytown, specifically serving as the consul for Hamburg and Bremen.

28. Louis N. Feipel, "The Navy and Fili-

bustering in the Fifties, Part III: The Bombardment of Greytown, Nicaragua, 1854," *United States Naval Institute Proceedings* 44, no. 6, Whole No. 184 (June 1918), 1222, https://hdl.handle.net/2027/chi.42906954?urlappend=%3Bseq=1292%3Bownerid=13510798903444908-1338; *ibid.*, 1222–3. Both of the agreements referred to were temporary, pending a formalization of Greytown's status in an upcoming Anglo-American treaty. That treaty eventually called for Greytown's return to Nicaragua, but Nicaragua rejected the treaty. As the little port's strategic significance and commercial potential beguiled more Americans, this possibility seemed increasingly remote. See, for instance, Senator Edward Everett's comments in Chapter 4.

29. *New York Times*, July 29, 1854.

30. Converting mid-19th century dollar amounts to "today's" equivalents is critical to understanding this story. But statistics for such conversions didn't become reliable until 1913. So, a 1913-to-2022 calculation was used here to represent 1850s dollars in 2022. Because the 19th C. suffered from bouts of deflation as well as inflation, using 1913 as a base results in only about a ten percent lower figure than if using the less reliable 1850s figures. These 1913-to-2022 conversions were made in 2021 with a free, convenient "calculator" on the site of the Federal Reserve Bank of Minneapolis, https://www.minneapolisfed.org/about-us/monetary-policy/inflation-calculator, which had the estimates for 2022 up on their site by at least August of 2022. The Bureau of Labor Statistics' Consumer Price Index Inflation Calculator gives more up-to-date figures, but the difference is negligible, https://www.bls.gov/data/inflation_calculator.htm. *New York Tribune*, August 26, 1854.

31. *New York Tribune*, August 2, 1854; Wood and Kirkland, *A Memorial … of the Sufferers … of Greytown* (1859), 14, https://hdl.handle.net/2027/loc.ark:/13960/t4dn4zd2m?urlappend=%3Bseq=16.

32. *Correspondence Between … Department of State and the Minister of Bremen*, 9, https://hdl.handle.net/2027/ucl.b3984741?urlappend=%3Bseq=677%3Bownerid=9007199276160643-835; Wood and Kirkland, *A Memorial … of the Sufferers … of Greytown* (1859), 38, https://hdl.handle.net/2027/loc.ark:/13960/t4dn4zd2m?urlappend=%3Bseq=40.

33. *New York Tribune*, August 3, 1854, 3; *New York Times*, August 5, 1854.

34. *New York Tribune*, August 3, 1854.

35. *New York Times*, August 5, 1854.

36. *Message from the President of the United States Communicating, in Compliance with a Resolution of the Senate, Information Respecting the Bombardment of San Juan de Nicaragua*. 33rd Cong., 1st sess. S. Exec. Doc. 85, serial 702, 4, https://hdl.handle.net/2027/ucl.b3984526?urlappend=%3Bseq=540%3Bownerid=9007199276160944-584; *New York Times*, May 26, 1854.

37. *New York Tribune*, August 2, 1854.

38. Joseph W. Fabens to William L. Marcy, June 16, 1854, *Information Respecting the Bombardment of San Juan de Nicaragua*, 17, https://hdl.handle.net/2027/ucl.b3984526?urlappend=%3Bseq=553%3Bownerid=9007199276160944-597.

39. Solon Borland to William L. Marcy, May 30, 1854, *ibid..*, 3–4, https://hdl.handle.net/2027/ucl.b3984526?urlappend=%3Bseq=539%3Bownerid=9007199276160944-583.

Chapter 2

1. J.B. Lockey, "Diplomatic Futility," *The Hispanic American Historical Review* 10, no. 3 (August 1930): 265, https://www.jstor.org/stable/2506375.

2. E.G. Squier to Francis Parkman, March 20, 1849, typescript from Parkman Papers at Massachusetts Historical Society, quoted in Sharon Hartman Strom, "'If Success Depends Upon Enterprise': Central America, U.S. Foreign Policy, and Race in the Travel Narratives of E.G. Squier," *Diplomatic History* 35, no. 3 (June 2011): 413; Terry A. Barnhart, *Ephraim George Squier and the Development of American Anthropology* (Lincoln: University of Nebraska Press, 2005), 154; Strom, "'If Success Depends Upon Enterprise,'" 413; Barnhart, *Squier and … American Anthropology*, 149.

3. William R. Manning, ed., *Diplomatic Correspondence of the United States: Inter-American Affairs*, vol. 3, *Central America, 1831–1850* (Washington, DC: Carnegie Endowment for International Peace, 1933), 38, https://hdl.handle.net/

2027/uva.x030346174?urlappend=%3Bseq=72%3Bownerid=27021597765709020-76.

4. *Ibid.*, 50.

5. "American Atlantic and Pacific Ship Canal Company: Charter and Act of Incorporation of the American Atlantic & Pacific Ship Canal Company, as amended," (New York: Wm. C. Bryant, 1852), 5–9, https://iiif.lib.harvard.edu/manifests/view/drs:7411823$1i; Manning, *Diplomatic Correspondence*, 3: 364–65, https://hdl.handle.net/2027/uva.x030346174?urlappend=%3Bseq=408%3Bownerid=27021597765709020-414.

6. Squier to Clayton, May 8, 1850, Mary Wilhelmine Williams, E. George Squier, and John M. Clayton, "Letters of E. George Squier to John M. Clayton, 1849–1850," *The Hispanic American Historical Review* 1, no. 4 (1918): 430; *ibid.*, 429, https://www.jstor.org/stable/2505893.

7. T.J. Stiles, *The First Tycoon: The Epic Life of Cornelius Vanderbilt* (New York: Knopf, 2009), 179; *ibid.*, 179–80.

8. Barnhart, *Squier and … American Anthropology*, 151; "San Juan De Nicaragua," *Harper's New Monthly Magazine* 10, no. 55, December 1854, 51, https://hdl.handle.net/2027/hvd.hnybh1?urlappend=%3Bseq=63%3Bownerid=27021597768256921-67; John Bigelow, *Breaches of Anglo-American Treaties*, 51, https://books.google.com/books?id=l-YrAQAAIAAJ&newbks=1&newbks_redir=0&printsec=frontcover&pg=PR3&dq=Breaches+of+Anglo-American+Treaties+A+Study+in+History+and+Diplomacy+Bigelow+OR+Google&hl=en#v=snippet&q=%22the%20Indian%20King%20as%20sovereign%20over%2.

9. "San Juan de Nicaragua," *Harper's*, 51; Mary Wilhelmine Williams, *Anglo-American Isthmian Diplomacy 1815–1915* (Washington: American Historical Association, 1916), 80, https://hdl.handle.net/2027/mdp.39015001695215?urlappend=%3Bseq=100%3Bownerid=13510798891368862-104; Kenneth Bourne, *Britain and the Balance of Power in North America: 1815–1908* (London: Longmans, 1967), 177.

10. Ephraim George Squier, *Travels in Central America, Particularly in Nicaragua: With a Description of Its Aboriginal Monuments, Scenery and People, Their Languages, Institutions, Religion, &C.*, vol. 1 (New York: D. Appleton & Company, 1853), 85–88, https://hdl.handle.net/2027/umn.31951002321630q?urlappend=%3Bseq=119%3Bownerid=13510798903081448-123.

11. *Ibid.*, 87.

12. Christie to Palmerston, May 15, 1849, The National Archives of Great Britain (acronym TNA), F.O. 53/45, 61–95; Richard W. Van Alstyne, "The Central American Policy of Lord Palmerston, 1846–1848," *The Hispanic American Historical Review* 16 (1935–36): 343–44; *ibid.*, 344, https://www.jstor.org/stable/2507558; TNA FO 53/46 Mosquito Land Grant Claim, 5; Squier, *Travels in Central America*, 1:88, https://hdl.handle.net/2027/umn.31951002321630q?urlappend=%3Bseq=122%3Bownerid=13510798903081448-126.

Chapter 3

1. Arthur D. Howden Smith, *Commodore Vanderbilt: An Epic of American Achievement* (New York: McBride, 1927), 164, as quoted in Jay Sexton, *Debtor Diplomacy: Finance and American Foreign Relations in the Civil War Era, 1837–1873* (Oxford: Clarendon Press, 2005), 66; William R. Manning, ed., *Diplomatic Correspondence of the United States, Inter-American Affairs 1831–1860*, vol. 7, *Great Britain, 1831–1860* (Washington: Carnegie Endowment for International Peace, 1936), 333, https://hdl.handle.net/2027/uva.x002447434?urlappend=%3Bseq=371%3Bownerid=27021597765709459-375.

2. Sexton, *Debtor Diplomacy*, 65.

3. Baring Brothers to Thomas W. Ward, October 15, 1850, reel 63: Letterbook, April 1848 to April 1851, Baring Brothers Archive, Manuscript Division, Library of Congress, as quoted in T.J. Stiles, *The First Tycoon: The Epic Life of Cornelius Vanderbilt* (New York: Alfred A. Knopf, 2009), 191.

4. *Ibid.*; *London Times*, October 15, 16, 1850, as quoted in Stiles, *The First Tycoon*, 191.

5. Sexton, *Debtor Diplomacy*, 67; *New York Herald*, November 16, 1850.

6. Charter of … the … Ship Canal Company, 22, https://iiif.lib.harvard.edu/manifests/view/drs:7411823$1i; John M. Clayton and Henry Lytton Bulwer, "The Clayton-Bulwer Treaty," *The Advocate of Peace* (1894–1920) 62, no. 3 (March 1900),

66–67, http://www.jstor.org/stable/25751541; Crampton to Everett (Inclosure) in letter Crampton to Russell, February 13, 1853, The National Archives of the United Kingdom (acronym TNA), *British and Foreign State Papers* vol. 42, 1852–53, 174–75, https://babel.hathitrust.org/cgi/pt?id=hvd.hjl35v&view=image&seq=206; *ibid*.

7. Manning, *Diplomatic Correspondence*, 4:235, https://hdl.handle.net/2027/txu.059172149398109?urlappend=%3Bseq=289%3Bownerid=13510798887257568-299.

8. Charles H. Brown, *Agents of Manifest Destiny: The Lives and Times of the Filibusters* (Chapel Hill, 1980), 260; Scroggs, *Filibusters and Financiers*, 83, https://hdl.handle.net/2027/mdp.39015005233559?urlappend=%3Bseq=103%3Bownerid=13510798890071585-107. Scroggs, probably for convenience's sake, used the word "presidents" here, when, in fact, until 1854, all Nicaragua's leaders were called either Head of State or Supreme Director; Wyke to Clarendon, Guatemala City, July 29, 1855, F.O. 15/85, No. 38, quoted in Richmond F. Brown, "Charles Lennox Wyke and the Clayton-Bulwer Formula in Central America, 1852–1860," *The Americas* 47, no. 4 (April 1991): 430, https://doi.org/10.2307/1006684.

9. Charter of … the … Ship Canal, 4–5, 25, 27–28, https://iiif.lib.harvard.edu/manifests/view/drs:7411823$1i; David I. Folkman, *The Nicaragua Route* (Salt Lake City: University of Utah Press, 1972), 73.

Chapter 4

1. Manning, *Diplomatic Correspondence*, 3:334, https://hdl.handle.net/2027/mdp.39015074697460?urlappend=%3Bseq=380%3Bownerid=1351079889258 1512-420; *ibid*., 337.

2. *New York Herald*, November 10, 1853.

3. G.P.R. James to Lord Clarendon, December 11, 1854, The National Archives of the United Kingdom (acronym TNA), FO 5/602, 407–08.

4. Dr. James Green to Lord Clarendon, July 4, 1853, FO 53/46, Mosquito Land Grant Claims, 166-7 (TNA); Henry Grant-Foote to Lord Clarendon, June 4, 1853, FO 53/46 C328465 (TNA); Henry Grant-Foote to Lord Clarendon, June 16, 1853, FO 53/46 C328465 (TNA).

5. "Passengers Sailed list for the May 5, 1853, *Star of the West's* New York departure," *New York Times*, May 6, 1853: J.G. Bryce and D. Keeling, https://www.sfgenealogy.org/californiabound/cb242.htm; "New York Passenger Lists, 1820–1891," FamilySearch, *Northern Light* arrival from San Juan del Norte, June 24, 1853, Image 198, Line 9, J.G. Bryce, https://www.familysearch.org/ark:/61903/3:1:-939V-5N73-C?i=197&wc=MX62-XP8% 3A165774901&cc=1849782; "New York Passenger Lists, 1820–1891," FamilySearch, *Prometheus* arrival at New York, June 9, 1853, from San Juan del Norte (Greytown): Image 259, Line 5, Loomis L. White, Line 6, D.F. Keeling, https://www.familysearch.org/ark:/61903/3:1:939V-5KS7-G6?i=258&cc=1849782&personaUrl=%2Fark%3A%2F61903%2F1%3A1%3A275N-QKT.

6. *New York Tribune*, August 29, 1854. Bryce is not mentioned by name in this article, but, from other sources, it is clearly him; Samuel S. Wood and William P. Kirkland, *The Greytown and Nicaragua Transit Company Controversy* (New York: John A. Grey, 1859), 27; *ibid*. 27–28, https://hdl.handle.net/2027/ien.35556043846179?urlappend=%3Bseq=27. (This is a slightly different version of the pamphlet cited elsewhere, entitled: *a Memorial to the Congress of the United States, on Behalf of the Sufferers from the Bombardment and Destruction of Greytown*. It is also dated 1859.)

7. Webster to Graham, March 18, 1852. British Foreign Office, *Correspondence with the United States Respecting Central America, 1849–56*. (London: Harrison, 1856), 141–42, https://hdl.handle.net/2027/nnc1.cu01564889?urlappend=%3Bseq=157%3Bownerid=270215977689 61117-181.

8. Manning, *Diplomatic Correspondence* 4:298, https://hdl.handle.net/2027/txu.059172149398109?urlappend=%3Bseq=352%3Bownerid=13510798887257568-372. Archived copy undated, but probably sent in July of 1852.

9. Karl Bermann, *Under the Big Stick: Nicaragua and the United States Since 1848* (Boston: South End Press, 1986), 35.

10. Manning, *Diplomatic Correspondence*, 4:298–99, https://hdl.handle.net/2027/txu.059172149398109?urlappend

=%3Bseq=352%3Bownerid=13510798887257568-372.

11. Malmesbury to Crampton, July 16, 1852, British Foreign Office. *Correspondence ... Respecting Central America, 1849–56,* 176, https://hdl.handle.net/2027/nnc1.cu01564889?urlappend=%3Bseq=192%3Bownerid=27021597768961117-216; Russell to Crampton, January 19, 1853 (No. 141.), 202–04, https://hdl.handle.net/2027/nnc1.cu01564889?urlappend=%3Bseq=218%3Bownerid=27021597768961117-242.

12. *Message from the President of the United States Communicating a Report from the Secretary of State, Embodying the Substance of Recent Communications from the British Minister on the Subject of the Inter-Oceanic Canal, by the Nicaragua Route, February 19, 1853,* 32d Congress, 2d Session, Senate, Ex. Doc. No. 44, 1, serial 665, page 5, https://hdl.handle.net/2027/uc1.b3983603?urlappend=%3Bseq=185%3Bownerid=9007199276158887-189; *ibid.,* page 1, https://hdl.handle.net/2027/uc1.b3983603?urlappend=%3Bseq=181.

13. Crampton to Russell, February 21, 1853, British Foreign Office, *Correspondence ... Respecting Central America, 1849–56,* 218, https://hdl.handle.net/2027/nnc1.cu01564889?urlappend=%3Bseq=234%3Bownerid=27021597768961117-258.

14. *Appendix to the Congressional Globe,* March 21, 1853, 32nd Cong., 3d sess. Senate, Special Session—Clayton-Bulwer Treaty, 284–90, https://hdl.handle.net/2027/hvd.32044103136669?urlappend=%3Bseq=302%3Bownerid=27021597764568840-320; *New York Times,* October 16, 1855.

15. Marcy to Ingersoll, June 9, 1853, Manning, *Diplomatic Correspondence,* 7:83–84, https://hdl.handle.net/2027/mdp.39015074697353?urlappend=%3Bseq=125%3Bownerid=13510798892612374-129.

16. Marcy to Borland, June 17, 1853, Manning, *Diplomatic Correspondence,* 4:42, https://hdl.handle.net/2027/txu.059172149398109?urlappend=%3Bseq=96%3Bownerid=13510798887257568-102.

17. *Ibid.*

18. *New York Herald,* November 10, 1853.

19. "San Juan," *Harper's New Monthly Magazine,* December 1854, 50, https://hdl.handle.net/2027/hvd.hnybh1?urlappend=%3Bseq=62%3Bownerid=27021597768256921-66.

20. Alpheus Spring Packard, Jr., "Cross-Fertilization," *The New International Encyclopedia,* vol. 5 (New York: Dodd, Mead, 1905), 614, https://books.google.com/books?id=m4NRAAAAYAAJ&q=The+mixture+of+the+European+races#v=snippet&q=The%20mixture%20of%20the%20European%20races&f=false. (Excerpted from the passage beginning, "The mixture of the European races" and ending with "and the results not harmful.")

21. *New York Times,* January 30, 1857.

22. *New York Times,* January 5, 1854.

23. A.K. McClure, *Old Time Notes of Pennsylvania,* vol. 1 (Philadelphia: The John C. Winston Company, 1905), 181–82, https://hdl.handle.net/2027/pst.000064033426?urlappend=%3Bseq=249%3Bownerid=27021597770128732-257. (For an excellent summary of Cooper's confrontation with Morton McMichael, editor of the *Philadelphia North American and United States Gazette,* see the *New York Tribune,* September 27, 1854; for the exchange of letters involved, see the *Semi-Weekly Courier and New-York Enquirer,* September 30, 1854.)

24. *Richmond Dispatch,* November 27, 1854. James Shields is the only person to be a U.S. Senator from three different states: Illinois (1849–1855); Minnesota (1858–1859); and Missouri (1879–1879).

25. *New York Times,* January 12, 1854; Mayorga to Marcoleta, February 19, 1854, Manning, *Diplomatic Correspondence,* 4:389, https://hdl.handle.net/2027/txu.059172149398109?urlappend=%3Bseq=443%3Bownerid=13510798887257568-463.

26. Marcoleta to Marcy, March 20, 1854, Manning, *Diplomatic Correspondence,* 4:389–91.

27. *Ibid.,* 408, https://hdl.handle.net/2027/txu.059172149398109?urlappend=%3Bseq=462%3Bownerid=13510798887257568-492.

28. *Ibid.,* 408–09.

29. *New York Herald,* November 17, 1854; Marcoleta to Marcy, November 22, 1854, Manning, *Diplomatic Correspondence:* 4:425–427, https://hdl.handle.net/2027/txu.059172149398109?urlappend=%3Bseq=479%3Bownerid=13510798887257568-509.

30. Marcoleta to Marcy, November 22, 1854, 426; Marcy to Marcoleta, November

30, 1854, 65–66, https://hdl.handle.net/2027/txu.059172149398109?urlappend=%3Bseq=119%3Bownerid=13510798887257568-125.

31. *New York Herald,* November 17, 1854.

32. *New York Times,* December 15, 1854.

33. The Editors of Encyclopaedia Britannica, "Filibustering," *Encyclopedia Britannica,* March 22, 2018, https://www.britannica.com/topic/filibustering; Albert K. Weinberg, *Manifest Destiny: A Study of Nationalist Expansionism in American History* (Baltimore: Johns Hopkins Press, 1935), 210; "Frank Pierce and Major-General Scott," *The United States Democratic Review* 31, October 1852, 300, https://hdl.handle.net/2027/coo.31924080777406?urlappend=%3Bseq=324; "Annexation," *The United States Magazine, and Democratic Review* 17 no. 85, July and August, 1845, 5, https://hdl.handle.net/2027/mdp.39015018403736?urlappend=%3Bseq=17%3Bownerid=13510798886850569-21; Lexico, Powered by Oxford, https://www.lexico.com/en/definition/manifest_destiny.

Chapter 5

1. *Message from the President of the United States, Communicating Reports in Relation to the Condition of Affairs in Central America, May 15, 1856,* U.S. Congressional Serial Set, Volume 858 (U.S. Government Printing Office, 1856), House Of Representatives, 34th Congress, 1st sess., Ex. Doc. No. 103, 63, https://hdl.handle.net/2027/ucl.b3984619?urlappend=%3Bseq=639%3Bownerid=9007199276160931-853.

2. *Message from the President of the United States, Communicating, in Compliance with a Resolution of the Senate, Information in Relation to the Transactions Between Captain Hollins, of the United States Ship* Cyane, *and the Authorities at San Juan De Nicaragua, December 20, 1853,* 10–13, 33rd Congress, 1st. sess., Senate. Executive, Doc. No. 8, https://hdl.handle.net/2027/ucl.b3984518?urlappend=%3Bseq=536. What appears on pages 10 through 13 of this document is the after-report by the *Cyane's* captain, George Hollins, on the events that the narrative will now cover. Most relevant here is his description of the first ejectment. This he describes, among other things, as destroying multiple buildings when another account said it was two, while most give it as involving only one. Moreover, and more confusingly, one of the buildings (or *the* building) destroyed apparently did not even belong to the ATC but to a nonaffiliated American named George W. McCerren. Greytown residents would later describe him as a "keeper of a boarding-house" who erected this building on Punta Arenas outside the area leased by the ATC, and "without the consent or authority of the local government … and refused to pay the usual license as paid by all other hotels and bar-rooms in the town." For simplicity's sake, the incident will hereafter be said to have involved one building, without reference to ownership. (See Wood, *The Greytown and Nicaragua Transit Company Controversy,* 6, https://hdl.handle.net/2027/ien.35556043846179?urlappend=%3Bseq=6.)

3. *New York Herald,* April 1, 1853. Any naval officer who commands a ship is addressed by naval custom as "captain" while aboard in command, regardless of actual rank. Hollins' official rank was commander, a senior officer rank, above lieutenant commander but below captain.

4. Ibid.

5. Ibid.

6. Ibid.

7. *Transactions Between Captain Hollins … and the Authorities at San Juan de Nicaragua,* 11–12, https://hdl.handle.net/2027/ucl.b3984518?urlappend=%3Bseq=537; *New York Herald,* April 1, 1853.

8. *New York Herald,* April 1, 1853.

9. *Transactions Between Captain Hollins … and the Authorities at San Juan De Nicaragua,* 11, https://hdl.handle.net/2027/ucl.b3984518?urlappend=%3Bseq=557.

10. *New York Herald,* April 1, 1853; Albany (NY) *Argus,* April 2, 1853.

11. Albany (NY) *Argus,* April 2, 1853; *Transactions Between Captain Hollins … and the Authorities at San Juan de Nicaragua,* 39, https://hdl.handle.net/2027/ucl.b3984518?urlappend=%3Bseq=585.

12. Wood, *A Memorial … on Behalf of the Sufferers … of Greytown,* 39, https://hdl.handle.net/2027/loc.ark:/13960/t4dn4zd2m?urlappend=%3Bseq=41.

13. Clarendon to Crampton, July 22, 1853, British Foreign Office, *Correspondence ... Respecting Central America, 1849–56*, 256, https://hdl.handle.net/2027/nnc1.cu01564889?urlappend=%3Bseq=272%3Bownerid=27021597768961117-322.

14. *Ibid.*, 258.

15. Marcy to White, August 9, 1853, *Department of State, Domestic Letters (Sep 1, 1852–Sep 29, 1853)* 41 (NARA Record Group 59, M40).

16. Crampton to Clarendon, August 22, 1853, as quoted in James J. and P. Patience Barnes, *Private and Confidential: Letters from British Ministers in Washington to the Foreign Secretaries in London, 1844–67* (Selinsgrove, PA: Susquehanna University Press, 1993), 80–81.

17. *New York Tribune*, August 3, 1854.

18. *Information Respecting the Bombardment of San Juan de Nicaragua*, 9, https://hdl.handle.net/2027/ucl.b3984526?urlappend=%3Bseq=545.

19. *New York Herald*, February 28, 1857.

20. Henry A. Wise to George Booker, June 16, 1854 (letter pages 3 & 4), George Booker Collection (RLT Bay 107, items 1–43 c.1), David M. Rubenstein Rare Book & Manuscript Library, Duke University. If history remembers Henry Wise at all it is from five years later when, as Virginia governor, he could have commuted John Brown's death sentence for the Harper's Ferry raid but chose not to.

21. *New York Tribune*, August 9, 1854.

Chapter 6

1. James C. Dobbin to George N. Hollins, June 10, 1854, *Information Respecting the Bombardment of San Juan de Nicaragua*, 21, https://hdl.handle.net/2027/ucl.b3984526?urlappend=%3Bseq=557; *New York Times*, February 28, 1857. On September 8, 1855, the *Pittsburgh Gazette* reprinted an article from the *New York Commercial Gazette* which carried a version of this letter including the sentence: "The latter [meaning Hollins] is all right." The *Commercial Gazette* implied that this meant Hollins "was made 'all right,'" i.e., that he was let in on the plot to destroy the port for commercial reasons and agreed to go along. On September 7, *Buffalo* [NY] *Commercial* carried the same version of the letter, with that sentence italicized.

2. *Information Respecting the Bombardment of San Juan de Nicaragua*, 23–24, https://hdl.handle.net/2027/ucl.b3984526?urlappend=%3Bseq=559.

3. *Ibid.*, 25–26, https://hdl.handle.net/2027/ucl.b3984526?urlappend=%3Bseq=561; Barnes, *Private and Confidential: Letters from British Ministers*, 107; *Correspondence Between ... Department of State and the Minister of Bremen*, 12, https://hdl.handle.net/2027/uc2.ark:/13960/t3125sm8z?urlappend=%3Bseq=14. (Here, Bremen minister Henri Wiedemann is stating in January 1855 that "the then existing government of San Juan handed in their resignation of authority to the English consul, and was thus dissolved."); *Information Respecting the Bombardment of San Juan de Nicaragua*, 18, https://hdl.handle.net/2027/ucl.b3984526?urlappend=%3Bseq=554.

4. *British and Foreign State Papers*, vol. 46 (Great Britain: H.M. Stationery Office, 1865), 880–81, https://hdl.handle.net/2027/ucl.c037896647?urlappend=%3Bseq=928%3Bownerid=116013559-934. On August 30, 1854, about six weeks after Greytown's razing, the *New York Times* published a letter it entitled "An Apology for Commander Hollins," signed FIAT JUSTITIA." ("Let Justice Be Done.") The author wrote that Hollins' "not doubly equal" phrase "has been distorted into the ebullition of a braggadocio—he simply meant to convey the idea that the presence of a force twofold that of his own would have furnished a valid excuse for neglecting or declining to carry out the infamous instructions, and so saved his beloved country the disgrace of the ordered bombardment." The author went on to say that "this is written without the knowledge of Commander Hollins, but you may rest assured it reflects his true sentiments."

5. *Nashville Union and American*, August 4, 1854, reprinted from the *New York Herald*, n.d.

6. *Ibid.*

7. W.D. Jolley, *Log of HMS Bermuda, July 1—Dec. 6, 1854.* Records of HM Ships, ADM 54—Admiralty: Supplementary Ships' Logs, ADM 54/28—*BERMUDA*, July 1—Dec. 6, 1854, The National Archives of the United Kingdom (acronym TNA),

July 13, 1854; "The Destruction of Greytown," *The Illustrated London News*, 16, August 19, 1854, 151.

8. *Information Respecting the Bombardment of San Juan de Nicaragua*, 29, https://hdl.handle.net/2027/uc1.b3984526?urlappend=%3Bseq=565.

9. Alexander McCready Wood, *Alexander Wood to Samuel Smith Wood, July 15, 1854*, Letter. *Samuel Smith Wood Papers (MS 1083)*, Manuscripts and Archives, Yale University Library, (Jan-Jul, 1854), 13, https://archives.yale.edu/repositories/12/resources/3990. This URL is to the home page of the Wood Papers. According to the Public Services Department at the Manuscripts and Archives Division of the Yale University Library, the library cannot "provide a url ... for direct access to download the files in the Samuel Smith Wood Papers." However, the library "would instruct anyone who would like access the [digitized] files to register [with the library, at mssa.assist@yale.edu] and agree to our user terms, and we would then send the files to them."

10. *Wood Family Pedigree* (1906 typescript), Samuel Smith Wood Papers, Yale University Library, ("Wood Family Pedigree," 1906), 11–12.

11. George N. Hollins, *Log of the USS Cyane: Mar. 1, 1853–Sept. 6, 1854* (Washington: National Archives and Records Service, Records of the Bureau of Naval Personnel, Record Group 24, General Service, General Service Administration, 1970. OCLC Number: 19465127.), July 15, 1854.

12. *New York Times*, July 25, 1854.

13. *New York Times*, July 31, 1854.

14. Henry A. Wise, *Henry Wise to George Booker, August 14, 1854*, Letter. Nineteenth Century Southern Political Leaders, Series A: Holdings of the Virginia Historical Society, William L. Barney, editor, Reel 44, Series III, 0719. The Mosquito grant scheme was sometimes called the "Cooper Project" because, as noted, a sitting senator named James Cooper (Whig-PA) was president of the grant-holding company (see Chapter 3); Henry A. Wise, *Henry Wise to George Booker, June 21, 1856*, Letter.

15. Manning, *Diplomatic Correspondence*, 7:107, https://hdl.handle.net/2027/uva.x002447434?urlappend=%3Bseq=145%3Bownerid=27021597765709459-149; ibid.., 109, https://hdl.handle.net/2027/uva.x002447434?urlappend=%3Bseq=147%3Bownerid=27021597765709459-151; James Buchanan and John Bassett Moore, ed., *The Works of James Buchanan, Comprising His Speeches, State Papers, and Private Correspondence 1853–1855*, vol. 9 (Philadelphia & London, 1908–1911), 242, https://hdl.handle.net/2027/mdp.39015009282529?urlappend=%3Bseq=264%3Bownerid=13510798889828142-270.

16. Manning, *Diplomatic Correspondence*, 7:578–79, https://hdl.handle.net/2027/uva.x002447434?urlappend=%3Bseq=617%3Bownerid=27021597765709459-628.

17. *New York Tribune*, August 29, 1854. (This article was written only six weeks after the razing. It names as culpable three men against whom no direct evidence was found during the course of this research: Attorney General Caleb Cushing, Navy Secretary James Dobbin, and John W. Forney, clerk of the House of Representatives.)

Chapter 7

1. *New York Tribune*, August 8, 1854; *Natchez Weekly Courier*, April 7, 1847; *New York Tribune*, August 8, 1854.

2. *Loudon* (TN) *Free Press*, August 23, 1854.

3. *New York Times*, July 29, 1854; *ibid.*, August 1, 1854.

4. *New York Times*, August 1, 1854, "Greytown Again."

5. *Ibid.*; *ibid.*, "The Revelation and Responsibility"; *ibid.*, "Greytown Again."

6. *The Liberator*, August 11, 1854.

7. Ibid.

8. Ibid.

9. *Nashville Tennessean*, October 4, 1854. While often called "The Lay of San Juan," (a lay being a narrative poem), it doesn't seem original to this event, although its ultimate origins couldn't be traced.

10. "His Labor Done. Grove L. Johnson Closes His Speech," *The San Francisco Morning Call*, September 18, 1894, 8. (See middle of second column, referencing "the Storming of Greytown" and quoting two lines of the poem); *Alexandria* (VA) *Gazette*, November 2, 1891. When two

American sailors were killed resisting police in Valparaíso, Chile, President Benjamin Harrison said he would resign if reparations were not demanded. "A Repetition of ... the Bombardment of Greytown Is Not Desired," the paper stated, and then reprinted the poem. (See first column, near bottom.)

11. *New York Tribune,* August 10, 1854; Library of Congress, "About New-York Tribune," *Chronicling America,* https://chroniclingamerica.loc.gov/lccn/sn83030214/.

12. *New York Tribune,* August 10, 1854.

13. *Ibid.*

14. *Ibid.*; Russell to Crampton, January 19, 1853 (No. 141 & 142), British Foreign Office. *Correspondence ... Respecting Central America, 1849–56,* 204, https://hdl.handle.net/2027/nnc1.cu01564889?urlappend=%3Bseq=220%3Bownerid=27021597768961117-244; *New York Tribune,* August 10, 1854.

15. Marcoleta to Marcy, July 28, 1854, Manning, *Diplomatic Correspondence,* 4:413, https://hdl.handle.net/2027/txu.059172149398109?urlappend=%3Bseq=467%3Bownerid=13510798887257568-497.

16. Wood, *The Greytown and Nicaragua Transit Company Controversy,* 27–28, https://hdl.handle.net/2027/ien.3555604384617 9?urlappend=%3Bseq=27; *New York Tribune,* August 29, 1854; Marcoleta to Marcy, May, 4, 1854, Manning, *Diplomatic Correspondence ,* 4:408, https://hdl.handle.net/2027/txu.059172149398109?urlappend=%3Bseq=462%3Bownerid=13510798887257568-492.

Chapter 8

1. Ward, "Physical Courage, Moral Cowardice Found in Kinney," *Corpus Christi Caller-Times,* January 18, 1959, 1-G. Hortense Warner Ward (1898–1977) received two Rockefeller Foundation grants to research Kinney for a biography that never materialized; Edwin Oscar Gale, *Reminiscences of Early Chicago and Vicinity* (Chicago: Fleming H. Revell, 1902), 161–162, https://books.google.com/books?newbks=1&newbks_redir=0&id=ER4VAAAAYAAJ&q=pearson#v=snippet&q=Pearson%2C%20who&f=false; Hubert Howe Bancroft, *The Works of Hubert Howe Bancroft,* vol. 35, *California Inter Pocula* (British Columbia: History Company, 1888), 406, https://books.google.com/books?id=esVQAQAAIAAJ&q=Hiram+pearson#v=snippet&q=Hiram&f=false.

2. Ward, "Physical Courage, Moral Cowardice Found in Kinney," 1-G & 2-G.

3. Henry S. Beebe, *The History of Peru* (Peru, Illinois: J.F. Linton, Printer and Publisher, 1858), 156–57. http://www.gutenberg.org/files/36524/36524-h/36524-h.htm; Coleman McCampbell, "H.L. Kinney and Daniel Webster in Illinois in the 1830's," *Journal of the Illinois State Historical Society (1908–1984)* 47, no. 1 (Spring 1954): 36, http://www.jstor.org/stable/40189348; *Transactions of the Illinois State Historical Society for the Year 1904* (United States: Illinois State Historical Society, 1904): 441n, https://archive.org/stream/transactionsofil1904illi#page/441/mode/1up; McCampbell, "Kinney and Webster in Illinois": 36; Beebe, *The History of Peru,* 156–57.

4. Daniel Webster, Fletcher Webster, *The Private Correspondence of Daniel Webster,* vol. 2 (Boston: Little, Brown, and Co., 1857), 21, https://hdl.handle.net/2027/uc2.ark:/13960/t8qb9xc3x?urlappend=%3Bseq=31; McCampbell, "Kinney and Webster in Illinois," 37, quoting from "A Rambler in the West," by anon, 136, which was reprinted in Mitchell S. Augustus, *Illinois in 1837* (Philadelphia: S. Augustus Mitchell, Grigg & Elliot, 1837), https://hdl.handle.net/2027/pst.000020056759?urlappend=%3Bseq=142%3Bownerid=13510798902984881-162. Fletcher's first name was also Daniel, but he went by this, his middle name.

5. McCampbell, "Kinney and Webster in Illinois," 37.

6. *Pittsburg Gazette,* September 22, 1837, reprinted from the *Hennepin* (IL) *Journal,* n.d.

7. Howard Louis Conrad, *Nathaniel J. Brown: Biographical Sketch and Reminiscences of a Noted Pioneer* (Chicago: Byron S. Palmer Printing Co., 1892), 15, https://books.google.com/books?id=9eFYAAAAMAAJ&q=young+lady#v=snippet&q=lady%20herself&f=false.

8. Ward, "Physical Courage, Moral Cowardice Found in Kinney," 2-G; Beebe, *The History of Peru,* 157.

9. McCampbell, "Kinney and Webster in Illinois," 44.
10. Ibid.
11. Claude Moore Fuess, *The Life of Caleb Cushing*, vol. 2 (New York: Harcourt, Brace and Company, 1923), 92–93, https://hdl.handle.net/2027/mdp.39015026645823?urlappend=%3Bseq=120%3Bownerid=13510798882304480-124.
12. Joseph Milton Nance, *After San Jacinto: The Texas-Mexican Frontier, 1836–1841* (University of Texas Press, 2011), 406.
13. Tracy Moorman, "The Abduction of Philip Dimitt, Did Kinney Mark Patriot for Death?" *Corpus Christi Caller-Times*, January 18, 1959, 91.
14. Ibid.
15. Carlyn Osborn, "The Changing Mexico-U.S. Border," Worlds Revealed: Geography & Maps at the Library of Congress, December 18, 2015, https://blogs.loc.gov/maps/2015/12/the-changing-mexico-u-s-border/.
16. Darwin Payne, "Camp Life in the Army of Occupation: Corpus Christi, July 1845 to March 1846." *The Southwestern Historical Quarterly* 73, no. 3 (1970): 327, http://www.jstor.org/stable/30238071; Richard H. Wilson, "The Eighth Regiment of Infantry," (New York: Maynard, Merrill & Co. 1891), 513, https://history.army.mil/books/R&H/R&H-8IN.htm; Bartee Haile, "Corpus Christi Founder Was a World-Class Scoundrel," *The Courier* (of Montgomery County, Texas), September 7, 2012, https://www.yourconroenews.com/neighborhood/moco/opinion/article/Corpus-Christi-founder-was-a-world-class-scoundrel-9267261.php.
17. Sean Cunningham, "The Most Bizarre Presidential Scandals," Esquire, July 16, 2008, https://www.esquire.com/news-politics/news/a4846/bizarre-scandals-0808/.
18. "William Rufus King, 13th Vice President (1853)," United States Senate, https://www.senate.gov/about/officers-staff/vice-president/VP_William_R_King.htm. King, Pierce's vice president, died of tuberculosis shortly after taking the oath of office. Pierce spent his entire term without a vice president. There is some circumstantial evidence that King and James Buchanan were lovers. See: Thomas Balcerski, "The 175-Year History of Speculating About President James Buchanan's Bachelorhood. Was His Close Friendship with William Rufus King Just That, or Was It Evidence That He Was the Nation's First Gay Chief Executive?" Smithsonian Magazine, August 27, 2019, https://www.smithsonianmag.com/history/175-year-history-examining-bachelor-president-james-buchanans-close-friendship-william-rufus-king-180972992/.
19. *New York Times*, May 2, 1855, reprinted from the *New York Post*, n.d.; World Wide Words, https://www.worldwidewords.org/qa/qa-sof1.htm.
20. Barnes, *Private and Confidential: Letters from British Ministers*, 143.
21. Roy Franklin Nichols, *Franklin Pierce, Young Hickory of the Granite Hills* (Philadelphia, University of Pennsylvania Press, 1931), 225–26.
22. Franklin Pierce, Inaugural Address, Yale Law School, Lillian Goldman Law Library, The Avalon Project, Documents in Law, History and Diplomacy, https://avalon.law.yale.edu/19th_century/pierce.asp; *The Liberator*, August 11, 1854, reprinted from the *National Era*, n.d.
23. *New York Tribune*, August 30, 1854; *Semi-Weekly Courier and New-York Enquirer*, September 2, 1854.
24. *New York Tribune*, September 6, 1854.
25. *Wilmington* [NC] *Journal*, September 1, 1854.
26. Kinney to Norton, November 8, 1854, Milford Phillips Norton Papers, Misc. Letters, 1842–1855, Archives and Information Services Division, Texas State Library and Archives Commission; Charles G. Norton, "Kinney Organized First Fair in Texas Here 86 Years Ago," *Corpus Christi Caller-Times*, May 25, 1938, 9. The eighth in a series of 12 articles about H.L. Kinney that Norton wrote for the paper. This 1938 *Corpus Christi Caller-Times* series is very similar in content to the six-part series Charles Norton did for the *Austin Times and the Texas Democrat* just a year before.
27. Charles G. Norton, *Milford Phillips Norton, Pioneer of Bayou City*, 17, Milford Phillips Norton Papers, Archives and Information Services Division, Texas State Library and Archives Commission, 17. This is a circa 1938 unpublished 21-page typescript. Perhaps it is filed under "Norton (Charles G.) Literary Effort." A copy

may also be held by La Retama Central Library, Corpus Christi.

28. Norton, "Kinney Organized First Fair in Texas Here 86 Years Ago," *Corpus Christi Caller-Times,* May 25, 1938; Dan L. Thrapp, *Encyclopedia of Frontier Biography,* vol. G–O (Lincoln, Neb: University of Nebraska Press, 1991), 785; Charles G. Norton, "Kinney Goes to War, Returning Later to Trade," *Austin Times and the Texas Democrat,* June 18, 1937, the fourth of six installments of a condensed sketch of "Col. H.L. Kinney, a Texian History Forgot." This 1937 *Austin Times and the Texas Democrat* series is very similar in content to the 12-part series Charles Norton did for the Corpus Christi Caller-Times just a year later.

29. Charles G. Norton, "Kinney Goes to War, Returning Later to Trade," *Austin Times and the Texas Democrat,* June 18, 1937.

30. James Myer to H.L. Kinney, April 12, 1854, Milford Phillips , Misc. Letters, 1842–1855, Archives and Information Services Division, Texas State Library and Archives Commission; M.P. Norton to H.L. Kinney, April 24, 1854, *ibid.*

31. Norton, *Pioneer of Bayou City,* Norton Papers, 16; J.W. Wilbarger, *Indian Depredations in Texas: Reliable Accounts of Battles, Wars, Adventures, Forays, Murders, Massacres, Etc., Together with Biographical Sketches of Many of the Most Noted Indian Fighters and Frontiersmen of Texas* (Austin, Texas: Hutchins Printing House, 1889), 69, https://archive.org/details/indiandepredatio00wilb/page/68/mode/2up?q=.

Chapter 9

1. Hubert Howe Bancroft, *The Works of Hubert Howe Bancroft, California Inter Pocula,* vol. 35 (San Francisco, CA: The History Company Publishers, 1888), 264, https://hdl.handle.net/2027/loc.ark:/13960/t7sn0jd0d?urlappend=%3Bseq=276; *ibid.,* 406, https://hdl.handle.net/2027/loc.ark:/13960/t7sn0jd0d?urlappend=%3Bseq=418.

2. Kinney to Norton, November 8, 1854, Norton Papers, Misc. Letters; *New York Herald,* November 17, 1854.

3. *New York Herald,* November 17, 1854.

The grant size figure given here as 25 million acres is close to the most common of 22.5 million acres.

4. *Prospectus of the Central American Company, Organized October 16th, 1855, on the Basis of 22,500,000 Acres of Land and a Capital of $5,625,000.* (Philadelphia: Printed by F.W. Thomas, 1855.)

5. Franklin Pierce, *The State of the Union: Being a Complete Documentary History of the Public Affairs of the United States, Foreign and Domestic, for the Year 1854* (Washington: Taylor & Maury, 1855), 11, https://archive.org/stream/stateofunionbein02wash#page/10/mode/2up. This was not delivered as a speech but rather as a document sent to Congress.

6. *Ibid.*

7. *Ibid.*

8. *Ibid.*

9. *New York Tribune,* December 5, 1854.

10. Franklin Pierce, *The State of the Union ... for the Year 1854,* part 4, The Navy, 88.

11. *Washington Daily Globe,* December 5, 1854.

12. *Baltimore Sun,* December 12, 1854.

13. Cong Globe, 33d Cong. 2d sess., vol. 31, Appendix, 1855, Washington D.C. January 11, 1855, 71, https://digital.library.unt.edu/ark:/67531/metadc30790/m1/85/.

14. Cong Globe, 33d Cong. 2d sess., 951, as quoted in David P. Currie, *The Constitution in Congress: Descent Into the Maelstrom, 1829–1861* (Chicago: University of Chicago Press, 2005), 119–20.

15. *Ibid.,* 952, as quoted in Currie, *The Constitution in Congress,* 120; *ibid.,* 119.

16. Kinney to Norton, December 12, 1854, Norton Papers, Misc. Letters; *New York Times,* December 15, 1854.

17. *New York Times,* December 15, 1854.

18. *New York Herald,* December 23, 1854. A Kitchen Cabinet is a collection of unofficial advisors a president consults in parallel with the official cabinet. The term dates to Andrew Jackson's administration and is still used today.

Chapter 10

1. Barnes, *Private and Confidential: Letters from British Ministers,* 111; Alfred Hasbrouck, "Gregor McGregor and the Colonization of Poyais, Between 1820 and

1824," *The Hispanic American Historical Review* 7, no. 4 (1927): 457, https://doi.org/10.2307/2505996. Hasbrouck spells the surname as McGregor, as do some others; but most give it as MacGregor.

2. "The King of Con-Men: The Biggest Fraud in History Is a Warning to Professional and Amateur Investors Alike," *The Economist*, December 22, 2012, https://www.economist.com/christmas-specials/2012/12/22/the-king-of-con-men; Maria Konnikova, "The Conman Who Pulled Off History's Most Audacious Scam," *BBC Online*, January 27, 2016, https://www.bbc.com/future/article/20160127-the-conman-who-pulled-off-historys-most-audacious-scam.

3. Michael Rafter, *Memoirs of Gregor M'Gregor: Comprising a Sketch of the Revolution in New Grenada and Venezuela, with Biographical Notices of Generals Miranda, Bolivar, Morillo and Horé, and a Narrative of the Expeditions to Amelia Island, Porto Bello, and Rio De La Hache, Interspersed with Revolutionary Anecdotes*. (London: Printed for J.J. Stockdale, 1820), 44–45, https://hdl.handle.net/2027/hvd.hxg199?urlappend=%3Bseq=54%3Bownerid=27021597765554094-62; David Sinclair, *The Land That Never Was: Sir Gregor MacGregor and the Most Audacious Fraud in History* (Cambridge, MA: De Capo Press, 2004), 154.

4. Sinclair, *The Land That Never Was*, 174–75.

5. Michael Rafter, *Memoirs of Gregor M'Gregor*, 94–95, https://hdl.handle.net/2027/hvd.hxg199?urlappend=%3Bseq=106%3Bownerid=27021597765551656-120.

6. *Ibid.*, 107, https://hdl.handle.net/2027/hvd.hxg199?urlappend=%3Bseq=119%3Bownerid=27021597765551656-133; Sinclair, *The Land That Never Was*, 184; *ibid.*, 182.

7. Rafter, *Memoirs of M'Gregor*, 338, https://hdl.handle.net/2027/hvd.hxg199?urlappend=%3Bseq=358%3Bownerid=27021597765558094-372.

8. Sinclair, *The Land That Never Was*, 221. Sinclair identifies the king selling MacGregor the Poyais grant as George Frédéric Augustus II, but it was probably George Frédéric Augustus I; David Hunter Miller, *Treaties and Other International Acts of the United States of America*, vol. 5 (Washington, DC: United States Government Printing Office, 1937), 801n1, https://hdl.handle.net/2027/hvd.32044049916968?urlappend=%3Bseq=845%3Bownerid=116348476-937.

9. Thomas Young, *Narrative of a Residence on the Mosquito Shore, During the Years 1839, 1840, & 1841: With an Account of Truxillo, and the Adjacent Islands of Bonacca and Roatan*. (London, England: Smith, Elder, 1842), 91, https://hdl.handle.net/2027/hvd.32044024226540?urlappend=%3Bseq=103%3Bownerid=27021597764374283-119.

10. Sinclair, *The Land That Never Was*, 108; *ibid.*, 25–26.

11. *Ibid.*, 78–79; CPI Inflation Calculator, accessed January 30, 2022, https://www.in2013dollars.com/uk/inflation/1822?endYear=2020&amount=200000; "Ex-Rate, World Currency Exchange Rates and Currency Exchange Rate History," accessed January 30, 2022, https://ex-rate.com/convert/gbp/26000000-to-usd.html.

12. Sinclair, *The Land That Never Was*, 316–17; Thomas Strangeways, *Sketch of the Mosquito Shore: Including the Territory of Poyais, Descriptive* ... (Edinburgh, 1822), 63, https://books.google.com/books?id=iR0TAAAAYAAJ&q=globules#v=snippet&q=globules&f=false; Henry Brackenbury, "James Douglas, M.D., Surgeon Venturer," *Blackwood's Magazine*, January 1912, 100, https://archive.org/details/blackwoodsmagazi191edinuoft/page/100/mode/2up/.

13. Sinclair, *The Land That Never Was*, 316.

14. Louis L. Straney, *Securities Fraud: Detection, Prevention and Control* (Hoboken, NJ: John Wiley & Sons, 2011), 35.

15. Bryan Taylor, "The Fraud of the Prince of Poyais on the London Stock Exchange, Global Financial Data," November 18, 2020, https://globalfinancialdata.com/the-fraud-of-the-prince-of-poyais-on-london-stock-exchange; Walter Scott, ed., *The Edinburgh Annual Register*, vol. 16 (Edinburgh: John Ballantyne and Co., 1823), 281, https://hdl.handle.net/2027/umn.31951000729653y?urlappend=%3Bseq=771%3Bownerid=13510798902501424-863.

16. Malmesbury to Crampton, June 18, 1852, British Foreign Office, *Correspondence ... Respecting Central America, 1849–56*, 166, https://hdl.handle.net/2027/

nnc1.cu01564889?urlappend=%3Bseq=182%3Bownerid=27021597768961117-206.

17. *Ibid.*, Crampton to Malmesbury, July 4, 1852, 179, https://hdl.handle.net/2027/nnc1.cu01564889?urlappend=%3Bseq=195%3Bownerid=27021597768961117-219.

18. Alexander Keith Johnston, *Dictionary of Geography, Descriptive, Physical, Statistical, and Historical, Forming a Complete General Gazetteer of the World* [aka *Johnston's Gazetteer*] (London: Longman, Brown, Green, and Longmans, 1852), 296, https://hdl.handle.net/2027/coo1.ark:/13960/t8gf1cx1b?urlappend=%3Bseq=308. (Possibly readable only in Page by Page View, Plain Text View garbled); Alexander Keith Johnston, *Dictionary of Geography, Descriptive, Physical, Statistical, and Historical, Forming a Complete General Gazetteer of the World*, New Edition. (London: Longmans, Green, Reader and Dyer, 1868), 1030, https://hdl.handle.net/2027/wu.89097025118?urlappend=%3Bseq=1042. (Possibly readable only in Page by Page View, Plain Text View garbled.)

19. Edward Chancellor, *Devil Take the Hindmost: A History of Financial Speculation* (New York: Plume, 2000), 97. "Alley-men" is a short-hand reference to stock jobbers who operated in Change Alley near the London Stock Exchange because, according to historian John Harold Clapham, they were "less respectable" and, so, were forced to remain "without" the exchange, becoming the "'little-go' or 'alley' men of the early nineteenth century."

Chapter 11

1. Robert E. May, *The Southern Dream of a Caribbean Empire, 1854–1861* (Gainesville: University Press of Florida, 2002), 95; *New York Herald*, January 6, 1855.

2. Scroggs, *Filibusters and Financiers*, 102, https://hdl.handle.net/2027/mdp.39015005233559?urlappend=%3Bseq=122%3Bownerid=13510798890071585-126.

3. *New York Herald*, February 11, 1855. A PDF of the article has been in the author's collection since 2012, downloaded from "ProQuest Civil War Era" with this date given. However, this date may be incorrect. The Library of Congress's *Chronicling America* collection of digitized newspapers has no issue of the *Herald* for February 11, 1855, and neither does Ancestry's *Newspapers.com*; Robert E. May, *Manifest Destiny's Underworld: Filibustering in Antebellum America*. (Chapel Hill: University of North Carolina Press, 2002), 138–39; Manning, *Diplomatic Correspondence*, 4:447, https://hdl.handle.net/2027/mdp.39015074697346?urlappend=%3Bseq=501%3Bownerid=13510798892581513-537.

4. *New York Tribune*, March 1, 1855. While not directly relevant here, the *Tribune* went on to declare this pacific colonization description as "humbug.... Their aim is … to overrun and subjugate the existing states of Nicaragua and Costa Rica, in order to establish a new slave-driving, Anglo-Saxon republic… to repeat in central America the drama enacted in Texas. Slavery is becoming confined in the united states; even Kansas cannot satisfy its necessities, and new countries must be brought under its sway. When will the Lone Star or Twin Stars of central America be added to the spangled banner of the union?"; *New York Times*, March 22, 1855; *Prospectus of the Central American Company, Organized October 16th, 1855, on the Basis of 22,500,000 Acres of Land and a Capital of $5,625,000*. (Philadelphia: Printed by F.W. Thomas, 1855.)

5. *Boston Daily Advertiser,* April 25, 1855, as reprinted on pages 3 & 4 of a 12-page promotional brochure entitled *A Home in Nicaragua!: The Kinney Expedition* (New York, W.C. Bryant & Co., 1855), https://hdl.handle.net/2027/loc.ark:/13960/t6d22qn6q?urlappend=%3Bseq=3.

6. Ferrar seemed to be playing both sides of the filibuster fence, as a partner of Kinney and Fabens but also a high official in the Nicaraguan government. In any event, Fabens needed a Nicaraguan co-owner for the mining holdings because it was required of foreigner owners.

7. Norton, *Pioneer of Bayou City*, Norton Papers, 18.

8. *Ibid.*, 19. Lucien Birdseye was the grandfather of Clarence Birdseye, Jr., the man who invented in 1924 the quick-freezing process for consumer foods that is still used today.

9. Marcoleta to Marcy, June 2, 1855, Manning, *Diplomatic Correspondence*, 4: 464–466, with enclosure of: Cooper to Hop-

kins [read: Hipkins], May 30, 1855, 465, https://hdl.handle.net/2027/mdp.39015074697346?urlappend=%3Bseq=519%3Bownerid=13510798893627431-555.

10. *Ibid.*
11. *Ibid.*
12. *Ibid.*, 466, https://hdl.handle.net/2027/mdp.39015074697346?urlappend=%3Bseq=520%3Bownerid=13510798893627431-556.
13. Joseph Warren Fabens, Henry Lawrence Kinney, *Joseph W. Fabens and Henry L. Kinney Letters* [two], *1855,* New-York Historical Society Manuscript Collections: Fabens to Kinney March 13, 1855; Fabens to Judge Nicholson (draft?), March 16, 1855 Fabens to Kinney, March 17, 1855.
14. The deed-of-transfer resides in "Miscellaneous Manuscripts, Nicholson, A.O.P." at the New York Historical Society.
15. Scroggs, *Filibusters and Financiers,* 101, https://hdl.handle.net/2027/mdp.39015005233559?urlappend=%3Bseq=121%3Bownerid=13510798890071585-125.
16. *New York Times,* February 28, 1857.
17. Marcy to Ingersoll, May 9, 1855. DOS (RG 59) Microfilm pub #M40: Domestic Letters of the Department of State, vol. 44 (Apr 21-Dec 20, 1855), 32–33.
18. Hermann von Holst, *The Constitutional and Political History of the United States,* vol. 4, *1850–1854* (Chicago, 1881–1889), 263n1, https://hdl.handle.net/2027/pst.000018425291?urlappend=%3Bseq=281%3Bownerid=13510798901661125-293.
19. *Ibid.*, 262–63, https://hdl.handle.net/2027/pst.000018425291?urlappend=%3Bseq=280%3Bownerid=13510798901661125-292.
20. Carl Schurz, *The Reminiscences of Carl Schurz,* vol. 2 (New York: McClure, 1907), 162, https://hdl.handle.net/2027/uc2.ark:/13960/t47p8tp0w?urlappend=%3Bseq=194.
21. *New York Times,* May 12, 1855.
22. *Sacramento Daily Union,* December 5, 1855, reprinting an article from the *Washington Star,* October 15, 1855.
23. *New York Times,* May 16, 1855, reprinting an article from the *New York Post,* n.d.

Chapter 12

1. *New York Times,* May 8, 1855; *Baltimore Sun,* May 10, 1855.

2. Pierce to Boarman, May 25, 1855, Charles Boarman Letterbook, 1838–1858, Library of Congress, https://lccn.loc.gov/mm70053942.
3. May, *Manifest Destiny's Underworld,* 149; Boarman to Scott, May 30, 1855, National Archives and Records Administration, Letters Received by the Office of the Secretary of War (Entry 18) in Record Group 107, Records of the Office of the Secretary of War.
4. May, *Manifest Destiny's Underworld,* 149; Scott to S. [Samuel?] Cooper, Acting Sec. of War, May 31, 1855, National Archives and Records Administration, *Letters Received by the Office of the Secretary of War.*
5. Joachimson to Cushing, June 18, 1855, Caleb Cushing Manuscripts, Library of Congress, as quoted in John Belohlavek, *Broken Glass, Caleb Cushing and the Shattering of the Union* (Kent State University Press, 2005), 265; March to Cushing, January n.d., 1855, *ibid..*, 264.
6. *New York Times,* July 19, 1955, reprinting an article from the *New York Post,* n.d.
7. Abijah W. Thayer to William Sidney Thayer, May 2, 1855, William Sidney Thayer Papers, Library of Congress; *ibid.,* June 8, 1855, as quoted in James T. Wall, *Manifest Destiny Denied (*Washington, DC: University Press of America, 1981), 53–54; James B. Thayer to W.S. Thayer, August 3, 1855, Thayer Papers, Library of Congress, as quoted in Wall, *Manifest Destiny Denied,* 53.
8. *New York Times,* August 7, 1855, reprinting an article from the *New York Post,* datelined July 28, 1855; Marcoleta to Marcy, September 7, 1855, Manning, *Diplomatic Correspondence,* 4:476, https://hdl.handle.net/2027/txu.059172149398109?urlappend=%3Bseq=530%3Bownerid=13510798887257568-564.
9. *New York Times,* August 7, 1855, reprinted article from the *New York Post,* datelined July 28, 1855.
10. *New York Times,* June 25, 1855.
11. Fabens to Kinney, July 3, 1855, The National Archives of the United Kingdom (acronym TNA), Foreign Office Archives, Public Record Office (London) 5/622, f. 215.
12. *Ibid.*; Roy Franklin Nichols, *Franklin Pierce, Young Hickory of the Granite*

Hills (Philadelphia, University of Pennsylvania Press, 1931), 398.

13. *New York Times,* August 7, 1855, reprinted article from the *New York Post* (datelined 28 July 1855); Scroggs, *Filibusters and Financiers,* 106–107, https://hdl.handle.net/2027/mdp.39015005233559?urlappend=%3Bseq=126%3Bownerid=13510798890071585-130.

14. *New York Times,* August 7, 1855; Scroggs, *Filibusters and Financiers,*107, https://hdl.handle.net/2027/mdp.39015005233559?urlappend=%3Bseq=127%3Bownerid=13510798890071585-131.

15. *New York Tribune,* October 15, 1855; Scroggs, *Filibusters and Financiers,*107.

Chapter 13

1. Scroggs, *Filibusters and Financiers,* 107, https://hdl.handle.net/2027/mdp.39015005233559?urlappend=%3Bseq=127%3Bownerid=13510798890071585-131; *ibid.,* 128, quoting Walker's newspaper, *El Nicaraguense,* https://hdl.handle.net/2027/mdp.39015005233559?urlappend=%3Bseq=150%3Bownerid=13510798890071585-154.

2. Scroggs, *Filibusters and Financiers,* 129, https://hdl.handle.net/2027/mdp.39015005233559?urlappend=%3Bseq=151%3Bownerid=13510798890071585-155; *New York Herald,* January 30, 1856, quoting a correspondent of the *San Francisco Herald;* Scroggs, *Filibusters and Financiers,*129.

3. Scroggs, *Filibusters and Financiers,* 130, https://hdl.handle.net/2027/mdp.39015005233559?urlappend=%3Bseq=152%3Bownerid=13510798890071585-156; *New York Herald,* September 12, 1855; *Alta Daily California,* October 20, 1855, quoting the *Washington Star,* n.d.; *New York Times,* September 10, 1855.

4. Scroggs, *Filibusters and Financiers,* 130; *New York Times,* February 29, 1856.

5. Scroggs, *Filibusters and Financiers,* 130; *New York Times,* February 23, 1857.

6. Scroggs, *Filibusters and Financiers,* 131, https://hdl.handle.net/2027/mdp.39015005233559?urlappend=%3Bseq=153%3Bownerid=13510798890071585-157.

7. *Ibid.*

Chapter 14

1. Marcy to Ingersoll, June 9, 1853, in Manning, *Diplomatic Correspondence,* 7:81, https://hdl.handle.net/2027/mdp.39015074697353?urlappend=%3Bseq=123%3Bownerid=13510798892612374-127.

2. Marcy to Kinney, February 4, 1855, Manning, *Diplomatic Correspondence ,* 4:448n, https://hdl.handle.net/2027/txu.059172149398109?urlappend=%3Bseq=502%3Bownerid=13510798887257568-532.

3. Buchanan to Marcy, January 10, 1854, *Documents Relative to Central American Affairs and the Enlistment Question* (Washington, DC: C. Wendell,1856), 16, https://hdl.handle.net/2027/hvd.32044080434772?urlappend=%3Bseq=22%3Bownerid=27021597764375707-26. The Supreme Court case to which Buchanan referred, states, in part, as follows: "while the different nations of Europe respected the right of the natives, as occupants, they asserted the ultimate dominion to be in themselves; and claimed and exercised, as a consequence of this ultimate dominion, a power to grant the soil, while yet in possession of the natives. These grants have been understood by all, to convey a title to the grantees, subject only to the Indian right of occupancy. The history of America, from its discovery to the present day, proves, we think, the universal recognition of these principles." *Johnson's Lessee vs. Mcintosh* (1823, 8 Wheaton, 543), https://www.courtlistener.com/opinion/85404/johnsons-lessee-v-mcintosh/.

4. Clayton to Squier, May 7, 1850, Manning, *Diplomatic Correspondence,* 3:60, https://hdl.handle.net/2027/mdp.39015074697460?urlappend=%3Bseq=94%3Bownerid=13510798893619446-98; Rory Carroll, "Nicaragua's Green Lobby Is Leaving Rainforest People 'Utterly Destitute,'" *The Guardian,* November 26, 2006, https://www.theguardian.com/environment/2006/nov/26/famine.conservation.

5. *The National Era,* March 26, 1857.

6. Dallas to Marcy, July 1, 1856, Manning, *Diplomatic Correspondence,* 7:664, https://hdl.handle.net/2027/uva.x002447434?urlappend=%3Bseq=702; Dallas to Clarendon, July 31, 1856, in Manning, *Diplomatic Correspondence,* 678, https://hdl.handle.net/2027/uva.x002447434?urlappend=%3Bseq=716%3Bow

nerid=27021597765709459-738; Dallas to Marcy, August 29, 1856, in Manning, *Diplomatic Correspondence,* 684–85, https://hdl.handle.net/2027/uva.x00244 7434?urlappend=%3Bseq=724%3Bowner id=27021597765709459-746.

7. Marcy to Dallas, September 26, 1856, in Manning, *Diplomatic Correspondence,* 157–58, https://hdl.handle.net/2027/uva. x002447434?urlappend=%3Bseq=195.

8. Dallas to Marcy, October 17, 1856, in Manning, *Diplomatic Correspondence,* 689n2 (con't), https://hdl.handle.net/2027/ uva.x002447434?urlappend=%3Bseq=729.

9. Marcy to Dallas, November 10, 1856, in Manning, *Diplomatic Correspondence,* 161–62, https://hdl.handle.net/2027/uva. x002447434?urlappend=%3Bseq=199.

10. Ibid.

11. *New York Times,* February 9, 1857; ibid., February 23, 1857.

12. George Mifflin Dallas, Julia Dallas, ed., *Letters from London Written from the Year 1856 to 1860, in Two Volumes,* vol. 1 (London: R. Bentley, 1870), 227, https:// hdl.handle.net/2027/hvd.32044081155 483?urlappend=%3Bseq=246%3Bowner id=27021597765029858-250; Dallas to Cass, April 16, 1857, Manning, *Diplomatic Correspondence,* 7:697, https://hdl.handle. net/2027/uva.x002447434?urlappend=% 3Bseq=737%3Bownerid=2702159776570 9459-759.

13. Roy Franklin Nichols, "The Missing Diaries of George Mifflin Dallas," *The Pennsylvania Magazine of History and Biography* 75 (July 1951), 298, https://www. jstor.org/stable/20088272?origin=JSTOR- pdf. Email inquiries in 2021 to both the Historical Society of Pennsylvania, which published the Nichols piece, and the Rare Book & Manuscript Library of the University of Pennsylvania, which holds the Dallas papers, affirmed that they have never acquired any Dallas's letterbooks from his England posting.

14. British Foreign Office, *Correspondence with the United States Respecting Central America, 1856–60.* (London: Harrison, 1860), 309, https://hdl.handle.net/ 2027/mdp.39015063730470?urlappend=% 3Bseq=329%3Bownerid=113489622-328; ibid., 317, https://hdl.handle.net/2027/ mdp.39015063730470?urlappend=%3Bseq =337%3Bownerid=113489622-336.

15. Regis A. Courtemanche, "The Royal Navy and the End of William Walker," *The Historian,* 30, No. 3 (May 1968), 353–54, https://www.jstor.org/stable/24441212.

16. Ibid., 356–361.

17. Hamilton Fish to General Robert Cumming Schenck, April 26, 1873, *The Clayton-Bulwer Treaty and the Monroe Doctrine: A Letter from the Secretary of State to the Minister of the United States at London, Dated May 8, 1882, with Sundry Papers and Documents Explanatory of the Same* (Washington, DC: Government Printing Office, 1882), 163, https://hdl. handle.net/2027/mdp.35112104623485? urlappend=%3Bseq=167%3Bownerid=135 10799902183331-175.

18. Francis Wharton, ed., *A Digest of International Law of the United States, Taken from Documents Issued by Presidents and Secretaries of State, and from Decisions of Federal Courts and Opinions of Attorneys-General,* vol. 3 (Washington, DC: U.S. Government Printing Office, 1906), 34, https://hdl.handle.net/2027/hvd. 32044057607319?urlappend=%3Bseq=40 %3Bownerid=27021597764994918-44.

19. Ira Dudley Travis, *The History of the Clayton-Bulwer Treaty* (Ann Arbor: Publications of the Michigan Political Science Association 3, no. 8, 1900), 201–02, https:// hdl.handle.net/2027/coo1.ark:/13960/t56d 6dg15?urlappend=%3Bseq=219.

Chapter 15

1. *New York Herald,* January 30, 1857.

2. William Walker, *The War in Nicaragua* (United States: S.H. Goetzel, 1860), 25, https://hdl.handle.net/2027/uva.x000 680132?urlappend=%3Bseq=37%3Bown erid=27021597765711489-61; William O. Scroggs, "William Walker's Designs on Cuba," *The Mississippi Valley Historical Review* 1, no. 2 (Sep 1914): 204, https://www. jstor.org/stable/1894950. This page in this article establishes that the Pierce administration began its recognition of Walker's puppet regime in May 1856; Scroggs, *Filibusters and Financiers,* 215, https://hdl. handle.net/2027/mdp.39015005233559 ?urlappend=%3Bseq=237%3Bownerid= 13510798890071585-241. This page in this book establishes that the Pierce administration ended its recognition in September 1856, about two months after Walker

assumed the presidency in a dubious election.

3. *New York Times,* February 9, 1857; *New York Herald,* February 5, 1857. Franking is any official mark or signature on a letter or parcel to indicate that postage has been paid or does not need to be paid. The free franking privilege is extended to members of Congress, who can send official mail for free by simply affixing a signature facsimile to an envelope. From 1789, presidents and Congress had the free frank. It was abolished in 1873 but brought back for Congress in 1891 but not for sitting presidents. (See: Matthew E. Glassman, *Franking Privilege: Historical Development and Options for Change,* April 22, 2015 [Washington D.C.: Congressional Research Service], https://digital.library.unt.edu/ark:/67531/metadc505480/.)

4. *New York Herald,* January 29, 1857.
5. *Ibid.*
6. *Ibid.*
7. "Court Officers and Staff: Commissioners," *The Federal Judicial Center,* https://www.fjc.gov/history/adminis tration/court-officers-and-staff-commis sioners.
8. *New York Herald,* February 5, 1857.
9. *Ibid.*
10. *Ibid.*
11. *Ibid.*
12. *Ibid.*
13. McKeon to Cushing Telegram, February 4, 1857, Reel 2, Franklin Pierce Papers, Manuscript Division, Library of Congress, Washington, D.C.
14. Cushing to McKeon Telegram, February 4, 1857, Reel 2, Franklin Pierce Papers, Library of Congress.
15. *New York Herald,* February 6, 1857. The *New York Times* of same date says, "General Cazneau testified that he *had heard* President Pierce has a twelfth interest in the mosquito grant" (emphasis in original). The fraction given is perhaps telling. In the deed-of-transfer bribe document the three Pierce confidants, Sidney and Fletcher Webster and A.O.P. Nicholson, were given a quarter-share in all of the Kinney/Fabens/Ferrer holdings, current and future. "Each [man was] ... entitled to, one-third of such fourth part ... being an interest to each ... equal to one twelfth of the whole." So, if Pierce received a twelfth, as Cazneau insisted or suggested, then one of this trio would have had to give up his twelfth—or some other, informal arrangement would have been necessary. (The deed-of-transfer resides in "Miscellaneous Manuscripts, Nicholson, A.O.P." at the New-York Historical Society.)

16. *New York Herald,* February 6, 1857.
17. *New York Times,* February 10, 1857. The *Times* dated the letter, February 17, which has to be a typo, as it appeared in the paper on this date, the 10th.
18. *Ibid.*
19. Trina Yeckley, Archivist, National Archives at New York City, email to author, July 13, 2011: "Unfortunately, Southern District Commissioner's Court records were not retained during that time period. I examined the dockets of the circuit court and did not find a record of Joseph Fabens, Alexander Lawrence, or Henry Bolton. If they were indicted, they should appear in the docket."
20. *The Abridgment: Containing Messages of the President of the United States to the Two Houses of Congress with Reports of Departments and Selections from Accompanying Paper* 46, no. 3, United States: n.p., 1880. This contains an excerpt from "the Report of the Postmaster-General for 1851" on franking privilege abuse at that time, 987, https://hdl.handle.net/2027/uiug.30 112124137354?urlappend=%3Bseq=995%3Bownerid=115617131-999.

Chapter 16

1. *New York Tribune,* July 14, 1857; David Waddell, "Great Britain and the Bay Islands, 1821–61," *The Historical Journal* 2, no. 1 (1959): 72. http://www.jstor.org/stable/3020338; Regis A. Courtemanche, "The Royal Navy and the End of William Walker," *The Historian,* 30, No. 3 (May 1968), 350, https://www.jstor.org/stable/24441212.
2. *Maine Farmer,* May 6, 1858.
3. May, *Manifest Destiny's Underworld,* 210; *New York Herald,* May 31, 1858.
4. *New York Herald,* May 31, 1858.
5. *Ibid.*
6. Norton, *Pioneer of Bayou City,* Norton Papers, 19–20.
7. Ward, "Physical Courage, Moral Cowardice Found in Kinney," 2-G.

8. *Sacramento Daily Union,* May 29, 1858.

9. "The King of the Mountains," *San Francisco Examiner,* June 27, 1897, 9–10.

10. Ellen Klages, *Harbin Hot Springs: Healing Waters, Sacred Land* (Middletown, Calif., 1991), 85; Cooper to Young, May 24, 1858, CR 1234 1, Brigham Young office files, 1832–1878 (bulk 1844–1877), https://catalog.churchofjesuschrist.org/assets/0426a9a7-f589-4d37-8ead-0fa33a1e048f/0/0 (accessed: April 5, 2022); Young to Cooper, May 25, 1858, Brigham Young office files transcriptions, 1974–1978, Letterbooks, Letterbook Volume 4, 1858 April 7–June 27, Church History Library, https://catalog.churchofjesuschrist.org/assets/8ec25b34-79e7-49c4-b5d0-20a9442de79f/0/91 (accessed: April 5, 2022).

11. *Historical Department Journal History of the Church, 1830–2008;* 1850–1859; 1858 January-June, May 30, 1858. Church History Library, accessed April 5, 2022, https://catalog.churchofjesuschrist.org/assets/92b58715-229d-4181-9ab7-60ab9b5948c9/0/606. The material quoted here begins in the online version near the bottom of page 607 and jumps to 609, 608 being blank.

12. Kinney Proclamation Addressed to Brigham Young, dated September 20, 1855, Brigham Young office files, 1832–1878 (bulk 1844–1877), General Correspondence, Incoming, 1840–1877, General Letters, 1840–1877, I–K, 1855, H.L. Kinney letter, Church History Library, accessed April 5, 2022, https://catalog.churchofjesuschrist.org/assets/86a68b3d-132d-4411-aa0a-1c42e901dbee/0/0; Wilford Woodruff journals and papers, 1828–1898, Wilford Woodruff Journals, 1833–1898, Wilford Woodruff journal, 1854 January–1859 December, May 26, 1858, 310 (very bottom of page), Church History Library, accessed April 5, 2022, https://catalog.churchofjesuschrist.org/assets/ed47e448-2936-4a1d-a4d8-4b5f96a8d1ac/0/309.

13. *Journal History,* June 11, 1858, 661, accessed April 5, 2022, https://catalog.churchofjesuschrist.org/assets/92b58715-229d-4181-9ab7-60ab9b5948c9/0/660; ibid., June 12, 1858, 671, accessed April 5, 2022, https://catalog.churchofjesuschrist.org/assets/92b58715-229d-4181-9ab7-60ab9b5948c9/0/670 ; ibid., June 16, 1858, 705, accessed April 5, 2022, https://catalog.churchofjesuschrist.org/assets/92b58715-229d-4181-9ab7-60ab9b5948c9/0/704. Quoted material jumps to 707, 706 being blank; Cooper to Young, June 21, 1858, Brigham Young office files, 1832–1878 (bulk 1844–1877), General Correspondence, Incoming, 1840–1877, General Letters, 1840–1877, Co-Dam, 1858; John B. Cooper letter; Church History Library, accessed April 5, 2022, https://catalog.churchofjesuschrist.org/assets/a249d099-7e7d-4f0c-93ff-4df9ac90ed2e/0/0; *New York Tribune,* July 30, 1858.

14. Anonymous Letter, February 17, 1859, Brigham Young office files, 1832–1878 (bulk 1844–1877), General Correspondence, Incoming, 1840–1877, General Letters, 1840–1877, A, 1859; Church History Library, accessed April 5, 2022, https://catalog.churchofjesuschrist.org/assets/be2bca28-0da1-4792-ac3c-f73545e6cefe/0/0; Cooper to Smith, *Journal History,* April 16, 1859, 517, accessed April 5, 2022, https://catalog.churchofjesuschrist.org/assets/6356ac4d-c36f-483c-b90e-37ce4fa02547/0/516.

Chapter 17

1. *Durand v. Hollins,* 8 F. Cas. 111 (C.C.S.D.N.Y. 1860) (No. 4,186), https://law.resource.org/pub/us/case/reporter/F.Cas/0008.f.cas/0008.f.cas.0111.2.pdf.

2. The missing case file citation is: *Durand v. Hollins,* RG 21, NY-1071, Docket 354.

3. McKeon to Streeter, March 16, 1855. Record Group 60, Department of Justice, Attorney General's Papers, Letters Received, National Archives. Box 14(?); Borland to Marcy, May 30, 1854, *Information Respecting the Bombardment of San Juan de Nicaragua,* 3, https://hdl.handle.net/2027/ucl.b3984526?urlappend=%3Bseq=539.

4. McKeon to Streeter, March 16, 1855; *Durand v. Hollins,* 8 F. Cas. 111.

5. Dobbin to Hollins, June 10, 1854, *Information Respecting the Bombardment of San Juan de Nicaragua,* 21, https://hdl.handle.net/2027/ucl.b3984526?urlappend=%3Bseq=557.

6. McKeon to Cushing, March 21, 1855, Record Group 60: General Records of the

Notes—Chapter 17

Department of Justice, Letters Received, 1809–1870 (Source Chronological Files), Entry A1 9, National Archives at College Park, MD.

7. *Nashville Union,* September 29, 1857, reprinted an article from the *New York Journal of Commerce,* n.d.

8. *Baltimore Sun,* September 21, 1857.

9. *New York Tribune,* September 19, 1857.

10. Kenneth E. Shewmaker, "'Congress Only Can Declare War' and 'The President Is Commander in Chief': Daniel Webster and the War Power." *Diplomatic History* 12, no. 4 (1988): 395; Arthur Meier Schlesinger, Jr., *The Imperial Presidency* (Boston: Houghton Mifflin, 1973), 56, https://books.google.com/books?newbks=1&newbks_redir=0&id=zbLO9aNL6ncC&q=dignity+for+formal+#v=snippet&q=%22irresponsible%22%20group&f=false; *New York Tribune,* September 19, 1857.

11. Arthur Meier Schlesinger, Jr., *The Imperial Presidency* (Boston: Houghton Mifflin, 1973), 56, https://books.google.com/books?newbks=1&newbks_redir=0&id=zbLO9aNL6ncC&q=dignity+for+formal+#v=snippet&q=utmost%20clarity&f=false.

12. *Durand v. Hollins,* 8 F. Cas. 111, https://law.resource.org/pub/us/case/reporter/F.Cas/0008.f.cas/0008.f.cas.0111.2.pdf.

13. Arthur Meier Schlesinger, Jr., *The Imperial Presidency,* 50, https://books.google.com/books?newbks=1&newbks_redir=0&id=zbLO9aNL6ncC&q=dignity+for+formal+#v=snippet&q=%22rise%20to%20the%20dignity%22&f=false.

14. Tyler to Webster, October 13, 1841, in John Tyler and Lyon Gardiner Tyler, *The Letters and Times of the Tylers,* 2 (Richmond: Whittet & Shepperson, 1884–96), 127, https://hdl.handle.net/2027/cool.ark:/13960/t2m623g9m?urlappend=%3Bseq=151. Some sources give the date of the letter as October 14.

15. Shewmaker, "'Congress Only Can Declare War,'" *Diplomatic History,* 402.

16. *Ibid.*; Frederick Walpole, *Four Years in the Pacific: In Her Majesty's Ship "Collingwood," from 1844 to 1848,* vol. 1 (United Kingdom: 1850), 6, https://hdl.handle.net/2027/njp.32101019614781?urlappend=%3Bseq=28%3Bownerid=27021597768246516-34. Walpole defines "paying with the fore-topsail," as a "cant phrase among sailors for not paying at all."

17. Kenneth R. Stevens, "Of Whaling Ships and Kings: The Johanna Bombardment of 1851," *Prologue: The Journal of the National Archives* 18 (Winter 1986) National Archives and Records Service, General Services Administration: 243.

18. *Ibid.,* 244; *ibid.*

19. *Ibid.,* 245–247; *New York Times,* February 4, 1852; Stevens, "Of Whaling Ships and Kings," *Prologue, 18,* Winter 1986, 247.

20. Stevens, "Of Whaling Ships and Kings," *Prologue, 18,* Winter 1986, 247.

21. Everett to Mooers, December 17, 1852. General Records of the Department of State. Domestic Letters, RG 59.

22. Shewmaker, "'Congress Only Can Declare War,'" 404; Stevens, "Of Whaling Ships and Kings," *Prologue, 18,* Winter 1986, 248.

23. Michael J. Garcia, Caitlain Devereaux, Lewis Andrew Nolan, Meghan Totten, and Ashley Tyson, *The Constitution of the United States of America Analysis and Interpretation,* aka CONAN. (Washington, DC: Congressional Research Service, Library of Congress, U.S. Government Publishing Office Washington, 2017), 497; J. Reuben Clark, *The Right to Protect Citizens in Foreign Countries by Landing Forces: Memorandum of the Solicitor for the Department of State, October 5, 1912* (2d rev. ed. Washington: U.S. Government Printing Office, 1929), 57, https://hdl.handle.net/2027/mdp.39015062380293?urlappend=%3Bseq=69%3Bownerid=3228489-75. Stevens, "Of Whaling Ships and Kings," *Prologue, 18,* Winter 1986, 248.

24. James Buchanan, *Works of James Buchanan, 1856–1860,* vol. 10, (Philadelphia: J.B. Lippincott Company, 1909), 361, https://hdl.handle.net/2027/uc2.ark:/13960/t15m6296v?urlappend=%3Bseq=383.

25. Clark, *The Right to Protect Citizens in Foreign Countries,* 48, https://hdl.handle.net/2027/mdp.39015062380293?urlappend=%3Bseq=60%3Bownerid=3239861-66.

26. Milton Offutt, *The Protection of Citizens Abroad by the Armed Forces of the United States* (Baltimore: Johns Hopkins Press, 1928), 33.

27. Francis D. Wormuth, Edwin Brown Firmage, and Francis P. Butler, *To Chain the Dog of War: The War Power of Congress in History and Law* (Dallas: Southern Methodist University Press., 1986), 140–141; *ibid.*, 133.

28. Hans Schmidt, *Maverick Marine, General Smedley D. Butler and the Contradictions of American Military History* (Lexington: University Press of Kentucky, 1987), 61.

29. *Ibid.*, 62.

30. Mayo to Morelos Zaragoza, April 9, 1914, RG 45/659, as quoted in Robert E. Quirk, *An Affair of Honor: Woodrow Wilson and the Occupation of Veracruz* (Lexington: Published for the Mississippi Valley Historical Association [by] University of Kentucky Press, 1962), 26, https://archive.org/details/affairofhonorwoo00quir.

31. James M. Lindsay, "TWE Remembers: The Tampico Incident," Council on Foreign Relations, April 9, 2013, https://www.cfr.org/blog/twe-remembers-tampico-incident; Quirk, *An Affair of Honor*, 50.

32. *New York Times*, April 16, 1914.

33. *New York Times*, April 18, 1914. A substantial effort was made to find the source of this "hen roost robbery" quote attributed to Palmerston but without success. The *Times*, however, used a similar turn of phrase in a scathing indictment of Pierce after Greytown, saying on July 29, 1854, that "there is not much likelihood that he will ever send our navy upon any more dangerous exploit than robbing some coterminous [coextensive in boundaries, scope, or duration] hen-roost, or burning some Indian hut, or kidnapping some negro fugitive."

34. *Congressional Record, House*, February 27, 1917, 4412–13, https://www.govinfo.gov/content/pkg/GPO-CRECB-1917-pt5-v54/pdf/GPO-CRECB-1917-pt5-v54-3.pdf, This is a 99-page PDF, covering February 27 & 28, 1917. King's speech begins on page 4412; *Jamestown* [N.D.] *Weekly Alert*, March 15, 1917, 6.

35. Edward S. Corwin, *The President: Office and Powers. History and Analysis of Practice and Opinion* (New York: New York University Press, 1940), 246. As noted in the body text, this quote also appeared in the 1941 edition (also on page 246) but changed in the 1948 edition, the new version remaining in the subsequent editions. (See 1948, page 241; 1957, page 198; and 1984, page 228). Click these links to see the difference between the first version, as represented by the 1940 edition (https://hdl.handle.net/2027/mdp.39015070264430?urlappend=%3Bseq=266%3Bownerid=13510798887814544-280) and the second version, as represented by the 1948 edition (https://hdl.handle.net/2027/uc1.b3965300?urlappend=%3Bseq=275%3Bownerid=9007199256164431-269).

36. "Japan Follows U.S. Precedent on Damages," *Boston Globe*, January 18, 1940, p. 12.

37. Nina Strochlic, "'Argo' in the Congo: The Ghosts of the Stanleyville Hostage Crisis, Operation Dragon Rouge." The Daily Beast, Updated July 12, 2017. Published Nov. 23, 2014. https://www.thedailybeast.com/argo-in-the-congo-the-ghosts-of-the-stanleyville-hostage-crisis.

38. "Timing of the U.S.-Belgian Operation Has Raised Some Serious Questions," *New York Times*, November 29, 1964, 236.

39. *Ibid.*

40. *Ibid.*

41. The Editors of Encyclopaedia Britannica, "Moise Tshombe," *Encyclopedia Britannica*, November 6, 2020, *https://www.britannica.com/biography/Moise-Tshombe*; Richard Reeves, *President Kennedy: Profile of Power* (Norwalk, CT: Easton Press, 2000), 492; Clifton Fadiman and André Bernard, *Bartlett's Book of Anecdotes* (Norwalk, CT: Easton Press, 2003), 317.

42. *Public Papers of the Presidents of the United States* (United States: Federal Register Division, National Archives and Records Service, General Services Administration, 1974), 552; "An Incident at Greytown," *Indianapolis Star*, May 5, 1972.

43. Lee H. Hamilton, Daniel K. Inouye, *Report of the Congressional Committees Investigating the Iran/Contra Affair* (1987), 474, https://hdl.handle.net/2027/mdp.39015040112453; Timothy E. Flanigan, *Authority to Use United States Military Forces in Somalia* (1992), 9–10, https://www.justice.gov/file/20526/download; Jack L. Goldsmith III, *Deployment of United States Armed Forces to Haiti* (2004), 31, https://www.justice.gov/file/18876/download; Alberto R. Gonzales, *Legal Authorities Supporting the Activities of*

the *National Security Agency Described by the President* (2006), 9, https://www.justice.gov/archive/opa/docs/whitepaperonnsalegalauthorities.pdf; Karl R. Thompson, *Authority to Order Targeted Airstrikes Against the Islamic State of Iraq and the Levant* (2014), 17, https://www.justice.gov/olc/opinion/file/1108686/download.

44. Matthew Waxman, "Remembering the Bombardment of Greytown," Lawfare, July 13, 2019, https://www.lawfareblog.com/remembering-bombardment-greytown.

45. William P. Rogers, "Congress, the President, and the War Powers," *California Law Review* 59, no. 5 (1971): 1197n17, https://doi.org/10.2307/3479587; "Samuel Freeman Miller and Supreme Court of the United States" (*U.S. Reports: In Re Neagle, Petitioner, 135 U.S. 1. 1889*, Periodical), https://www.loc.gov/item/usrep135001/.

46. Peter Margulies, "Taking Care of Immigration Law: Presidential Stewardship, Prosecutorial Discretion, and the Separation of Powers," *Boston University Law Review* 94, no. 105 (2014): 149; *ibid.*, 150n257; *ibid.*, 141n203, http://www.bu.edu/bulawreview/files/2014/03/MARGULIES.pdf.

47. Fred F. Manget, "Presidential War Powers (A Constitutional Basis for Foreign Intelligence Operations)," NARA, Record Group 263: Records of the Central Intelligence Agency, 1894–2002. Series: Articles from "Studies in Intelligence," 1955–1992. File Unit: Summer 1987: 10-114–7, 96, https://research.archives.gov/id/7283242; Ellen C. Collier, *Instances of Use of United States Armed Forces Abroad, 1798–1989*, Washington, DC: Congressional Research Service, December 4, 1989) University of North Texas Libraries, UNT Digital Library, 3, https://digital.library.unt.edu/ark:/67531/metadc992714/.

48. Jennifer K. Elsea, Thomas J. Nicola and Michael J. Garcia, *Congressional Authority to Limit U.S. Military Operations in Iraq*, (Washington D.C.: Library of Congress. Congressional Research Service, July 11, 2007), CRS-11–CRS-12, from the University of North Texas Libraries, https://digital.library.unt.edu/ark:/67531/metadc816938/; Jennifer K. Elsea, *Congressional Authority to Limit Military Operations*, (Washington D.C.: Library of Congress, Congressional Research Service, February 19, 2013), 9, from the University of North Texas Libraries, https://digital.library.unt.edu/ark:/67531/metadc462751/.

49. Michael J. Garcia, etc., *The Constitution of the United States of America: Analysis, and Interpretation*, aka CONAN, 2017, 630–31, https://www.govinfo.gov/content/pkg/GPO-CONAN-2017/pdf/GPO-CONAN-2017.pdf.

50. Austin Wright, "How Barbara Lee Became an Army of One," *Politico*, July 30, 2017, https://www.politico.com/magazine/story/2017/07/30/how-barbara-lee-became-an-army-of-one-215434; Barbara Lee, et. al., to Bob Corker and Bob Menendez, May 15, 2018, 1, https://lee.house.gov/imo/media/doc/Lee%20bipartisan%20AUMF%20principles%20letter%20May%202018.pdf.

51. *War Powers Resolution: Hearings Before the Committee on Foreign Relations, United States Senate, Ninety-fifth Congress, on a Review of the Operation and Effectiveness of the War Power Resolution, July 13, 14, and 15, 1977.* (United States: U.S. Government Printing Office, 1977), 508; *ibid.*, 508–09n30, https://www.google.com/books/edition/War_Powers_Resolution/YGod1zwLeUkC?hl=en&gbpv=0.

52. *Use of U.S. Armed Forces in Foreign Countries, II: Instances of Use of U.S. Armed Forces Abroad, 1798–1945, Congressional Record (Bound Edition)*, 91st Congress, 1st Session, Volume 115, Part 13 (Senate: June 23, 1969), 16841, https://www.govinfo.gov/content/pkg/GPO-CRECB-1969-pt13/pdf/GPO-CRECB-1969-pt13-2-2.pdf. This 1945 document was entered into the *Congressional Record* during a 1969 debate on the Vietnam War. The list begins on page 16840. It lists about 160 instances. For the 2022 list, see: https://sgp.fas.org/crs/natsec/R42738.pdf.

Chapter 18

1. Will Soper, "Revisiting Nineteenth-Century U.S. Interventionism in Central America: Capitalism, Intrigue, and the Obliteration of Greytown," *American Nineteenth Century History* 18, No. 1 (2017), 19–44, https://doi.org/10.1080/14664658.2017.1319633.

2. Jennifer K. Elsea, *Congressional Authority to Limit U.S. Military Operations in Iraq*, Summary page, updated July 11, 2007, https://digital.library.unt.edu/ark:/67531/metadc816938/.

3. Kevin R. Kosar, "Why I Quit the Congressional Research Service: How Congress's Dysfunction Has Degraded Its Own In-House Think Tank," *Washington Monthly*, January/February 2015, https://washingtonmonthly.com/magazine/janfeb-2015/why-i-quit-the-congressional-research-service/.

4. Schiff to Soper, September 13, 2018, enclosing an undated copy of the response Schiff's district office received from Barbara Torreon of the CRS in response to my questioning the accuracy of the Greytown entry in the CRS's "Instances" list of U.S. military interventions. (Author's collection.)

5. Email exchange, Soper to Shenkman to Soper, September 21, 2018, in re my proffered op-ed for *History News Network* and his acceptance. (Author's collection.)

6. Will Soper, "Can an Amateur Historian Rewrite History?" History News Network, October 23, 2018, https://historynewsnetwork.org/article/170070. All of HNN's content is "licensed Under Creative Commons 3.0 [https://creativecommons.org/licenses/by/3.0/]. Readers Are Free to copy, distribute, transmit, and adapt HNN content provided that HNN is clearly identified as the source. ... You must give appropriate credit [see above], provide a link to the license [https://creativecommons.org/licenses/by/3.0/legalcode], and indicate if changes were made [none were]."

Chapter 19

1. *Wiggins V. United States*, 3 Ct. Cl. 412 (1867), 420, https://cite.case.law/ct-cl/3/412/.

2. Ibid., 424.

3. Hollins, *Log of the USS* Cyane: *Mar. 1, 1853–Sept. 6, 1854*, July 15, 1854; *Congressional Globe* (30), March 2, 1855, 1095, https://digital.library.unt.edu/ark:/67531/metadc30789/m1/1137/?q.

4. *Journal of the Senate*, December 31, 1855, 24, https://memory.loc.gov/cgi-bin/ampage?collId=llsj&fileName=047/llsj047.db&recNum=23&itemLink=r?ammem/hlaw:@field(DOCID+@lit(sj04720))%230470025&linkText=1; *Wiggins V. United States*, 422, https://cite.case.law/ct-cl/3/412/. (See also, *Grant v. United States*, 1 Ct. Cl. 41 (1863) https://cite.case.law/ct-cl/1/41/3529531/.)

5. Charles Covell, *The Law of Nations in Political Thought* (New York: Palgrave Macmillan, 2009), 91–92; Charles G. Fenwick, "The Authority of Vattel," *The American Political Science Review* 7, no. 3 (August 1913), 407, https://www.jstor.org/stable/1944965.

6. Emer de Vattel, *The Law of Nations, Sixth American Edition*, Book 3, chapter 15, section 232 (Philadelphia, PA: T. & J.W. Johnson, 1844), 402, https://hdl.handle.net/2027/uc1.32106009089639?urlappend=%3Bseq=495%3Bownerid=9007199272265105-499.

7. Charles Augustus Trautmann-Perrin and Marie Louise Trautmann-Perrin, *Collection of Printed Materials Related to the Claim of Maria* [read: Marie] *Louise and Trautman Perrin Over the Destruction of Their Property During the Bombardment of San Juan Del Norte (Greytown), Nicaragua, by the U.S. Sloop* Cyane *on July 13, 1854* (Boston: Massachusetts Historical Society, Call Number: Box L-1868. Location: Manuscript), *Document 3—Statement of Losses Sustained*, 1; Document 2, Appeal to Secretary of State Seward, 1, http://balthazar.masshist.org/cgi-bin/Pwebrecon.cgi?v1=1&ti=1,1&Search%5FArg=Marie%20Louise%20Perrin&Search%5FCode=FT%2A&CNT=10&PID=CcKN5Z877uAs-licoLR-32TAYg&SEQ=20220412121810&SID=1. (Author's note: This collection, five documents in all, was archived with just penciled numbers at the top of each document. Since the collection doesn't otherwise specifically identify them, I gave them the following descriptive names in the citations in this chapter: *Document 1—Letter Appealing for Influence*; *Document 2—Appeal to Secretary of State Seward*; *Document 3—Statement of Losses Sustained*; *Document 4—Petition to the U.S. Court of Claims*; *Document 5—Letter Appealing for a Loan*.)

8. *Document 1—Letter Appealing for Influence*, 2; *Document 5—Letter Appealing for Loan*, 1; Tufts University Digital Library, The Boston Directory (Boston: Adams, Sampson & Co, 1865), http://bcd.

lib.tufts.edu/view_text.jsp?urn=tufts:central:dca:UA069:UA069.005.DO.00021&chapter=d.1865.su.Perrin; *Declaration of Intention and Petition for Naturalization of Trautman Perrin*, National Archives and Records Administration, Boston, RG 21, Stack area C, Row 24, Compartment U8-C6-3; *Gopsill's Philadelphia City Directory for 1871*, 1132, www.ancestry.com/imageviewer/collections/2469/images/2867561?usePUB=true&_phsrc=QSo191&_phstart=successSource&usePUBJs=true&pId=1185880248.

9. *Document 2—Appeal to Secretary of State Seward*, 1; *Document 5—Letter Appealing for Loan*, 1.

10. Seward to Sumner, February 26, 1868, in *Document 2—Appeal to Secretary of State Seward* (including Seward's reply), 3.

11. Ibid.; Travers Twiss, *The Law of Nations Considered as Independent Political Communities: On the Rights and Duties of Nations in Time of Peace* (Oxford: Clarendon Press, 1861), 275, https://hdl.handle.net/2027/mdp.35112102839240?urlappend=%3Bseq=333%3Bownerid=13510798902176162-359.

12. Seward to Sumner, February 26, 1868, *Document 2—Appeal to Secretary of State Seward*, 3.

13. *Document 2—Appeal to Secretary of State Seward*, 1; *Perrin v. United States*, U.S. Court of Claims, 4 Ct. Cl. 543 (1868), 543, https://cite.case.law/ct-cl/4/543/.

14. *Wiggins v. United States*, 3 Ct. Cl. 412 (1867), 422, https://cite.case.law/ct-cl/3/412/; *Perrin V. United States*, U.S. Court of Claims, 4 Ct. Cl. 543 (1868), 544, https://cite.case.law/ct-cl/4/543/; ibid., 545.

15. *Perrin V. United States*, U.S. Court of Claims, 4 Ct. Cl. 543 (1868), 547.

16. *Perrin V. United States*, 79 U.S. 315, 12 Wall. 315, 20 L. Ed., 412 (1870). https://cite.case.law/us/79/315/; *The Petition of Marie Louise Perrin and Trautman Perrin, Praying for Compensation*, 44th Cong., 1st sess., S. Rep. No. 464. July 13, 1876, serial 1668, #693–#695, https://hdl.handle.net/2027/uc1.b3985273. The 1884 petition was similar.

17. *Perrin v. United States*, U.S. Court of Claims, 4 Ct. Cl. 543 (1868), 547–48; *National Board of Young Men's Christian Ass'n v. United States*, 396 F.2d 467, 470 (1968) aff'd 395 U.S. 85 (1969), https://cite.case.law/f2d/396/467/2148531/.

18. "U.S. Strikes 'Terrorist' Targets in Afghanistan, Sudan," CNN, August 20, 1998, www.cnn.com/U.S./9808/20/clinton.02/index.html; *Presidential Notification of the U.S. Strikes in Afghanistan Against a Series of Camps and Installations Used by the Usama Bin Ladin Organization, and in Sudan Where the Bin Ladin Organization Has Facilities, and Extensive Ties to the Government*, 105th Congress, 2d Session House Document 105–308, www.gpo.gov/fdsys/pkg/CDOC-105hdoc308/html/CDOC-105hdoc308.htm; James Risen, "Question of Evidence: A Special Report. to Bomb Sudan Plant, or Not: A Year Later, Debates Rankle," *The New York Times*, October 27, 1999.

19. *El-Shifa Pharmaceutical Industries Co. V. United States*, 55 Fed. Cl. 751 (2003), 754, https://cite.case.law/fed-cl/55/751/.

20. "Lewinsky Completes Second Day of Testimony," CNN, August 20, 1998, www.cnn.com/ALLPOLITICS/1998/08/20/lewinsky/; Christopher Hitchens, "A Rejoinder to Noam Chomsky," *The Nation*, October 4, 2001, www.thenation.com/article/archive/rejoinder-noam-chomsky/; Marc Lacey, "Look at the Place! Sudan Says, 'Say Sorry,' but U.S. Won't," *The New York Times*, October 20, 2005, www.nytimes.com/2005/10/20/world/africa/look-at-the-place-sudan-says-say-sorry-but-us-wont.html.

21. *El-Shifa Pharmaceutical Industries Co. v. United States*, 55 Fed. Cl. 751 (2003), 766, https://cite.case.law/fed-cl/55/751/#p766.

22. Ilana Tabacinic, "The Enemy-Property Doctrine: A Double Whammy?," 62 *U. Miami L. Rev.* 601 (2008), 603n20, http://repository.law.miami.edu/umlr/vol62/iss2/12; *El-Shifa Pharmaceutical Industries Co. v. United States*, 55 Fed. Cl. 751 (2003), 770; Tabacinic, "The Enemy-Property Doctrine," 611–12, quoting, in part, *United States v. Pacific Railroad*, 120 U.S. 227 (1887), 239, https://cite.case.law/us/120/227/#p239; Tabacinic, "The Enemy-Property Doctrine," 612n96.

23. Tabacinic, "The Enemy-Property Doctrine," 613; *El-Shifa Pharmaceutical Industries Co. v. United States*, 378 F.3d 1346 (Fed. Cir. 2004), 1356–1357, https://cite.case.law/f3d/378/1346/2201631/

#p1356; Tabacinic, "The Enemy-Property Doctrine," 603; Andrew Clapham, *War*, Clarendon Law Series (London: Oxford University Press, 2021), 220.

24. *The Congressional Globe*, May 18, 1872, 3621, https://hdl.handle.net/2027/ucl.c109461612?urlappend=%3Bseq=47%3Bownerid=113854763-51.

25. "The Senator Who Wanted to Override Grant's Veto," *Detroit Free Press*, March 27, 1873, 3.

26. Ulysses S. Grant, *The Papers of Ulysses S. Grant, February 1–December 31, 1872*, vol. 23 (Carbondale: Southern Illinois University Press, 1967), 152–153, https://scholarsjunction.msstate.edu/usg-volumes/23/.

27. U.S. Congress, Senate, Committee on Claims Petition of Doctor J. Milton Best, 43rd Cong., 1st sess., 1873, S. Rep. 126, serial 1586, 2, 4, https://hdl.handle.net/2027/hvd.hjlf1g?urlappend=%3Bseq=355%3Bownerid=2702159776 5906096-375.

28. *Ibid.*, 6, 7.

29. *Ibid.*, 8.

30. *Mitchell v. Harmony*, 54 U.S. 115 (1851), https://cite.case.law/us/54/115/; *(William S.) Grant v. United States*, 1 Ct. Cl. 41 (1863), https://cite.case.law/ct-cl/1/41/3529531/; *Wiggins v. United States*, 3 Ct. Cl. 412 (1867); George Orwell, *1984* (San Diego, CA: Harcourt Brace Jovanovich, 1983), 147.

31. Petition of Doctor J. Milton Best, 9.

32. Washburne to Grant, *The Papers of Ulysses S. Grant*, vol. 23, 154, https://msstate.contentdm.oclc.org/digital/collection/USG_volume/id/23581/rec/24.

33. I.F. R., "United States Court of Claims. Brown v. the United States," *The American Law Register*, vol. 20, no. 3 (1872), 184, www.jstor.org/stable/3303292.

34. *United States v. Pacific Railroad*, 120 U.S. 227 (1887), 234, quoted in Brian Angelo Lee, "Emergency Takings," 114 *Mich. L. Rev.* 391 (2015), 452, https://repository.law.umich.edu/mlr/vol114/iss3/2.

35. Stephen I. Vladeck, "Enemy Aliens, Enemy Property, and Access to the Courts," *Lewis and Clark Law Review* 11, 2007, American University, WCL Research Paper No. 08–21, 989, permalink: https://papers.ssrn.com/sol3/papers.cfm?abstract_id=1020269; "Dictum," Nolo's Free Dictionary of Law Terms and Legal Definitions, www.nolo.com/dictionary/dictum-term.html; *United States v. Caltex (Philippines), Inc.*, 344 U.S. 149, 154 (1952), 154, https://cite.case.law/us/344/149/#p154.

36. *Caltex (Philippines), Inc. v. United States*, 120 Ct. Cl. 518 (1951), 548, https://cite.case.law/ct-cl/120/518/#p548.

37. *Mitchell v. Harmony*, 54 U.S. 115, 13 How. 115, 14 L. Ed. 75 (1851), 135, https://cite.case.law/us/54/115/#p135.

Chapter 20

1. Norton, "Kinney Tries Colonization in Nicaragua," *Austin Times* and the *Texas Democrat*, July 2, 1937; Ward, "Physical Courage, Moral Cowardice Found in Kinney," G2.

2. *Democratic Press* (Eaton, OH), February 7, 1861, reprinted from the *New York Times*, February 4, 1861.

3. *Ibid.*; "Joseph Livingston White," Find A Grave, accessed November 10, 2021, http://www.findagrave.com/cgi-bin/fg.cgi?page=gr&GRid=23556010; *Detroit Free Press*, July 16, 1861.

4. *Webster's Revised Unabridged Dictionary* (1913), quoted on *Dictionary.net*, http://www.dictionary.net/appurtenance.

5. Hewson A. Ryan, "Before the Falklands—the Swan Islands," Christian Science Monitor, originally published May 14, 1982, https://www.csmonitor.com/1982/0514/051429.html; "Swan Islands," Encyclopedia Britannica, November 16, 2015, https://www.britannica.com/place/Swan-Islands.

6. David Pletcher, The *Diplomacy of Trade and Investment: American Economic Expansion in the Hemisphere, 1865–1900* (Columbia, Mo.: University of Missouri Press, 1998), 162–67; J. Warren Fabens, *"The Last Cigar" and Other Poems*. (United States: M.L. Holbrook & Company, 1887), https://archive.org/details/thelastcigarothe00fabe/page/n7/mode/2up.

7. "Solon Borland (1811–1864)," Encyclopedia of Arkansas, accessed April 9, 2022, https://encyclopediaofarkansas.net/entries/solon-borland-1595/.

8. Madeleine B. Stern, *Purple Passage: The Life of Mrs. Frank Leslie* (United States: University of Oklahoma Press, 1953), 69–70. Squier's wife claimed his mental state

was deteriorating before their divorce and her remarriage. But an earlier ex-husband had also wound up in an insane asylum.

9. Hollins to Du Pont, March 4, 1855, *The Papers of Samuel Francis Du Pont, 1803–1865*, Hagley Museum and Library, Wilmington, Delaware; Du Pont to Henry Winter Davis, August 7, 1854, *Du Pont Papers*. Du Pont became famous during the Civil War and for his efforts to modernize the navy. Dupont Circle in Washington, D.C. is named after him.

10. Hollins to Du Pont, June n.d., 1859, *Du Pont Papers*; Hollins to Du Pont, September 22, 1859, *ibid*.

11. The Gilder Lehrman Institute of American History, "one of the great archives in American history," with more than 70,000 items, says in the background information to a letter Hollins wrote in 1863 that it was Hollins who "disguised himself as a woman," https://www.gilderlehrman.org/content/john-h-winder. An equally reputable source, the Mariners' Museum and Park in Newport News, Virginia, giving a more detailed account, says that Hollins' ersatz better half was the son of "former Speaker of Maryland's House of Delegates." The son was said to have made a passable "French Lady." https://blog.marinersmuseum.org/2020/08/confederate-pirates-capture-of-steamer-st-nicholas/.

12. John V. Quarstein, "The First Ironclad Emerges: Battle of the Head of Passes," The Mariners' Museum and Park, Mariners' Blog, July 9, 2020, source: *A History of Ironclads: The Power of Iron Over Wood*, John V. Quarstein (Charleston, SC: History Press, 2006), https://blog.marinersmuseum.org/2020/07/the-first-ironclad-emerges-battle-of-the-head-of-passes/.

13. "Death of Commodore Hollins," *Washington Post*, January 21, 1878.

14. HMdb.org (Historical Marker Data Base), https://www.hmdb.org/m.asp?m=9828; George S. Hillard, "Fletcher Webster," in *Harvard Memorial Biographies*, vol. 1, ed. Thomas Wentworth Higginson (Cambridge: Sever and Francis, 1866), 30. https://quod.lib.umich.edu/m/moa/abj7370.0001.001/43.

15. *Chicago Tribune*, September 9, 1865.

16. Claude Moore Fuess, *The Life of Caleb Cushing*, 2 (New York: Harcourt, Brace and Company, 1923), 227, https://hdl.handle.net/2027/mdp.39015026645823.

17. *New York Times*, May 31, 1910; Galveston Daily News, December 24, 1869 reprinted from the *New York Herald*; *Brooklyn Daily Eagle*, April 3, 1907, 28; *The Harvard Graduates' Magazine* 19, September 1910, 170, http://books.google.com/books?id=h4EBAAAAYAAJ&q=Sidney+Webster#v=snippet&q=Sidney%20Webster&f=false.

18. *New York Times*, May 31, 1910.

19. Sidney Webster, *Franklin Pierce and His Administration* (New York: D. Appleton and Company, 1892), 16, https://hdl.handle.net/2027/hvd.32044011783982?urlappend=%3Bseq=22%3Bownerid=3680677-26; *ibid.*, 19, https://hdl.handle.net/2027/hvd.32044011783982?urlappend=%3Bseq=25%3Bownerid=3680677-29.

20. "United States Census, 1880," database with images, FamilySearch (https://www.familysearch.org/ark:/61903/1:1:-M6SM-W58: 14 January 2022), Perrin Charles Trautmann, Charleston [read: Chas. A. Trautmann-Perrin], Charleston, South Carolina, United States; citing enumeration district, sheet, NARA microfilm publication T9 (Washington, D.C.: National Archives and Records Administration, n.d.), FHL microfilm.

21. Samuel Smith Wood, *Samuel Wood to Alexander and Samuel Wood, Jr., July 5, 1855,* Letter. From Yale University Library, Manuscripts and Archives, *Samuel Smith Wood Papers* (MS 1083), 46, https://archives.yale.edu/repositories/12/resources/3990. This URL is to the home page of the Wood Papers. According to the Public Services Department at the Manuscripts and Archives Division of the Yale University Library, the library cannot "provide a URL ... for direct access to download the files in the Samuel Smith Wood Papers." However, the library "would instruct anyone who would like access the [digitized] files to register [with the library, at mssa.assist@yale.edu] and agree to our user terms, and we would then send the files to them"; Robert Seager, II., "The Samuel S. Wood Papers," *The Yale University Library Gazette* 34, no. 4 (1960), 169–72, http://www.jstor.org/stable/40857860; Alexander McCready

Wood, *Alexander Wood to Samuel Smith Wood, October 13, 1854*, Letter. *Samuel Smith Wood Papers* (MS 1083), ms_1083_s01_b001_f0007, 19; Seager, "The Samuel S. Wood Papers," 172–73; Samuel Smith Wood, *Samuel Wood to Alexander Wood, September 5, 1855*, Letter. *Samuel Smith Wood Papers* (MS 1083), ms_1083_s01_b001_f0010, 8–9.

22. Seager, "The Samuel S. Wood Papers," 173; Samuel Smith Wood, *Samuel Wood to Alexander Wood, November 9, 1855*, Letter. *Samuel Smith Wood Papers* (MS 1083), 41; Samuel Smith Wood, *Samuel Wood to Alexander Wood, April 8, 1856*, Letter. *Samuel Smith Wood Papers* (MS 1083), ms_1083_s01_b001_f0011, 22.

23. Seager, "The Samuel S. Wood Papers," 175.

24. Alexander McCready Wood, *Alexander Wood to Samuel Smith Wood, October 7, 1857*, Letter. *Samuel Smith Wood Papers* (MS 1083), ms_1083_s01_b001_f0013, 22.

25. Seager, "The Samuel S. Wood Papers," 175.

26. William P. Kirkland, *W. P. Kirkland to Samuel Smith Wood, July 26, 1859*, Letter. *Samuel Smith Wood Papers* (MS 1083), 33; Seager, "The Samuel S. Wood Papers," 176.

27. *Ibid.*, 177.

Bibliography

The Abridgment: Containing Messages of the President of the United States to the Two Houses of Congress with Reports of Departments and Selections from Accompanying Papers 46, no. 3, United States: n.p., 1880. (Contains an excerpt from "the Report of the Postmaster-General for 1851" on franking privilege abuse at that time.)

"Annexation." *The United States Magazine, and Democratic Review* 17, no. 85, July and August, 1845. https://hdl.handle.net/2027/mdp.39015018403736.

Appendix to the Congressional Globe. March 21, 1853, 32nd Cong., 3d sess. Senate, Special Session—Clayton-Bulwer Treaty.

Augustus, Mitchell S. *Illinois in 1837.* Philadelphia: S. Augustus Mitchell, Grigg & Elliot, 1837. https://hdl.handle.net/2027/pst.000020056759.

Bancroft, Hubert Howe. *The Works of Hubert Howe Bancroft.* Vol. 35. *California Inter Pocula.* San Francisco: The History Company Publishers, 1888. https://books.google.com/books/about/The_Works_of_Hubert_Howe_Bancroft_Califo.html?id=esVQAQAAIAAJ.

Barnes, James J., and Patience P. *Private and Confidential: Letters from British Ministers in Washington to the Foreign Secretaries in London, 1844–67.* Selinsgrove, PA: Susquehanna University Press, 1993.

Barney, William L., editor. Nineteenth Century Southern Political Leaders, Series A: Holdings of the Virginia Historical Society, microfilm, 47 reels.

Barnhart, Terry A. *Ephraim George Squier and the Development of American Anthropology.* Lincoln: University of Nebraska Press, 2005.

Beebe, Henry S. *The History of Peru.* Peru, Illinois: J.F. Linton, 1858. http://www.gutenberg.org/files/36524/36524-h/36524-h.htm.

Belohlavek, John. *Broken Glass, Caleb Cushing and the Shattering of the Union.* Kent State University Press, 2005.

Bermann, Karl. *Under the Big Stick: Nicaragua and the United States Since 1848.* Boston: South End Press, 1986.

Bigelow, John. *Breaches of Anglo-American Treaties: A Study in History and Diplomacy.* New York: Sturgis & Walton Company, 1917. https://books.google.com/books?id=1-YrAQAAIAAJ&newbks=1&newbks_redir=0&printsec=frontcover&pg=PR3&dq=Breaches+of+Anglo-American+Treaties:+A+Study+in+History+and+Diplomacy+Bigelow+OR+Google&hl=en#v=onepage&q=Breaches%20of%20Anglo-American%20Treaties%3A%20A.

Boarman, Charles. *Charles Boarman Letterbook.* Library of Congress. https://lccn.loc.gov/mm70053942.

Booker, George. *George Booker Collection* (RLT Bay 107, items 1–43 c.1). David M. Rubenstein Rare Book & Manuscript Library, Duke University.

Boston City Directories Search Service. Accessed March 5, 2022. https://bcd.lib.tufts.edu.

Bourne, Kenneth. *Britain and the Balance of Power in North America: 1815–1908.* London: Longmans, 1967.

Brackenbury, Henry. "James Douglas, M.D., Surgeon Venturer." *Blackwood's Magazine.* January 1912, 94–110. https://archive.org/details/blackwoodsmagazi191edinuoft/page/n5/mode/2up.

Brigham Young Office. *Brigham Young*

Office Files, 1832–1878 (bulk 1844–1877). Call Number: CR 1234-1. https://catalog.churchofjesuschrist.org/record/02e985d2-0e16-45c3-8891-986d21e20b37/0?view=browse.

British Foreign Office. *British and Foreign State Papers*. Vol. 42. 1852–53. London: William Ridgway, 1864, 169. https://hdl.handle.net/2027/hvd.hj135v.

———. *British and Foreign State Papers*. Vol. 46. 1855–1856. London: William Ridgway, 169, Piccadilly, 1865. https://hdl.handle.net/2027/ucl.c037896647?urlappend=%3Bseq=9%3Bownerid=116013559-13.

———. *Correspondence Respecting Central America, 1856–60*. London: Harrison, 1860. https://hdl.handle.net/2027/mdp.39015063730470.

———. *Correspondence with the United States Respecting Central America (1849–56)*. London: Harrison, 1856. https://hdl.handle.net/2027/nnc1.cu01564889.

Brown, Charles H. *Agents of Manifest Destiny, the Lives and Times of the Filibusters*. University of North Carolina Press, 1980.

Brown, Richmond F. "Charles Lennox Wyke and the Clayton-Bulwer Formula in Central America, 1852–1860." *The Americas* 47, no. 4 (April 1991): 411–45.

Buchanan, James, and John Bassett Moore, ed. *The Works of James Buchanan. Comprising His Speeches, State Papers, and Private Correspondence*. Vol. 10. 1856–1860. Philadelphia: J.B. Lippincott Company, 1909. https://hdl.handle.net/2027/uc2.ark:/13960/t15m6296v.

Caltex (Philippines), Inc. v. United States. 120 Ct. Cl. 518 (1951). https://cite.case.law/ct-cl/120/518/.

Chancellor, Edward. *Devil Take the Hindmost: A History of Financial Speculation*. New York: Plume, 2000.

Charter and Act of Incorporation of the American Atlantic & Pacific Ship Canal Company, as Amended.... New York: Wm. C. Bryant, printers, 1852. https://iiif.lib.harvard.edu/manifests/view/drs:7411823$1i.

Clapham, Andrew. *War*. Clarendon Law Series. London: Oxford University Press, 2021.

Clark, J. Reuben. *The Right to Protect Citizens in Foreign Countries by Landing Forces: Memorandum of the Solicitor for the Department of State, October 5, 1912*. 2d rev. ed. Washington, D.C.: US Government Printing Office, 1929. https://hdl.handle.net/2027/mdp.39015062380293.

Clayton, John M., and Henry Lytton Bulwer. "The Clayton-Bulwer Treaty." *The Advocate of Peace (1894–1920)* 62, no. 3 (1900): 66–67. http://www.jstor.org/stable/25751541.

Collier, Ellen C. *Instances of Use of United States Armed Forces Abroad, 1798–1989*. Washington, D.C.: Congressional Research Service, December 4, 1989. University of North Texas Libraries, UNT Digital Library. https://digital.library.unt.edu/ark:/67531/metadc992714/.

The Congressional Globe. The *Globe*, as it is usually called, contains the congressional debates of the 23rd through 42nd Congresses (1833–73). https://memory.loc.gov/ammem/amlaw/lwcg.html.

Conrad, Howard Louis. *Nathaniel J. Brown: Biographical Sketch and Reminiscences of a Noted Pioneer*. Chicago: Byron S. Palmer Printing Co., 1892. https://books.google.com/books/about/Nathaniel_J_Brown.html?id=9eFYAAAAMAAJ.

Corwin, Edward S. *The President: Office and Powers. History and Analysis of Practice and Opinion*. New York: New York University Press, 1940, 1941, 1948 (https://hdl.handle.net/2027/ucl.b3965300?urlappend=%3Bseq=17%3Bownerid=9007199256164431-11), 1957 (https://hdl.handle.net/2027/mdp.39015000554785), 1984.

"Court Officers and Staff: Commissioners." *The Federal Judicial Center: History of the Federal Judiciary, Judicial Branch*. Accessed April 8, 2022. https://www.fjc.gov/history/administration/court-officers-and-staff-commissioners.

Courtemanche, Regis A. "The Royal Navy and the End of William Walker." *The Historian* 30, no. 3 (May 1968): 350–365. https://www.jstor.org/stable/24441212.

Covell, C. *The Law of Nations in Political Thought*. New York: Palgrave Macmillan, 2009.

CPI Inflation Calculator. Accessed April 8, 2022. https://www.in2013dollars.com/uk/inflation/1822?endYear=2020&amount=200000.

Currie, David P. *The Constitution in Con-*

gress: Descent Into the Maelstrom, 1829–1861. Chicago: University of Chicago Press, 2005.

Cushing, Caleb. "Caleb Cushing Papers." Library of Congress. LCCN Permalink: https://lccn.loc.gov/mm78017509.

Dallas, George Mifflin. *Letters from London, Written from the Year 1856 to 1860*. Edited by Julia Dallas. Vol. 1. London: Bentley, 1870.

Declaration of Intention and Petition for Naturalization of Trautman Perrin. National Archives and Records Administration, Boston, RG 21, Stack Area C, Row 24, Compartment U8-C6–3.

Deed-of-Transfer from Kinney to Nicholson and Fletcher and Sidney Webster. New York Historical Society. Residing in "Miscellaneous Manuscripts Nicholson, A.O.P."

Despatches from United States Consuls in San Juan Del Norte, Nicaragua, 1851–1906. United States: Department of State, National Archives and Records Service, 21 microfilm reels. OCLC Number: 145079238.

"The Destruction of Greytown." *The Illustrated London News*. Vol. 16, August 19, 1854.

Documents Relative to Central American Affairs and the Enlistment Question. Washington, D.C.: C. Wendell, Printer, 1856. https://hdl.handle.net/2027/hvd.32044080434772.

Du Pont, Samuel Francis. *The Papers of Samuel Francis Du Pont, 1803–1865*. Hagley Museum and Library, Wilmington, Delaware.

Durand v. Hollins. 8 F. Cas. 111 (C.C.S.D.N.Y. 1860) (No. 4,186). https://law.resource.org/pub/us/case/reporter/F.Cas/0008.f.cas/0008.f.cas.0111.2.pdf.

Dycus, Stephen, William C. Banks, Peter Raven-Hansen and Stephen I. Vladeck. *National Security Law*. 7th Edition. New York: Wolters Kluwer, 2020.

El-Shifa Pharmaceutical Industries Company v. United States. 55 Fed. Cl. 751 (2003). https://cite.case.law/fed-cl/55/751/.

———, 378 F.3d 1346 (Fed. Cir. 2004). https://cite.case.law/f3d/378/1346/2201631/.

Elsea, Jennifer K., Michael J. Garcia and Thomas J. Nicola. *Congressional Authority to Limit Military Operations*. Washington, D.C.: Library of Congress. Congressional Research Service, February 19, 2013. https://digital.library.unt.edu/ark:/67531/metadc462751/.

———. *Congressional Authority to Limit U.S. Military Operations in Iraq*. Washington, D.C.: Congressional Research Service, July 11, 2007. https://digital.library.unt.edu/ark:/67531/metadc816938/.

———. "Moise Tshombe." *Encyclopedia Britannica*. November 6, 2020. https://www.britannica.com/biography/Moise-Tshombe.

———. "Swan Islands." *Encyclopedia Britannica*. November 16, 2015. https://www.britannica.com/place/Swan-Islands.

Fabens, J. Warren. *"The Last Cigar" and Other Poems*. United States: M.L. Holbrook & Company, 1887. https://archive.org/details/thelastcigarothe00fabe/page/n7/mode/2up.

Fabens, Joseph Warren, and Henry Lawrence Kinney. *Joseph W. Fabens and Henry L. Kinney Letters* [two], *1855*. New-York Historical Society Manuscript Collections. OCLC Number: 708221502.

Fadiman, Clifton, and André Bernard. *Bartlett's Book of Anecdotes*. Norwalk, CT: Easton Press, 2003.

Feipel, Louis N. "The Navy and Filibustering in the Fifties, Part III: The Bombardment of Greytown, Nicaragua, 1854." *United States Naval Institute Proceedings* 44, no. 6, Whole No. 184 (June 1918). https://hdl.handle.net/2027/chi.42906954?urlappend=%3Bseq=1283%3Bownerid=13510798903444908-1329.

Fenwick, Charles G. "The Authority of Vattel." *The American Political Science Review* 8, no. 3 (1914): 375–92. https://www.jstor.org/stable/1946172.

"Find a Grave: World's Largest Gravesite Collection." https://www.findagrave.com.

Fish, Hamilton, to General Robert Cumming Schenck. April 26, 1873. *The Clayton-Bulwer Treaty and the Monroe Doctrine: Letter from the Secretary of State to the Minister of the United States at London, Dated May 8, 1882, with Sundry Papers and Documents Explanatory of the Same...* Washington, D.C.: Government Printing Office, 1882.

https://hdl.handle.net/2027/mdp.35112104623485.
Flanigan, Timothy E. *Authority to Use United States Military Forces in Somalia* (1992). https://www.justice.gov/file/20526/download.
Folkman, David I. *The Nicaragua Route*. Salt Lake City: University of Utah Press, 1972.
"Frank Pierce and Major-General Scott." *The United States Democratic Review* 31, October 1852. https://hdl.handle.net/2027/coo.31924080777406.
Fuess, Claude Moore. *Daniel Webster*. Vol. 2. Boston: Little, Brown and Company, 1930.
―――. *The Life of Caleb Cushing*. Vol. 2. New York: Harcourt, Brace and Company, 1923. https://hdl.handle.net/2027/mdp.39015026645823.
Gale, Edwin Oscar. *Reminiscences of Early Chicago and Vicinity*. Chicago: Fleming H. Revell, 1902. https://hdl.handle.net/2027/uc2.ark:/13960/t1mg7rf7f.
Garcia, Michael J., Caitlain Devereaux, Lewis Andrew Nolan, Meghan Totten, and Ashley Tyson. *The Constitution of the United States of America Analysis and Interpretation (aka CONAN)*. Washington, D.C.: Congressional Research Service, Library of Congress, US Government Publishing Office, 2017. https://www.govinfo.gov/content/pkg/GPO-CONAN-2017/pdf/GPO-CONAN-2017.pdf.
General Records of the Department of Justice, Letters Received, 1809–1870 (Source Chronological Files), Entry A1-9, National Archives at College Park, MD. RG 59.
General Records of the Department of State. Domestic Letters. National Archives at College Park, MD. RG 59.
The Gilder Lehrman Institute of American History. https://www.gilderlehrman.org.
Gilman, Daniel Coit, Harry Thurston Peck, and Frank Moore Colby, eds. *The New International Encyclopedia, Vol. 5*. New York: Dodd, Mead, 1905. https://books.google.com/books?id=m4NRAAAAYAAJ&vq.
Glassman, Matthew E. *Franking Privilege: Historical Development and Options for Change*. April 22, 2015. Washington, D.C.: Congressional Research Service.

https://digital.library.unt.edu/ark:/67531/metadc505480/.
Goldsmith III, Jack L. *Deployment of United States Armed Forces to Haiti* (2004). https://www.justice.gov/file/18876/download.
Gonzales, Alberto R. *Legal Authorities Supporting the Activities of the National Security Agency Described by the President* (2006). https://www.justice.gov/archive/opa/docs/whitepaperonsalegalauthorities.pdf.
Gopsill's Philadelphia City Directory, 1871 (16 mm.). FamilySearch Family History Library, United States & Canada, 2nd Floor, Film 1000897, Item 3, Image Group Number 8321660. https://www.familysearch.org/search/catalog/2057911?availability=Family%20History%20Library.
Gore, W.R. "The Life of Henry Lawrence Kinney." Master's thesis, University of Texas, 1948.
Grant, Ulysses S. *The Papers of Ulysses S. Grant*. 31 vols. Mississippi State University, University Libraries, Institutional Repository. https://scholarsjunction.msstate.edu/usg-volumes/.
Grant (William S.) v. United States. 1 Ct. Cl. 41 (1863). https://cite.case.law/ct-cl/1/41/3529531/.
Hamilton, Lee H., Daniel K. Inouye. *Report of the Congressional Committees Investigating the Iran/Contra Affair* (1987), https://hdl.handle.net/2027/mdp.39015014635240?urlappend=%3Bseq=3%3Bownerid=13510798889954506-7.
Hasbrouck, Alfred. "Gregor McGregor and the Colonization of Poyais, Between 1820 and 1824." *The Hispanic American Historical Review* 7, no. 4 (1927): 438–59. https://doi.org/10.2307/2505996.
Hillard, George S. "Fletcher Webster." *Harvard Memorial Biographies Vol. 1*. Edited by Thomas Wentworth Higginson. Cambridge: Sever and Francis, 1866, 21–30. https://quod.lib.umich.edu/m/moa/abj7370.0001.001/43.
Historical Department of the Church of Jesus Christ Latter-day Saints. *Journal History of the Church, 1830–2008*. Call Number: CR 100 137. https://catalog.churchofjesuschrist.org/record/3ffad93a-5200-4a7e-9d68-2f4e42a13188/0?view=browse.
Hollins, George N. *Log of the USS Cyane:*

Mar. 1, 1853–Sept. 6, 1854. Washington: National Archives and Records Service, Records of the Bureau of Naval Personnel, Record Group 24, General Service, General Service Administration, 1970. OCLC Number: 19465127.

A Home in Nicaragua! The Kinney Expedition. New York, W.C. Bryant & Co., 1855. https://hdl.handle.net/2027/loc.ark:/13960/t6d22qn6q?urlappend=%3Bseq=1.

Johnson's Lessee v. McIntosh. 21 U.S. 543, Supreme Court of the United States, 1823 (8 Wheat. 543). https://www.courtlistener.com/opinion/85404/johnsons-lessee-v-mcintosh/.

Johnston, Alexander Keith. *Dictionary of Geography, Descriptive, Physical, Statistical, and Historical, Forming a Complete General Gazetteer of the World* [aka *Johnston's Gazetteer.*] London, 1852. https://hdl.handle.net/2027/cool.ark:/13960/t8gf1cx1b. (Possibly readable only in Page by Page View at this link, Plain Text View garbled.)

———. *Dictionary of Geography, Descriptive, Physical, Statistical, and Historical, Forming a Complete General Gazetteer of the World, New Edition.* [aka *Johnston's Gazetteer.*] London: Longmans, Green, Reader and Dyer, 1868. https://hdl.handle.net/2027/wu.89097025118. (Possibly readable only in Page by Page View at this link, Plain Text View garbled.)

Jolley, W.D. *Log of HMS Bermuda, July 1—Dec. 6, 1854.* Records of HM Ships, ADM 54—Admiralty: Supplementary Ships' Logs, ADM 54/28—*BERMUDA.* July 1—Dec. 6, 1854. The National Archives of the United Kingdom.

King, Edward John. *Congressional Record, House.* February 27, 1917, 4412–13. https://www.govinfo.gov/content/pkg/GPO-CRECB-1917-pt5-v54/pdf/GPO-CRECB-1917-pt5-v54-3.pdf. (This is 99-page PDF for the dates of February 27 & 28, 1917, running from page 4369 to 4468. King's speech begins on page 4412 and ends on 4413.)

Klages, Ellen. *Harbin Hot Springs: Healing Waters, Sacred Land.* Middletown, Calif., 1991.

Lee, Brian Angelo. "Emergency Takings," *114 Mich. L. Rev.* 391 (2015). https://repository.law.umich.edu/mlr/vol114/iss3/2.

Lockey, J.B. "Diplomatic Futility," *The Hispanic American Historical Review* 10, no. 3 (August 1930): 265–94. https://www.jstor.org/stable/2506375.

Manget, Fred F. "Presidential War Powers (A Constitutional Basis for Foreign Intelligence Operations)." NARA, Record Group 263: Records of the Central Intelligence Agency, 1894–2002. Series: Articles from "Studies in Intelligence," 1955–1992. File Unit: Summer 1987: 10-114–7. https://research.archives.gov/id/7283242.

Manning, William R, ed. *Diplomatic Correspondence of the United States: Inter-American Affairs. Vol. 7: Great Britain, 1831–1860.* Washington, D.C.: Carnegie Endowment for International Peace, 1936. https://hdl.handle.net/2027/uva.x002447434.

———. *Diplomatic Correspondence of the United States. Inter-American Affairs 1831–1860.* Washington, D.C.: Carnegie Endowment for International Peace, 1932–39, 12 vols. https://catalog.hathitrust.org/Record/006685374.

———. *Diplomatic Correspondence of the United States. Inter-American Affairs. Vol. 3: Central America, 1831–1850.* Washington, D.C.: Carnegie Endowment for International Peace, 1933. https://hdl.handle.net/2027/uva.x030346174.

———. *Diplomatic Correspondence of the United States. Inter-American Affairs. Vol. 4: Central America, 1851–1860.* Washington, D.C.: Carnegie Endowment for International Peace, 1934. https://hdl.handle.net/2027/txu.059172149398109.

Margulies, Peter. "Taking Care of Immigration Law: Presidential Stewardship, Prosecutorial Discretion, and the Separation of Powers." *Boston University Law Review* 94, no. 105 (2014): 105–169. http://www.bu.edu/bulawreview/files/2014/03/MARGULIES.pdf.

May, Robert E. *John A. Quitman, Old South Crusader.* Baton Rouge: Louisiana State University Press, 1985.

———. *Manifest Destiny's Underworld: Filibustering in Antebellum America.* University of North Carolina Press, 2004.

———. *The Southern Dream of a Caribbean Empire, 1854–1861.* Gainesville: University Press of Florida, 2002.

McCampbell, Coleman. "H.L. Kinney and Daniel Webster in Illinois in the 1830's." *Journal of the Illinois State Historical Society (1908–1984)* 47, no. 1 (1954): 35–44. http://www.jstor.org/stable/40189348.

McClure, A.K. *Old Time Notes of Pennsylvania*. Vol. 1. Philadelphia: John C. Winston Company, 1905. https://hdl.handle.net/2027/pst.000064033426.

Message from the President of the United States, Communicating, in Compliance with a Resolution of the Senate, Information in Relation to the Transactions Between Captain Hollins, of the United States Ship Cyane, and the Authorities at San Juan De Nicaragua, December 20, 1853. 33rd Congress, 1st. sess., Senate. Executive Doc. No. 8. https://hdl.handle.net/2027/ucl.b3984518?urlappend=%3Bseq=527%3Bownerid=9007199276160585-565.

Message from the President of the United States, Communicating Reports in Relation to the Condition of Affairs in Central America, May 15, 1856, US Congressional Serial Set. Volume 858 (US Government Printing Office, 1856), House of Representatives, 34th Congress, 1st Sess., Ex. Doc. No. 103, Series 858. https://hdl.handle.net/2027/ucl.b3984619?urlappend=%3Bseq=577%3Bownerid=9007199276169212-577.

Message from the President of the United States Communicating, in Compliance with a Resolution of the Senate, Information Respecting the Bombardment of San Juan De Nicaragua. 33rd Congress, 1st sess., S. Exec. Doc. 85. https://hdl.handle.net/2027/ucl.b3984526?urlappend=%3Bseq=537%3Bownerid=9007199276160944-581.

Message from the President of the United States Communicating a Report from the Secretary of State, Embodying the Substance of Recent Communications from the British Minister on the Subject of the Inter-Oceanic Canal, by the Nicaragua Route, February 19, 1853. 32d. Congress, 2d sess., Senate, Ex. Doc. No. 44, 1. 665. https://hdl.handle.net/2027/ucl.b3983603?urlappend=%3Bseq=181.

Message of the President of the United States, Communicating a Report of the Secretary of State, in Compliance with a Resolution of the Senate of the 17th Ultimo, Calling for Copies of Certain Correspondence and Other Papers Relative to the Republics of Nicaragua, Costa Rica, the Mosquito Indians, and the Convention Between the United States and Great Britain of April 19, 1850. Congressional Serial Set, S. Exec. Doc. No. 25, 34th Cong., 1st sess. (1856). https://digitalcommons.law.ou.edu/cgi/viewcontent.cgi?article=2285&context=indianserialset.

Message of the President of the United States Communicating, in Compliance with a Resolution of the Senate, the Correspondence Between the Department of State and the Minister of Bremen, on the Subject of Claims for Losses Alleged to Have Been Sustained by Subjects of the Hanse Towns at the Bombardment of Greytown. 35th Cong., 1st Sess., Senate, Ex. Doc. No. 10. Senate Documents. Volume 112. United States Senate: U.S. Government Printing Office, 1858. https://hdl.handle.net/2027/uc2.ark:/13960/t3125sm8z?urlappend=%3Bseq=3.

Miller, David Hunter. *Treaties and Other International Acts of the United States of America*. Vol. 5. Washington, D.C.: US Government Printing Office, 1937.

Miller, Samuel Freeman, and the Supreme Court of the United States. *U.S. Reports: In Re Neagle, Petitioner, 135 U.S. 1.* 1889. Periodical. https://www.loc.gov/item/usrep135001/.

Mitchell v. Harmony. 54 U.S. 115 (1851). https://cite.case.law/us/54/115/.

Moore, J. Bassett, and F. Wharton Moore. *A Digest of International Law*. Vol. 4. Washington, D.C.: US Government Printing Office, 1906. https://hdl.handle.net/2027/osu.32435025543695.

Nance, Joseph Milton. *After San Jacinto: The Texas-Mexican Frontier, 1836–1841.* University of Texas Press, 2011.

National Archives and Records Administration. "Guide to Senate Records: Chapter 6, Records of the Committee on Claims and Other Claims Committees." https://www.archives.gov/legislative/guide/senate/chapter-06.html.

The National Archives of the United Kingdom (acronym TNA). Foreign Office Archives, Public Record Office (London).

Nat'l Bd. of YMCAs v. United States. 396 F.2d 467 (1968) aff'd 395 U.S. 85 (1969). https://cite.case.law/f2d/396/467/2148531/.

"New York Passenger Lists, 1820–1891," database with images, FamilySearch (https://familysearch.org/ark:/61903/3:1:939V-5KS7-G6?cc=1849782&wc=MX62-NWL%3A165774001: 21 May 2014), 127–4 Jun 1853–17 Jun 1853 > image 259 of 629; citing NARA microfilm publication M237. Washington, D.C.: National Archives and Records Administration, n.d.

"_____," database with images, FamilySearch (https://familysearch.org/ark:/61903/3:1:939V-5N73-C?cc=1849782&wc=MX62-XP8%3A165774901: 21 May 2014), 128–18 Jun 1853–16 Jul 1853 > image 198 of 723; citing NARA microfilm publication M237. Washington, D.C.: National Archives and Records Administration, n.d.

Nichols, Roy Franklin. *Franklin Pierce, Young Hickory of the Granite Hills*. Philadelphia: University of Pennsylvania Press, 1931.

_____. "The Missing Diaries of George Mifflin Dallas." *The Pennsylvania Magazine of History and Biography* 75 (July 1951): 295–338.

Norton, Charles G. "Col. H.L. Kinney, a Texian History Forgot." *Austin Times and the Texas Democrat*. Archives and Information Services Division, Texas State Library and Archives Commission. There were six installments of this series, running from May 28 to July 2, 1937. This 1937 *Austin Times and the Texas Democrat* series is very similar in content to the 12-part series Charles Norton did for the *Corpus Christi Caller-Times* just a year later.

_____. *Milford Phillips Norton, Pioneer of Bayou City*. Milford Phillips Norton Papers. Archives and Information Services Division, Texas State Library and Archives Commission. This is a circa 1938 unpublished 21-page typescript. It is possibly filed under "Norton (Charles G.) Literary effort."

_____. Twelve Installments On The Life Of H. L. Kinney. *Corpus Christi Caller-Times* (Corpus Christi, Texas). The articles ran from May 16 to May 31, 1938. This 1938 *Corpus Christi Caller-Times* series is very similar in content to the six-part series Charles Norton did for the *Austin Times and the Texas Democrat* just a year earlier.

Norton, Milford Phillips. *Papers, Misc. Letters, 1842–1855*. Archives and Information Services Division, Texas State Library and Archives Commission.

Offutt, Milton. *The Protection of Citizens Abroad by the Armed Forces of the United States*. Baltimore: Johns Hopkins Press, 1928.

Orwell, George. *1984*. San Diego: Harcourt Brace Jovanovich, 1949, 1983.

Payne, Darwin. "Camp Life in the Army of Occupation: Corpus Christi, July 1845 to March 1846." *The Southwestern Historical Quarterly* 73, no. 3 (1970): 326–42. http://www.jstor.org/stable/30238071.

Perrin v. United States. 79 U.S. 315, 12 Wall. 315, 20 L. Ed. 412 (1870). https://cite.case.law/us/79/315/.

Perrin v. United States. US Court of Claims, 4 Ct. Cl. 543 (1868). https://cite.case.law/ct-cl/4/543/.

The Petition of Marie Louise Perrin and Trautman Perrin, Praying for Compensation. 44th Congress, 1st sess., Senate Report No. 464. July 13,1876, United States Congressional serial set. 1668 (1875–76.), #693. https://hdl.handle.net/2027/ucl.b3985273?urlappend=%3Bseq=693%3Bownerid=90071992 76155056-709.

Pierce, Franklin. *Franklin Pierce Papers*. Manuscript Division, Library of Congress, Washington, D.C.

_____. "Inaugural Address." Yale Law School, Lillian Goldman Law Library. *The Avalon Project, Documents in Law, History and Diplomacy*. https://avalon.law.yale.edu/19th_century/pierce.asp.

_____. "The State of the Union: Being a Complete Documentary History of the Public Affairs of the United States, Foreign and Domestic, for the Year 1854." Washington: Taylor & Maury, 1855. December 4, 1854. https://www.presidency.ucsb.edu/documents/second-annual-message-8.

Pletcher, David. *The Diplomacy of Trade and Investment: American Economic Expansion in the Hemisphere, 1865–1900*. Columbia: University of Missouri Press, 1998.

Presidential Notification of the U.S. Strikes in Afghanistan Against a Series of Camps and Installations Used by the Usama Bin Ladin Organization, and in Sudan

Where the Bin Ladin Organization Has Facilities, and Extensive Ties to the Government. 105th Congress, 2d sess. House Document 105-308. http://www.gpo.gov/fdsys/pkg/CDOC-105hdoc308/html/CDOC-105hdoc308.htm.

Prospectus of the Central American Company, Organized October 16th, 1855, on the Basis of 22,500,000 Acres of Land and a Capital of $5,625,000. Philadelphia: F.W. Thomas, 1855.

Public Papers of the Presidents of the United States. United States: Federal Register Division, National Archives and Records Service, General Services Administration, 1974.

Quirk, Robert E. *An Affair of Honor; Woodrow Wilson and the Occupation of Veracruz.* Lexington: Published for the Mississippi Valley Historical Association [by] University of Kentucky Press, 1962. https://archive.org/details/affairofhonorwoo00quir.

R., I.F. "United States Court of Claims. Brown v. the United States." *The American Law Register* 20, no. 3 (1872): 172–90. https://www.jstor.org/stable/3303292.

Rafter, Michael. *Memoirs of Gregor M'Gregor: Comprising a Sketch of the Revolution in New Grenada and Venezuela, with Biographical Notices of Generals Miranda, Bolivar, Morillo and Horé, and a Narrative of the Expeditions to Amelia Island, Porto Bello, and Rio De La Hache, Interspersed with Revolutionary Anecdotes.* London: J.J. Stockdale, 1820. https://hdl.handle.net/2027/hvd.hxg199.

Reeves, Richard. *President Kennedy: Profile of Power.* Norwalk, CT: Easton Press, 2000.

Remini, Robert Vincent. *Daniel Webster: The Man and His Time.* United Kingdom: W.W. Norton, 1997.

Rogers, William P. "Congress, the President, and the War Powers." *California Law Review* 59, no. 5 (1971): 1194–1214. https://doi.org/10.2307/3479587.

Romney, Edyth Jenkins. *Brigham Young Office Files Transcriptions, 1974–1978.* Call Number: MS 2736. https://catalog.churchofjesuschrist.org/record/69c289c7-aa19-42a8-a522-851f178f9f47/0?view=browse.

"San Juan De Nicaragua." *Harper's New Monthly Magazine* 10, no. 55, December 1854. https://hdl.handle.net/2027/hvd.hnybh1?urlappend=%3Bseq=62%3Bownerid=27021597768256921-66.

Schlesinger, Jr., Arthur Meier. *The Imperial Presidency.* Boston: Houghton Mifflin, 1973. https://www.google.com/books/edition/_/zbLO9aNL6ncC?hl=en&gbpv=0.

Schmidt, Hans. *Maverick Marine, General Smedley D. Butler and the Contradictions of American Military History.* Lexington: University Press of Kentucky, 1987.

Schurz, Carl. *The Reminiscences of Carl Schurz.* Vol. 2. New York: The McClure Co., 1907. https://hdl.handle.net/2027/uc2.ark:/13960/t47p8tp0w.

Scott, Walter, ed. *The Edinburgh Annual Register.* Vol. 16. Edinburgh: John Ballantyne and Co., 1823. https://hdl.handle.net/2027/umn.31951000729653y.

Scroggs, William O. *Filibusters and Financiers: The Story of William Walker and His Associates.* New York: Macmillan Co., 1916. https://hdl.handle.net/2027/mdp.39015005233559.

———. "William Walker's Designs on Cuba." *The Mississippi Valley Historical Review* 1, no. 2 (Sep 1914): 198–211. https://www.jstor.org/stable/1894950.

Seager, Robert, II. "The Samuel S. Wood Papers." *The Yale University Library Gazette* 34, no. 4, April (1960): 166–77. https://www.jstor.org/stable/40857860.

Senate Journal. https://memory.loc.gov/ammem/amlaw/lwsj.html.

Sexton, Jay. *Debtor Diplomacy: Finance and American Foreign Relations in the Civil War Era, 1837–1873.* Oxford, England: Clarendon Press, 2005.

Shewmaker, Kenneth E. "'Congress Only Can Declare War' and 'The President Is Commander in Chief': Daniel Webster and the War Power." *Diplomatic History* 12, no. 4 (1988): 383–410. https://doi.org/10.1111/j.1467-7709.1988.tb00034.x.

Sinclair, David. *The Land That Never Was: Sir Gregor MacGregor and the Most Audacious Fraud in History.* Cambridge, MA: De Capo Press, 2004.

Smith, Arthur D. Howden. *Commodore Vanderbilt: An Epic of American Achievement.* New York: McBride, 1927.

"Solon Borland (1811–1864)," Encyclopedia of Arkansas, accessed April 8, 2022. https://encyclopediaofarkansas.net/entries/solon-borland-1595/.

Soper, Will. "Can an Amateur Historian Rewrite History?" History News Network, October 23, 2018, https://historynewsnetwork.org/article/170070.

———. "Revisiting Nineteenth-Century U.S. Interventionism in Central America: Capitalism, Intrigue, and the Obliteration of Greytown," *American Nineteenth Century History* 18, no. 1 (2017): 19–44. https://doi.org/10.1080/14664658.2017.1319633.

Squier, E.G. "Nicaragua, an Exploration from Ocean to Ocean." *Harper's New Monthly Magazine* 11, no. 65, October 1855: 577–590. https://hdl.handle.net/2027/ucl.b00054155 8?urlappend=%3Bseq=589%3Bownerid=13510798903573473-651.

———. *Travels in Central America, Particularly in Nicaragua: With a Description of Its Aboriginal Monuments, Scenery and People, Their Languages, Institutions, Religion, &c.* Vol. 1. New York: D. Appleton & Company, 1853. https://hdl.handle.net/2027/umn.31951002321630q.

Squier, George, and John M. Clayton. "Letters of E. George Squier to John M. Clayton, 1849–1850." Edited by Williams, Mary Wilhelmine. *The Hispanic American Historical Review* 1, no. 4 (1918): 426–34. https://www.jstor.org/stable/2505893.

Stern, Madeleine B. *Purple Passage: The Life of Mrs. Frank Leslie.* University of Oklahoma Press, 1953.

Stevens, Kenneth R. "Of Whaling Ships and Kings: The Johanna Bombardment of 1851," *Prologue: The Journal of the National Archives* 18 (Winter 1986): National Archives and Records Service, General Services Administration, 241–49.

Stiles, T.J. *The First Tycoon: The Epic Life of Cornelius Vanderbilt.* New York: Knopf, 2009.

Straney, Louis L. *Securities Fraud: Detection, Prevention and Control.* Hoboken, NJ: John Wiley & Sons, 2011.

Strangeways, Thomas. *Sketch of the Mosquito Shore:* Edinburgh: William Blackwood, 1822. https://hdl.handle.net/2027/hvd.32044019372838?urlappend=%3Bseq=9%3Bownerid=27021597764372877-13.

Strom, Sharon Hartman. "'If Success Depends Upon Enterprise': Central America, U.S. Foreign Policy, and Race in the Travel Narratives of E.G. Squier." *Diplomatic History* 35, no. 3 (June 2011): 403–43. https://doi.org/10.1111/j.1467-7709.2011.00958.x.

Tabacinic, Ilana. "The Enemy-Property Doctrine: A Double Whammy?" 62 *U. Miami L. Rev.* 601 (2008). http://repository.law.miami.edu/umlr/vol62/iss2/12.

Thayer, William Sidney. *William Sidney Thayer Papers, 1835–1901* (bulk 1835–1895). Library of Congress. https://lccn.loc.gov/mm78042689.

Thrapp, Dan L. *Encyclopedia of Frontier Biography.* Vol. G–O. Lincoln: University of Nebraska Press.

Thompson, Karl R. *Authority to Order Targeted Airstrikes Against the Islamic State of Iraq and the Levant* (2014). https://www.justice.gov/olc/opinion/file/1108686/download.

Transactions of the Illinois State Historical Society for the Year 1904. United States: Illinois State Historical Society, 1904. https://archive.org/details/transactionsofil1904illi/page/n8/mode/1up.

Trautmann-Perrin, Charles Augustus, and Marie Louise Trautmann-Perrin. *Collection of Printed Materials Related to the Claim of Maria Louise and Trautman Perrin Over the Destruction of Their Property During the Bombardment of San Juan Del Norte (Greytown), Nicaragua, by the U.S. Sloop* Cyane *on July 13, 1854.* Massachusetts Historical Society, Call Number: Box L-1868; Location: Manuscript. http://balthazaar.masshist.org/cgi-bin/Pwebrecon.cgi?v1=1&ti=1,1&Search%5FArg=Collection%20of%20Printed%20Materials%20Related%20to%20the%20Claim%20of%20Maria%20Louise%20and%20Trautman%20Perrin&Search%5FCode=FT%2A&CNT=10&PID=Z19RYxrS15I_eK3obtQw8uNDI&SEQ=2. (Author's note: This material, five documents in all, was archived with just penciled numbers at the top of each. Since the collection doesn't otherwise specifically identify them, I gave them these descriptive names in the citations here: "Document 1—Letter Appealing for Influence"; "Document 2—Appeal to Secretary of State Seward"; "Document

3—Statement of Losses Sustained"; "Document 4—Petition to the US Court of Claims"; "Document 5—Letter Appealing for a Loan.")

Travis, Ira Dudley. *The History of the Clayton-Bulwer Treaty*. Vol. 3, no. 8. Ann Arbor: Michigan Political Science Association, 1900. https://hdl.handle.net/2027/cool.ark:/13960/t56d6dgl5.

Tufts [University] Digital Library. *The Boston Directory*. Boston: Adams, Sampson & Co., 1865. http://bcd.lib.tufts.edu/view_text.jsp?urn=tufts:central:dca:UA069:UA069.005.DO.00021&chapter=d.1865.su.Perrin.

Twiss, Travers. *The Law of Nations Considered as Independent Political Communities: On the Rights and Duties of Nations in Time of Peace*. Oxford: University Press/Clarendon Press, 1861. https://hdl.handle.net/2027/mdp.35112102839240.

Tyler, John, and Lyon Gardiner Tyler. *The Letters and Times of the Tylers*. Vol. 2. Richmond: Whittet & Shepperson, 1884–96. https://hdl.handle.net/2027/cool.ark:/13960/t2m623g9m.

"United States Census, 1880." Database with images. FamilySearch. Citing NARA microfilm publication T9. Washington, D.C.: National Archives and Records Administration. Accessed January 15, 2022. https://www.familysearch.org/search/collection/1417683.

United States v. Caltex (Philippines), Inc.. 344 U.S. 149, 154 (1952). https://cite.case.law/us/344/149/.

United States v. Pacific Railroad. 120 U.S. 227 (1887). https://cite.case.law/us/120/227/.

Use of U.S. Armed Forces in Foreign Countries, II. Instances of Use of U.S. Armed Forces Abroad, 1798–1945, Congressional Record (Bound Edition). 91st Congress, 1st sess., vol. 115, no. 13. Senate: June 23, 1969. https://www.govinfo.gov/content/pkg/GPO-CRECB-1969-pt13/pdf/GPO-CRECB-1969-pt13-2-2.pdf. This is a 110-page PDF for the date of June 23rd, 1969, running from page 16802 to 16858. The list begins on page 16840 and ends on 16843.

Van Alstyne, Richard W. "The Central American Policy of Lord Palmerston, 1846–1848." *The Hispanic American Historical Review* 16, no. 3 (1936): 339–59. https://www.jstor.org/stable/2507558.

Vattel, Emer de. *The Law of Nations Sixth American Edition*. Philadelphia: T. & J.W. Johnson, Law Booksellers, 1844. https://hdl.handle.net/2027/ucl.32106009089639.

Vladeck, Stephen I. "Enemy Aliens, Enemy Property, and Access to the Courts." *Lewis and Clark Law Review*. Vol. 11, 2007, American University, WCL Research Paper No. 08-21. Permalink: https://papers.ssrn.com/sol3/papers.cfm?abstract_id=1020269.

von Holst, Hermann. *The Constitutional and Political History of the United States*. Vol. 4, 1850–1854. Chicago. https://hdl.handle.net/2027/pst.000018425291.

Waddell, David. "Great Britain and the Bay Islands, 1821–61." *The Historical Journal* 2, no. 1 (1959): 59–77. http://www.jstor.org/stable/3020338.

Walker, William. *The War in Nicaragua*. Mobile, AL: S.H. Goetzel, 1860. https://hdl.handle.net/2027/mdp.39015005287399.

Wall, James T. *Manifest Destiny Denied*. Washington, D.C.: University Press of America, 1981.

Walpole, Frederick. *Four Years in the Pacific: In Her Majesty's Ship "Collingwood," from 1844 to 1848*. Vol. 1. United Kingdom: 1850. https://hdl.handle.net/2027/njp.32101019614781.

Walsh, Mike. *Mike Walsh Papers*. New-York Historical Society. Manuscript Collections, 1840–1865.

War Powers Resolution: Hearings Before the Committee on Foreign Relations, United States Senate, Ninety-fifth Congress, on a Review of the Operation and Effectiveness of the War Power Resolution, July 13, 14, and 15, 1977. United States: U.S. Government Printing Office, 1977. https://www.google.com/books/edition/War_Powers_Resolution/YGodlzwLeUkC?hl=en&gbpv=0.

Webster, Daniel, and Fletcher Webster. *The Private Correspondence of Daniel Webster*. Vol. 2. Boston: Little, Brown, and Co., 1857. https://hdl.handle.net/2027/uc2.ark:/13960/t8qb9xc3x.

Webster, Fletcher. Letter to his wife quoted on battlefield marker. HMdb.org (Historical Marker Data Base). August 30, 1862. https://www.hmdb.org/m.asp?m=9828.

Webster, Sidney. *Franklin Pierce and His*

Bibliography

Administration. New York: D. Appleton and Company, 1892. https://hdl.handle.net/2027/hvd.32044011783982?urlappend=%3Bseq=5%3Bownerid=3705771-9.

Weinberg, Albert K. *Manifest Destiny: A Study of Nationalist Expansionism in American History.* Baltimore: Johns Hopkins Press, 1935.

Wharton, Francis, ed. *A Digest of International Law of the United States, Taken from Documents Issued by Presidents and Secretaries of State, and from Decisions of Federal Courts and Opinions of Attorneys-General.* 2nd edition, vol. 3. Washington: 1887. https://hdl.handle.net/2027/hvd.32044057607319.

Wiggins v. United States. 3 Ct. Cl. 412 (1867). https://cite.case.law/ct-cl/3/412/.

Wilbarger, John Wesley. *Indian Depredations in Texas.* United States: Statehouse Books. 1985. https://www.google.com/books/edition/_/qqdAAQAAMAAJ?hl=en&gbpv=1.

Wilde, Oscar. *Intentions.* United States: T.B. Mosher, 1904. https://books.google.com/books?id=DqElAAAAMAAJ&q=.

Williams, Mary Wilhelmine. *Anglo-American Isthmian Diplomacy 1815–1915.* Washington, D.C.: American Historical Association, 1916. https://hdl.handle.net/2027/mdp.39015062922193.

Wilson, Richard H. "The Eighth Regiment of Infantry." New York: Maynard, Merrill & Co., 1891. https://history.army.mil/books/R&H/R&H-8IN.htm.

Wood, Samuel Smith. "Samuel Smith Wood Papers (MS 1083)." Manuscripts and Archives, Yale University Library. https://archives.yale.edu/repositories/12/resources/3990. According to the Public Services Department at the Manuscripts and Archives Division of the Yale University Library, the library cannot "provide a URL … for direct access to download the files in the Samuel Smith Wood Papers." However, the library "would instruct anyone who would like access to the [digitized] files to register [with the library, at mssa.assist@yale.edu] and agree to our user terms, and we would then send the files to them."

Wood, Samuel S. [Smith] and W.P. Kirkland. *The Greytown and Nicaragua Transit Company Controversy.* New York: John A. Grey, 1859. https://hdl.handle.net/2027/ien.35556043846179. (This is a slightly different version of the pamphlet cited below, titled *A Memorial to the Congress of the United States, on Behalf of the Sufferers from the Bombardment and Destruction of Greytown, Etc.*. and also dated 1859.)

_____, William P. Kirkland. *A Memorial to the Congress of the United States, on Behalf of the Sufferers from the Bombardment and Destruction of Greytown, or San Juan Del Norte, by the U.S. Sloop-of-war* Cyane, *on the 13th July, A.D. 1854; and Narrative of Events Which Transpired at That Place Between the Years 1852 and 1854.* New York: J.A. Gray, 1859. https://hdl.handle.net/2027/loc.ark:/13960/t4dn4zd2m. (This is a slightly different version of the pamphlet cited above, titled *The Greytown and Nicaragua Transit Company Controversy* and also dated 1859.)

Woodruff, Wilford. *Wilford Woodruff Journals and Papers, 1828–1898.* History Catalog of the Church of Jesus Christ of Latter-day Saints. Call Number: MS 1352. Accessed April 8, 2022. https://catalog.churchofjesuschrist.org/record/400c3266-ede2-43cf-9a24-50153adebbeb/0?view=summary.

Woods, James M. "Expansionism as Diplomacy: The Career of Solon Borland in Central America 1853–1854," *The Americas: Quarterly Review of Inter-American Cultural History* 40, no. 3 (January 1984), 399–415.

Wormuth, Francis D., Edwin Brown Firmage, and Francis P. Butler. *To Chain the Dog of War: The War Power of Congress in History and Law.* Dallas: Southern Methodist University Press., 1986.

Wright, Austin. "How Barbara Lee Became an Army of One." *Politico*, July 30, 2017. https://www.politico.com/magazine/story/2017/07/30/how-barbara-lee-became-an-army-of-one-215434.

Young, Thomas. *Narrative of a Residence on the Mosquito Shore, During the Years 1839, 1840, & 1841: With an Account of Truxillo, and the Adjacent Islands of Bonacca and Roatan.* London: Smith and Elder, 1842. https://hdl.handle.net/2027/hvd.32044024226540.

Index

Numbers in **_bold italics_** indicate pages with illustrations

Accessory Transit Company 7, 22–23, 27–28, 34, 37, 39, 59, 61–62, 87, 117, 132, 174, 194, 196, 205*n*2; accused of backing Shepherd grant scheme 45–46; called "important agency" in razing 66; distances from Shepherd grant scheme 100–101; eases Fabens in as commercial agent 20–21; Greytown cancels lease of 17; Greytown reportedly destroyed on behalf of 64, 69; Hollins blocks ejectment of 52–53; leased Punta Arenas from Mosquito Protectorate 17, 54; located on Greytown's Punta Arenas 15; in "mortal feud" with Greytown merchants 15, 19, 49; 51; offshoot of canal company 5, 35; plan to take-over of Greytown rumored 101; purports Greytowners stole food from 55–57; recruits 50-man force to thwart Kinney 114; remains on Punta Arenas 55; White lied about Punta Arenas lease of, 49, 54–55; *see also* Nicaragua Transit Company
Adrian, Thomas 138
The Aeneid 81
Albright, Madeleine 179
Al-Qaeda 165, 173
Amelia Island 95–96
American Atlantic and Pacific Ship Canal Company *see* Canal Company
American hotel **_10_**
American Nineteenth Century History: printed author's 2017 Greytown article 3
American Party 189
Anglo-Honduran treaty (1859) 126–129
Anglo-Nicaraguan convention (1860) 126–129
Anglo-Saxonism 43–44, 210*n*4

An Apology for Commander Hollins 204*n*4
Aubrey, William P. 77–78
Aulick, John H. *see* Selim, Sultan
Austin Times and the Texas Democrat 84, 208*n*28
Authority to Order Targeted Airstrikes Against the Islamic State of Iraq and the Levant (2014) 162
Authority to Use United States Military Forces in Somalia (1992) 162
Authorization for Use of Military Force 162, 165, 168, 171
author's 1982 Greytown pitch letter **3**

Baez, Buenaventura 188–189
Baltimore Sun 89, 149
Banks, William C. 4
Baring Brothers & Co. 33
Bartlett's Book of Anecdotes 161
Beebe, Henry S. 73, 76
Bell, Peter Hansborough 84
Belohlavek, John 112
Benjamin, Judah P. 189
Benton, Thomas Hart 107
Berger, Raoul 166
Bermann, Karl 39
HMS *Bermuda*: present during Greytown bombardment 59–61, 68
Best, J. Milton *see* Grant, Ulysses S.; Howe, Timothy O.; Vattel, Emer de
Bigelow, John 28
bin Laden, Osama 179–180
Birdseye, Lucien 103–104, 210*n*8
Black Hawk War 72
Black River Grant 98–99, 122; *see also* Poyais
Bloomfield, Thomas 153
Boarman, Charles: asks Army's Winfield

237

238 Index

Scott for aid 111; Pierce orders to stop Kinney 110–111; *see also* Scott, Winfield
Bolivar, Simón 95
Booker, George: asks Wise for Shepherd grant advice 57; Wise implicates Borland in Shepherd grant scheme 62; *see also* Wise, Henry A.
Borland, Solon 19, 42, 46, 56, 58–59, 62, 68, 92, 156; asks eighth of Shepherd grant to secure confirmation 82; conduct excoriated by *New York Times* 66–67; Hollins' defense uses claim of that Greytowners usurped port 147–148; involvement in Shepherd speculation suggested 57; pays 50 armed Americans to protect transit company 23; possible involvement in Paladino murder 14–15, 22; post–Greytown life 189; prior career 9–12; recommends Greytown population be exterminated 24; reportedly helped plan Greytown's fate 64; thwarts Smith's arrest with gun 18; as U.S. minister *12*–13; visits Fabens' Greytown home 20–21; wounded slightly by Greytown mob 21
Boston Atlas 15
Boston Globe 159
Bourne, Kenneth 28
Boyce, W.W. 178
Boyd, Stephen E. 163
Boyle, Edward R. 103–104
Bremen 21, 198*n*27, 204*n*3
Britannica 48, 161
British Honduras (aka Belize) 28, 98–99, 122
Brookin, Major 144, 146
Brooklyn Daily Eagle 193
Brown, Nathaniel J. 75
Bryce, James G. 46, 71, 201*ch*4*n*6; background 38; convinces some Greytowners to tie holdings to Shepherd grant 38; Keeling eclipsed by 38; Shepherd brother's agent 37; *see also* Keeling, David Francis; Shepherd grant
Buchanan, James 80, 123, 125, 144–146, 207*n*18, 212*ch*14*n*3; alarmed by Mormons 138; assumes Marcy will disavow Hollins' actions 63; insists only Congress can declare war 155–156; says Anglo-Honduran/Nicaraguan treaties "entirely satisfactory" 128–129
bungos **6**, 9, 13–15, 18, 25, 61, 138, 195; description of 5
Butler, Francis 156

Caicos Islands 112, 114
Caltex (Philippines), Inc. v. United States (1951): Claims Court decision overturned by Supreme Court 186
"Can an Amateur Historian Rewrite History?": author's op-ed 4; referenced by authors of *National Security Law* 4; reprint of 170–172
Canal Company 5, 32, 34, 66; called a mere "speculation" 33; incorporated in 1849 5; Squier suggests buy Shepherd grant 36; White transfers rights of to Accessory Transit 35
Cape Gracias á Dios 96
Cape Horn 9, 25
Cass, Lewis 80; Buchanan's secretary of state 125
Castillo Rapids 9
Cazneau, William L. 214*n*15; testifies at Fabens' hearing 134–135
Central American 117
Central American Company *see* Central American Land and Mining Company; Cooper project
Central American Land and Mining Company 37, 45, 57, 69, 71, 86–87, 89, 101, 103, 120, 142; Accessory Transit denies connection with 100; Borland connivance with suggested 82; Greytowners persuaded to transfer titles to 38; Kinney chosen by to lead expedition 83; Kinney ostracized by 102; Marcoleta calls "a fraud" 46–47; *see also* Cooper project
Chamorro, Don Fruto 42
Chancellor, Edward 99
Christie, W.D. 30–31, 36
CIA 160, 188; *see also* Manget, Fred F.
Cicilline, David N. 163
Clapham, Andrew 182
Clarendon, Lord 54–55, 63, 122–123; acquiesces when Senate quashes grant articles 125; agrees that treaty validate Mosquito grants 124; begins 1856 treaty talks with Dallas 124; *see also* Dallas, George Mifflin; Marcy, William L.
Clark, Henry D. 65
Clark, J. Reuben: justified executive interventions 155–156
Clark, Mrs. 65
Clarkson, Colonel 144–146
Clayton, John 27, 32; tells Squier Indians have no sovereign rights 123; tells Squier of Vanderbilt's canal interest 25–26
Clayton-Bulwer Treaty 32, 34, 129
Clinton, Bill 173, 180; El-Shifa factory destroyed by 179
CNN 180

Collier, Ellen C. 164
Committee on Claims 179, 182–184
Congressional Record 1, 158
Congressional Research Service 155, 166–167; 171–172; background of 164; chose not to address author's Greytown revelations 169; comments on Greytown and *Durand* 165; as "keepers" of the intervention list 168
Constitution 4, 69, 80, 88, 91, 156, 161–163, 166, 171, 174, 183; congressmen say Pierce violated 89–90; court decided president acted under 151; Hollins' defense said president acted under 149–150; newspapers say Pierce violated 65–66
Cooper, James 62, 92, 102–103 202n23; background of 45; as president of Shepherd grant company 44–45; rivalry with Kinney 104
Cooper, John B.: offered Kinney's Mosquito grant to Mormons 144, 146
Cooper project 62; why so called 205n14; *see also* Central American Land and Mining Company; Shepherd (aka Mosquito) grant
Corpus Christi 86, 103; during Mexican-American war 78–79; Kinney and partner considered founders of 77; Kinney holds fair in 83–84; Kinney returns to after filibuster 141–142
Corpus Christi Caller-Times 78, 84, 207n26
Corwin, Edward S. 217n35; declares *Durand* "leading precedent" for presidential interventions 159
Costa Rica 36, 39, 48, 210n4
Court of St. James's 123
Covell, Charles 175
Cox, Leander Martin 90
Crampton, John 55; describes Pierce's drinking 81; England can withdraw Canal Company protection 34; says White lied about Punta Arenas ownership 54; Shepherd grant scheme "humbug," like "Poyais swindle" 93
Crimean War 101
Cuba 48, 90, 188
Cuneo, Ernest 162
Currie, David P. 90
Cushing, Caleb 64, 76, 112, 135–136, 148, 192, 205n17; allegedly instigates Fabens and Kinney's arrest 107; arguments during Perrin suit 178; Daniel Webster borrows $3,000 from 75; denies Pierce knew of franked envelope or contents 134, 214n17; Fletcher refuses to repay Cushing his father's debt 87; led treaty delegation to China 106; opposition to Kinney scheme laid to unresolved debt 107, 109; personality of described 107–108; was Perrins' attorney in Greytown suit 178; Webster's indebtedness to reaches $10,000 76, 108–109
Cutler, Otis N. 183
USS *Cyane* 49–52, 55, 57–58, 63–64, 67–68, 70, 82, 88, 90, 92, 114, 117, 147, 149, 158–159, 174; descriptions of razing by 59–62; log of notes gunpowder at Punta Arenas destroyed 61–62; Marines from prevent ejectment of Accessory Transit 53; returned to Greytown to exact apology and reparations 56; sent to prevent ejectment of Accessory Transit 17

USS *Dale* 154
Dallas, George Mifflin 123, 126, 213n13; appointed to negotiate Central America treaty with British 122; and Clarendon validate Mosquito grants in draft treaty 124–125; Kinney's Philadelphia attorney when indicted at 110; *see also* Clarendon, Lord; Kinney, Henry Lawrence
Dallas, Susan 126
Dallas-Clarendon treaty 98, 127–128, 138, 193; articles to validate Mosquito land grants 122, 124–125; Clarendon acquiesces in grant articles expunging 125; Marcy inexplicably drops objections to Indian grants 123–124; Pierce appoints George Mifflin Dallas 122
HMS *Dee* 61
deed-of-transfer 131, 214n15; used by Kinney to bribe three officials 106–107
De Forrest, William H. 173–174
De Miranda, Francisco 94
Democratic Party convention of 1852 80–81
Democratic Review 48
De Niro, Robert 180
Deployment of United States Armed Forces to Haiti (2004) 162
Detroit Free Press 188
Devil Take the Hindmost 99, 210n19
Dexter, Harrington, & Co. 173
Dictionary of Geography, Descriptive, Physical, Statistical, and Historical, Forming a Complete General Gazetteer of the World see *Johnston's Gazetteer*
Digest of International Law of the United States 128

240   Index

Dimitt, Philip 77–78
Dobbin, James C. 63–64, 92, 190, 205*ch*6*n*17; defends Hollins' actions at Greytown 89; orders *Cyane* to Greytown 49, 58, 148,150; tells Hollins of arrest 82–83
Douglas, Stephen A. 38, 80
Du Pont, Samuel Francis 190, 222*n*9
Durand, Calvin 4, 62, 147, 150, 158, 173; sues Hollins for losses at Greytown 83
Durand, W. Cecil 158, 217*n*33
Durand v. *Hollins* (1868) 147, 149–150, 163, 167; cited in War Powers Act debate 165–166; Congressional Research Service expounds on 164; congressman cites in WWI debate 158–159; excerpts from decision 151; origin and significance 4; used to justify executive interventions 159–162, 164; *see also* In re Neagle; *Slaughter-house cases*
Dycus, Stephen 4

Economist 93
El-Shifa Pharmaceutical Industries Co.: Sudanese factory President Clinton destroyed 173
El-Shifa Pharmaceutical Industries Co. v. United States (2003): background and legal arguments 179–181; suit owner of factory brought after Clinton attack 179; *see also* Clinton, Bill; *Wag the Dog*
El-Shifa Pharmaceutical Industries Co. v. United States (2004): factory owner's appeal, legal arguments made during 181–182
El Toro Rapids 9
"Emergency Takings" 185
Emerson, J. Terry 166
Emma: Kinney sails for Greytown on 112; wrecks in Caicos Islands 112–114
"Enemy-Property Doctrine: A Double Whammy?" 181–182, 186
Engel, Eliot L. 163
Everett, Edward 34, 37, 43; says Greytown is like Hanse independent city-states 41, 151; says Greytown "will be an American town" 42

Fabens, Joseph W. 23, 49, 56–57, 59–60, 109–110, 112, 116, 118, 120; abandons Kinney to join William Walker 119; accused of violating U.S. neutrality as Walker recruiter (1857) 130; aids Kinney in bribing three officials 105–107; background 20–21; description of court proceeding (1857) 130–136; escapes indictment 136, 214*n*19; harbors Borland from mob at home 21–22; Hollins and agree on reparations demands 58; joins Kinney's filibuster 92; Kinney and accused of violating U.S. neutrality (1855) 107; life after Kinney and Walker filibusters 188–189; remains with Kinney in his new colonization scheme 102, 105; U.S. Commercial Agent at Greytown *20*; unsuccessfully exhorts *Northern Light* passengers to "take" town 21–22
Federal Reserve Bank of Minneapolis 199*n*30
Fenwick, Charles G. 175
Ferrar, Fermín 102, 106; note on relationship of with government and filibusters 210*n*6
Field, Stephen Johnson 185; dictum in *Pacific Railroad* became law later 186
Fifth Amendment *see* Takings Clause
filibustering 62, 76, 89, 91–93, 100–101, 107, 113–116, 120, 127, 130, 133, 138–139, 141, 143, 176, 193–194; descriptions of concept and examples of 48
Fillmore, Millard 41, 70
Firmage, Edwin 156
Fish, Hamilton 192–193; criticizes Mosquito grant articles in treaties 128
Fisher, Louis 171
Folkman, David 35
Foote, Henry S. 10–11
Forney, John W. 64, 205*n*17
Fort Hamilton 111, 116
Fort Schuyler 111
Frank Leslie's Illustrated Newspaper 190
Frémont, John C. 19–20

Garfield, James A. 182
Gavitt, Jonathan 187–188
George Frédéric Augustus I 96
SS *George Law* 118
Gold Rush 5, 25, 61, 72, 86
Goldwater, Barry 166
Graham, John 116
Graham, William Alexander 39, 153
Granada, Nicaragua 8, 116,
Grand Turk Island 114
Grant, Ulysses S. 25; fellow Republicans challenge veto of Best's award 183; vetoes award to loyal Civil War property owner 181–184
Grant-Foote, Henry 37
Grant [William S.] v. United States (1863) 184; property destroyed to keep enemy seizing is compensable 174
Greece 152; *see also* Johanna

Index

Green, Dr. James 37
Greytown *2*
Greytown Harbor 7, 13, 15, 19, 28, 61, 195
Guano Islands Act of 18 October 1856 188
Guardian 123

Haly, S.T. 43, 46, 120; partner in Mosquito grant 31; and Shepherd brothers traded with Mosquitos 29–31
Hanse towns of Germany 19, 151; description of 198*n*27; Greytown compared to by Edward Everett 41; Lord Malmesbury says Greytown seeks to emulate 40
Harbin, James Madison "Matt" 143–144, 146
Harper's *New Monthly Magazine*: describes American Anglo-Saxons as "great composite race" 43; describes Greytown's "miserable insignificance" 28; describes "mortal feud" between Greytown and Transit Company 16–17, 19, 49; Squier describes Paladino meeting 7
Hillard, George Stillman 192
Hipkins, William 104
History News Network 4, 169; *see also* "Can an Amateur Historian Rewrite History?"
Hitchens, Christopher 180
Hoffman, Dustin 180
Hollins, George N. 17, 55–57, 63, 67, 70, 92, 158–159, 173–174, 203*n*2, 203*n*3, 222*n*11; actions defended by Pierce 88–89; anonymous letter apologizing for actions of 204*n*4; arrested in damages case 82–83; background 50–*51*; bombards and torches Greytown 59–62; damages case against dismissed 151; damages case strategy discussed 147–150; demands reparations and apology from Greytown 58–59; destroys gunpowder to prevent use by townspeople 61–62; dismisses British captain's protest 59; post–Greytown life and death 190–191; prevents ejectment of transit company 50–54; *see also Durand v. Hollins*
Holm, Richard 160
A Home in Nicaragua! The Kinney Expedition 102
Honduran Bay Islands 127, 138
Honduras 7, 12, 16, 24, 39, 97, 99, 127, 138, 188–189; Anglo-Honduran treaty preserves British Mosquito grants 126–129
Howe, Timothy O.: argues against Grant's veto of damages award 182–183; notes property "deliberately destroyed" is compensable 184; *see also* Grant, Ulysses S.; Vattel, Emer de
H.R.1004—Prohibiting Unauthorized Military Action in Venezuela 163
Huerta, Victoriano 157
Huntress 114

Idris, Salah El Din Ahmed Mohammed: owner of El-Shifa factory 179; *see also El-Shifa Pharmaceutical Industries Co. v. United States* (2003); *El-Shifa Pharmaceutical Industries Co. v. United States* (2004)
Illinois-Michigan Canal 73, 75
Imperial Presidency 150
In re Neagle (1890): to protect federal officials, expanded to citizens overseas 159, 163; *see also Durand v. Hollins*; *Slaughter-house cases*
India (natural) rubber 187
Ingersoll, Joseph 42, 122, 123
Instances of Use of United States Forces Abroad 1, 164, 168–169, 171
Isthmus of Nicaragua 5, 25, 32
Isthmus of Panama 25, 195

Jamaica 5, 30, 114
James, G.P.R. 37
USS *Jamestown* 139–141
Jamestown [ND] *Alert* 158
Japan: invokes Greytown when denying reparations 159–160
Johanna 154; considered uncivilized by U.S. 154; Navy commander lobbies unsuccessfully for Selim reimbursement 154–155; protests U.S. whalers not paying 153; as source of U.S. whaling ships resupply 152; Selim takes U.S. captain prisoner 153; U.S. Navy bombards island twice 154; U.S. Navy captain demands reparations 154; U.S. treats differently than "civilized" Greece 152, 154; *see also* Shewmaker, Kenneth E; Stevens, Kenneth R.
Johnson, Wm. Cost 91–92, 102
Johnson vs. Mcintosh (1823): Supreme Court case denying Indians sovereign land rights 123; 212*ch*14*n*3
Johnston's Gazetteer 99
Jolley, W.D. 59–60
Journal of American History 2
Journal of Commerce 67

Karp, Matt 171
Keeling, David Francis 43–44; back-

Index

ground of 37; bought half Shepherd grant 36; eclipsed by Judge Bryce 38; *see also* Bryce, James G.; Shepherd grant
Kennedy, C.H. 139–141
Kennedy, John F. 161
Kennedy, Joseph C.G. 11
Kerr, John Bozman 34, 39; deplores White's "loose" talk 40; reports neighbors fear Nicaragua "already lost" to U.S. 40; succeeds Squier as minister to Nicaragua 34
King, Edward John 158–150
King, Jonas 152, 155; *see also* Shewmaker, Kenneth E.
King, William R. 207n18; endorsement aids Pierce's election 80
King Street, Greytown, looking Northward *52*
King Street, Greytown, looking Southward *50*
Kinney, Henry Lawrence 89, 92–94, 98, 100–101, 103, 108–109, 122–123, 125–126, 130, 134–136; accused of betraying neighbor to Mexicans 77–78; arrested for violating U.S. neutrality 107; arrives in Texas 77; assisted U.S. and Texas forces in war 79; befriended by future president General Franklin Pierce 79; bribes three federal officials 105–107; contemplates selling grant to Mormons 138; criticizes Walker to subordinates, Walker orders hanged 120–121; description of failed attempt by to seize Greytown 139–141; deserted by Fabens, who joins Walker 119; during Mexican-American War offered "smorgasbord of vices" 79; early life 72; elected Greytown's civil and military governor 117; engages Milford Norton as lawyer and agent 83; establishes Kinney's Ranch with Aubrey 77; failed state fair leaves deeply in debt 84; fails in attempt to sell grant to Mormons 142–146, 215n11; Federal vessels blockade expedition ship 110–111; and 500 "colonizers" prepare to steam for Greytown 102; flees Illinois as boom collapses 76; Fletcher Webster denounces 112; forms rival Nicaraguan Land and Mining Company 102; hopes to ally with Walker 118–119; Illinois real estate powerhouse 72–*73*; informs Walker of Shepherd grant purchase 120; invests heavily for Webster through son 74; lawyer convinces to seek opportunities from President Pierce 85–86; leaves Daniel financially distressed 75–76; meets Fletcher, son of legendary Daniel Webster 74; meets with president at least twice 91; moves to Honduras' Ruatán Island 138; murdered in Mexico 187; returns to Corpus Christi, finances described 141–142; rivalry with Senator Cooper 104; self-anointed "colonel" 72; Shepherd grant company ostracizes 102; Shepherd grant company taps to lead expedition 87; and smaller group steal away in schooner *Emma* 112–114; spared from hanging 121; tolerated by Texans despite Mexican trading 78
Kinney, Somers 187
Kinney's 1852 fair 84; *see also* Lone Star Fair
Kinney's Ranch 77
Kirkland, W.P. 71, 195
kitchen cabinet 92, 208n18
Konnikova, Maria 93
Know-Nothings 189
Krock, Arthur: invokes *Durand* defending U.S. Congo intervention 160–161

Lake Nicaragua 5, 9, 25
lake steamer *8*
Lamar, Mirabeau Buonaparte 78, 139
Lansing, Robert: cites Greytown as precedent for U.S. Mexican intervention 157
Law of Nations 175, 178
Lawrence, Abbott 32
Lawrence, Alexander C. 131–132, 214n19
"The Lay of San Juan" 68–69, 205ch7n9, 205–206ch7n10
Lee, Barbara 165
Lee, Brian Angelo 185
Lee's Summit, Missouri 147
Legal Authorities Supporting the Activities of the National Security Agency Described by the President (2006) 162
Leslie, Frank 189
Lewinsky, Monica 173, 180
Liberator: comments on razing and reprints other papers comments 67–69
Liverpool 29–31
Lockey, J.B. 24
London Times 33
Lone Star Fair 141; *see also* Kinney's 1852 fair
Lord, Thomas 100
Lumumba, Patrice 160–161

MacGregor, Gregor 93–95, 208–209n1, 209n8; Poyais fraud of 96–98; Poyais

Index

Mosquito grant scheme of similar to Kinney's 93–**94**
Machuca Rapids 8–9
Malmesbury, Earl of 99, 100, 122; believes Greytowners seek Hanseatic-like independence 40–41; insists on Poyais grant protection in treaty 98
CSS *Manassas* 191
Manget, Fred F.: *Durand* sanctioned "about 200" executive interventions 164
manifest destiny 28, 47–48
Manning, John A. 149
March, Charles W. 112
Marcoleta, José de 70–71, 100, 103–105; learns of Mosquito colonization scheme 45–47; Nicaraguan minister to U.S. 39; recruits mercenaries to block Kinney 114
Marcy, William L. 23, 43, 45–46, 49, 54, 57, 59, 63, 71, 80, 103–105, 107, 131, 134, 147–148, 151; calls White out on Punta Arenas lie 55; finally questions peaceful intent of Kinney 101, 210n3; Greytowners must redress food theft 56; inexplicably allows treaty to validate Mosquito land grants 123–125; insists Greytown still part of Nicaragua 42; insists Mosquito Indians can't sell their land 122–123; reprimands Borland 10, **11**, 12–13; says Kinney scheme is "peaceful pursuit" 47; sends *Cyane* to prevent transit company ejectment 50
Margulies, Peter 163–164
Maria 153
Marsh, George Perkins 152
Martin, T.J. 53
Mason, James 174
May, Robert E. 3, 101, 111, 139
Mayo, Henry T. 157
McCampbell, Coleman 73, 75–76
McClure, A.K. 45
McCullough, Ben 145
McKeon, John 104, 110, 114, 150; arrests Fabens second time for violating neutrality act 130; arrests Kinney and Fabens for violating neutrality act 107; Fabens' 1857 neutrality violation hearing 130–136; Hollins defense strategy during Durand's suit 147–149
McMichael, Morton 45
Meagher, Thomas Francis: asks if president was "interested" in Mosquito grant 133–135: background 131; Fabens' lead attorney during 1857 hearing 131; reveals Sidney Webster used presidentially-franked envelope 133–134, 214*ch*15n3

Memoirs of Gregor M'Gregor see Rafter, Michael
memorial 61, 192, 195–196; definition of 70; of Greytown sufferers 71; of owners of gunpowder destroyed by Hollins 174; of vessel *United States* owner 110, 116
Metropolitan Club 161
Mexican-American War 65, 92, 80, 84, 117; role of Corpus Christi and Kinney in 78–79
Mexico 1, 25, 48, 75, 85, 99, 187; Greytown as pretext for 1914 U.S. intervention in 157–158; Kinney and Mexican-American War 78–79; Kinney's relationship with 77–78
Michigan Law Review 185
Millar, William: describes murder of Paladino 13–15; questions Borland about confrontation at Fabens' house 22
Miller, David Hunter 96
Miller, Samuel Freeman 159
Miskito Indians preparing tortoise shell **29**
Mitchell v. Harmony (1851): dictum in found sounder than in *Pacific Railroad* 184, 186
Mooers, Charles C. 153–155
Moorman, Travis 78
Morgan, Charles 46, 100, 132
Mormon History Journal 146
Mormons 138, 142–144, 187; offered Mosquitia to escape persecution 146; *see also* Young, Brigham
Mosquito grant *see* Shepherd (aka Mosquito) grant
Mosquito Indians 41, 96; British establish protectorate for 16; English traded with for 200 years 16; never conquered by the Spanish 16; U.S. denies sovereign rights of to lands occupied 17, 122–123, 212*ch*14n3
Mosquito Protectorate 23, 27–30, 39, 45–47, 69–70, 82, 96, 99, 102, 104, 117, 124, 128, 138, 142, 144, 170; Britain cedes to Nicaragua and Honduras 126; as Britain's sanctuary for Mosquito Indians 16; British agree to end if Indians' welfare is guaranteed 41; called a "subterfuge" by U.S. 17; Greytown reattached to after 1848 British seizure of 19; Hondurans and Nicaraguans fear proposed U.S. colony in 48; transit company fears Kinney in might jeopardize monopoly 100; transit company leased Punta Arenas from 17; Walker declares part of Nicaragua 120
Myer, James 84–85

244 Index

Nashville Tennessean 68, 205*ch*7*n*9
The Nation 180
National Archives and Records Administration: search for *Durand v. Hollins* case file unsuccessful 147
National Board of Young Men's Christian Ass'n v. United States (1968): battle damage suit dismissed based on *Perrin* 179
National *Era*: notes British Mosquito titles based only on grants 123–124; predicts Greytown razing was pretext for annexation 82; writes Greytown razed under false pretense 67
National Security Law 4
Nelson, John L. 114
Nelson, Samuel: "riding circuit" presides over *Durand v. Hollins* 147, 151; see also *Durand v. Hollins*
Neutrality Act 47–48, 91, 101, 107, 110–111, 130–132, 188
The New International Encyclopedia 44, 202*n*20
New York Commercial Advertiser 68
New York Herald 11, 33–34, 36, 43–44, 47–48, 50–53, 59, 67, 87, 92, 100–101, 130–134, 139–140, 214*n*15
New-York Historical Society 105–106, 214*n*15
New York Journal of Commerce 149
New York Mirror 68
New York Post 68, 81, 109, 112–114, 117, 120
New York Times 1, 12, 19–20, 42, 44–45, 47–48, 62–66, 91–92, 102, 109, 115–117, 120–121, 125–126, 131, 136, 154, 157–158, 160, 179, 180, 187, 191–193, 204*n*4, 214*n*15
New York Tribune 4, 11, 17, 20, 22–23, 33, 38, 56–57, 64–65, 69–71, 82, 88, 92, 102, 112–113, 117, 149, 170, 201*n*6
Nicaragua Land and Mining Company: second Kinney scheme 102
The Nicaragua Route 35
Nicaragua Transit Company (incorrect name sometimes given to Accessory Transit Company) 64, 198*n*19, 201*n*6, 203*n*2, 206*n*16; *see also* Accessory Transit Company
Nichols, Roy F. 126, 213*n*13; attributes Pierce's failings to death of young son 81–82; suggests Pierce possibly involved in Kinney filibuster 117
Nicholson, A.O.P. 134, 214*n*14; bribed by Fabens and Kinney **105**–106; gives good notice to Kinney expedition in newspaper 116
Nigger Emperor of Nicuragua [*sic*] **30**

1984 184
North American Newspaper Alliance 162
SS *Northern Light* 15, 18–20, 22–23, 25
Norton, Charles G. 207*n*26, 207*n*27, 207*n*28; details Kinney's debt from failed state fair 84; grandson of Kinney's attorney 83; Kinney still "fairly wealthy" after filibuster 141; Kinney's borrowing for expeditions 103; Kinney's relationship with grandfather, Milford Norton 83; Kinney's sources of wealth 85
Norton, Milford P.: encourages Kinney to go to Washington 85; Kinney "drew drafts" on, forcing asset sales 103; Kinney reports selection as expedition leader to 86–87; Kinney's attorney and agent 83; reassures Kinney's creditors Birdseye and Boyle 103
Nott, Charles C., Sr. 185
Nueces Strip 77–79

SS *Ocean Bird* 111, 117, 142
Offutt, Milton 156
Organization of American Historians 2
Orwell, George 184
O'Sullivan, John L. 148

Paladino, Antonio 17, 46, 56, 198*n*14; animosity between steamboat captain Smith and 7–8; Borland reportedly encouraged Smith in murder of 15; description of and prospective trip with ex-minister Squier 5; historical significance of deadly clash between Smith and 13–14; letter seconds accounts of murder of 15; Squier's eulogy for 14; *see also Routh*; Smith, T.T.
Palmerston, Lord 32, 158; considers revalidating Shepherd grant 31; fears southward U.S. expansion 28
Panic of 1837 75–76, 195
Panic of 1857 195
Patton, Edward 17–18
USS *Pawnee* 191
Pearson, Hiram: Kinney promises to visit in San Francisco 86; ties to Kinney in Illinois 72; as vice president of Central American Land and Mining 87; *see also* Kinney, Henry Lawrence
Pearson, William 155–156; bombarded Johanna twice 154; exacted reparation for Mooers from Selim 154
Peckham, Rufus 90
Perrin: name appears in *El-Shifa* (2003) decision 16 times 181

Index

Perrin, Marie Louise (aka Trautmann-Perrin, Marie Louise) 178–179, 219*n*7; alternate name explained 176; becomes U.S. citizen 176; "a confirmed invalid" by 1868 176; moves to Charleston, S.C. 193–194; secures passport 193; Seward notes "very temporary" sojourn of at Greytown 177, 185; sought reparations for Greytown losses 62, 175–177

Perrin, Trautman(n) (aka Trautmann-Perrin, Charles Augustus) 158, 175, 178–179, 219*n*7; alternate name explained 176; becomes U.S. citizen 176; moves to Charleston, S.C. 193–194; secures passport 193; Seward notes "very temporary" sojourn of at Greytown 177, 185; sought reparations for Greytown losses 62, 176–177; two reparations appeals to Committee on Claims fail 178–179

Perrin v. United States (1868) 62, 158; background 175–177; case strategy 177–178; importance of in U.S. military damages cases 173–174, 179–182, 186; referenced 16 times in *El-Shifa* (2003) 181; *see also El-Shifa Pharmaceutical Industries Co. v. United States* (2003); *El-Shifa Pharmaceutical Industries Co. v. United States* (2004)

Perrin v. United States (1870): Supreme Court upholds Court of Claims defeat 178–179

Peru, Illinois: Kinney's center of operations 72–76

Phoenix 152

Pierce, Bennie 81–82

Pierce, Franklin 13, 18–19, 56, 68, 86, 90–91, 93–94, 105–108, 130–132, 141, 149–150, 169, 172, 189, 193, 208*n*18; accused of usurping Congress' war powers 65–66; ambiguous relation to Kinney scheme 110–111, 116–117, 130; Anglo-American Central American treaty 122; background 79; befriends Kinney during Mexican-American War 79; defends Greytown razing 87–89, 208*n*5; description of character 81–82; knowledge of letter in free-franked envelope denied 135; meets with Kinney as expedition leader 100; newspapers, congressmen criticize Greytown razing 88; possible interest in Mosquito grant 133, 134–135; remains friends with Sidney Webster despite taking bribe 136–137; reported to own one-twelfth of Mosquito grant 135; secretary's envelope free-franked by 136–137, 214*ch*15*n*3; wins 1852 presidential election 48, **80**–81; *see also* presidential franking privilege; Webster, Sidney

Polk, James K. 38, 79, 110

USS *Portsmouth* 49

Powell, L.W. 145–146

Poyais 112–113, 115, 209*n*8; British defend specious bonds of 98–99; earlier British scheme similar to Kinney's 93; greatest fraud in history 93; history of 93–98; and Kinney scheme become connected 94; post-scandal legacy 98–99; *see also* Black River Grant; Dallas-Clarendon treaty; MacGregor, Gregor

President: Office and Powers see Corwin, Edward S.

presidential franking privilege 131, **133**–134, 214*ch*15*n*3, 214*n*20; *see also* Pierce, Franklin; Webster, Sidney

Protection of Citizens Abroad by the Armed Forces of the United States 156

Punta Arenas 18–19, 40, 51; at heart of Greytown/transit company feud 15, **16**, 17; Marcy sends warship to prevent further dismantlings 50, 52–55; transit company won't move, town dismantles one building 49, 203*n*2; White lies to Marcy, denying Greytown owns 49

Quirk, Robert 157
Quitman, John 38

Rafter, Michael 94, 97; calls MacGregor's self-glorification "aberration of human intellect" 96

Rappleye, Charles 2

Raven-Hansen, Peter 4

the razing of Greytown **60**

Reeves, Richard 161

Report of the Congressional Committees Investigating the Iran/Contra Affair (1987) 162

Republic of Texas 77

"Revisiting Nineteenth-Century U.S. Interventionism in Central America: Capitalism, Intrigue, and the Obliteration of Greytown": author's 2017 *American Nineteenth Century History* article 3, 168

Richmond Dispatch 45, 202*n*24

The Right to Protect Citizens in Foreign Countries by Landing Forces 155–156

Rivas, Patricio: puppet head of William Walker's filibuster government 121

river steamer **8**

246 Index

Robert Charles Frédéric: English consul annuls all grants issued by 30–31; Mosquito king who sold grant to Shepherds, Haly 29–30
Rogers, Wm. H. 21–22
Rogers, William P. 163
Routh 13–15, 17–18, 21–23, 25; description of route 7, 9; *see also* Paladino, Antonio; Smith, T.T.
Ruatán Island 127, 138, 143
Rudler, A.J. 128
Rusk, Thomas Jefferson 84, 100
Russell, Lord 40–41; suggests England and America both colonize Mosquito Protectorate 70

Sacramento Daily Union 109
St. Nicholas 191
Salmon, Nowell 127–128
Samuel Smith Wood papers 194, 205*ch*6*n*9, 222*n*21
San Francisco Daily Union 142
San Francisco Examiner 143
San Juan de Nicaragua 42, 46, 67; as alternate name for Greytown 19; *see also* San Juan del Norte
San Juan del Norte 5, 27–28, 144, 166; as alternate name for Greytown 19; *see also* San Juan de Nicaragua
San Juan del Sur 9–10
Santo Domingo *see* Fabens, Joseph
Schatzell, John P.: Kinney deeply in debt to 84, 141–142
Schiff, Adam 169, 171, 219*ch*18*n*4
Schlesinger, Arthur M., Jr.: commenting on Greytown and *Durand v. Hollins* 150–151; *see also* Shewmaker, Kenneth E.
Schmidt, Hans 157
Schurz, Carl: on character of Caleb Cushing 108
Scott, Joseph 22, 55–57
Scott, Winfield 80–81; role in blocking Kinney's expedition 111; *see also* Boarman, Charles
Scroggs, William O. 100, 106, 117–121, 201*ch*3*n*8, 213*n*2; Washington was inveigled into razing Greytown 4, 100–101
Seager, Robert II: wrote article on Samuel Wood from papers 194–196
Second Battle of Bull Run: Fletcher Webster mortally wounded at 192
Selim, Sultan 156; clashed with U.S. whalers over supplies payments 152–155; *see also* Johanna
Semi-Weekly Courier and New-York Enquirer 68, 89; 202*n*23; accuses Borland of colluding with Kinney scheme 82
Seward, William H. 174; enunciates core premise governing Perrins' damage suit decision 177, 179, 185
Shenkman, Rick 169
Shepherd, Peter 28; *see also* Shepherd grant
Shepherd, Samuel 28; *see also* Shepherd grant
Shepherd (aka Mosquito) grant 47, 87, 92, 96, 98, 100, 104, 109, 122, 127, 133–135, 138, 187, 191, 193, 205*n*14 208*n*3; Anglo-American draft treaty validates Poyais grant and 124; British equate Shepherd scheme with their Poyais fraud 93; colony planned by U.S. owners of 43–45; Greytown was part of 38, 91; Keeling buys half of 36; Kinney claims to buy 120; Kinney tries to sell to Mormons 142–146; Marcy inexplicably allows treaty consideration of 124–125; owned by Shepherd brothers and Haly 30; part-owner of seeks advice from friend 57; Squier suggests Vanderbilt buy 36; two transit officials on board of 46; voided by Walker 120; *see also* Central American Land and Mining Company; Cooper project
Shewmaker, Kenneth E.: on incremental erosion of Congress' war powers 150, 152, 155; *see also* Johanna; Schlesinger, Arthur M.
Shields, James 45, 202*n*24
Sketch of the Mosquito Shore, Including the Territory of Poyais 97
Slaughter-House cases (1873): with *Durand* and *In re Neagle* justifies executive war powers 163
Smith, George A. 146
Smith, T.T.: arrest thwarted by Borland 17–18; described 7; murders black riverman 13–15; *see also* Borland, Solon; Paladino, Antonio; *Routh*
solicitation by H.L. Kinney to Brigham Young **145**
Soper, Will 169–171
Squier, Ephraim George 5, **6**, 7, 14, 25, 28–31, 34, 40, 46, 58, 123, 189–190; anxious over Vanderbilt's obtrusive aide Joseph White 27; background 24; negotiated canal contract for Vanderbilt 26; suggests Vanderbilt buy Shepherd grant 36
Squier, Frank 190
SS *Star of the West* 7

Index

Stevens, Kenneth R.: writes of Johanna incident 153–155; *see also* Johanna
Stevenson, H.L. 49
Stiles, T.J. 27, 33
stock jobbing: pejorative for questionable securities transactions 69, 93
Strangeways, Thomas: fictional author of *Sketch of the Mosquito Shore* 97; *see also* MacGregor, Gregor; Poyais
Streeter, Farris B. 147
Sumner, Charles 177
Supreme Court of the United States 123, 128, 147, 160–161, 163, 166, 171, 175, 178–179, 181–182, 184–186, 212*ch*14*n*3
USS *Susquehanna* 191

Tabacinic, Ilana 181–182, 186
Take Care Clause (of the Constitution) 163
Takings Clause (of Fifth Amendment) 182, 185; *El-Shifa* (2004) court finds *Perrin* "seminal" in takings jurisprudence 181; invoked by Cushing in *Perrin* case 178; private property taken for public use requires compensation 174; *Wiggins* found compensable but not *Perrin* under 178
Taney, Roger 186
Taylor, Zachary 79
SS *Tennessee* 131, 132
Texas state fair of 1852 83; description of 84; a Kinney "land-selling scheme" 84; *see also* Kinney, Henry Lawrence; Lone Star Fair
Thayer, Abijah 113; *see also* Thayer, William Sydney
Thayer, James 113–114; *see also* Thayer, William Sydney
Thayer, William Sydney: a Kinney confident also covering him for *Post* 112, *113*–114, 117
Thorpe, D.W. 143–144
Thrapp, Dan L. 84
To Chain the Dog of War 156
Torreon, Barbara Salazar 169, 172
Travis, Ira Dudley 128–129
trespass 62; description of three types of 83
Tshombe, Moise 161
Twiss, Travers 177
Tyler, John 151, 216*n*14

SS *United States* 116, 142; ship Kinney chartered 102
U.S. Circuit Court 147, 160–161, 214*n*19
U.S. Civil War 131, 174, 177–178, 181–182, 184–185, 189, 191–194, 196, 210*n*3

U.S. Commissioner's Court 132
U.S. Court of Claims 174, 178–179, 184–185
U.S. Court of Federal Claims 179–180
U.S. Senate Committee on Claims: Perrins' two requests for reparations denied by 178–179; Senator on argues Best's property taken for public use 182–184
United States v. Caltex (Philippines) Inc. (1952): dictum in *Pacific Railroad* held as law by 185
United States v. Pacific Railroad (1887) 181; in which dictum disregards three previous precedent cases 185–186

Vanderbilt, Cornelius 36, 131–132; approaches British banks for canal financing 32–33; canal denounced as cover for inland-only route 34; water route across Nicaragua secured for *26*–27
Vattel, Emer de 179, 181–182, 184–186; background and importance of 174–175; *see also* Grant, Ulysses S.; Howe, Timothy O.
Venezuela 96, 163, 176; MacGregor moves to after Poyais debacle, receives pension from 98; MacGregor offers services to against Spain 94
Vera Cruz *see* Japan; Wilson, Woodrow
USS *Vixen* 111
Vladeck, Stephen I. 4; commenting on dicta in *Pacific Railroad* 185
von Holst, Hermann 107–108

Wag the Dog: *El-Shifa* filing cites as parallel to Lewinsky scandal 180–181; fake war distracts from presidential sex scandal 180; *see also* Clinton, Bill; *El-Shifa Pharmaceutical Industries Co. v. United States* (2003)
Walker, Patrick 30, 36, 96
Walker, William 104–105, 114, 116, 118; background and early success of in Nicaragua *115*; British and Hondurans foil third filibuster of 127; execution of by Hondurans 128; Kinney interacts with 119–121; regime recognized briefly by U.S. 130, 213–214*ch*15*n*2
War 182
War Powers Resolution 162–163, 165–166, 168
Ward, Hortense Warner 75, 78, 84; researched Kinney in the 1950s 72, 206*n*1
Warren, Earl 166
Washburne, Elihu B. 184

Washington Star 109, 120
Washington Union 105, 109, 116
Waxman, Matthew 162
Webster, Daniel (orator, statesman) 34; authorizes force against Johanna 152; debt dispute with Caleb Cushing 75–76, 108–109; prohibits force in Greek dispute 152; recognizes Greytown's right to "punish wrong-doers" 19, 54; son, Fletcher, buys land from Kinney for 74–76
Webster, Daniel (Fletcher's son, Daniel's grandson) 113
Webster, Edward 76
Webster, Fletcher 110, 113, 116, 191, 206*n*4; bribed by Kinney 105–107; buys land from Kinney for father **74**; denounces Kinney 112; joins Kinney's filibuster 76; killed in Civil War 192; refuses to repay father's Cushing debt 108–109
Webster, Julia 75
Webster, Sidney 64, 112, 134, 136; bribed by Kinney 106–107; Pierce and remain friends 137; post-administration life 192–193; private secretary to President Pierce **106**; used Pierce-franked envelope to acknowledge bribe 131, 133; *see also* Pierce, Franklin; presidential franking privilege
Webster-Crampton Treaty 39, 41–42, 98
Weinberg, Albert K. 48
Wheeler, John 89, 91
White, Joseph L. 36–37, 57, 82, 92, 101, 104; background of 27; deceives Marcy about ownership of Punta Arenas 49, 54–55; disclosed as a director of Shepherd grant company 46, 100; murdered by business rival 187–188; offers to bribe Nicaraguans 39; propounds Accessory Transit Greytown takeover 58, 204*n*1; purportedly behind Greytown razing 58, 62, 64, 69; Squier reports overbearingness of 27; Vanderbilt and seek English investment 32–33; transfers canal rights to Accessory Transit 34–35;
U.S. minister Kerr decries character of 40
White, Loomis L. 37
Wiedemann, Henri 198*n*27, 204*n*3; describes Paladino murder 13–15; German diplomat aboard *Routh* 13; seeks to mollify Borland after assault 21
Wiggins, James S. 173–174
Wiggins *v. United States* (1867) 173, 184, 186; event that led to 174; why resulted in compensation and *Perrin* did not 175, 178
Wilbarger, J.W. 85
Wiley, George: calls Paladino murder "cowardly and brutal" 15; described Borland's clash with Greytown authorities 18
Williams, Mary Wilhelmine 28
Wilmot, David 174
Wilson, Woodrow 158–150; uses Greytown as pretext for Vera Cruz intervention 157–158
Wise, Henry A. 62, 204*n*20; advises Shepherd-grant investor 57; suggests Borland implicated in Shepherd grant scheme 57; *see also* Booker, George
Wood, Alexander 61, 194
Wood, Leonard 157
Wood, Mary Ann 61, 195
Wood, Samuel Smith: background 61; memorials to Congress fail 71; post–Greytown life 194–196
Wood, Samuel Smith, Jr. 195
Woods, James M. 13
Wormuth, Francis 156

Yale University Library Gazette 194
Young, Brigham 138, 142, 145–146; declines grant purchase 144; Kinney proffered sale of Shepherd grant to 143; *see also* Latter-Day Saints; Mormons; Saints

Zacharie, James W. 116, 142